Social Representations
and the Social Bases of Knowledge

Swiss Monographs in Psychology

Edited by the Swiss Psychological Society
Volume 1

Mario von Cranach, Willem Doise
and Gabriel Mugny
(Editors)

Social Representations
and the Social
Bases of Knowledge

Hogrefe & Huber Publishers
Lewiston, NY Toronto Bern Göttingen

Library of Congress Cataloging-in-Publication Data

Social representations and the social bases of knowledge / edited by
   Mario von Cranach, Willem Doise, Gabriel Mugny.
        p. cm. — (Swiss monographs in psychology : v. 1)
   Includes bibliographical references and index.
   ISBN 0-88937-070-2 : $40.00
   1. Social perception. 2. Social role. 3. Knowledge, Sociology
of. I. Cranach, Mario von. II. Doise, Willem, 1935–
III. Mugny, Gabriel. IV. Series.
HM132.S5724 1992
306.4'2—dc20   91-44436
                                                    CIP

Canadian Cataloguing in Publication Data

Main entry under title:
Social representations and the social bases of
   knowledge
(Swiss monographs in psychology ; v. 1)
Includes bibliographical references and index.
ISBN 0-88937-070-2
1. Knowledge, Sociology of. 2. Social psychology.
I. Cranach, Mario von. II. Doise, Willem, 1935–
III. Mugny, Gabriel. IV. Series.
BD175.S63 1992   306.4'2   C92-093066-2

© Copyright 1992 by Hogrefe & Huber Publishers
P.O. Box 51
Lewiston, NY 14092

12–14 Bruce Park Ave.
Toronto, Ontario M4P 2S3

ISBN 3-456-82105-0
ISBN 0-88937-070-2
Hogrefe & Huber Publishers
Lewiston, NY Toronto Bern Göttingen

Table of Contents

PART III.
KNOWLEDGE AND THE SOCIAL-CULTURAL ENVIRONMENT

PART IV.
SOCIAL PRACTICES AND THE DYNAMICS OF SOCIAL REPRESENTATIONS

List of Contributors

Rolf Ammann
Dittlingerweg 10
CH – 3005 Bern

Joannis Avramakis
Psychologisches Institut
Universität Bern
Laupenstrasse 4
CH – 3008 Bern

Ernest E. Boesch
Drosselweg 8
D – 6601 Scheidt-SB

Felice Carugati
Università degli Studi di Parma
Facolta' di Lettere e Filosofia
Istituto di Psicologia
Borgo Carissimi, 10
I – 43100 Parma

Mario von Cranach
Psychologisches Institut
Universität Bern
Gesellschaftsstrasse 49
CH – 3012 Bern

Hans Peter Dachler
Hochschule St. Gallen
für Wirtschafts-, Rechts- und
Sozialwissenschaften
Guisanstrasse 12
CH – 9010 St. Gallen

Hanns-Dietrich Dann
Institut für Psychologie II
Friedrich-Alexander-Universität
Erlangen-Nürnberg
Erziehungswissenschaftliche Fakultät
Regensburger Strasse 160
D – 8500 Nürnberg

Pierre R. Dasen
Université de Genève
Faculté de Psychologie et des Sciences de
l'Education
24, rue Général-Dufour
CH – 1211 Genève 4

Annamaria Silvana de Rosa
Università degli Studi di Roma
LA SAPIENZA
Dipartimento di Psicologia dei Processi
Sviluppo e Socializzazione
Via dei Marsi, 78
I – 00185 Roma

Willem Doise
Université de Genève
Faculté de Psychologie et des Sciences de
l'Education
24, rue Général-Dufour
CH – 1211 Genève 4

Francesca Emiliani
Università degli Studi di Bologna
Dipartimento di Scienze dell'Educazione
Via Zamboni, 34
I – 40126 Bologna

August Flammer
Psychologisches Institut
Unviersität Bern
Laupenstrasse 4
CH – 3008 Bern

Uwe Flick
Technische Universität Berlin
Sekr. DO 303
Institut für Psychologie
Dovestrasse 1–5
D – 1000 Berlin 10

Michèle Grossen
Université de Neuchâtel
Faculté des Lettres
Seminaire de Psychologie
Espace Louis-Agassiz 1
CH – 2000 Neuchâtel

Gerhard Kaminski
Psychologisches Institut
Universität Tübingen
Friedrichstrasse 21
D – 7400 Tübingen

Lenelis Kruse
Psychologisches Institut
Universität Heidelberg
Hauptstrasse 47–51
D – 6900

Alfred Lang
Psychologisches Institut
Universität Bern
Laupenstrasse 4
CH – 3008 Bern

Ivana Markova
University of Stirling
Department of Psychology
Stirling FK9 4LA
Scotland

Luisa Molinari
Università degli Studi di Bologna
Dipartimento di Scienze dell'Educazione
Via Zamboni, 34
I – 40126 Bologna

Jean Marc Monteil
Laboratoire de Psychologie Sociale
de la Cognition
Université Blaise Pascal
F – 63000 Clermont-Ferrand

Serge Moscovici
Ecole des Hautes Etudes
en Sciences Sociales
Laboratoire de Psychologie Sociale
44, rue de la Tour
F – 75116 Paris

Gabriel Mugny
Université de Genève
Faculté de Psychologie et des Sciences de
l'Education
24, rue Général-Dufour
CH – 1211 Genève 4

Juan Antonio Pérez
Université de Genève
Faculté de Psychologie et des Sciences de
l'Education
24, rue Général-Dufour
CH – 1211 Genève 4

Anne-Nelly Perret-Clermont
Université de Neuchâtel
Faculté des Lettres
Seminaire de Psychologie
Espace Louis-Agassiz 1
CH – 2000 Neuchâtel

Monica Rubini
Università degli Studi di Bologna
Dipartimento di Scienze dell'Educazione
Via Zamboni, 34
I – 40126 Bologna

Klaus Scherer
Université de Genève
Section de Psychologie
24, rue Général-Dufour
CH – 1211 Genève 4

Wolfgang Scholl
Institut für Wirtschfats- und Sozialpsychologie
Georg-August-Universität
Gosslerstr. 14
D – 3400 Göttingen

Maria Luisa Schubauer-Leònie
Université de Genève
Faculté de Psychologie et des Sciences de
l'Education
24, rue Général-Dufour
CH – 1211 Genève 4

Marie-Noelle Schurmans
Université de Genève
Faculté de Psychologie et des Sciences de
l'Education
24, rue Général-Dufour
CH – 1211 Genève 4

Susanne Schwarz
Psychologisches Institut
Universität Heidelberg
Hauptstrasse 47-51
D – 6900 Heidelberg

Gün R. Semin
Vrije Universiteit Amsterdam
Faculty of Psychology and Pedagogics
De Boeleaan 1081
NL – 1081 Amsterdam

Norbert Semmer
Psychologisches Institut
Universität Bern
Gesellschaftsstrasse 49
3012 Bern

Beat Thommen
Rosenweg 11
CH – 2555 Brügg bei Biel

Franziska Tschan
Psychologisches Institut
Universität Bern
Gesellschaftsstrasse 49
CH – 3012 Bern

Introduction

This book results from a scientific undertaking, the main aim of which was to explore the social foundations of knowledge. But the book itself can be considered as evidence supporting one thesis developed by some participants in that undertaking who argued that cognitive products are also generated through societal communicative dynamics. Indeed the chapters of this book were initially presented as contributions to the first international congress organized by the Swiss Association of Psychologists. The congress was conceived as a response to the most fundamental social need, the need for communication.

The basic need to be fulfilled was not only the urgent desire of researchers to let colleagues share their most recent results. The essence of the need was also institutional. For many years the Swiss Association of Psychologists has tried to stimulate scientific communication. Important initiatives were the launching of the Swiss Journal of Psychology, the regular meetings of young researchers; their youth being defined through the freshness of ideas. However these initiatives have not always been successful. The Journal went through a crisis and participants in the meetings of young researchers sometimes were not numerous. Furthermore, even after seven hundred years of cultural and linguistic Helvetian pluralism another peculiar phenomenon often happened during these scientific meetings of psychologists: regularly members of linguistic regional groups left the conference room together and this seemed to happen more often when the speaker did not belong to their own linguistic group (p: .05). This strange phenomenon was considered by the Executive Committee of the Association as an instance of communicative behavior which did not fit in the frame of scientific universality. And the members of the Committee who had learned about the cognitive effects of social interactions thought it necessary to further them between autochthonous scholars from different linguistics regions.

As a result of the efforts of the Committee, chaired by Professor Meinrad Perrez, a proposal was accepted by ballot of the members of the General Meeting of the Association. The basic idea was that communication amongst Swiss scholars would be facilitated when using a language foreign to all of them: the English language. But everybody knows that linguistic competence functions differently according to specific communicative situations and the crux of the problem was to create encounter situations which would facilitate the use of the new scientific coin. Which situation would better serve that purpose than a situation in which Swiss researchers would be invited to communicate results of their research to foreigners with whom they share similar interests?

A necessary condition for realizing such a communication situation was to define a theme on which Swiss researchers would surely have messages to communicate. Of course every researcher has many things to communicate, but communication is more effective when a minimum of shared meaning preexists for the participants in the situation. An area of study was therefore defined offering reference points familiar to Swiss and foreign researchers. The members of the Executive Committee thought that social psychology as practised in Berne and Geneva could offer such reference points and therefore three social psychologists from these universities were invited to initiate this series of congresses which should be authentically Swiss but satisfying international standards. It was agreed upon from the beginning that these three social psychologists would receive the necessary funds to invite several foreign colleagues considered by them as first rate interlocutors for the specific theme of the congress.

So much for the social origins of a planned series of biannual international congresses to be organized by scholars appointed by the Executive Committee of the Swiss Association of Psychologists. To stick to the requirements, these congresses should be borne upon a theme researched by several Swiss scholars who have established a network of professional contacts with foreign colleagues; their organization should be under the shared responsibility of colleagues of at least two Swiss universities from different linguistic regions; foreign colleagues have to be invited and priority should be given to communications in English.

The authors of these lines were invited to convene the first congress. They agreed rapidly on the general theme of the meeting: social representations and social bases of knowledge. In Berne and Geneva significant bodies of research have been carried out for about twenty years, often in collaboration with foreign colleagues, in the areas of goal oriented action, sociocognitive development, social influence and social representations. At a very general level all this research illustrates the notion that analyses of social interaction conditions and of shared meaning systems are essential for studying exhaustively the basic phenomena dealt with in the aforementioned subareas of social psychology. Such an assumption is also guiding much research in the field of applied social psychology.

Four more specific themes were retained for organizing the main sections of the congress. One important criterion for defining them was the readiness of distinguished foreign colleagues to deliver main contributions on the topic. All these main contributions have been adapted for this book together with other selected contributions satisfying usual criteria of quality and relevance. It is hoped that this procedure will benefit the work of Swiss colleagues through presenting it in a more general framework.

The theme of the first session was epistemological. In his opening address to the congress, S. Moscovici expanded on the opposition between scientific knowledge and common sense or myths. He argued that this opposition persists in scientific thinking itself and gives rise to the creation of "scientific myths". The second contribution to the opening session was delivered by M. von Cranach and proposed a synthetic view on the links between social, cognitive and conative dynamics.

The theme of the second session was concerned with the situational dynamics intervening in the genesis or actualization of cognitive competences and of social cognitions

and representations. In his contribution, J. M. Monteil articulated assumptions on the intervention of such situational dynamics with more current postulates on the neurological bases of cognition. His contribution can be considered as an argumentation in defense of the social and societal study of cognition.

For introducing the third session on cognitions and the sociocultural environment, our colleagues E. Boesch and G. Kaminski attempted to frame knowledge in two broader settings. The first contributor to the session introduced a more cultural perspective and the second dealt with ecological problems.

Finally the embedding of knowledge in social practice was the topic of the fourth session which allowed H. D. Dann to develop his ideas on subjective theories of teachers and P. Dachler to report on the different meanings of leadership in organizations.

The structure of the conference in four main sessions (a fifth session assembled papers without explicit links to the central theme of the congress) provided the organizers with the means to distribute the numerous other contributions according to their links with the invited papers. Of course this resulted in a kind of prototypical classification weighting the different links one single paper could entertain with the themes of more than one session. Only a fuzzy sets logic can generate a satisfying classification system in such cases allowing the same element to be part of different classes. But such a logic is difficult to use when deciding on a timetable of a congress or on the contents list of a book. Therefore we finally decided to introduce some changes in the attribution of papers to the different sections of the book, but each section begins with the invited papers which are followed by a series of related papers in alphabetical order.

Let us conclude with a more personal remark. It was a real pleasure for two Genevans and one Bernese to collaborate. Of course the Genevans are very familiar with what French common sense calls "le système D", which is a highly complex way of organizing things unknown in other cultures. As this system seems unfamiliar to German Swiss (von Cranach, personal communication) we were rather concerned about the issue of our collaboration. But if this culture gap has been successfully bridged, it is from the efforts and the goodwill of the local organizers, particularly H. Bolliger and G. Ochsenbein, and through the very efficacious assistance of R. Winkelmann. The English of many chapters of this book has been substantially improved due to the linguistic skills of Mary Valach. We acknowledge also very gratefully the financial help of the Swiss Academy of Human Sciences.

Mario von Cranach
Willem Doise
Gabriel Mugny
Université de Genève

Part I.

The Social Bases of Knowledge

The Psychology of Scientific Myths

Serge Moscovici

If it is true that nowadays, in the face of the rising flux of televised images, newspaper prose and works of fiction, science resembles a town with flooded streets, the inquisitive observer, wondering about the reason for this strange phenomenon and the name given to it, must recognize that its notions cannot possibly enlighten us.

We live, and this has to be declared aloud, in a world in which myths are overabundant and freely proliferate. Their vision fascinates us, we speak their language. But why are we attracted towards that world of images rather than towards the world of concepts? To justify this preference we could enumerate the benefits we derive from myths. What do they bring to our lives, our actions, our minds? What do they achieve that could not be done as well or better by science and philosophy in order to inform, enrapture and guide millions of people whom they address and for whom they are created? Our questions remain unanswered and we awkwardly conclude that if myths multiply, circulate and are sold, it is because people are disoriented, badly informed, or because they just love myths. Incoherent and ill-woven as their web may be, they cling to that mass of fables whose magic action bears little relevance to the mystery of the means of communication. To know why is beyond the possibilities of explanation which are ours today.

Unable as we are to explain the strange prosperity of myth creation in general, we are at least able to illuminate them in a particular area where they scandalize: the word is not too strong. Their number has reached such a puzzling eminence as one would judge the thing to be sheer impossibility. I am speaking of scientific myths. Three or four recent examples of the universe, e. g. viruses, left and right brains, the Big Bang, the death of the universe, have combined to make more striking the manifestations of the problem under examination. Their close relationship to one of the most resounding epidemics of recent years; the link between virus and AIDS together with the

worldwide success of books, such as those by Changeux or Hawkins, gives more scope to the prospect of a psychology of scientific myths. This still has to be created, since our science touches upon it only occasionally and in passing, but I think that it has to be taken further and examined methodically.

The very phrase "scientific myths" is as puzzling as a round square or an atheistic religion. It points to the paradox we have to consider as being at the starting point of this psychology. In fact we like to relegate myths into the past. We boast that they have been eliminated by science. They are the remnants of an archaic system of thought which tried to classify the data of reality and apply its own explanations, such as origins or impersonations: phenomena we can now explain much better. The heredity of species, the fecundity of the soil, diseases, the birth of planets and so on, are things we understand fairly well today without the help of occult force, beneficent or maleficent intents. When traces of them are found in a book or in conversation, we fall a prey to an obscure or rather ancient impression recurring in our minds. It has never been erased, but we have rejected it to the point of oblivion and indifference. We have the impression of going backwards and crossing once more a frontier, retracing our steps in time to meet an obsolete system of thought. In doing so, we fail to recognize the difference between this system and science.

This is not noticeable from the contents but from the form when hearing someone say "This is a myth", meaning a belief which is neither true nor reasonable. The same applies to ill-digested, warped or distorted scientific facts. One is led to conceive scientific myths as a deviation from knowledge, and even a pathology of thought either by default or excess. By default, in losing the sense of the limits between a firm thought and a loose thought, a whole truth and a half a truth. By excess, when reason yields to its understanding of everything from a single theory which is always complete and sometimes satisfactory in a logical sense. Or, to speak clearly, when explanation is applied without retaliation to everything that exists in the universe. Let us say that the most obvious and least questionable mark of scientific myths is this combination of ignorance of the frontiers and logical completeness. One could even say that their failing is not to have any.

Despite the extraordinary progress and diffusion of the sciences, the myths that one assumed to be relieved of have not been eliminated but are actually prospering. Whilst acknowledging this, it seems more interesting to ask who has shown the way. Who more or less directly conceives myths? Are we dealing with those who François Jacob calls "fanatics or popularizers"? The answer depends on an observation which is in itself questionable. Some myths inspired by biology have been launched into the French-speaking world through books such as Monod's *Le hasard et la nécessité*, Changeux's *L'Homme neuronal*, Gros's *La civilisation du gène*, Ruffié's *Le sexe et la mort*, among others. Popular literature encourages this way of thinking which makes us see myths along the grain of scientific discoveries. These authors are not content with presenting research work and theories which bring to light and explain hitherto ill-understood phenomena. They seem to venture dangerously beyond the boundaries of science proper. They tread in a no man's land which is shaped by a whole corpus of ideas fashioning the no man's image of science and the scientist's image of daily thought. The choice of such terms as "indeterminacy", "relativity", "Oedipus complex" and "black hole" enables them to play on several registers of images. Reverence towards great scientists and the authority which is recognized in these heroes of culture, give those ideas an ascendancy which is not to be denied, even if he who expresses them speaks only for himself. The thermal death of the universe, the duality of left and right brains, neuronal Man with a capital M, the death of the father; we know that these are not scientific discoveries but myths and derivations rather than deviations from the former. As for myth-makers in the modern world, a fine bunch of Nobel Prizes could be found among them.

All this can give offence, I know. Let us confess that things would be easier if one could say that there are the myths which recede on the one hand, and science which progresses on the other. Here, the poor popularizers and the man in the street elaborating these myths; there, the scientists fighting them. But we have to face facts. The same men produce in one and the same motion both scientific discoveries and myths; a paradox which psychology takes up. Why a paradox? This is a moot question. It could still be avoided by saying that scientists are seduced like everybody else by original images. They have to answer the ultimate questions of life, or else they feel like everybody the lures of publicity and best-sellers. As true as these reasons are, they remain unsatisfactory. Though it is more risky, let me remind you of a demarcation which is seldom put forward today but contains all other demarcations and keeps its energy intact in our culture. *It is not to be denied that science resumes underhand the inveterate distinction between esoteric and exoteric knowledge.* Its location is on the side of the former class of knowledge which, according to Bacon, is presented in a puzzling fashion, taught to those who are qualified for it and understood only by a small number of people. It is privileged insofar as it is credited with the faculty of producing new ideas, so that, all things considered, it represents the only mode of thinking and the correct one, which all other modes of knowledge are not. In other respects, the things dealt with by scientists are surrounded by an aura of secrecy, inasmuch as they are not immediately approachable as things of ordinary experience are, but only now and again.

Explicitly or not, this demarcation states an *interdict of knowing*. On one hand access is prohibited to what is instituted as knowledge apart from the rest, supposed to remain opaque to vulgar understandings. This is conveyed by a widespread conviction: not everybody is capable of grasping scientific notions, or they are reserved for those who have been given special training enabling them to decipher them. It is claimed that one *cannot* know them, yet it is believed that one *must* not know them. And I am convinced that the passage from *you shall not know* to *you cannot know* is the source of many pedagogic difficulties. On the other hand, like philosophies and religions before, the interdict inculcates the belief that it is not only dangerous but impossible to divulge this information, these expressions and methods because of their nature. Consequently it is unadvisable and even forbidden to communicate them to the public at large. Spinoza called this kind of communication ad *captum vulgi* or more frequently *ad captum alicujus*. This quasi prohibition is deeply rooted nowadays when you think of the contempt attached to the words popularization or popular science, or when you see how suspicious the scientists who try to propagate scientific notions appear: an activity which is strongly censured, and hardly tolerated in those of respectable age who are supposed to have spent their creative energy.

Under these two aspects the interdict of knowing is at the core of the psychology which is puzzling us here. For the paradox springs from transgressing it, going beyond the permitted information and producing exoteric knowledge. It expresses this stepping over the demarcation line which is an exigence of culture as well as an event of thought. This is an event which occurs at a given time in the evolution of a field of research when a new world of knowledge emerges, and when experts are tempted to share their discoveries with a wider public and even conquer an authority which they had not before. Though this will to conquer is always conveyed in modest terms, it is nevertheless obstinately pursued. For being recognized by the public brings about some non-scientific benefits which are enough to justify transgressing the interdict that science, as a rule, obeys.

Why make so much of the interdict of knowing?, you will ask. It is because it introduces my point of view. Most scientific theories account for scientific myths by a need for compensation. The latter are pseudo-sciences, destined to answer the questions which have always preoccupied man, be they ethical, philosophical or logical, e.g. the cause of certain diseases, the origin of the universe, free will, and so on. Science has no answer to these questions, but does not prevent us from requiring from it more than it can give and interpret its informations in an unauthorized sense, combining e. g. cognitive science and biology in order to draw conclusions that each discipline alone would reject. Other theories would consider these myths as the results of a work of substitution. The material with which they are created stems of course from the sciences themselves. But it is used in a different context, taken outside its strict limits. For instance the story of the thermal death of the universe comes from the application of the second principle of energy to the universe as a whole, something which is excluded by thermodynamics. Some evolutionist myths are based on a natural selection which is extended to culture. The effect produced is that of a vast unicoloured coherent system in which shades of meaning are sacrificed and explanations given in blocks without caring for particular facts. Our epoch has pushed to perfection the art of manufacturing ersatz; the falsification is at times difficult to detect. If we wrongly believe that we are liberated from myths, this is because they are based on the same premises as science, but they do not respect the limits fixed by it.

Much is true in these theories, yet, to fathom what is true, reports, interviews and field studies would be necessary. The viewpoint I was alluding to sees in them some tools of communication which allow one to pass from one class of knowledge to another. More exactly, to pass from less familiar esoteric knowledge to familiar exoteric knowledge such as is implicitly circulating through society. One could even contend that, manufactured and perfected with undeniable skill, myths are neither pseudo-sciences whose unreality is unmasked at a given time, nor false sciences which entangle the link of thought to reality. *They are cognitive operators capable of going round the mentioned interdict and transforming two incompatible pieces of knowledge into each other.* Indeed we do not believe our own eyes when we notice how long-lived they are. This is because we neglect an absolutely essential factor motivating the fascination they exert. In fact they open the door to a forbidden world and thought, and they themselves are for their conceptors forbidden fruit.

One of the hypotheses which has been directing our research for a long time is that the object of psychosocial theory is to associate representations and communications. Here and there it has become something banal, taken for granted. However, it is not so banal when we get to the core of the problem and when we consider how the hypothesis is used, but I shall not elaborate on this point because that is, as they say, another story. "To associate representations and communications" means, clearly, that the former are fashioned in the course of the latter and not shaped beforehand and then selected and diffused, as it is sometimes conceived in human sciences. It does not mean that representations are prepared in order to be communicated in the same way as advertising is. Like money, they acquire shape and value by circulating and have value only as long as they circulate. Without going into details, theory would hold that there are three communication systems, each of which brings about a corresponding social representation (See: Doise, 1987; Farr, 1987; Strauss, 1952).

Roughly, as far as science is concerned, the first system which is common to propaganda and education imposes a representation determined by science and cuts up the existing representations in society about the same reality. Thus, as shown by Vergès (1987), the economic representations taught to pupils during the scholastic year isolate and rearrange the images and notions they had at the beginning. On one hand, owing to a movement of autonomy, economics appears as a field of autonomous representations; on the other hand, owing to a movement of articulation, the ideas and images concerning that reality are connected and concentrated. Consequently, at the end of the year, the items of knowledge relating for instance to consumption, do not simply refer to the act of purchasing but are integrated into a greater coherent field in connection with such items as "goods", "income", "purchasing power" and "standard of living". You observe that at one and the same time the associations between the items are more definite and the vocabulary is contracted, which indicates a stronger cohesion and a comparative isolation of the representation. Without being a double of economic knowledge, it is nevertheless affected by it.

The second communication system which I have called fusion resembles the flux of a contagion, the daily exchange of conversation, rumour, a television programme or a newspaper article which follows events and coordinates them statistically. In this case, the notions and images of science are absorbed and assimilated by the circulating social representations. The result is nonplussing if you consider that it leaves its mark on opinion. Thus on the front page of *Le Monde* of January 7, I can read:

"There is still time to prevent the virus of suspicion producing more severe effects". Or in the literary columns of January 27, about a book by Sternhell: "The Jerusalem historian had announced that he would shadow the downward progress of the virus at the time of Vichy". Here we are not dealing with a metaphor but with a leitmotiv of images that contemporary representations use irreverently and which is understood by everyone. By searching deeper, one notices that they are superimposed on older social and economic images.

I come now to the third communication system called propagation, which aims mostly at harmonizing a group's representations with those of science, reducing opposition and minimizing the discrepancies between them. In short, altering them so as to incorporate novel unusual information into the field of existing notions and judgements. In fact, and here is a precise thesis, this is the system in which scientific myths are born so as to bring knowledge related to the extraordinary and unfamiliar into contact with knowledge related to the ordinary and familiar. Exceptional ideas and facts, think of the Big Bang, of journeys into the solar system, are of incomparable, even puzzling richness. When they break into the system, they sometimes prove disturbing, but in truth they answer a more profound necessity. Now it is a question of converting existing representations so as to attune them to a new vision, e.g. that of psychoanalysis, statistical mechanics or biology. And you cannot convert anything without dramatizing what is routine, using widespread beliefs and practices as moulds, and combining the new elements with the initial representations of daily life. Thus operating an unexpected convergence between two realities belonging to two distinct modes of understanding causes an almost visual contact which makes you grasp things in a new way. The impression which is then confirmed is that of a transformation that makes the esoteric acceptable and intelligible by stripping it of its disconcerting elements. As for instance the scandal of gravity, a force acting at a distance, is covered by the current representation of attraction and repulsion.

If I can affirm substantially that scientific myths achieve a compromise by changing the comparatively unfamiliar into the comparatively familiar, I still have to indicate how. This will allow me to give some theoretical substance to the psychology of myths, to pass from the general viewpoint to its particular applications. I shall briefly evoke a law, then specific rules and their concrete illustrations.

Let us then come to the last and sternest exercise which consists in enumerating the operations by which scientific propositions are transformed in contact with social representations and an expert thought is changed into a naive thought directly connected with immediate life and experience. This does not mean giving them a vulgar, popular shape, but arguing, as one used to say, *ex concessis*, sheltered under a shared position and *ad hominem*, taking into account the images and notions of individuals and groups. To that purpose, a repetitive discourse must be given shape, i. e. a discourse repeating what comes from science and common sense, making some occasional adjunctions or suppressions which break its uniformity. Their aim is to cover up contradictions and prepare compromises between opposite ideas. Now the possibility of making compromises, as Bartlett contended, is an exclusive trait of social thought, in any case being discarded by science. No doubt this discourse uses ready-made and second hand approximate phrases. Myths however emerge from it, thanks to an extraordinary collective skill, in order to give full flight to propositions and images without falsifying them, to find unity throughout the representations and to avoid the literality of statements without giving up truth. In fact this discourse can be recognized by the joint use of allusions and compromises. Indeed, having recourse to allusive words: entropy in the myth of the thermal death of the universe, D. N. A. for the myth of genetics, charisma for that of the leader, or to allusive formulas: principle of indeterminacy, $E = mc^2$, discreetly indicates the link to a world of concepts. Only those who know them understand what they refer to, and this very fact gives value to some statements in the eyes of those for whom the allusion conjures up a relationship of thought.

Beyond the device of allusion, here are the four rules of compromise which I think I have observed at work in scientific myths.

a) The first rule is to use propositions in an equivocal way, changing them into two-sided propositions, that is having a strange side and a familiar side.

$$(1)\ X = Z - \begin{bmatrix} = X = Y \\ Z\ Y \\ \neq X \neq Y \end{bmatrix}$$

My first example will be the myth of the thermal death of the universe which always begins with the statement "The second law of thermodynamics is universal". It is well known what the equivocation consists of. To be called universal, a law, i. e. that of gravity, has to apply to every system of physical objects in certain conditions fixed by science. In that case, we can say that we are really dealing with the second law of thermodynamics ($X = Y$). But if, according to the common viewpoint, we have a statement about the universe as a whole, then we deal with another law: not of thermodynamics, but of one of its representations. I shall not dwell on the recourse to equivocation which is so frequent and so difficult to rule out, for no scientific term is so firmly defined that this recourse becomes impossible.

b) The second rule is to avoid directly contradicting a familiar proposition by avoiding contradicting its implications. Its formal expression is the following:

$$(2)\ X = Y - Y = Z - [\,X = Z\,] - X \neq Z - [\,X \neq Y\,]$$

It can be illustrated by the avoidance of the contradiction between two propositions which are found in the myth of the left and right brains.

1. The opposition between the two brains explains the difference between the bio-psychological qualities of individuals, etc.
2. The opposition between the occupations is explained by the faculties individuals have acquired. The implication is that the differences between chemists, engineers and other scientists, and artists come from their training, not from their physiological equipment. The propositions between square brackets are those which have to be covered up without being explicitly pronounced. This appears from the following text, an extract from *The Aquarius Conspiracy* which recounts the myth: "For tens of thousands of

left-brained engineers, chemists, psychologists, and for their more imaginative, more spontaneous right-brained colleagues, drugs were a passport to Xanadu, especially in the nineteen sixties". Here the rule has the consequence that it allows one to distinguish between "right-brained" and "left- brained" occupations with specific traits and list in them well-known, therefore concrete types.

c) The third rule to bring a "strange" proposition closer to a "familiar" proposition consists in seeming to repeat it, while in fact an apparently negligible expression is added to or substracted from it.

$$(3) \ X = Y - [\ Y = a + b \ ] - X = a - [\ X \neq Y \ ]$$

Let us resume the myth of the thermal death of the universe. However fictive it may seem, it introduces the notion of evolution into the common representation of a stable intemporal universe. But, as in every representation of our culture in that respect, instead of being neutral, as science would have it, the evolution occurs in the sense of a degradation. And here is the proposition of an English astronomer who, like other scientists, has contributed to the birth of the myth. He affirms that "entropy in the universe must always increase so that all change will eventually cease, and this ending will come in a finite time – the universe is running down and must eventually come to a stop". Thus the first proposition, which is "strange" for science and common sense, at the beginning describes an evolution. A negligible assertion "so that all change will eventually cease" metamorphoses it into a general, fatal evolution at whose termination you again find the universe stable, but, as you know, dead. This changes the common representation of the universe which was hitherto in use, since its stability is a terminal yet non permanent state. But this also changes the proposition of science into a proposition of myth, since it states that entropy in the universe must always increase; an inadequate statement of the law. The second law of thermodynamics in fact says nothing about the universe any more than does the law of minimal action. At most one could find in it an implication relating to the universe, on the condition that one knows to what extent the latter could be regarded as an isolated system.

d) The fourth rule would be to introduce between two propositions, one "strange", the other "familiar", an assertion cognate with both which, without contradicting the former, becomes incompatible with it by adding information, however negligible, and ultimately safeguarding the latter, that which is already familiar.

$$(4) \ X = Y - X \neq a - Y = a + b - X \neq Y$$

Here is an example. In the last century, biologists gave up the idea of evolution in a straight line. There is no longer any scale of nature. Instead we are presented with an amply ramified genealogical tree from which we can read the (mostly hypothetic) lines of ascent and descent between the species of living beings. Thus we step from a known representation, that of a fixed scale, to one which is not so well-known, that of evolution. This theory of organic evolution has become the starting-point of scientific and political myths. Therefore you can see what the two propositions which are still incompatible despite the lapse of time would be: on one side the development of a complex genealogical tree of the species, on the other, the linear sequence of living beings. Thus, in everything that concerns the origin and evolution of man, you again find the proceedings which I shall illustrate by an example taken from *L'Homme neuronal*. The assertion cognate with these two biological propositions is borrowed from studies about the development of animals and children. Changeux writes that chimpanzees, like children aged two to four, build up graphic collections or coloured blocks but do not go beyond that stage. Whereupon he asserts: "With man, the development goes on", as if there was an immediate succession and one could pass from big chimp to small man. Curiously the point is made with regard to organic evolution, but in filigree the scale of nature of the common representation is preserved.

That such rules exist conceals a fascinating conclusion. If the irruption of a new myth is a miracle, this miracle really happened through thermodynamics, evolution, psychoanalysis, political economy, and the rest. By compromises as systematic as they were strong, science has metamorphosed common representations, for, despite ourselves, our beliefs and practices have been upset. It has itself undergone a metamorphosis as its esoteric stock of knowledge has been swallowed little by little, digested and assimilated by the mass of exoteric knowledge. Nowadays we are not even aware of its presence because it has become the limit of our horizon. During this double metamorphosis, neither reason nor logic were respected as they should have been. That is the reason why we are ready to explain its results in terms of errors, of return of archaic elements, of pressure of affects and the debauch of imagination. Thus ascribing those results to prerational mechanisms, as a consequence of a recession and lapse in the work of reason.

This is why the psychology of scientific myths would be a psychology of prerational mental and social life. In my opinion, it is not adequate to view things in such a way, remaining fettered by stereotypes and clichés. Without much difficulty, we can recognize in it neither a disruption nor a recession but a continuation of science by other means when it has reached a certain stage and its discoveries are indispensable if one wants to go beyond by enriching the cognitive and practical possibilities of the majority of people. Between the two branches of the dilemma "nothing but science" and "the science of nothing, i. e., ignorance", there is room for many other alternatives. We have seen that rules serve to create alternative phrases and images shared by scientists and non-scientists alike. If you do not endorse the general contempt for social thought, then you can suppose that we deal with post-rational mechanisms constructing a discourse "ad captum alicujus" which extends, in a sense, the discourse of reason and science. And which opens up their books of secrets to society at large.

One could surmise that there is a post-rational development of the child who has reached the Piagetian age of reason but does not stop there. This has something to do with the strange proclivity of the mind solicited to communicate with others, to explore reality and discuss truth with the living and the dead. Needless to say, from my point of view, the psychology of scientific myths, if it deserves to be pursued, should open a window on that post-rational intelligence which is no less mysterious than its opposite. I would even say that it is more mysterious since it intervenes every time we have to trespass the limits of what we know and what we do.

References

W. Doise (1987): Pratiques scientifiques et représentations sociales: que faire de la psychologie de Piaget? Cahiers du Centre de Recherches interdisciplinaires de Vaucresson, 3, 89–108.

R. M. Farr (1987): The science of mental life. A social psychological perspective. Bulletin of the Psychological Society, 40, 1–17.

L. Strauss (1952): Persecution and the art of writing. The University of Chicago Press, Chicago and London.

P. Vergès (1987): A social and cognitive approach to economic representation in W. Doise, S. Moscovici (eds.): Current Issues in European Social Psychology, vol. II, Cambridge, Cambridge University Press, 271–305.

The Multi-Level Organisation of Knowledge and Action
– An Integration of Complexity

Mario von Cranach

1. Introduction

This book is organized around the concept of social representations, which are social images, ideas or theories of the world; and the idea that knowledge rests on a social basis. I want to expand this idea, and I want to enclose some additional notions so that we arrive at a more complete picture. In its essence, my argument contains three assertions: 1. that it is the main function of knowledge to steer action; 2. that all human action and information-elaboration,* including knowledge, proceeds simultaneously on several levels constituted by the individuals and their social systems; and 3. that knowledge and action are pillars of human social co-evolution. In this paper I shall elaborate and justify these assertions and I shall try to show some of their theoretical and methodological consequences. In the first part, I shall mainly refer to problems of knowledge and action in general; in the second part, I shall be concerned with their multi-level organisation in human self-active systems.

A social representation is the organized knowledge on the level of a social system, concerning a certain topic. But what is knowledge? From a formal or technical point of view (e. g. speaking of computers) knowledge can be defined as *stored information.* When we deal with human beings as we do in psychology, this definition is still formally correct, but it must be understood in a liberal and extended sense: we must see that knowledge has qualitative implications, that human knowledge implies e. g. sensations and emotions, that we need to distinguish various classes of knowledge etc.

– In the course of my presentation, I shall formulate a number of theses. Let me emphasize in the beginning, that most of these are not very original. They contain ideas which have already been known; some of them if taken alone are even trivial. Why then, bring them up? Because these ideas, although widely agreed upon, are not widely followed; their consequences are not taken seriously. I point to these principles to develop their consequences. My presentation is therefore programmatic. In my statements and considerations, I am starting out from the research experiences of our group, using them occasionally as examples; but it is not my principal aim to report about our research.

2. General characteristics of knowledge and action

2.1. Let me begin with the example of an empirical study which I performed with Beat Thommen and Rolf Ammann some years ago. (Thommen, Ammann & von Cranach, 1988. See Thommen, v. Cranach, Ammann, this vol.). We reconstructed the social representations of two schools of psychotherapy. We then observed some of their member therapists in therapy-sessions, investigated their action-related cognitions by use of self-confrontation methods, and finally we tried to reconstruct the therapy-relevant knowledge. The results show how these schools, through the knowledge they pass on to their individual members during socialisation, control the individual actions.

Regarding this research, three points which are somehow related to the assertions I made before, are salient for my present problem:

1. In order to perform this study, it was necessary to distinguish, in theory and method, between the social representations of these schools and their reflection in the knowledge of the individual therapists. We had to distinguish between *social* and *individual social representations* or between *individual* and *social knowledge.*

---

* By this term, I want to avoid the computer analogy which is hidden in the term "information processing."

2. The psychotherapeutic schools can be considered as acting social systems, be it on an international, a national or local level: They can be sub-divided into partial organisations or groups, and these again into individuals. Whenever a school acts, it does so through the actions of its sub-groups and its members. There is activity within and among all of these levels, which is at least partly coordinated through the schools' social representations.

Let us move now from the example to more abstract formulations. Human individuals and human social systems are members of a class of living systems (which includes a great variety of animals and their societies), which I have called *self-active systems* because they steer and energize their activity out of themselves, although of course in interaction with their environment. These self-active systems are the subject of my first thesis.

I. Self-active carrier-systems and knowledge
Knowledge comes into existence in the history of self-active systems; it serves their adaptation and survival. Therefore, *any self-active system must be in possession of knowledge, and any knowledge is bound to a self-active carrier-system.*

The identification of the carrier-system and of the conditions of its existence is necessary for the full understanding of its knowledge. What I mean, is that knowledge is necessary for the survival of self-active systems and that where there is knowledge, there must be a self-active carrier-system.

But why should it be necessary to identify the carrier-system and its needs? To answer this question, let me give another example. People in West Germany and also in Switzerland discuss the hot and permanent political issues of abortion and of traffic speed limits. Both are related to the values of life and of freedom, but this relationship seems paradoxical. "Conservatives" use the value of life to reject abortion and the value of freedom to sustain free traffic; the "progressives" argue just the other way round. We understand these cognitive structures better when we investigate the interests, alliances and histories of conservative and progressive groups, the ideology of which forms the basis of individual attitudes. In other words, to know its function for a certain carrier-system on a certain level, helps to understand a social representation.

3. As the individuals used their knowledge to guide their actions, so did the schools if we look at them as units. Their social representations determined for example, how they trained and supervised their individual members.

2.2. Implicit in our discussions so far, there is another conclusion, which I formulate as a thesis:

II. Human multi-level systems
Human self-active systems are organized on many levels; we distinguish between *the individual level and several social levels*. All of these systems carry knowledge.

2.3. Knowledge is stored information, so it presupposes the existence of a memory-system (Miller, 1978). Psychologists have concentrated on the internal memory of the individual organism, and mostly neglected the external storing of information, which is important at least in the human case (see however the contribution of A. Lang, this volume). The properties of the memory determine what information is encoded in which way and how it is preserved and retrieved. Therefore, the question for the memory is in no ways trivial for the scientific investigation of knowledge. To formulate this idea in a short thesis:

III. Memories
The knowledge of self-active systems is determined by their internal and external memories in which it is stored.

2.4. In the preceeding discussion, I have repeatedly mentioned the function of knowledge for action. Today, psychologists often tend to treat knowledge as well as cognition, as if these would be self-sufficient and existed for their own sake, "l'art pour l'art" so to speak. Of course, this cannot the case. Self-active systems do not live through thinking and collecting information, but through directed behaviour and acting: acting on the environment, to adapt it to the needs of the system; and acting on themselves to adapt to the environment. To achieve a given or selected end, directed behaviour must be ordered or structured in a particular way. In order to to this, the system must know, at least partly, the aim and the way to achieve it, and it must perceive its own states and the environment, a perception which is again based on knowledge. (This is common insight of any modern action theory.) This is the primary, the survival function of knowledge, for which it came into the world. Since this function is so often overlooked, I should like to stress it as a thesis.

IV. Primary knowledge function: Action
Human self-active systems, individual or social, exist through acting on their environment and on themselves. This presupposes knowledge. *Knowledge serves action* and that is its primary function.

2.5. Of course there is a second function. Once a system has acquired broader knowledge and a good capacity to elaborate information, there is a tendency to use these achievements for their own further development and for the fun of their use. Furthermore, a system may seek to interpret and understand the world and itself also where it does not directly help it to act. So we can observe at all levels of human systems, that information elaboration and knowledge become valuable per se. They could not survive on this function alone, but it helps their internal organization and development. In the long run, it becomes a great advantage to think in stock. – Thus, societies who can afford it, sustain scientific subsystems consisting of individual scientists for which thinking and knowing is, to a degree, rewarding per se. For this function I have formulated another thesis:

IV. Secondary knowledge function
On each level, knowledge is sought, elaborated and ordered for its own value, and for a better understanding of the world. In this function, it helps the systems internal differentiation and integration, furthers its development and enlarges its action capacities.

Why do I put so much stress on the distinction of these two functions? It is my impression that in research on knowledge, and also in the study of social representations, the action function is very often neglected. The question of which function a representation serves should be part of its investigation, and it can only be answered in regard to a specific carrier system. And the same representation, (same as to topic or content) can serve different functions at different levels, as we have seen before.

2.6. Let us now take a look at the relationship between knowledge and action. In a very simple way, I have formulated it in thesis VI.

VI. Knowledge and action
Action is steered by knowledge, and knowledge is confirmed or changed through action.

Now this is really trivial and I can not imagine any colleague in the field of cognitive or action psychology who would deny it. The action steering function of knowledge, as already contained in thesis IV has been elaborated in many scientific concepts: in Oshanin's "operative representation system", which Hacker (1986) explicitly names "anticipatory activity – guiding memory representation", and which he breaks down in details according to their structure and function. (Hacker Tab. 4.6, p. 123); or in Klix' (1984) model of action planing, or Dörner's (1988) attempted synthesis which is more oriented to the motivational aspects ("intention regulation") of the relationship; and in the formal computer-oriented model of the "production process" (Opwis, 1988). The second part of my statement, the function of action for knowledge is less often considered; it forms an important part of Piaget's theory, who introduced it into developmental psychology (e. g. Piaget 1970), and a central aspect of learning in the psychology of work (see Hacker, 1986: "changes of mental regulation through work activities"). The view appears much less accentuated, however, in cognitive psychology, and there I have found more stress on the function of confirmation than on innovation.

Both aspects are very much neglected however, in social psychology; neither in the field of "social representations" nor in that of "naive psychology" or "subjective theory" does it receive much attention.

Let us end with the notion that the dynamic interplay between knowledge and action, or better from knowledge to action to change of knowledge to new action etc. can be represented in the figure of a spiral (a very old idea indeed), the slope of which symbolizes the development of the system (Fig. 1). The interplay of knowledge and action is an important aspect, maybe even the motor of mental development. We shall come back to this topic in a later section of this paper.

2.7. In all of these considerations, it is our aim to disentangle the web of multi-level knowledge and action, but before we can finally turn to this task, there is still another aspect to be considered. Individual knowledge is not immediately translated into action. In order to become effective, it must be elaborated and transformed into a multitude of cognitive processes. This is why we introduced, in the study I described in paragraph 2.1., "action-related cognitions" between "individual social representations" and the execution of the act. The details of this translation process form the object of various models. There is a common assumption among them: the application of knowledge demands its transformation into cognitive, affective and motivational processes which are tightly adapted to the specifics of the situation. Consider, e. g., the second example of paragraph 2.1.: Conservatives and progressives behave as if they would follow different rules which determine which value, life or freedom, should be applied to which topic, abortion or traffic speed limit. To put it in more general terms, human knowledge systems contain different, inconsistent or even contradictory items. To use them in the production of consistent action, people use (that is a hypothesis) "application rules" which relate a given piece of knowledge to a given set of circumstances.

Likewise, action is not immediately transformed into knowledge. Before that can happen, it must be evaluated by the acting system. An evaluation is a process in which the memories of the act, its goal, plan and execution, its external circumstances and its effects are compared with the action system's original expectations and its internalized standards. Again, evaluations have salient qualitative properties, well illustrated by the strong emotional component of individual action evaluation. In fact, from these considerations we must conclude that whenever we study the connection between knowledge and action, we must look for processes. To express it in a thesis:

VII. Processes as links between knowledge and action
In order to steer action, knowledge must be transformed into information elaboration processes which tend to be distinguished by specific qualities. In order to transform actions into knowledge, action effects and experiences must be evaluated.

The most important methodological conclusion drawn from this statement is that research on the relationship between knowledge and action must be *process-oriented*, and that researchers must take care *not to miss the qualities involved*.

3. Multi-level knowledge and action

3.1 So far, we have mainly dealt with general characteristics of knowledge and action, and various aspects of their relationship. Let us now turn to problems of multi-level organisation. Putting together the assumptions from thesis I and thesis II, we arrive at the conclusion:

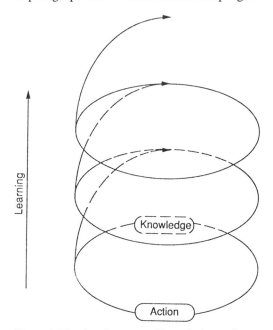

Figure 1. The development of knowledge and action.

VIII. Multi-level knowledge and action

Human knowledge is multi-level knowledge and human action is multi- level action.

What are the levels of the self-active systems with which we actually want to deal? Fig. 2 gives a survey of our proposition. Let me briefly explain what I mean, proceding up from the individual towards society. At the basis you find the *individual* subject, gifted with its full human outfit as there is e. g. self-reflexivity, emotionality, action-competence and social responsibility. The *interaction* of individuals creates system-like structures, *interaction systems* which are not yet self-active, and which do not necessarily contain social relationships and social structure. Self-active social systems evolve when interaction is enduring or repeated, so that it creates room for the development of patterns of interaction, social bonds, common knowledge (a joint history) and common interests and goals. They can begin in the *acquaintanceship*, the most rudimentary form of a human self-active social system. A *dyad* is a stable self-active unit of two persons, e. g. a couple involved in an intimate relationship. The structure of the *informal group*, which comprises of more than two individuals and

can include dyads, is much more complicated, because processes can form networks, and subgroups (e. g. coalitions) are possible. Personal relationship is also an important characteristic of the informal group.

In *formal groups*, all of these characteristics are maintained, but in addition, a new element comes into existence, namely formalization. Formalization means that at least some of the system's social structures are formally defined, and that the effectiveness or validity of processes is bound to the observation of prescribed forms: a demand, question or order e. g. must be delivered in the appropriate form to be considered. Formalized groups are normally parts of organizations, or they are rather large groups. I believe that the criterion of formalization for the classification of groups is more important than that of size.

Formalization is the essential characteristic of *organizations*. Another one consists of the inclusion of material outfit and production means in its structure, which is, to a lesser degree, already found in groups. All the organization's essential processes and structures are formally defined, but since organizations include groups and individuals, there are also informal processes on the group and individual

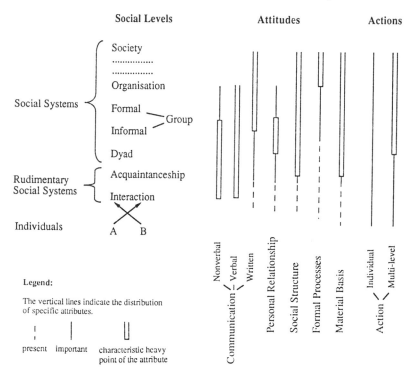

Figure 2. Human self-active systems: a classification of levels (vertical lines indicate qualitative characteristics).

level. (Similar classifications can be found in the literature; e. g. Weinert, 1981, pp. 128–129).

3.2. We find particular kinds of systems on each level of organization. Multi-level organization of knowledge and action does not only mean that the processes run off at all of these levels, but that they form a joint enterprise. For a given system, the others are not just a part of the environment, but coordinated systems on the same level, or super-systems, or sub-systems. They are co-actors, although it must be seen that they co-act in different combinations and that there are exceptions: that there is occasionaly lower level action without higher level action; and that co-actors can simultaneously be opponents or competitors. The particularities of this co-acting will be discussed later. Here I want to point out a presupposition of acting and co-acting: that each level is in possesion of an appropriate outfit to perform processes which serve the necessary sub-functions of knowledge and action. To put it into a statement:

IX. Subfunctions of knowledge and action
On all levels, systems are organized so as to secure the necessary sub-functions of knowledge and action.

What are these functions? They are partly contained in Miller's (1978) classification of the functions of living systems, and in our own publications (v. Cranach, Ochsenbein, Valach,

1986). Tab. 1 shows the division we found useful, although this should not be considered a complete or definitive classification. This is what we believe a system must be able to do in order to act and to co-act. We consider the division between energizing and steering fundamental, but we stress the fact that steering and energizing processes interact; there is e. g. energizing through goal setting or planning. There is also the coordination of the functions of knowledge and action and its sub-functions, which I have already discussed.

3.3. How do multi-level systems co-act? (This is the essence of our considerations). I want to look at this problem from three viewpoints: how the action of the system becomes organized; how the coherence between the levels is achieved; and what the differences and similarities are between the processes on the various levels.

Actions of social systems show us, to a greater or lesser degree, unified over-all patterns. Seen from a certain distance and as a whole, the manoeuvres of a sailing ship, the production of a factory, even the co-operation within a family or the functioning of university departments show coherence and unidirectedness to an astounding degree, even if we take the inevitable frictions, conflicts and misunderstandings into full account; and that is why social goals are achieved at all. How is the multi-level action of social systems integrated into a common structure? Like all actions,

Table 1. Subfunctions of knowledge and action.

Knowledge	Action	
Encoding		
	Steering	Energizing
Storing	Situational orientation	Beginning behavior
	– Perception of environment	
	– Self-monitoring attribution	Reinforcing (additional) energy)
Decoding	Goal determination	Inhibiting (less energy)
	Planning	Stopping behavior
	Starting execution	Energizing of
		– Conflict resolution
	Execution control	– Change of direction
		etc.
	Stopping execution	
	Final evaluation	

multi-level social acts must follow plans or blueprints. The socially defined blueprint of an action is the task. Tasks are knowledge on the social level. They are, it is well known, built up from interdependent sub-tasks of different content, which together form a hierarchical order. In the case of a multi-level action, the task is projected on the structure of the given social system which has to perform it. The projection appears in the form of distributed knowledge: the system and its parts know the task and who has to do what, so there is a correspondance between the task and the distributed knowledge of the system. On this basis, the social system develops information-elaboration processes which are sequentially and hierarchically structured as action-related information tends to be. (See e.g. Volpert, 1982). These processes steer the multi-level execution of the act.

Let me use the manoeuvres of a sailing yacht as an example (v. Cranach et al., 1986). Most of these manoeuvres constitute well defined tasks rehearsed in sailing books and journals. Such a task is projected on the typical crew structure (Fig. 3), consisting of skipper, helmsman, navigator, sailors at various working stations etc. The crew which knows the manoeuvre (or in the case of training, at least the skipper should know it *for the crew*!), translates and elaborates this knowledge in the form of thoughts and commands, which correspond in their content to the sub-functions of action mentioned in thesis IX: perceptions, goals, plans etc. are elaborated and transmitted. (Thoughts and commands are of course, processes, remember thesis VII.) These thoughts and communications steer the execution of the manoeuvre in the form of individual actions and of cooperation. I will try to summarize all these ideas in thesis

X. Structure of social systems' actions
In the actions of social systems, the knowledge contained in the task is projected on the structure of the system; the subsystems translate it into action related cognitive and communicative processes, which steer the execution of the act.

3.4. There is another property of this process which needs to be discussed. Think of my example of the sailing yacht: when the skipper makes a decision, he decides as a person, but also as a member of the crew. In other words, the crew as a whole decides through him, because his social position is the location of the decision function. All of the knowledge, information elaboration, energizing and action execution must finally be actualized in individual persons, because it is individuals who know, think, strive and act; and still, if we reduce these processes to sheer individual processes, they lose their functional meaning, and finally even the social systems get lost in our ideas (not in reality). To avoid the reductionistic fallacy which is to frequent in the scientific discussion, let me formulate the following:

XI. Social and individual processes
The processes of knowledge and action of a social system are finally always realized through individual processes; but they cannot be reduced to individual processes without loss of their social functions and of the social system.

Therefore, social representations are always based on individual representations (of social origin), and group action involves always individual actions, although they are more than individual representations and actions.

3.5. How is the coherence between the levels, the unified structure of multi-level actions, established? In our example the individual goals, plans etc. of the skipper are transmitted through his commands, or to state it in more general terms, cognitive and motivational processes are transmitted through communication processes. These are intermediate processes, which mediate between levels, and simultaneously they make up the social form of information elaboration. This is a complicated relationship, but it has important implications which I should like to explain.

In generalizing thesis XI, we can pretend that higher level processes are simultaneously lower lever processes; and that lower level processes run off in the frame of higher level processes. Thus, many, if not most individual acts are parts of social systems' acts, as we can show with numerous examples. Lower level processes are often determined by higher level processes: the level of individual effort can be a function of a group norm, as we know from research in the psychology of work. A general form of this connection is that of a feedback circle, in which the result of a social process acts as a standard for the individual process, which in turn contributes to the setting of this standard. Another example would be the behaviour of people in a panicking crowd. (These problems are the target of our present research about energization in group action.) Higher level processes are of course also determined by the results of lower level processes; thus the motivation of the group can be affected by the complaints of an individual member.

In all of these cases, *it are the processes which link the levels*. The problem of the modern statistical technique of "multi-level data analysis" ("Mehrebenenanalyse", v. Saldern 1986) lies in the fact that it operates with aggregations of data over levels (means, standard deviations etc.), in which the dynamics of the processes get lost, just as the regulative dynamic of a feedback circle gets lost if we restrict our analysis to the standard value. Let me finish these considerations with the thesis

XII. Connections between higher and lower level-processes
The processes on the various levels are interconnected. Processes of higher levels are often simultaneously processes on lower levels, (and are always processes on the individual level, thesis XI;) and they are often determined by the outcome of lower-level processes. Processes on lower levels run off in the context of higher-level processes as their parts.

3.6. I have tried to show that it is justified to speak of action and knowledge, as well as individuals and social systems. However, individuals, groups, organizations, etc. are not the same; how similar and how different are the processes on the various levels? Let us once again look at our example of group action, the manoeuvre of the sailing yacht (Fig. 3). As we have seen, there is knowledge, elaboration of information and action on two levels: the individuals think and act; the group communicates and co-operates. In other words, similar functions of steering and of execution are per-

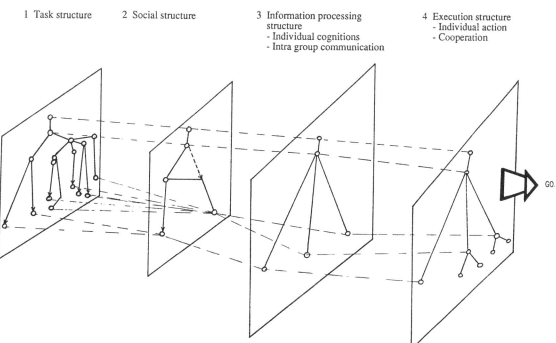

Figure 3. From task to execution: the multi-level structure of the actions of social systems.

formed on different levels through qualitatively different processes. They are similar because they have to serve the same function and because they are partly transmitted from level to level: functional analogy and homology. They are different because they are produced by systems of very different structure and quality. Therefore, I propose:

XIII. Similarities and differences
Processes on different levels can be similar because of homologies and functional analogies, and different because of their different underlying structures.

For this reason, cross level comparison is a useful heuristic device for the study of multi-level processes.

Let me illustrate this thesis with some research examples. The first refers to investigations of our research group, (Ochsenbein, v. Cranach, Tschan, 1990). These studies were aimed at the function of self-monitoring in action steering: under what circumstances will an acting system monitor its own information-processing?

During recent years, we developed a theory of "self-monitoring" which included assumptions about the functions of action related cognitions. On this basis, we predicted when certain cognitions should be consciously monitored. To test these hypotheses, we developed a specific type of experiment. We constructed an "action parcours", into which we implanted

problems located at certain points which were distributed over sequence and hierarchy. These required conscious information elaboration. In a series of experiments, these predictions were tested and sustained (Ochsenbein, 1989). Regarding our group action studies, we assume, in the context of a heuristic strategy, similarity between individual cognitions and group communication. On the basis of analogical hypotheses, we can predict what should be communicated in group action. These predictions have in fact, been repeatedly confirmed, and the experiments also yielded additional information about information elaboration in groups. The connection of the two studies is depicted in Fig. 4.

This is an example of a similarity based on homology and functional analogy, an example from the realm of action. Let us now turn to the problem of similarities between knowledge functions on different levels. In thesis III, I have stressed the importance of memory functions for knowledge, but how can we conceive of the memory of human multi-level systems? The research on the "Transactive Memory" by Daniel Wegner and his group give us an answer. It fits perfectly into our framework (Wegner, 1986). Let me report the essence of the theory in Wegner's own words.

"A Transactive Memory System is a set of individual memory systems in combination with the communication that takes place between the individuals." (P. 186) Wegner then

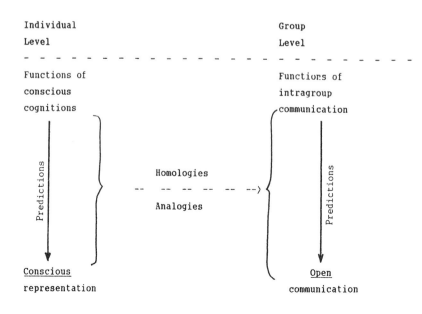

Figure 4. Similarities between individual conscious cognition and open group communication in action-situations: *Logic of the predictions.*

distinguishes between internal and external encoding and decoding and makes it clear that the use of the internal individual memory requires that an item of information is stored together with a label, while external encoding requires that the location of the item is encoded internally with the label. (E. g. In which book did I read about oral tradition in ancient Indian philosophy?) Now to the transactive memory: "Other people can be locations of external storage for the individual ... This allows both people to depend on communication with each other for the enhancement of their personal memory stores. At the same time, this interdependence produces a knowledge holding system that is larger and more complex than either of the individuals own memory systems ... The transactive memory system, in short, is more than its individual component systems." (P. 189–190) "The transactive memory system of a group involves the operation of the memory systems of the individuals and the processes of communication that occur within the group. Transactive memory is therefore not traceable to any of the individuals alone, nor can it be found somewhere "between" individuals. Rather, it is a property of a group. This unique quality of active memory brings with it the realisation that we are speaking of a constructed system, a mode of group operation that is build up over time by its individual constituents. Once in place the transactive memory system can have an impact on what the group as a whole can remember, and as a result, on what individuals in the group remember and regard as correct even outside the

group. In short, transactive memory derives from individuals to form a group information processing system that eventually may return to have a profound influence upon its individual participants" (P. 191 direct quote). It should be clear now that the transactive memory is a multi-level system, with internal and external coding on the individual level, and communication and external coding on the social levels. Furthermore, it becomes obvious that its establishment is an important part of the development of social systems, which occurs through its internal communication and its actions. Once established, the functioning of the transactive memory becomes crucial for the existence of the social system, just as the functioning of the individual memory becomes crucial for the individual person. Without memory there is no knowledge, no action and no identity.

Wegner and his colleagues have studied the transactive memory mainly on the level of dyads, but of course, it is also an essential component of organisations. Our modern organisations greatly depend upon external storage. Perhaps the most fascinating case of internal storage is the oral tradition of religious and philosophical thought in Ancient India (between 750 and 350 B. C.), ideas which were so sacred and secret that they could not be written down. In the Braman-Schools, students learned these texts by heart in up to 12 years of study and passed them on from generation to generation, for about 1000 years. Specific systems of memory training were developed, and the constant change of colloquial lan-

Figure 5. Coevolution
of individual and
group.
□ Link between levels
— Individual processes
- - Group processes

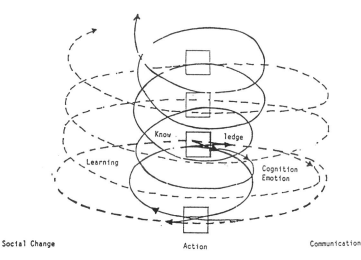

guage, a threat to the mystic quality of the texts, provoked the development of a scientific grammar and phonetics system, as a kind of meta-memories for the text. (Rüstau 1988 p. 16–17). The development of systems of formal rules is, of course, a characteristic of organisations.

Let us formulate these ideas in another thesis:

XIV. Multi-level (transactive) memory
The knowledge of human self-active systems is stored in their multi-level memories. These operate as a systematic combination of individual memory processes, externally storing and transactively coding through communication. Each system on each level has its own characteristics.

Regarding the problems of memory, let us go back to those of similarity and differences between levels. Obviously we agree with Wegner on the idea that intergroup communication is functionally equivalent but qualitatively different from individual cognition. Let us illustrate this with an example on the level of social organizations. As I have pointed out before, one of its characteristics consists of the formalization of processes, so that information elaboration is formalized communication. Franziska Tschan, in her investigation of an organizational act, has investigated the system of formalized social markers which were used in communicating so that the members would not get lost in the organizational jungle (Tschan, this volume).

3.7. In the beginning of my paper, I stated that I consider knowledge and action as pillars of human social co-evolution. Now I am in the position to explain what I meant. Let us depict the development of systems as a series of nested spirals. Each spiral corresponds to a level in the multi-level process, the individual or a social level. Viewed from above, these processes would appear circular since they consist of a sequence of repeated and formally similar stages, but since they change in content and course, be it gradually or by leaps, the gradient of the spiral is produced which symbolizes developmental change in our model. In thematically distinguished realms, the spirals are interconnected by switching stations, where the process may jump from one track to another.

Figure 5 shows a very simple version of the model, the co-evolution of one individual within (only) one group; the two levels are connected by only two switching stations, namely "knowledge" and "action". (The complicated processes within the switching stations are left unconsidered for the moment.)

How does the model operate? Here is a short description (Fig. 6). We begin with the switching station "knowledge". In processes of socialization and social influence, A (the actor) has aquired, adapted and internalized the social representation of his group G. As "individual social representations", they are now part of his own knowledge system. From a combination of this knowledge and his perceptions of his environment and himself, he

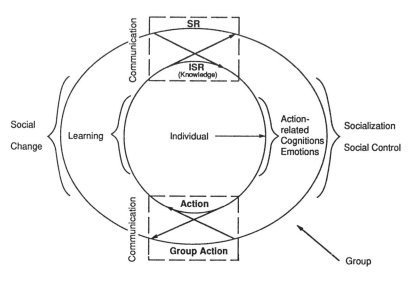

Figure 6. Nested circular processes in multi-level social coevolution.
SR = social representations.
ISR = individual social representations

develops action-related cognitions which guide his action in various forms, such as situational orientation, planning, execution control etc. (He also provides for the energization of his action, but these processes are left unconsidered for the moment). Next he performs the act. Since he operates in the context of his group, his action is also part of a group action. From the various feedback he receives during the action and from his results, and after one or many of these circles, gradually or abruptly, his knowledge, and consequently his action, changes. Sooner or later his changed knowledge is transfered to the group level, and the group's social representations are changed.

Let us now look at the events on the group level. The group (G) is an acting unit which performs actions (or goal directed behaviour, if you prefer) as a whole. (Of course all its processes are two-level processes, operating simultaneously on the individual and on the group level.) From a functional point of view, G's action is analogous (to a degree) to A's actions: G starts out from knowledge, its social representations feed into its elaboration of information, namely action- related communication. The latter guides the act in forms of establishment of goals, planning, execution and control of the act. Gradually, G's knowledge basis is changed ("social change"). The levels are connected at the crossing points of knowledge and action.

To formulate a last thesis:

XV. Multi-level social coevolution
Knowledge and action are essential components of multi-level social co-evolution.

The model can be extended to cover more than two levels (v. Cranach & Tschan, 1989), or to include other theoretical viewpoints. The research on "minority influence" (Moscovici, 1976) can easily be included into the model. And last but not least, with co-evolution we grasp a part of the historical process into which all social research should fit.

4. An outlook to application

Psychological research should also be practical and useful in the end. My presentation has been a theoretical one indeed, still I believe –

and I am now turning to the practitioners – that the multi-level approach is a very useful tool to resolve practical problems. Why and how? First, in practical work, diagnosis, consulting, or trying to induce change, we have to deal very often with multi-level problems. That is well known in family therapy, but it is equally true for other situations. In educational consulting, a school-child is an individual within a family, and within a class within a school within a community and so on, and all of these levels may simultaneously be important. Second, our theory suggests that we study these systems from the viewpoint of their interests, aims and goals, and that gives us a very useful starting point for our diagnosis and intervention. Third, from our perspective, we see the child's school achievement as a result of the joint co-production of himself, family, teacher, class, school, etc.; we can find a way out of the individualism which leads so easily to the attribution of personal causation and guilt to events wich are in fact products of social systems. Fourth, we can see ourselves as part of the system we are investigating, an insight which protects us against mistakes and helps our planning. I believe these ideas are practical, but to use them in practice, we must first learn how. That is a fascinating endeavour – but it is a topic for another paper.

References

Cranach, M. von & Tschan, F. (1990). Mehrstufigkeit im zielgerichteten Verhalten von Organisationen. In: R. Fisch und M. Boos (Hrsg.), *Vom Umgang mit Komplexität in Organisationen.*

Cranach, M. von, Ochsenbein, G. & Valach, L. (1986). The group as a self-active system. *European Journal of Social Psychology, 16*, 193–229.

Dörner, D. (1988). Wissen und Verhaltensregulation. In: H. Mandl & H. Spada (Hrsg.), *Wissenspsychologie* (S. 264–282). Berlin: VEB Deutscher Verlag der Wissenschaften.

Hacker, W. (1986). *Arbeitspsychologie.* Berlin: VEB Deutscher Verlag der Wissenschaften.

Klix, F. (Hrsg.). (1984). Ueber Wissensrepräsentation im menschlichen Gedächtnis. In: *Gedächtnis-Wissen-Wissensnutzung.* Berlin: VEB Deutscher Verlag der Wissenschaften.

Miller, J.G. (1978). *Living Systems.* New York: McGraw Hill.

Moscovici, S. (1976). *Social Influence and Social Change*. London: Academic Press.

Ochsenbein, G. (1989). Analoge Funktionen offener Informationsverarbeitung in menschlichen selbst-aktiven Systemen. *Zeitschr. f. Sozialpsychologie, 20*, H. 1, 27–37.

Opwis, K. (1988). Produktionssysteme. In: H. Mandl & H. Spada (Hrsg.) *Wissenspsychologie* (S.74–98). München-Weinheim: PVU.

Oshanin, D. A. (1976). Dynamisches operatives Abbild und konzeptuelles Modell. *Probleme und Ergebnisse in der Psychologie, 59*, 37–48.

Piaget, J. (1970). Piaget's Theory. In: P. H. Mussen (Ed.) *Carmichael's Handbook of Child Psychology*. New York: Wiley.

Rüstau, H. (1988). Die Genesis der altindischen Philosophie. In: R. Moritz, H. Rüstau & G. R. Hoffmann (Hrsg.) *Wie und wann entstand Philosophie in verschiedenen Regionen der Erde?* (S. 16–17). Berlin: Dietz Verlag.

Saldern, M. von (Hrsg.). (1986). *Mehrebenenanalyse*. Weinheim/München: PVU.

Thommen, B., Ammann, R. & Cranach, M. von (1988). *Handlungsorganisation durch soziale Repräsentationen*. Bern: Hans Huber.

Volpert, W. (1982). The Model of the Hierarchical-Sequential Organization of Action. In: W. Hacker, W. Volpert, M. v. Cranach (Eds.), *Cognitive and Motivational Aspects of Action* (pp. 35–51). Amsterdam, North Holland Publishers. Berlin: VEB Deutscher Verlag der Wissenschaften Berlin.

Wegner, D. M. (1986). Transactive Memory: A Contemporary Analysis of the Group Mind. In: B. Mullen & G. R. Goethals (Eds.) *Theories of Group Behaviour*, (pp. 185–208). New York: Springer Verlag.

Weinert, A. B. (1981). *Lehrbuch der Organisationspsychologie*. München: Urban & Schwarzenberg, München 1981.

Who Pays the Bill? The Language of Social Representation*

Lenelis Kruse & Susanne Schwarz

1. The language of social representation

Who pays the bill in the restaurant? Who changes
the tire? No question, it is the man!
Who washes the dishes, who comforts the child? Of
course, it is the woman who does it!
Real men don't eat quiche, and real women don't
pump gas, and boys don't cry and girls don't fight.

Do we still expect women and men, boys and
girls to behave like that? Or have our conceptions, our norms, our expectations of what men
and women do or don't do changed during the
course of Women's Lib and feminist movements or even legislation towards equal rights
for women and men? Have the roles of women
and men changed, have the behaviours related
to these roles changed? What about emancipated women in management positions, what
about new men, or new fathers who run a
household?

At least in our society, but probably worldwide, gender-roles, gender-related norms and
behavioural expectations are in a state of
change. People nowadays have different beliefs and attitudes concerning gender-appro-
priate roles and behaviours from those who
lived 20 years ago. Our conception of what a
woman is and should do is probably much different from the conception our grandmothers
once held and our mothers still hold. And the
conception we share with our friends may be
rather different from the concepts about
gender-adequate roles and behaviours that
groups of conservative catholics hold.

These are some of the issues dealt with in a
larger research project at the University of
Heidelberg, that was part of the Heidelberg-
Mannheim Research Group whose members
and their projects focus on "Language Use in
Social Context".

In our research project "Social Representation and Language" we have tried to specify
and elaborate Moscovici's theory or concept of
social representation (cf. Moscovici 1961; Farr
& Moscovici 1984) with respect to the problem
of how social representations become manifest
in language behaviour, in both speech production and comprehension. The object we have
chosen to study social representations is *the
man* and man-woman relationships.

Conceptions about the sexes, sex and gender
roles, role-appropriate behaviours and male-
female relationships are good candidates for
the study of social representations. They can
be conceived of as subjective theories, interpretive schemata, belief systems that have the
status of "représentations collectives" (Durkheim 1970), i. e. are existent above and beyond
individual cognitions as properties of a community or society as a whole or at least of larger
social groups.

We have chosen Alfred Schütz's (1971) notion of the "common stock of knowledge" to
denote this property of a social representation.
On the one hand, a social representation or
common stock of knowledge is *collectively
shared* by all members of the community (e. g.
that humans exist as men and women, that
women and men are different in some respects,
similar in others, and that they occupy different roles in a society). On the other hand, conceptions of sex and gender differ or are *differently represented* in different groups. Members
of conservative groups or political parties may
still be convinced that men are stronger, more
intelligent, just better than women and that
this can be traced to genetic causes. Other
groups may not agree with this notion but may
still hold that a woman's place is in the kitchen
but not at the lectern of a social psychology
conference.

Distinctive features of this common stock of
knowledge are, that it is "taken for granted",
that it serves as a common interpretive schema
as well as a means of communication. We ex-

* The research reported here was made possible by a research grant from the Deutsche Forschungsgemeinschaft
and was carried out by the authors, Franc Wagner and Ernst Weimer.

pect group-specific modes of social representations to exist or develop when issues are socially controversial or when they are in a process of change (such as concepts of unemployment, AIDS, the use of nuclear energy and gender relationships). From this point of view, social representations may also be used to identify and label different groups, e. g. as "Greens", "No-Nukes", as "Chauvis" or "Hooligans". Social representations then serve as *identity markers* which, following Henry Tajfel's theory of social identity (cf. Tajfel, 1978), may be used to identify with a membership group or to discriminate against an outgroup.

But how do we know who or which groups share which stock of knowledge or belief system in which situations or circumstances?

We expect that this primarily happens by means of *language*, rather than by non-verbal gestures, sheer force etc. Speech should, therefore, be a dominant mode of the manifestation of a social representation. Language is the most important mediator and constituent of social representations; it is in *communication* that persons, events, relationships are *cognitively* and *verbally* constructed. It is also by verbal communication that social representations are negotiated, questioned and confirmed. This happens mainly in face-to-face interaction, but also through the *media*, through newspapers and magazines, through radio and television.

Moscovici has stressed that social representations are subject to *creative processes*, that they are always in the making (1988, p.219). He has also emphasized, that the theory of social representation is a theory of social thinking and *communication*, but neither he nor most of the other researchers in Europe who have taken up the concept of social representation, have taken the communication aspect so seriously as to study verbal behaviour of individuals and groups. Nor are social psychologists in general interested in the language of social interaction. An exception is the most recent work by G. Semin and K. Fiedler (1988,1989) and their associates. Thus, the general neglect of the linguistic aspect in research was the motive for our research.

Being interested in how people, sharing different aspects of the social representation of man, differ in their language behaviour, we first had to find ways of assessing the *collective*

character of the social representation of man *independent of individual cognitions*, attitudes, beliefs and speech acts. For this purpose, we assumed that social representations manifest themselves not only in verbal and non-verbal actions of *individuals*, that is, to use Karl Mannheim's terms, in the *subjective culture* (1970), but become manifest also in the *objective culture*, in literature, movies, works of art, buildings, etc. We thus turned to print media, to magazine and journal texts as examples of the objective culture, which, even though created by individuals, gain a kind of *supra-individual* existence, and may serve as external memories of a common stock of knowledge, potentially accessible to all members of a society.

2. Text analysis: Interactions between women and men

Widely read German magazines were taken and screened over a period of six months in order to select texts which adressed problems of the man, of the male role and of male-female relationships.

Texts from different German magazines were analyzed

1) with respect to representations of male- or female-role-specific behaviours, experiences, emotions, and
2) with respect to typical sequences of interactions between men and women.

Units of analysis where those parts of the texts that presented interactions of a man and a woman. The analysis was done by means of a model based on the concept of *frame*, as developed by Fillmore (1976) and van Dijk (1977), because it deals with both the *cognitive structure* of an interactional episode or scenario (specifying social roles and typical role-related actions) and with the *linguistic structure* matching such episodes in a *prototypical* way.

In order to analyze the interactions between men and women we used a three level *hierarchical category system* that was constructed to represent the themes and scenes of man-woman interactions.

Verb concepts with pertaining semantic roles, in our case male or female roles as logical subject and logical object, represent the lowest level of this category system. Each verb concept stands for several concrete verbs used in the texts.

Two to four verb concepts constitute a *subcategory* (e. g. "seeking help" or "giving help"). Four subcategories are combined to a *supracategory* which can be taken as comprehensive categories of experience and behaviour.

Four supracategories have been chosen:

– *Associative Behaviour* (with the subcategories seeking help, giving help, cultivating social contact, establishing a relationship);
– *Dissociative Behaviour* (with subcategories intimidation, self-protection, opposition, using force);
– *Evaluative Behaviour* (with subcategories positive and negative sanctions, self-enhancement and self-abasement);
– *Emotional Experience* (with subcategories sympathy, antipathy, joy, uneasiness).

3. Results

515 texts from 72 different German magazines were analyzed and 3090 single acts were subjected to the coding procedure. The question to be answered by way of the text analysis concerns the linguistic manifestation of typical male and female patterns of behaviour and experience as well as man-woman interactions as presented in media texts. The results obtained were rather conclusive.

In 52.9% of the coded acts a man was in the role of the logical subject, in 47.1% it was a woman. Yet, for the various modes of behaviour and experience the frequency distribution was quite different: Women are primarily presented by means of the category Emotional Experience (with 45.9% of all acts with women in the role of the logical subject). They are least presented (10%) in terms of Evaluative Behaviour.

Men, on the contrary, are more often described by means of Dissociative Behaviour (30.3%), least often in terms of Emotional Experience (20.3%).

Looking at the categories more closely we find that within the category of Associative Behaviour, 60.9% of all acts are initiated by men, only 39.1% by women. With Emotional Experience, however, the distribution is almost reversed: 66.8% of all acts have women in the role of the subject against 33.2% of men. The differences between men and women are even more pronounced for the category of Evaluative Behaviour (25.6% women versus 74.4% men in the subject role).*

A more detailed analysis of the four categories in terms of sub-categories and verb concepts reveals even more conspicuous differences, as we have also looked at how often a woman is presented in the object role when a man is in the subject role and vice versa, e. g. a man asks a woman for help or a woman asks for help from a man.

Here we can only give a summary report of this part of the analysis: for more detailed results cf. Kruse, Weimer & Wagner (1988). As to the category of Associative Behaviour it seems, at least in widely read magazine articles, that women are characterized as seeking help, while men are seen in the complementary role as those who give help, who are empathetic with respect to women and who grant them moral support. Men are described as conquerors and wooers, as those who establish and intensify intimate relationships. It is the man who initiates contact, while it is the woman, who is seen in the role of the passive receiver of man's kind acts.

For the next category, Dissociative Behaviour, we also found evidence that the social representation of men and women, as reflected in the magazine texts, is in accordance with the typical gender-role stereotype: Men are verbally portrayed as intimidating, threatening, using force, women being their targets and victims. Women on the other hand, are described in terms of behaviour patterns that are complementary to those of men: they engage in more passive, reactive behaviours to protect and to defend themselves against men.

For the category Emotional Experience we find that emotions, such as feelings of sym-

---

* Critical χ^2 for all differences 10.83, p<.001.

pathy and antipathy, of joy and uneasiness, seem to be a matter for women rather than men. Women are significantly more often portrayed as showing both: feelings of affection and love and affects, such as hate and anger towards men.

Thus, in general, the results are rather unambiguous: Consistent with data from numerous studies on sex- and gender-stereotyping (Broverman et al. 1972; Spence et al. 1975) we find that women are described by means of positively and negatively evaluated modes of emotional experience; they are depicted in the role of victims and seeking help. Complementary to the female role of victim, men are characterized as pursuers. They demand, threaten and forbid. They are frequently seen as using force and shunting needs and wishes of their partners. Furthermore, men are portrayed as those who give help to helpless women, who show empathy and give them actual and moral support. Women, however, very often respond to such actions by more passive modes of opposition or by resigning completely.

What about the New Man, the Emancipated Woman? They do not show in our sample of print media. Role relationships between men and women are still presented in traditional clichés: men act, women react; women seek help, men give help; men play the active part in courtship behaviour, women are the receivers of such acts.

4. Verbal recall of frame-(in)consistent episodes

The results of the media study served as a starting point for a series of experimental studies which focussed on the *subjective* culture, i.e. on individual cognitions, images and speech behaviours expressed by individual members of the society.

How do individuals perceive, comprehend and verbally recall gender-related acts and role-relationships that are either *consistent* or *inconsistent* with the gender-related frames found in the media texts?

4.1 First Experiment

For our first experiment, two different stories were constructed (1) about a young man and a young woman who meet while being on vaca-

tion, (2) about a girl and her boyfriend and what happened between them during a weekend. These stories were composed of episodes with gender-related actions (such as "seeking help") that were either frame-consistent (i.e. "the young woman is seeking help") or frame-inconsistent ("the young woman is initiating contact"). The proportion of frame-consistent to frame-inconsistent episodes was $1:2$.

In accordance with a number of studies on the processing and recall of schema-consistent or -inconsistent information (cf. Kintsch & Greene, 1978, or Snyder & Uranowitz, 1978) we hypothesized that subjects asked to summarize the stories would differ with respect to the *recall* of the frame-consistent and inconsistent episodes and to *mistakes* and *insecurities* (such as corrections, slips of tongue, change of subject role, etc.) when verbally reconstructing the story.

Subjects (18 women and 18 men between 18 and 65 years of age) were asked (in individual trials) to read the first story. After a filler task of two minutes they were requested to summarize the story. The *free recall* of the story was then followed by a *cued recall*, where the experimenter asked specific questions concerning the actors of specific episodes, e. g. "who was asking for help". The same procedure was followed for the second story.

4.2 Results

We looked at several variables as indicators for the effectiveness of the social representation of man or male-female relationships when recalling verbal material consistent or inconsistent with the particular representation or frame:

(1) number of recalled acts, (2) change of subject roles, (3) substitution of subject role or sex markers, (4) corrections, slips of the tongue etc., (5) pauses, (6) uncertainties.

1) With respect to the *number* of acts and experiences that were remembered or verbally recalled no differences were found between frame-consistent and inconsistent acts.

2) We had expected that Ss might perhaps *change the subject role* in accordance with the culturally accepted frame or schema, e. g., change the episode "She asked him,

whether she could sit at his table" into "he asked her, whether he could sit at her table". This hypothesis, however, could not be confirmed, neither for the free recall part of the task nor for the cued recall. One has to keep in mind, however, that "change of subject role" is a rather severe mistake, considering the short time lapse between reading and recalling the story and would thus have been a very strong indicator for the effectiveness of a frame.

3) A less strong indicator was *substitution of sex markers*, i. e., instances where Ss would talk about "they" or "both of them" instead of referring to a particular person, using the personal pronoun (he/she) or the proper name of the protagonists. There was, in fact, a strong effect for both texts. Inconsistent acts were significantly more often reconstructed without specifying the sex of the actor. While this effect should have disappeared completely in the cued recall task, we still obtained a significant effect for one of the texts; 96% of substitutions occurred with inconsistent episodes, only 4% with consistent ones.

Indicators (4) – (6) could be summarized as *uncertainties* (corrections, slips of the tongue, stuttering, phrasing a sentence as question etc.). We expected to find more uncertainties with inconsistent phrases. This was corroborated for corrections and slips (e. g., when Ss started a sentence using a particular subject role, then stopped to start over again): 91% of corrections and slips occurred when recalling inconsistent episodes, only 9% with consistent ones (in the first text). This effect could be interpreted as a kind of negotiation between two competing frames: the frame-inconsistent episode just read, and the culturally shared frame of what women and men actually do.

Thus, trying to study social representations of male-female relationships as part of the subjective culture, i. e., as they are represented in individual minds and become manifest in individual speech behaviour, we found that there is a tendency to reconstruct texts in a way that they are in accordance with culturally shared frames of gender-typical modes of behaviour and experience found in samples of the objective culture. The strongest indicator of this tendency was the substitution of sex-specific nouns and pronouns by neutral plural phrases in those episodes that did not comply with the culturally valid or shared representation of male-female relationships.

The first experiment raised a number of interesting questions which we then tried to tackle within a second experiment.

5. Group specific differences in verbal recall and text production

In setting up the second experiment, one of the objectives was to control for the memory effect which we assumed was responsible for the rather weak effects of the social representation (qua frame) on the reproduction of texts. In accordance with research on memory of, e. g., scripted versus non-scripted activities (cf. Graesser et al. 1980) we hypothesized that a longer period of time between reading the text and reconstruction task would make the culturally shared frames more salient and would result in more frame-consistent reproductions of originally frame inconsistent episodes at a later point of measurement.

5.1 Second Experiment

We thus repeated the first experiment, using only the first text, and again had our Ss (40 male students, between 20 and 35 years of age) go through the recall and the cued recall task immediately after reading the text. In addition, however, Ss were called by telephone a week later and were asked to reconstruct the text once more.

5.2 Results

We found, in fact, significant differences with respect to change of subject roles for frame-consistent versus frame-inconsistent episodes. (So, after all, it wasn't the young woman who payed the bill, but the young man.) At instances where this "strong" effect was only marginally significant, namely at the condition of immediate recall, it was "substituted" by significant results with respect to the weaker effect , i. e. substitution of specific sex markers.

In summary, the results of the second experiment provide rather convincing evidence that our Ss *reconstruct* rather than just *reproduce* the text on the basis of collectively shared representations of man-woman relationships.*

In order to further test these findings and to avoid effects of text memory completely, Ss in the second experiment were not only asked to reproduce a text but also to *produce* their own story. They were given a list of verbal phrases (verb concepts) together with a macrostructure for a story consisting of five episodes. Ss were asked to tell a story using the verb concepts in the sequence given in the instructions.

The verbal phrases had been chosen according to the results of the media analysis, i.e. pertaining to verb concepts and categories which we had found were used more often with either men or women in the subject role, i.e. were part of gender-typical frames. As culturally shared frames they can be taken as a facet of the social representation of men (and women).

The stories were tape-recorded and analysed with respect to frame-consistent or -inconsistent use of gender roles with the particular verb phrases. Who is reported to pay the bill, the man or the woman? Who starts the conversation? Who fixes the bike?

Before reporting the findings, another variable has to be introduced that was analyzed in this experiment. As emphasized above, our research on social representation had as its aim to study both the collectively shared and *group specific* modes of the social representation of the man. The question raised in the context of this experiment is whether Ss who belong to social groups with more traditional or conservative norms and attitudes with respect to men would differ from members of social groups with more modern, liberal attitudes in the way they handle frame-consistent and -inconsistent episodes in the story-production as well as in the story-reconstruction task.

To investigate these potential differences we had recruited half of our Ss from rather conservative student corporations and the other half from liberal and progressive groups, such as the "Green-Alternatives" (people associated with the Greens, the peace-movement etc.).

In order to further ascertain these group differences a German version of the Sex-Role Orientation Scale" (Krampen, 1979, adopted from Brogan & Kutner, 1976) was applied to distinguish Ss with a traditional from those with a liberal sex-role orientation.

The results clearly show that, in fact, Ss belonging to student corporations behaved in a more conservative way. They constructed stories that significantly more often combined the verbal phrases with male or female subject roles in a frame-consistent way (192) than did Ss from the green-alternative groups (124). The differences were significant at the .05 level.

Analyzing the results of the story-reproduction task as to group differences it became evident that it is only the Ss of the student corporation group who were responsible for the significant results concerning change of subject role and/or substitution of sex markers in a frame-consistent way. The Ss from the "Green-alternative" groups seem to be more flexible in accepting either frame-consistent or -inconsistent episode constructions and are ready to reproduce them respectively.

Considering these results, it appears that we are now well on the way to finding some answers to the questions (1) of how social representations existing in a society become manifest in the language of its members, and (2) how these speech patterns may covary with group membership, i.e., are representative of people sharing different aspects of a social representation about an issue which is no longer consensually constructed by all members of a society. Having found alternative representations of both the man and the man-woman relationship our next step must now be to turn to so-called "alternative" media which may be expected to reflect the representations of their readers.

---

* An alternative interpretation, as suggested by M. v. Cranach, could read that subjects reconstruct nothing but their everyday experience.

Who Pays the Bill? The Language of Social Representation

29

Literature

Brogan, D. & Kutner, N. G. (1976). Measuring sex-role orientation: A normative approach. *Journal of Marriage and the Family, 38*, 31–40.

Broverman, I. K., Vogel, S. R., Broverman, D. M., Clarkson, D. M. & Rosenkrantz, P. S. (1972). Sex-role stereotypes: A current appraisal. *Journal of Social Issues, 28*, 59–78.

van Dijk, T. A. (1977). Context and cognition: Knowledge frames and speech act comprehension. *Journal of Pragmatics, 1*, 211–232.

Durkheim, E. (1970). *Individuelle und kollektive Vorstellungen.* In E. Durkheim, Soziologie und Philosophie (S. 45–83). Frankfurt/M.: Suhrkamp. (Original 1898)

Farr, R. & Moscovici, S. (eds) (1984). *Social representations.* Cambridge: Cambridge University Press.

Fillmore, C. J. (1977). Scenes-and-frame semantics. In A. Zampoli (ed.), *Linguistic structures processing* (pp. 55–82). Amsterdam: North-Holland.

Graesser, A. C., Woll, S. B., Kowalski, D. J. & Smith, D. A. (1980). Memory for typical and untypical actions in scripted activities. *Journal of Experimental Psychology: Human Learning and Memory, 6*, 503–515.

Kintsch, W. & Greene, E. (1978). The role of culture-specific schemata in the comprehension and recall of stories. *Discourse Processes, 1*, 1–13.

Krampen, G. (1979). Eine Skala zur Messung der normativen Geschlechtsrollen-Orientierung (GRO-Skala). *Zeitschrift für Soziologie, 3*, 254–266.

Kruse, L. Weimer, E. & Wagner, F. (1988). What men and women are said to be: Social represen-

tation and language. *Journal of Language and Social Psychology, 7*, 243–262.

Mannheim, K. (1970). *Wissenssoziologie.* (Soziologische Texte, Bd. 28). Berlin: Luchterhand.

Moscovici, S. (1961) *La Psychanalyse, son image et son public.* Paris: PUF.

Moscovici, S. (1988). Notes toward a description of social representations. *European Journal of Social Psychology, 18*, 211–250.

Schütz, A. (1971). Strukturen der Lebenswelt. In I. Schütz (Hrsg.), *Alfred Schütz. Gesammelte Aufsätze Bd. 3.* (S. 153–170). Den Haag: Martinus Nijhoff.

Semin, G. R. & Fiedler, K. (1988). The cognitive functions of linguistic categories in describing persons: social cognition and language. *Journal of Personality and Social Psychology, 54*, 558–568.

Semin, G. R. & Fiedler, K. (1989). Relocating attributional phenomena within a language cognition interface: The case of actors' and observers' perspective. *European Journal of Social Psychology, 6*, 491–508.

Snyder, M. & Uranowitz, S. W. (1978). Reconstructing the past: some cognitive consequences of person perception. *Journal of Personality and Social Psychology, 36* (9), 941–950.

Spence, J. T., Helmreich, R. L. & Stapp, J. (1975). Ratings of self and peers on sex-role attributes and their relation to self-esteem and conceptions of masculinity and feminity. *Journal of Personality and Social Psychology, 32*, 29–39.

Tajfel, H. (1978). Social categorization, social identity and social comparison. In H. Tajfel (ed.), *Differentiation between social groups: Studies in the social psychology of intergroup relations* (pp. 33–47). Monterey: Brooks/Cole.

On Social Representations of Emotional Experience: Stereotypes, Prototypes, or Archetypes?*

Klaus R. Scherer

In collaboration with colleagues in many different countries, we have recently conducted several questionnaire studies of actual experiences of major emotions, obtaining self reports on the recall of antecedent situations, physiological symptoms, expressive behavior, control attempts, and subjective feeling states. The results showed a large amount of universality in antecedents and reactions in comparing eight European countries (Scherer, Wallbott, & Summerfield, 1986), major differences between Japan, the USA, and the European sample in a comparison of these three major cultural groups (Scherer, Wallbott, Matsumoto, & Kudoh, 1989; Matsumoto, Kudoh, Scherer, & Wallbott, 1988), and a complex mixture of universality and cultural specificity in an ongoing study of cultures on all five continents, with 37 countries studied to date (Wallbott & Scherer, 1986/1989). While emotion theorists stressing the biological functions and the phylogenetic continuity of the emotion system happily point to the substantial amount of universality shown by the data, and anthropologists and cross-cultural psychologists undertake to interpret the pattern of cultural differentiation observed, many psychologists suggest, often in a slightly deprecating tone, that such self report data might reflect "nothing but stereotypes or social representations of the emotions" and are unlikely to reveal much of value for the "scientific" study of emotion.

Stimulated by the theme of the congress upon which this volume is based, social representation, I will attempt in this paper to evaluate the merits of this claim and to inquire more generally into the status of verbal reports of emotional experiences. There can be little doubt about the existence of shared social representations of the emotions, including their nature and function as well as their appropriateness in specific situations. The very existence of language differences in emotion labels and in psychiatric categories concerning affective disorders (i.e. abnormal emotional behaviors) is a direct consequence of these representations, which, with the exception of some anthropologists (Levy, 1984; Lutz & White, 1986) have so far received little attention from emotion researchers. On the other hand, there can also be little doubt about the fact that the actual emotion episodes consist of highly individualistic patterns of situation appraisal, physiological arousal, expressive behavior, control attempts, and phenomenological experience. Obviously, self reports of recalled emotion episodes are located between these two extremes of cultural codification and unique individual experience. If only by the force of having to use a culturally proscribed category system in the form of language-specific terms to describe antecedent situations, reactions, and emotion categories, social representations of emotions will necessarily influence the account given. Furthermore, memory storage of the event and the retrieval processes are affected by emotion representation, as is the evaluation of the episode in a specific social group and cultural context. Most importantly, social representations are likely to have affected the very elicitation, unfolding, and control of the emotional episode.

There can be little doubt, then, that verbal report of emotion experiences will necessarily reflect social representations of emotion. The question becomes whether this is in some way an artifact that impedes the "scientific" study of emotion or whether, on the contrary, the study of emotion would be incomplete without taking this factor into account. I will first attempt to explore which psychological concepts might be most profitably employed in this context to evaluate the interaction of stored memories of biological and psychological processes and of social representations of affect in shaping verbal reports of emotional experience.

* I am much indebted to Ursula Hess and Pierre Philippot for valuable comments on the manuscript.

In reviewing the literature on social representation, I was struck by the relative lack of concern with emotional phenomena in this domain. Given the long tradition of social science concern with this phenomenon which dates back to Durkheim, and the leading role the concept has always played in European social psychology (see Scherer, in press), the absence of explicit treatment of emotion is surprising. As in other areas of psychology, emotion seems to have been neglected in comparison with cognitive or social interactional phenomena. This is all the more striking since many of the major studies of social representation, such as on psychoanalysis (Moscovici, 1961/1976), on social cognition and intergroup relations (Doise, 1988), and on a variety of other topics (see Jodelet, 1989), touch on phenomena with strong affective components. Given the absence of a role model, my lack of expertise in this area, and the patent difficulties of reaching agreement on a definition of the term social representation (Doise, 1985, 1988), I will not attempt a definition or description of social representations of emotion. Rather, I will stick to three proven concepts: stereotypes, prototypes, and archetypes. I will briefly describe how these concepts could be used in the study of verbal accounts of emotional experience. I assume, then, that individual cognitive representations of emotional experiences are determined by underlying social representations of emotion that will manifest themselves in stereotypes and prototypes, and possibly even in archetypes.

The notion of "stereotype" which is very much established in scientific terminology and in everyday language, does not fare much better than social representation in terms of agreement among social psychologists as to its definition. Many authors agree that stereotyping implies such cognitive features as extreme category width, levelling and sharpening, overgeneralization, polarization and the like. However, some authors see stereotypes as a device for cognitive economy and stress the "kernel of truth". Others do not make much of a distinction with respect to "prejudice" and use the term for ill-founded categorizations often with a negative bias. It may be best to accept this latter connotation which corresponds to the current usage of the concept. In other words, let us assume that stereotypes consist of at least

partly incorrect categorizations and inferences, maybe with a tiny kernel of truth, which are shared among specific subgroups of society and thus may strongly affect cognitive processing. The social representations of emotion may contain such stereotypes which might have been created by cultural lore, literary invention, or the needs of specific cultural values or sanctioning systems. If anything, stereotypes should be culture-specific. Thus, we need to examine closely the cross-cultural differences found in our comparative studies in order to determine whether these are likely to be due to stereotypes rather than to actual cultural differences in emotion elicitation and/or emotional reactions. Since stereotypes are acquired in the life-long process of socialization, and since these processes may be highly specific for groups of individuals due to differential parental influence, subculture context, and media exposure, we would expect that stereotypes differ strongly between groups and individuals within a particular culture.

Undoubtedly, narrative accounts of emotional experiences will contain some stereotypes concerning emotion elicitation and emotional reaction. However, if it could be shown that verbal reports of emotional experiences contained *only* stereotypes in the sense defined above, the use of this kind of research material would indeed be compromised. While it might yield interesting insights into one form of social representation and raise important questions about the relationship of social representation to reality, it would not be very useful to study emotional processes.

The notion of "prototypes" has become very popular in recent years, following the pioneering work by Rosch and her associates on categorization. Fehr and Russell (1984) on the one hand and Shaver, Schwartz, Kirson, & O'Connor (1987) on the other hand, have extended the idea to the emotion domain, claiming that the so-called fundamental emotions are prototypes at the basic level of emotion categorization. These authors view emotion categories as fuzzy sets which include criteria such as antecedents, responses, and self-control procedures. In an empirical study of emotion experiences, Shaver and his collaborators find consistent groupings of these facets for the major emotions and conclude that emotion prototypes constitute people's implicit models of emotion processes and serve to organise and store emotional experiences. It is likely, then, that these prototypes represent at the same time modal patterns of situation-appraisal-emotion relationships, biologically based patterns of response modality configurations, feeling states at the psychological level, and the social representations of these underlying processes.

Most psychologists working on emotion would probably agree that verbal emotion reports are strongly influenced by emotion prototypes. They might not agree, however, on the relative contribution and importance of the factors or determinants enumerated above. All of these, including the biological processes at the level of control or regulation attempts, are subject to cultural influences. Thus, cultural comparison per se may not be sufficient to determine their relative contribution. In particular, biologically oriented emotion researchers would want assurance that the basic physiological reaction patterns, which they suspect to be phylogenetically continuous, could be demonstrated through verbal report.

I suggest using the notion of "archetypes" in this context. This is based on Jung's concept of fundamental forms of representation, obviously without being too concerned with the specific symbols he proposed. More specifically, I propose to use the term "archetype" to refer to the cognitive representations of phylogenetically continuous associations between specific types of situations, differentiated emotional states, and biologically determined, adaptive response configurations. These would, when filled with culturally specific content such as values, rules, interaction strategies, specific objects, frequency of specific events, verbal labelling and the like, turn into prototypes with the accompanying social representation of the emotion categories. In fact, the universally stable core of the prototypes collected in many different cultures might well represent such archetypes and could be usefully employed to structure the search for phylogenetically continuous emotional processes.

To summarize: I suggest that verbal reports of emotion experiences are affected by three types of cognitive representations – archetypes, prototypes, and stereotypes. Emotion archetypes correspond to the cognitive representation of phylogenetically continuous and interculturally universal emotion mechanisms based on strong and repeated individual experience and cultural transmission on a very fundamental level of commonly shared experience. Emotion prototypes encompass archetypes but in addition, reflect culture-specific emotion-eliciting situations and values, as well as culturally controlled ways of emotion expression and feeling (display and feeling rules). Emotion stereotypes can reflect a kernel of truth based on archetypes and stereotypes but are mostly characterized by beliefs about emotion processes that are specific to individuals and groups, and which may reflect group-specific ideologies (e. g. hippie culture need for constant happiness, or emotion repression by ascetic sects).

In order to be able to properly interpret verbal emotion reports collected in questionnaire research, we would like to identify the underlying type of cognitive representation. In view of the lack of clear criteria this may seem like a fairly hopeless undertaking. However, we should not give up too early. I suggest that fine-grained interpretation of cross-culturally comparative data sets may give us at least some clues as to relative importance of particular types of representation for specific aspects of the emotion reports. Specifically, I suggest to use measures of effect size for differences between individuals, groups, cultures, and different basic emotions as an index for the presence of archetypes, prototypes, or stereotypes.

– Archetypes: Since the basic emotions are considered to be highly differentiated on the level of eliciting situation, physiological symptoms, behavioral expression and subjective feeling state, we would expect very strong effect sizes for emotion differences in this case. Given the phylogenetically continuous nature of the mechanisms presumed to underlie archetypes and their universality, we should find very small effect sizes for culture differences. Needless to say, the variance due to group differences should be negligible.

– Prototypes: We believe emotion prototypes to be considerably influenced by cultural values, norms, and lifestyles, with respect to both elicitation and experience. In consequence, we should expect fairly sizeable effect sizes for culture differences if verbal reports have been influenced by prototypic representations. This should not, however, reduce the effect size for emotion differences. If anything, cultural categorization and regulation should increase differences between basic emotions. Thus, we would want to have evidence for strong emotion difference main effects to infer the effect of emotion prototypes. Effect size for individual differences (together with error) should be relatively small but could well be quite a bit larger than in the case of archetypes, assuming that cultural effects may be less uniform than biological effects in the way they shape individual emotion experiences.

– *Stereotypes:* The most important index for the existence of stereotypes would seem to be the existence of strong effects for group factors such as sex, education, occupation, religion, etc., which are unlikely to be based on real differences in emotional experience (something which is admittedly enormously difficult to establish). We may expect emotion and culture difference effect sizes to be fairly small since it is likely that different groups and individuals have different stereotypes in different cultures and for different emotions (which should reduce the effect size for the latter). However, it cannot be excluded that under certain circumstances stereotypes may strengthen and sharpen existing differences between cultures and/or emotions and thus inflate effect sizes for the latter. A major difficulty in diagnosing the presence of stereotype effects is that we know little about the nature of the social groups that would need to be identified in order to find similar social representations.

Furthermore, in many empirical studies, little attention is given to such group variables beyond age and sex.

It should be noted that archetype, prototype, and stereotype effects are not mutually exclusive. On the contrary, it is quite likely that all three are present in any one verbal emotion report. In consequence, all we can attempt to do is to identify the relative strength of the respective type of cognitive representation. This may vary considerably over the different aspects of verbal emotion reports. For example, it is possible that reports of physiological symptoms are more strongly determined by archetypes (and are thus very similar across cultures; see also Rimé, Phillipot, & Cisamolo, 1990) while reports of expressive behavior in emotion situations depend more on prototypes (given the importance of cultural display rules).

I will conclude this paper by illustrating some of the preceding suggestions with data from our large 37 culture study (Wallbott & Scherer, 1986/1989). Figures 2–4 show means for different emotions and effect sizes for reported body temperature, laughing/crying, and body orientation respectively (these figures are based on data reported in Table 4 in Wallbott & Scherer, 1986/1989. Since no group effects were reported in this preliminary paper, these are included in the error variance.).

Judging by the effect size criteria suggested above, it would seem that a joy/happiness archetype may be responsible for the reports of laughing and feeling warm in joyful situations (see Figures 1 and 2): we find very strong emotion difference effect sizes (with joy being very different from all others), very small cul-

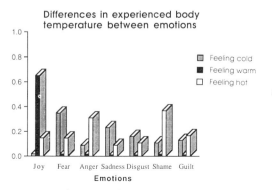

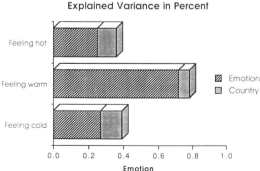

Figure 1. Differences in experienced body temperature between emotions.

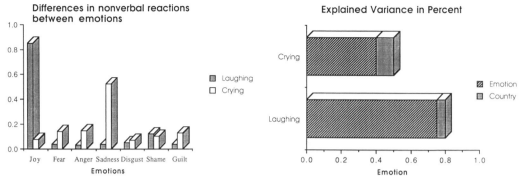

Figure 2. Differences in nonverbal reactions between emotions.

ture/country effect sizes, and a comparatively minuscule residual error (reflecting systematic individual and group differences in addition to error). It would seem that the warm glow and laughter with joy is indeed a universal phenomenon with little cultural constraint (we know the latter to be true from another variable, control/coping efforts, in the same study). Strangely enough, it is difficult to assume phylogenetic continuity, at least for laughter, given the controversy that surrounds the question of nonhuman smiling and laughing (van Hooff, 1972). However, it may well represent an emotional reaction pattern that is found particularly early in ontogenetic development, at least as far as smiling and laughter is concerned (see Geppert & Heckhausen, 1990; Scherer & Wallbott, 1990). This particular example may seem trivial, given its obviousness, which, alas, is the burden of many findings in social psychology, yet, it illustrates the use of effect size differences particularly well.

Crying in sadness, feeling hot in anger and shame, and feeling cold in fear (see Figures 1 and 2) are borderline candidates for archetypes: while the effect sizes for emotion are still much bigger than the culture/country effect

sizes, there is some cultural variation, (in the case of crying probably due to cultural display rules) and, in particular, there is quite a lot of individual variation (residual error, distance between shaded bars and 1.0 mark in the Figures).

The body orientation results shown in Figure 3 seem to suggest the operation of emotion prototypes, as defined above: there are clear emotion differences but the culture effect sizes are equally, if not more important, suggesting a strong role for cultural prescription or regulation/control in the case of this behavioral variable. As mentioned above, it is likely that all three types of representations have an influence in the examples cited but archetypes or prototypes are likely to be dominant. As suggested before, these effects seem to vary greatly between different modalities of the emotion response.

Examples for a clear operation of stereotypes are more difficult to find, partly due to the difficulty of identifying the relevant group variables as mentioned above. We hope that future analyses of the group variables that were collected in this intercultural study, e. g. religion, might help to provide some examples

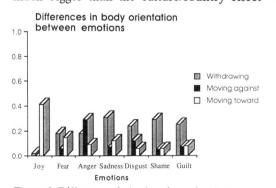
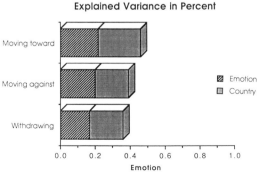

Figure 3. Differences in body orientation between emotions.

for stereotypes, using group difference effect size criteria. Another possibility to illustrate the operation of stereotypes, is to identify cases in which the verbal report for some subjects is clearly at odds with that of most other subjects. We can use the reported emotion-eliciting situations as a case in point. For example, we find that Japanese respondents report less body-related joy, fewer death and separation induced sadness episodes, less stranger-induced fear but much more stranger-induced anger, and fewer anger episodes induced by perceived injustice than in the European or US samples (Scherer et al., 1989). Many of these differences can be readily explained by different cultural norms and interactional practices as well as different demographic and economic patterns. Thus, it is unlikely that the differences we find are due to stereoptypes. Most likely they are good examples of culturally mediated prototypes. However, the fact that approximately 5% of the subjects reported that a fear experience was caused by a supernatural event (an even higher percentage is found for the English sample in the European study, see Scherer et al., 1986), could be more easily accounted for by the notion of shared stereotypes about the existence of the supernatural.

In conclusion, verbal reports of emotional experiences may be a privileged body of data to investigate different types of social representations and their effects. In any case, it would seem that the study of emotion cannot easily dispense with the use of verbal report of subjective experience, given that this modality may be our only route of access to some of the most important determinants and components of emotional state. One would obviously want to determine which parts of the verbal report of cognitive representation of emotion are due to shared social schemata or representations and to what extent these may be "socially constructed", i.e. independent of actually experienced emotional patterning (see Rimé et al., 1990). The present contribution attempts to suggest a conceptual framework and an analytical procedure for this task. Given the importance of intercultural comparison in this approach, future progress in this area will depend on the number and sophistication of cross-cultural studies on emotional experience.

References

Doise, W. (1985). Les représentations sociales: définition d'un concept. *Connexions*, *45*, 243–253.

Doise, W. (1988). Les représentations sociales: un label de qualité? *Connexions*, *51*, 99–113.

Fehr, B., & Russell, J. A. (1984). Concept of emotion viewed from a prototype perspective. *Journal of Experimental Psychology: General*, 113, 464–486.

Geppert, U., & Heckhausen, H. (1990). Ontogenese der Emotionen. In K. R. Scherer (Hrsg.). *Enzyklopädie der Psychologie. Band C/IV/3 Emotionen*. (pp. 115–214). Göttingen: Hogrefe.

Hooff, J. A. R. A. M. van (1972). A comparative approach to the physiology of laughter and smiling. In R. A. Hinde (Ed.), *Nonverbal communication* (pp. 209–241). Cambridge: Cambridge University Press.

Jodelet, D. (1989). *Les repésentations sociales*. Paris: PUF.

Levy, R. I. (1984). The emotions in comparative perspective. In K. R. Scherer & P. Ekman (Eds.), *Approaches to emotion*. (pp. 397–410). Hillsdale, N. J.: Erlbaum.

Lutz, C., & White, G. M. (1986). The anthropology of emotions. *Annual Review of Anthropology*, 15, 405–436.

Matsumoto, D., Kudoh, T., Scherer, K. R., & Wallbott, H. G. (1988). Antecedents of and reactions to emotions in the US and Japan. *Journal of Cross-Cultural Psychology*, *19*, 267–286.

Moscovici, S. (1961). *La psychanalyse. Son image et son public*. Paris: PUF (2eme éd., 1976).

Rimé, B., Philippot, P., & Cisamolo, D. (1990). Social schemata of peripheral changes in emotion. *Journal of Personality and Social Psychology*, *59*, 38–49.

Shaver, P., Schwartz, J., Kirson, D., & O'Connor, C. (1987). Emotion knowledge: Further exploration of a prototype approach. *Journal of Personality and Social Psychology*, 52, 1061–1086.

Scherer, K. R. (in press). Key developments in social psychology. In M. Dierkes, & B. Biervert (Eds.). *Social sciences in Western Europe*.

Scherer, K. R., & Wallbott, H. G. (1990). Ausdruck von Emotionen. In K. R. Scherer (Hrsg.). *Enzyklopädie der Psychologie. Band C/IV/3 Emotionen*. (pp. 345–422). Göttingen: Hogrefe.

Scherer, K. R., Wallbott, H. G., & Summerfield, A. B. (Eds.). (1986). *Experiencing emotion: A crosscultural study*. Cambridge: Cambridge University Press.

Scherer, K.R., Wallbott, H.G., Matsumoto, D., & Kudoh, T. (1988). Emotional experience in cultural context: A comparison between Europe, Japan, and the USA. In K.R. Scherer (Ed.), *Facets of emotion: Recent research.* (pp. 5–30). Hillsdale, NJ: Erlbaum.

Wallbott, H.G., & Scherer, K.R. (1986). How universal and specific is emotional experience? *Social Science Information*, *24*, 763–795 (reprinted in K.R. Scherer (Ed.), *Facets of emotion: Recent research.* Hillsdale, NJ: Erlbaum).

The Social Production of Knowledge

Wolfgang Scholl

In recent years, the psychology of knowledge has been strongly advanced in cognitive psychology. Yet, social cognition and the older cognitive theories in social psychology are primarily focussed on individual processes so that social aspects are insufficiently explored. It is proposed here that the production of new and more valid knowledge is largely a social process (sections 1, 3, 4), based on general principles of knowledge production (1) as well as on certain aspects of cognitive functioning (2).

1. General principles of knowledge production

Campbell (1974) developed the idea of knowledge production as an evolutionary process reaching from the behavior of protozoa to human science.

Evolution – even in its biological aspects – is a knowledge process ... The natural-selection paradigm for such knowledge increments can be generalized to other epistemic activities, such as learning, thought and science. (Campbell, 1974, p.413)

He argues that knowledge grows through cycles of blind variation and selective retention. Since new knowledge cannot be logically derived from previous knowledge, new experiences and ideas can only be created through relatively blind variation in ignorance of the likely results. The produced variations are then selected according to some external fitness criterion and a few are accepted as provisionally valid. Finally, a cumulation of experience and knowledge becomes possible through retention devices so that the better fitting solutions are preserved and transmitted before a new cycle begins.

The sequence of blind variation and selective retention is an abstraction from the biological evolution principles of mutation, environmental selection and genetic reproduction. According to Campbell, the mechanisms of cultural evolution fit into the same abstract principles. He discusses several knowledge producing mechanisms which may complement each other. Since the variation part of one mechanism is often guided by the retention result of another, variation is usually not so blind as it would be within one mechanism alone, but even then many variations are needed for improvement, i. e. even this guided variation is relatively blind.

In *trial-and-error learning* (or operant conditioning) unsystematic trials or curiosity behavior produce blind variation (v), reinforcement is the selection (s) device and habit formation the retention (r) mechanism.

In *vicarious learning* (or imitation) the risks of error at successive trials are deferred to casually observed others (v) and only the best suited ideas and behaviors of them are exercised (s) and stored, together with the resulting experience, in memory (r).

In *problem solving and creativity*, the trial-and-error process is located inside the brain; momentary associations, accidental analogies and mechanistic variations help to produce new ideas (v) which are tested and selected in thought (s) and then executed in reality, which is much more economical and less risky than immediate trial and error. The best ideas are stored prominently in memory (r).

Through *language and communication*, additional ideas and experiences can be symbolized and exchanged between different people (v), scrutinized and enlarged in discussions (s) and stored in transactive memories (Wegner, 1987), books or computers (r). Compared to individual decision-making the quality is enhanced and errors are reduced.

Cultural learning entails the clashing of diverging cultures or subcultures (v), the differential acceptance or diffusion of ideas, world views and technologies (s) and their transmission via socialization processes through proverbs, sagas, shared procedures, schooling and technical or artistic artifacts (r). Again, the complexity of life with its risks is thereby reduced; many achievements have neither to be invented nor to be tested but can simply be taken over.

Science is the prototype of knowledge acquisition with its permanent creation of new hypotheses or technical arrangements (v), elaborate testing methods and instruments (s) and its publishing and teaching practices (r). Its rigorous standards of argumentation, testing and publication rationalize the opportunities of language and communication on the one hand and cultural learning on the other.

The social aspects of knowledge production are dominant in imitation and in the last three mechanisms but they are also often important as social reinforcers in trial-and-error learning and as received idea stuff in problem solving. Since communication has a central relay function between individual and social knowledge production, its mechanisms shall be more deeply explored (sections 3 & 4). But first, some peculiarities of individual knowledge acquisition shall be reviewed.

2. Basic assumptions about individual knowledge acquisition

In psychology there are different theories on how human beings acquire knowledge about the world and themselves. But some assumptions are broadly accepted and can serve as a basis for later hypotheses about the social production of knowledge.

Knowledge acquisition is a constructive process. This position is held unanimously by symbolic interactionist, genetic and modern cognitive approaches as well as by diverse schools of philosophy of science. According to Piaget (1976) knowledge is constructed stepwise by equilibrating assimilation and accomodation, affirmation and negation, differentiation and integration.

Through differentiation and integration actors develop higher degrees of cognitive complexity with regard to specific areas (Seiler, 1980). Since human beings have no direct access to "reality", increases in valid knowledge take place through discrepancies between their images of reality, especially those between action expectation and perceived action result, which foster new endeavours of differentiation and integration of these images.

Knowledge processing is seen as motivated by curiosity (Berlyne, 1974), search for validity, need for structure or consistency and need for specific conclusions or wishful thinking, which control its beginning, direction and termination (Kruglanski, Baldwin & Towson, 1985). While curiosity and sometimes search for validity foster variation, consistency and often wishful thinking strengthen the retention of existing beliefs and thereby limit variation; selection is sharpened by search for validity but biased by wishful thinking and consistency.

The self-concept is presumably the most central knowledge structure within the total network of reality representations (Epstein, 1979). Thus, the knowledge of an actor is not only limited (Simon, 1957) but especially biased toward consistency with the (cognitive) self-image, toward enhancement of (affective) self-esteem and toward support for (conative) self-commitments or identities.

3. Knowledge production through communication

If the knowledge of any actor is limited and biased toward the self then much can be gained from a systematic *social* comparison of one's concepts, opinions, experiences and examinations. Through the exchange of information and the confrontation of opinions, blanks can be filled, simpler structures differentiated, unwarranted generalizations corrected, biases lessened and new perspectives discovered and elaborated. In terms of the blind-variation-selective-retention model unforseeable variations come into play through communication. The more diverse the knowledge bases of the participants, the larger the potential growth of knowledge.

Diverse knowledge bases mean cognitive dissensus. So it is not surprising that this potential is not fully utilized. Actors tend to terminate the social comparison, if the opinions and especially the basic cognitive structures of the others are relatively divergent from their own thinking (Festinger, 1954), because the equilibration process breaks down if too much accomodation is needed; i. e. they restrict the possible range of blind variation. Combining the growing potential of knowledge diversity or dissensus with its declining use we can derive the first central hypothesis: *The growth of knowledge through communication depends in a curvilinear (n) fashion on the amount of dissensus between the actors.* Almost nothing can be learned through communication if the knowledge bases of each participant are identical and almost nothing will be learned if they are very divergent; the optimal learning point lies in between, probably nearer to low dissensus than to high dissensus because of the accomodation problems. There is no direct empirical evidence for this curvilinear relationship of which the author is aware. Indirect evidence comes from Driver & Streufert (1969) and Katz & Allen (1982). The same curvilinear relation holds between the growth of knowledge through communication and the number of participants, because the communication difficulties grow faster with the number of communicators than the knowledge potential (Steiner, 1972, p. 96).

This curve is not the same for all circumstances. Several factors enlarge or diminish its width and height. Participants with high cognitive complexity can better assimilate and integrate divergent informations (Driver & Streufert, 1969). Time and motivation are two other important factors. The greater the dissensus, the more time and motivation is needed for learning from each other.

Even more important are the consequences of cognitive-affective-conative consistency. Consensus can be defined as *cognitive* congruence between two or more actors, mutual sympathy as *affective* congruence and mutual cooperativeness as *conative* congruence (Scholl, 1986). So sympathy/antipathy and cooperativeness/competitiveness have consistency effects on consensus/dissensus and vice versa. For instance, high sympathy and cooperativeness may suppress dissensus in cohesive groups so that problems are not sufficiently explored from different perspectives (Janis, 1972; Smith, Petersen, Johnson & Johnson, 1986). On the other hand, competitiveness is often induced by differential rewarding which leads to and is reinforced by growing antipathy so that communication will be reduced to unfruitful confrontations with lessened chances for mutual learning (Johnson, Maruyama, Johnson, Nelson & Skon, 1981).

The practical problem of social knowledge production therefore is to work on a rather low level of consensus while maintaining a rather high level of sympathy and cooperativeness, i. e. to allow for sufficient social variation while securing proper selective retention. Normative regulations which emphasize the value of an open confrontation of divergent opinions in a friendly and cooperative manner can help to reduce the likely inconsistency and to stabilize communication at an approximate optimum. Such regulations have been recommended by Maier (1967) for group problem solving, by Blake & Mouton (1970) for conflict management, by Hall (1971) for discussions and by Fisher & Ury (1984) for negotiations.

4. Power and knowledge

For the analysis of interaction and communication the second most important variable besides congruence is power (Scholl, 1986). In the discussion about power a conceptual distinction between power and influence seems necessary, so that power describes an actor effecting his will against the interests of others whereas influence refers to effects on other actors in line with their interests (like in counseling, helping, cooperation etc.) Without such a distiction almost all aspects in Social Psychology would be instances of power so that power would lose the status of a distinct variable, and

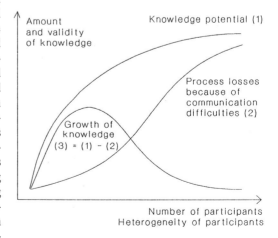

Figure 1. Knowledge production through communication.

the literature about the consequences of power, participation and control would yield irreconcilable results (Scholl, 1986; Scholl & Pelz, 1990).

The relation of power to knowledge has seldom been directly investigated; a negative effect of power on knowledge has been shown among others by Torrance (1955), Wilensky (1967) and Fodor & Smith (1982). Much indirect evidence has been assembled in participation research (Kiessler & Scholl, 1976; Miller & Monge, 1986). Participation and power equalization lead to more relevant knowledge and higher productivity.

Typical power reactions in processes of knowledge production are as follows: the more powerful often stop discussions if they see their interests endangered; people with deviant opinions come under conformity pressure or are driven out; information is held back or manipulated in favor of a preferred course of action; the less powerful are often reluctant to express their opinions freely. In terms of the blind-variation-selective-retention model, power exertion reduces the range of variation, biases the selection criteria and furthers one-sided retention. So the second central hypothesis is:

The amount and validity of knowledge production is more reduced the more the free interchange of opinions is impeded by power exertion or for the sake of power acquisition.

The invalidity of knowledge through power exertion tends to grow with time: (a) Power is often used for gaining more power resources which then raise the likelihood of further power exertion (Kipnis, 1976) with its detrimental effects on knowledge. (b) Power exertion is often accompanied by a devaluation of the victim (Kipnis, 1976) so that his future ideas and remarks are devalued too. (c) If the likelihood of false decisions is raised by power exertion, a subsequent correction is even less likely because of a self-esteem saving escalation tendency (Brockner, Houser, Birnbach, Lloyd, Deitcher, Nathanson & Rubin, 1986) of the power wielder which can hardly be corrected by the less powerful actors. (d) The use of expert power in manipulating the perception of others leads after a while to the same distorting effect in the power wielder because he begins to believe in his own propaganda (Higgins, 1981). (e) The exertion of power often leads to reactance (Brehm, 1966) and thereby to a decline of sympathy, cooperativeness and again information exchange. (f) Antipathy and competitiveness in turn raise the likelihood of power exertion and thus reinforce its negative effect on the social production of knowledge.

5. Outlook: Knowledge production in social systems

The outlined mechanisms of the social production of knowledge are assumed to hold true in all social systems: in groups, organizations, societal, political and economic systems as well as in scientific communities. Of course, the actual dynamic in such systems calls for a more complex model of knowledge production which is beyond the scope of this article (for a first attempt see Scholl, 1989). Yet, a few considerations shall be shortly added to illuminate the broader ramifications:

Because of its ubiquity in social systems power cannot only have negative effects on system efficiency via its adverse effects on knowledge production; often it is also used to secure the system's internal coordinability and its external defensibility which are necessary preconditions for its survival. Therefore, those systems should be most effective which reduce the use of power to a minimum necessary for coordination and defense and thereby impeding only marginally the system's production of knowledge which is helpful for its long run survival and evolution. (Of course, this is no panacea, because the evolution of a social system always leads to new problems.)

Since power is often not only used in this functional sense for the system but also to gain more power for oneself or for one's group (see 4a) the functional minimum tends to be overstepped. This leads to the hypothesized dysfunctions in knowledge production and losses in efficiency which lower the system members' acceptance of the taken decisions, of its proponents and in the end of the system itself. Totalitarian systems and planned economies are a case in point. There seems to exist a dialectical relationship between power and the social production of knowledge: power overcomes knowledge in the short run but succumbs in the long run, giving way to new insights, new power holders or even new social systems.

References

Berlyne, D. E. (1974). *Konflikt, Erregung, Neugier. Zur Psychologie der kognitiven Motivation.* Stuttgart: Klett.

Blake, R. L. & Mouton, J. S. (1970). The fifth achievement. *Journal of applied Behavioral Science, 6,* 413–426.

Brehm, J. W. (1966). *A theory of psychological reactance.* New York: Academic Press.

Brockner, J., Houser, R., Birnbach, G., Lloyd, K., Deitcher, J., Nathanson, S. & Rubin, J. Z. (1986). Escalation of commitment to an ineffective course of action: The effect of feedback having negative implications for self-identity. *Administrative Science Quarterly, 31,* 109–126.

Campbell, D. T. (1974). Evolutionary epistomology. In P. A. Schilpp (Ed.), *The philosophy of Karl Popper* (413–463). La Sylle, Ill.: Opencourt.

Driver, M. J. & Streufert, S. (1969). Integrative complexity: An approach to individuals and groups as inforamtion-processing systems. *Administrative Science Quarterly, 14,* 272–285.

Epstein, S. (1979). Entwurf einer integrativen Persönlichkeitstheorie. In S.-H. Filipp (Hrsg.), *Selbstkonzeptforschung – Probleme, Befunde, Perspektiven* (15–45). Stuttgart: Klett.

Festinger, L. (1954). A theory of social comparison processes. *Human Relations, 7,* 117–140.

Fisher, R. & Ury, W. (1984). *Das Harvard-Konzept. Sachgerecht verhandeln – erfolgreich verhandeln.* Frankfurt: Campus.

Fodor, E. M. & Smith, T. (1982). The power motive as an influence on group decision making. *Journal of Personality and Social Psychology, 42,* 178–185.

Hall, J. (1971). Decisions, decisions, decisions. *Psychology Today,* May, 51–54; June, 86–88.

Higgins, E. T. (1981). The "communication game": Implications for social cognition and persuasion. In E. T. Higgins, C. Herman & M. Zanna (Eds.), *Social cognition: The Ontario Symposium, Vol. I* (343–392). Hillsdale, NJ: Erlbaum.

Janis, I. L. (1972). *Victims of groupthink: A psychological study of foreign policy decisions and fiascoes.* Boston: Houghton-Mifflin.

Johnson, D. W., Maruyama, G., Johnson, R. T., Nelson, D. & Skon, S. (1981). Effects of cooperative, competitive, and individualistic goal structures on achievement: A meta-analysis. *Psychological Bulletin, 89,* 47–62.

Katz, R. & Allen, T. J. (1982). Investigating the Not Invented Here (NIH) syndrome: A look at the performance, tenure, and communication patterns of 50 R&D project groups. *R&D Management, 12,* 7–19.

Kiessler, K. & Scholl, W. (1976). *Partizipation und Macht in aufgabenorientierten Gruppen – Ein Feldexperiment zur Therie der organisatorischen Bedingtheit von Gruppenprozessen.* Frankfurt: Haag & Herchen.

Kipnis, D. (1976). *The powerholders.* Chicago: The University of Chicago Press.

Kruglanski, A. W., Baldwin, M. W. & Towson, S. M. J. (1985). Die Theorie der Laienepistomologie. In D. Frey & M. Irle (Hrsg.), *Theorien der Sozialpsychologie, Band III: Motivations- und Informationsverarbeitungstheorien* (293–314). Bern: Huber.

Maier, N. R. F. (1967). Assets and liabilities in group problem solving. *Psychological Review, 74,* 239–249.

Miller, K. I. & Monge, P. R. (1986). Participation, satisfaction, and productivity: A meta-analytic review. *Academy of Management Journal, 29,* 727–753.

Piaget, J. (1976). Piaget's theory. In B. Inhelder & H. H. Chipman (eds), *Piaget and his school* (11–23). New York: Springer.

Scholl, W. (1986). Soziale Interaktion – ein interdisziplinärer Bezugsrahmen. Beitrag zum 3. Hamburger Symposium zur Methodologie der Sozialpsychologie 1987: Universität Göttingen.

Scholl, W. (1989). Effizienz und die soziale Produktion von Wissen. Beitrag zur Tagung der Fachgruppe Sozialpsychologie in Bielefeld 1989: Universität Göttingen.

Scholl, W. & Pelz, J. (1990). Untersuchungen zur Unterscheidung von Macht und Einfluß. Vortrag auf dem *37. Kongreß der Deutschen Gesellschaft für Psychologie in Kiel.*

Seiler, T. B. (1980). Entwicklungstheorien in der Sozialisationsforschung. In K. Hurrelmann & D. Ulich (Hrsg.), *Handbuch der Sozialisationsforschung* (pp. 101–121). Weinheim: Beltz.

Simon, H. A. (1957). *Models of man.* New York: Wiley.

Smith, K. A., Petersen, R. P., Johnson, D. W. & Johnson, R. T. (1986). The effects of controversy and concurrence seeking on effective decision making. *The Journal of Social Psychology, 126,* 237–248.

Steiner, I. D. (1972). *Group process and productivity.* New York, London: Academic Press.

Torrance, E. P. (1955). Some consequences of power differences on decision making in permanent and temporary 3-man groups. In A. P. Hare, E. F. Borgatta & R. F. Bales (eds.), *Small groups, studies in social interaction* (482–491). New York: Knopf.

Wegner, C. M. (1987). Transactive memory. A contemporary analysis of the group mind. In B. Mullen & G. R. Goethals (eds.), *Theories of group behavior* (185–208). New York: Springer.

Wilensky, H. L. (1967). Organizational intelligence. New York: Basic Books.

Part II:

Social Situations
and the Actualization of Knowledge

Toward a Social Psychology of Cognitive Functioning: Theoretical Outline and Empirical Illustrations

Jean Marc Monteil

When scientific psychology applies itself to the study of knowledge, whether it be through the processes which permit its construction or those used in its mobilization, the dominant theoretical paradigm remains that of cognitive psychology. As in all scientific procedures the objective is to set out theoretical models and empirical facts. This dialectic is expressed through the confrontation of two approaches. The first, which is essentially "modelling" shares with artificial intelligence an interest in simulating more or less complex behaviour. The second, which is experimental, seeks the confirmation of its hypotheses in empiricism. We will not contest the validity of these theoretical and methodological orientations. They are both indispensable and fruitful and enable us to understand better man's mental activity. They present the problem of the acquisition, construction and use of knowledge in the following terms: on the one hand, a subject with cognitive properties which are assumed to be universal, on the other hand, an object endowed with intrinsic properties. One supposes, then, that the subject applies his universal properties to the intrinsic properties of the object. Research procedure consists in setting up, by simulation or experimentation, conditions in which one can observe the implementation of these properties during the processing of the object by the subject. The object may just as easily be a person or a physical object as a problem to resolve. In certain cases it is presented within a context which is varied in order to test the modifications of processing carried out by the subject. It must be admitted, in such a paradigm, that the social dimension is envisaged at best merely as a derived or reactive element. It will be noticed that a whole area of cognitive social psychology, inspired from social cognition, is inscribed in a general paradigm of this nature. The fact that the object (and therefore the information) is social does not distinguish the two psychologies – cognitive and social – it is simply accepted that the social factors complicate somewhat the models which are likely to explain cognitive functioning.

Contrary to this approach, another one of socio-determinist inspiration can be conceived, according to which cognitive competence and its development depend only on the influences of the environment and of the place occupied by the individual in social relationships. For the experimental social psychologist these two positions, if considered mutually exclusive, are quite obviously not very satisfactory. To my mind, neither the intra-individual level, nor that of social positions and societal relationships should be neglected. The one and the other must be taken into account. Social psychology rightly has the authority to carry out this union (Doise, 1982). This will be discussed later, for the moment let it suffice to note that the most recent neurobiological data argue for a consideration of the social dimension.

The social dimension of neuronal man

Knowledge is being gained which informs us about both the structure and the functioning of the brain which, up to very recently, was regarded as an impenetrable black box. Morever, some people consider that the development of neuroscience, of which the neurobiology of behaviour is a constituent, marks a veritable intellectual revolution: the neuronal revolution (Changeux, 1984). A body of research focusing on the central nervous system and the peripheral system as regards their structure, their genesis and their behavioural incidences, it is understandable that neuroscience also fascinates psychologists, sometimes to the point of leading them to adopt its reasoning without possessing any scientific expertise in this domain. It is for this reason that, rather than making psychology dependent on neuroscience, in an attempt to justify it, it is without any doubt more useful for a knowledge of human functioning to retain, from among the contributions of neuroscience, those which enable psychology to continue its participation in fundamental science all the while stressing its specificity. It seems to me that some of these contributions merit the interest of psychology and of social psychology in particular.

A neuronal postulate and cognitive approaches

If nowadays nobody disputes the fact that the development of the brain is the result of genetic programming everyone also agrees in recognizing that there is however in the human species, more than in any other species, a type of "play" in the production of the program. It is this play, known as epigenesis, which precludes discussion of a strict determinism: "Every human individual has inscribed in the very structure of his brain, by means of specific neuronal networks, the unique history, affective, social and cultural, which is his" (Lecourt, 1989). Moreover, certain studies illustrate strikingly this determining role of epigenesis. Let us reflect upon the study done on the Japanese brain which shows hemispheric specializations for the use of two writing systems, one alphabetic known as Kana which relies on the left hemisphere; the other which is ideogrammatic is known as Kanji and relies on the right hemisphere. In man, this indetermination component which is linked to epigenesis makes it possible to have an effect on the programme which itself is transmitted. In fact, the further up the evolutive ladder one moves the more the epigenetic component becomes important in the construction of individuals. The more important the epigenetic component the more the very structure of the nervous system is linked to the individual's history: "Man's central nervous system forms a kind of engram of his personal history, and the human individual, unique therefore un-clonable results from his social history ... this history is marked in physical structure since it is inscribed in the cerebral matter itself because of the importance of the epigenesis which will stabilise this or that circuit" (Prochiantz, 1989, p. 18).

If, as we have just seen, the social experience influences the construction of neuronal net-

works to the point of being indissociable from their development, psychologists of strict neuroscientific allegiance should find therein food for thought. Do they not, actually, postulate an identity between each individual mental state, situated in time space, and a specific neurophysiological state. Cognitive psychology which still maintains a distance with regard to neuroscience views this identity merely as occasional: functionalism is the name given to this idea. Such an idea makes it possible to reconcile two requirements: one concerning natural science which, as such, claims to share a materialistic or physicalistic ontology, the other maintaining a certain autonomy of psychological explanation vis-à-vis neuropsychology. Consequently it is difficult to make out the reasons why cognitive psychology would regard as outside its domain the social dimensions whose importance is accepted by science which serves as a point of comparison if not of reference. If physical matter marks the social history of the individual it becomes feasible that a symbolic "engram" of the social experience could exist in permanent memory and could intervene in the development and cognitive functioning of the human individual. It therefore seems difficult to exclude the social dimension from the study of the processes of knowledge: particularly if one considers, as cognitive psychology does, that a highly structured interiority exists and that it is necessary to seek explanations by well-ordered sequences of internal states.

If one accepts the framework of classical cognitivism for which propositional attitudes, i. e mental attitudes in relation to propositional contents such as believe that, wish that, for example, are real states which determine behaviour in organisms, one perceives the advantage of taking into account the social history of the subject, as this being at the very root of the development of the propositional contents. Seeking cognitive explanations focuses also on representations and mental states situated at the infra-personal levels. Fodor (1983) distinguished two autonomous systems, as it were, in cognition. One peripheral, is characterized by an isolated processing of information, the other, which is central, allows integrated inferences to occur. The first relates to the infra-personal level of cognition, the second to the personal level. In neither case can the social dimension be eliminated. In fact, in the first case it exists as a constituent element of the stimulus – the percept – and in the second case it can participate in the development of the concept. The distinction between percept and concept is to be understood here in terms of the distinctions proposed by Woodfield (1983). One question remains: that of the existence of two types of thought; one of limited content purely internal to the subject, the other of extensive content dependent on the environment of this same subject, as Putman (1988) tried to exemplify with his experiment on thought, known as "the twin earth". This indicates that two individuals could have the same internal psychology while having thoughts of different semantic content. Going even further, one could also envisage that the individuation of all thought content would depend on external factors, notably social ones. This externalist vision of cognition challenges cognitive psychology in the strict sense of the term while preserving the reality of mental attitudes.

Without going further, it seems worthwhile, as a conclusion to this brief incursion into the "neurocognitivist" field, to imagine the human individual, whatever the rivalry between the different approaches to cognition, as a socially inserted neurophysiological and psychological system. In its insertions it constructs mental representations, processes and stores information which can subsequently be called up (either automatically or consciously) in operations which aim to implement behaviour. In order to understand human cognitive functioning such a position implies that social insertions cannot be neglected. Because of the new importance attributed to this notion of social insertion, it will be fitting to furnish at least a minimal definition of it at the appropriate time.

Several social psychologies?

In one of its recent issues (1989) the European Journal of Social Psychology presents and deals with important epistemological questions with regard to the psychosocial study of human cognition. One finds therein, in fact, the confrontation of different points of view likely, in our opinion, to favour a problematic synthesis between cognitive science and social psychology. The first of these points of view

defended by Zajonc (1989) and Nuttin (1989) is drawn from natural science and puts forward explanations in terms of internal causal mechanisms in the individual. Social psychology, on the contrary, refuses an explanatory system based strictly on internal mechanisms and proposes a type of social constructionism approach (Gergen,1989). It attributes an essentially social origin to mental life. Closely linked to this notion, Harré (1989) considers, moreover, that cognitive psychology, which studies mental life at individual level, is only an illustration of what he calls the privatization of social dimension. These positions held by Gergen (1989) and Harré (1989) are, on the face of it, not very far removed from the psychological contructionism of Doise (1989) and Moscovici (1989). Nevertheless, for Gergen and Harré, the fact of viewing the psychological as basically social leads them, in the very name of the complexity of this social reality, to refuse experimental methods (advocated by Zajonc and Nuttin) and to suggest, for example, investigations using as a starting point the analysis of discourse. The constructionism of Doise and Moscovici, on the other hand, relies on methodological procedures of a psycho-logical nature.

On account of space restrictions it is not possible to elaborate on this epistemological debate within social psychology. However, even briefly mentioned, it enables one to pinpoint certain basic problems concerning the ideas, either explicit or implicit, of social psychologists regarding cognitive functioning. One can, for a start, ponder on the status of the social dimension in social psychology, a status which, to say the least, appears to be characterized in various ways. One must then note the absence of thorough reflection on the status of the cognitive, even though it is concerned with mental life and its products.

In Summarizing the main standpoints taken, all the points of view can be grouped under two main standpoints thereby making it possible to present the problem of the role of the social dimension in the psychology of cognition. In the first of these standpoints the social reality finds, as it were, its explanation in the individual, and psychological functioning itself finds the material basis of its explanation in the brain. The social reality here is reactive and derived from individual activity which is governed by physiological or neurophysiological laws. In the second standpoint, that of Doise and Moscovici, social interaction, communication, social meta systems imbued with norms and values, affect individual cognitive functioning and participate in the construction of new forms of knowledge. It remains, at this level, to identify the mechanisms and processes by which the social experience informs and affects cognitive functioning and therefore participates in the activity of knowledge. It is certainly not sufficient to say, as Vygostky, that the subject internalizes what he constructs first in the social reality, in order to explain this internalization process. As for the social representations which Moscovici terms authentic social realities, are they not, before being social, that is to say collective, mental representations unique to an individual? Transmitted, and communicated to other individuals by (as Moscovici says) the expedient of numerous microcontacts brought about by the daily life of individuals, they are transformed by the person who communicates them by means of public representations, then retransformed again to the point of expanding and becoming, in some cases, durable and resistant, thus forming these authentic social realities discussed by Moscovici. But it is necessary, here also, to reflect further on the generation of the first representation; which re-presents the problem of individual cognitive activity and its possible social determinants.

The various approaches and the subjects of study of social psychologists, even briefly mentioned, illustrate quite well a certain difficulty in apprehending the social dimension according to a common point of view and a univocal definition of its influence and of its cognitive administration.

What place does the social experience hold in the study of human cognitive functioning?

If we accept that social psychology possesses a specificity in its interest in understanding the functioning of man, as this man participates in and partakes of the social world, we should certainly be able, without great difficulty, to subscribe to the following proposition: to study the human individual from a psychosocial point of view is firstly to consider this individual as a socially inserted being and then to endeavour to construct systems of explanation which, of necessity, take these social insertions into account. The importance attached here to social insertion requires that a minimal definition of same be given. In a book soon to be published, the third in a series on the links between social conduct and cognition (Beauvois, Joule & Monteil, 1991), a first notional precision has been presented. We will define social insertion by the fact that the activities of the individual (his automatisms, his "conscious acts", his behaviour) are more or less determined by behaviour systems which implicate other individuals. An insertion can therefore be more or less strong. That being the case, in a relationship with any object the activities of the individual (whatever the activities) will be more or less determined by the behaviour system which governs the relationship with the object. As it determines activities this behaviour system will produce activities which can just as easily be "conscious acts" as automatisms, for example. One problem among others is that of the role played by these productions on subsequent behaviour in relation to the object as well as in relation to any other system. Dealing with this question of the role of these productions demands a consideration of the strength of the social insertions in which these productions apply.

This notion of insertion appears to us, on more than one count, essential to psychosocial specificity. We will be content here to emphasize its significance in a perspective linked to our own area of research. One can take as heuristically fruitful the idea that insertion forms the subject-matter of specific representations which guide and direct cognitive activity in present and future events including those which occur when the behaviour system has changed. In that case insertion would be endowed with properties of inertia.

Let us return for a moment to neuroscience. Behavioural neurobiology tells us that the social and affective history of individuals engrams in the cerebral matter itself. Now this social history is the result of successive insertions, more or less different, more or less permanent, more or less specific, but which, at any rate, exist. Consequently, it seems, from a logical point of view, perfectly acceptable to consider that if social and affective history finds its expression in the stabilization or the form of specific neuronal network it also finds its expression at symbolic level in man's permanent memory. Thus we arrive at the hypothesis that at the time of coding and storing information, emotional and social experience is closely associated with the corporal environment of the subject. There is good reason to believe that such a hypothesis is not absurd. To mention only the work of Tulving (1983) we know that what is stored corresponds not only to information as such but also to the way in which this information is processed and placed in memory. Emotional and social experience, both of which are in all likelihood linked, and endowed with a representational content, are to be situated in the domain of mental representations. Consequently, as Thomson and Janigian (1988) suggest, the human individual has a cognitive representation of his life in terms of events which occur, goals attained, failures ... etc, a schema of life, as it were, which like all schemas would act as a processing unit for information encountered later.

The notion of episodic memory is important here in recalling that information is coded both temporarily and with reference to that which places it in memory. This is why it would appear justifiable to think that the individual's history- in the sense that it depends on his insertions- forms a solid representation in the subject's memory. For this reason it is easy to activate and to mobilize in the form of response systems in the behavioural repertoire of the subject. For this to happen it is sufficient that the latter be in the presence of certain inputs or certain sociopsychological configurations functioning as regenerators of content indications in relation to previous social insertions. Therefore, more interest should certainly be taken in contextual information of episodic nature, in particular in the contextual trend of cognitive psychology. For what are very likely reasons of methodological convenience, greater importance is given to contextual information of a semantic nature. Consequently, it is understandable that this difficulty in considering the episodic dimension of human memory results in cognitive psychology maintaining the social history of man outside its area of research. This difficulty has, moreover, led it, in the study of the processes of knowledge, to envisage the social factors merely as a source of external variation, able, at best, to modulate behavioural responses but in no way to generate them.

Using the mnemonic system to understand and explain human behaviour is, and on this point agreement is sufficiently widespread, to consider it, as well as the information processing system which is linked to it, as socially inserted systems. This perspective leads inevitably to taking into account the social history of the subject so as to understand his cognitive behaviour and his social conduct. A requirement of this nature generates consequences, not only at the level of the theoretical models which support the scientific activity of the social psychologist, but also at the level of the experimental paradigms used, notably regarding the development of variables and their condition of manipulation.

Outline of a model and first experimental illustrations

Adopting the notion of socially inserted man implies drawing inferences from it at the level of study of his cognitive activity. If one accepts Tulving's idea that what is stored corresponds, not only to the information, but also to the way in which this information was processed and placed in memory, one can reasonably envisage that the subject encodes the information and the context of this information. The context of this information, in the notion of "inserted man", is composed, above all, of the social and emotional conditions in which the subject finds himself situated at the moment of being confronted with information processing or with the necessity of developing an attitude, a strategy, or even managing a mechanism so as to succeed in giving a coherence to his environment. The influence of "this context" is nothing new when one remembers the work initiated by Rosenzweig in 1933!

In short, in a learning situation the subject always finds himself confronted with the reality of a social insertion which accompanies the information to be processed. That being the case, constructing a rule or knowledge means constructing it in a specific insertion. What is placed in memory is a representation which associates the insertion, or the characteristics of the insertion, with the rule or the knowledge. One could envisage processing these representational contents separately but one would then have to accept a total independence of the information to be processed from the unity in which it is situated. This hypothesis would presuppose in the subject the existence of a capacity for cutting himself off from the environment, the implementation of which is as difficult to imagine on the neurophysiological level as on the psychological one. Does that mean that all information is for the subject always "ecologically" defined? In my opinion, certainly, and for the very reason of the existence of the subject as a socially inserted individual. The problem of knowing if the information is processed first at the level of sensorial memory, that is to say, at the early stages, or, indeed, processed at the level of working memory, does not make the slightest difference, knowing that it was encoded in a specific situation of insertion. One must therefore envisage the fact that the knowledge, the rules acquired by the subject and the processes which support this acquisition are constitutively dependent on the social conditions of their development.

And where does social psychology fit into all this, one might ask? Its existence is fully justified here since it is a matter of giving a dominating place to the social dimension in the construction and use of knowledge. When I say "construction" and "use" I consider that we are dealing with two distinct processes.

The literature on knowledge in social psychology sometimes neglects the distinction between acquisition and restitution. It is indeed necessary to note that the processes of acquisition are in keeping with information to be encoded, knowledge to be constructed and, therefore, that here the social dimension of which we speak is involved in and has something of the nature of this construction. The processes of restitution and mobilization reflect the attempts to establish a correspondence between current problem situations and formerly developed knowledge. This distinction is important. It determines, in fact, two research approaches, complementary certainly, but, nevertheless, heuristically separate. One aims to understand how, and by what mechanism, the social context affects constitutively cognitive constructions; the other focuses on two things:

a) To understand the activity of cognitive production by studying the modalities by which correspondences are made between current situations in which the subject is inserted, and which were constructed and stored at a certain time in the history of this same subject.

b) To identify and understand the activities brought into play when this correspondence is not established.

These two approaches have, of course, methodological implications that bring about strong constraints, notably at the level of experimental work. It is, thus, that proving experimentally the influence of social insertions on the development of rules or of knowledge, for example, presupposes first manipulating and creating the social conditions of acquisition of these rules and knowledge and then checking that the use of the latter for production purposes finds expression, all things being equal, in differences of attitude, strategy or performance, according to the manipulations carried out. This type of research approach is currently in operation in a program concerning the acquisition of script (Monteil, Versace in preparation). Insofar as empirical elements would appear to indicate the presence of social conditions in the experimentally controlled development of this cognitive schema, one would dispose of important information for undertaking research focusing strictly on the mechanisms by which this exertion of control, in the cognitive sense of the term, of social conditions takes place.

The notion, defended here, according to which all processing of information would take place under social insertion, raises, at the same time, the question of the link between "contextual" information of episodic nature and "contextual" information of semantic nature. Can one actually consider these two contextual structures, episodic and semantic, as dissociated or dissociable? The question remains open. Whatever the answer to that question may be, the general perspective adopted here implies also envisaging experimental paradigms which, in the first place, make it possible to control the social conditions of the development of knowledge and then expose the subject to scenes, capable or not, of entering into correspondence with what was previously constructed. It is easy to see where the difficulty lies in such a programme. It necessitates the processing by the subject of information under an experimentally controlled specific social situation so that its effects at the level of a cognitive activity, realized in situations which are either incongruent or congruent with the manipulated insertions, can then be measured.

The empirical elements which we are now going to provide must be perceived as indications of the relevance of becoming involved in a concern such as ours. Therefore it is more a matter of results reinforcing an exploratory undertaking than validating a theoretical body which is only slightly developed.

Some empirical data

I shall try to illustrate the relevance of the idea put forward here by referring to a series of recent studies (Monteil, 1988a; 1988b; 1989; 1991). These studies will, in the first place, show that cognitive performance can be drastically modified according to the social insertions with which the subjects are confronted. In the first experiment, two groups of French secondary-school pupils, displaying wide variations of academic levels, attended a biology class under two conditions: one condition of anonymity and one of individuation. In the first, the pupils were informed that nobody among them would be examined during the lesson; in the second, on the contrary, they were told that everyone would be examined. Half of the subjects were also publicly reminded of their academic level (good vs weak) while the other half were told that they were all of the same standard. The pupils did not know each other and so their ignorance of their respective levels ensured that the conditions were perfectly controlled. In fact no questions were asked during the lesson but all the pupils will subsequently be given a post-test of ten questions concerning this same lesson and their replies will be assessed by four independent judges. The subjects who were told they were of the same standard, i. e. those who were denied any explicit social comparison, achieved performances in keeping with their usual performance: the high-achievers succeeded, the weak pupils failed, regardless of the conditions of anonymity or individuation. On the other hand the results were very different in the condition where an explicit social comparison was made possible. The condition of anonymity showed both group of pupils obtaining comparable results, unlike the condition of individuation where the high-achievers performed well and the weak pupils performed badly (see Fig. 1).

In the second study only very high-achievers pupils participated in the experiment. But half of them were told that they had succeeded in an earlier task, the others were told they had failed; thus the academic status was experimentally manipulated and made salient for all the subjects. As in the previous experiment, anonymity and individuation were introduced. In accordance with predictions, the subjects in the condition of anonymity obtained equivalent performances regardless of the manipu-

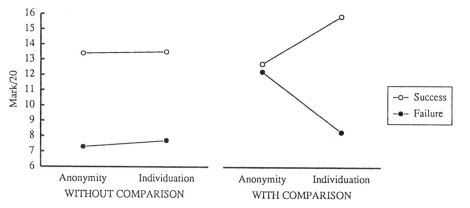

Figure 1. Means scores on the written control task following the teacher's lesson. Interaction between comparison, Social insertion, and Academic level.

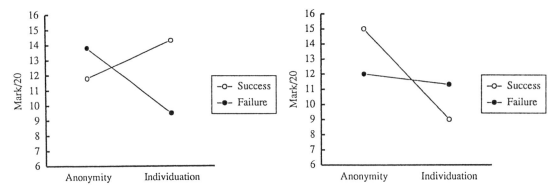

Figure 2. Interaction between Social insertion and Attribution of Success and Failure on the control task scores.

Figure 4. Social insertion and Attribution of success and failure on the post-test scores.

lated academic status (success or failure). In the position of individuation the subjects placed in the failure condition did not perform as well as the subjects placed in the success condition (see Fig. 2).

In the third study, carried out according to the same paradigm but using four different tasks ordered according to their academic prestige (Mathematics, Biology, History and Geography, Technical and Manual Instruction), it is shown that the interaction effect between academic status (success and failure) on the one hand, and social position (anonymity vs individuation) on the other, is much stronger with prestigious disciplines than with less valued ones (see Fig. 3).

In the fourth and fifth studies, again conducted according to the same paradigm, but this time with a population of weak pupils, a pattern of results was obtained which was the opposite of that obtained with high-achievers. The subjects to whom success was attributed

achieved very weak performances in the individuation conditions and improved performances in the conditions of anonymity, not only in tasks of simple restitution of information but also in tasks demanding the transformation of this information. The subjects placed in a failure condition remained insensitive to the conditions of individuation and anonymity, and obtained weak performances in accordance with their usual results (see Fig. 4).

This body of research shows clearly the influence of social insertions on individual cognitive functioning. Admittedly this account does not provide the explanations which can identify all the mechanisms which enable the social system to intervene in this functioning. However, on considering the results of the experiments mentioned and, firstly, those of the second and third experiments, it appears that one can begin to construct an outline of a theoretical model. The subjects of different protocols are either high-achievers or weak pupils,

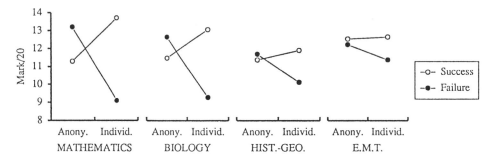

Figure 3. Interaction between Social insertion and Attribution of sucess on the control task scores, depending on the subject matter.

which has always been the case. Consequently, each one possesses what we will call a specific system of organic and mental dispositions constructed throughout their academic experiences which themselves are made up of successive sanctions and reinforcements in specific social insertions and generally distributed socially according to the level of success or failure. This system of mental and organic dispositions which is the fruit of successive, experiences placed in memory, is automatically activable and activated when the current social insertions present a sufficient level of salience. When the social scenes which define the insertions enter into correspondence with the elements of the dispositional system, which itself is linked to previous social insertions, and are in congruence with what has been stored in memory, they bring about, in the subject, the mobilisation of the dominant response system in his behavioural repertoire. One can, in this case, consider this response as almost automatic or, at the very least, as necessitating a very weak level of involvement of the attentional resources. That being all the more so when the current situation of insertion presents a strong social influence as is the case in the third study where the performances of success or failure appear all the more consonant with expectations as the academic discipline is prestigious. This is why the weak pupils, in our experiment, when put back into a configuration which matches their academic habitus, the fruit of numerous reinforcements, fail at the task, even if when placed in another configuration, they succeed. It is the same for high-achievers who continue to succeed whereas placed in another configuration they will fail.

Let us continue this reasoning and the corresponding experimental illustration. When the situation of insertion, under which the task is carried out, is incongruent with the dispositional system of the subject, which is the case for high-achievers to whom failure is attributed and which is made evident by means of comparison with others, the processing of this cognitive configuration demands the mobilization of considerable attentional resources and, therefore, a response at a semantic level, so as to give a meaning to this situation which can no longer be processed automatically. There is, in fact, incongruence between the present situation and what the subject has stored through earlier insertions. This new sociocognitive reality leads him to re-evaluate the situation and, therefore, to focus attention on the elements which are incongruent with his dispositional system. This focalisation would then lead him to construct a signification of the present situation, on the basis of which he would perform. In our experiments, the subject, in a situation of failure, made obvious by the condition of individuation, seems to undergo a real cognitive collapse. In the case where failure is attributed to him but where his anonymity is guaranteed, he manages, however, to conceal the inadequacy ascribed to him. These results make it possible, when the situation is incongruent with the dispositional system, to perceive the intervention of the signification, i.e, of the semantic level. It is with the results of the last experiments, carried out with weak pupils, that we can best illustrate our approach. These latter actually accomplish better performances in the condition of anonymity-success and weak performances in the condition success-individuation, unlike the good pupils. In the case of an attribution of failure, the conditions anonymity vs individuation have no effect, the performances, being, as usual, weak.

What can be said about these results? They confirm, in my opinion, the model outlined here. In a failure condition the situation mobilizes the usual response system of the subject: he fails. In a condition where success is attributed the situation is incongruent with the dispositional system; that being the case, the subject is led to re-evaluate the situation, he resorts to the semantic level and mobilizes, in order to process the situation, the knowledge stored in relation with the situations of academic resolution with which he was previously confronted; he also takes into account the elements of the current situation. This operation leads him to consider the situation of individuation (social visibility) as unfavorable and the situation of anonymity as favorable. His cognitive performance will then result from a connection which is socially indispensable for the signification which he attaches to the situation in which he finds himself.

This brief summary of a number of studies suggests that the social conditions which are imposed on the subject in a situation of constructing, or using knowledge, are certainly not without importance for the way in which the subject constructs or uses the knowledge. Otherwise how can one explain the influence of current insertions on his cognitive activity? These insertions seem to govern, either an "almost automatic" processing, or a controlled processing, of the problem situation: which in the two cases, can be interpreted as the result of an activity of correspondance of the characteristics of experimentally provoked situations with what has been previously stored during the development, here academic, of the subject. What is manipulated in the experiments presented are indeed true social insertions.

Conclusion

The exploratory nature of this work obviously does not allow one to put forward elements of conclusion of great scope. It authorizes, at most, the construction of a body of hypotheses likely to justify a research programme. Such is the present reality for us. In spite of the still too speculative dimension which underlies the propositions put forward, it is, nevertheless, possible to say that when social psychology takes on the study of cognitive functioning, it is not obliged to merge with cognitive psychology. If indeed its area of study is the thinking man, this thinking man is, first and foremost, a social being who maintains social contacts, participates in interactions, belongs to social groups, is the object of categorization; in short, he is a socially inserted being. Consequently it is difficult to imagine that this ensemble of characteristics can be held as negligible in the study of his cognitive functioning.

It is therefore at a dual level of investigation of human cognition that social psychology must assume its scientific responsibility. It must continue to devote itself to studying the effects of fundamental social situations such as situations of social comparison, inter-group relationships, social influence...etc, on behaviour so that one can better identify the most basic and most cognitively salient social insertions for all human individuals. Armed with this knowledge of the relationships between the individual and the collective it must promote and conduct a procedure aimed at apprehending the study of human cognition by taking account of the autobiographical dimension of

the individual i.e his social and affective history which is a product of the insertions presented or imposed by everyday life. The aim of this is to determine to what point human cognitive operations are socially penetrated or penetrable.

It will be acknowledged that, since these preoccupations are not necessarily of interest to other branches of scientific psychology, social psychology can therefore draw from them new reasons to assert its specificity.

References

Beauvois, J.L., Joule, R. & Monteil, J.M. (1991). *Perspectives cognitives et conduites sociales*. Vol. III. Fribourg: Delval.

Changeux, J.P. (1983). *L'homme neuronal*. Paris: Fayard.

Doise, W. (1982). *L'explication en psychologie sociale*. Paris: P.U.F.

Doise, W. (1989). "Constructivism in Social Psychology". *European Journal of Social Psychology*, 19, 389–400.

Fodor, J. (1983). *The modularity of Mind*. Cambridge: Bradford Books M.I.T. Press.

Gergen, M. (1989). "Induction and Construction: Teetering between Worlds". *European Journal of Social Psychology*, 19, 431–438.

Harré, R. (1989). "Metaphysics and Methodology: Some Prescriptions for Social Psychology Research". *European Journal of Social Psychology*, 19, 439–454.

Lecourt, D. (1989). "Introduction". In A. Prochiantz. *La construction du cerveau* (pp.1–17). Paris: Hachette.

Monteil, J.M. (1988a). "Marcajes sociales del nino en la institución escolar". In G. Mugny., J.A. Perez (Eds.), *Psicologia Social Del Desarrollo Cognitivo*.(317–324). Barcelona: Anthropos.

Monteil, J.M. (1988b). "Comparaison sociale, stratégies individuelles et médiations sociocognitives. Un effet de différenciation comportementale dans le champ scolaire". *European Journal of Psychology of Education*, 3, 3–18.

Monteil, J.M. (1989). *Eduquer et former. Perspectives psycho-sociales*. Grenoble: P.U.G.

Monteil, J.M. (1991). "Social regulation and individual cognitive function: effects of individuation individuation on cognitive performance.". *European Journal of Social Psychology* (in press).

Monteil, J.M; Versace, R. "The social experience and the construction of scripts: an experimental study" (in preparation).

Moscovici, S. (1989). "Precondition for Explanations in Social Psychology". *European Journal of Social psychology,* 19 , 407–430.

Nuttin, J.M. (1989). "Proposal for a Heuristic Quasi-Social Analysis of Social Behaviour: The Case of Harlow's 'Nature of Love'." *European Journal of Social Psychology,* 19, 371–384.

Prochiantz, A. (1989). *La construction du cerveau.* Paris: Hachette.

Putman, H. (1988). *Representation and Reality.* Cambridge: Bradford Books M.I.T. Press.

Rosenzweig, S. (1933). "The experimental situation as a psychological problem". *Psychol. rev,* 40, 337–354.

Thomson, S.C., Janigian, A.S. (1988). "Life Schemes: A Framework for Understanding the search for meaning". *Journal of Social and Clinical Psychology,* 7, 260–280.

Tulving, E. (1983). *Elements of Episodic memory.* Oxford: Oxford University Press.

Woodfield, A. (1983). *Thought and object.* Oxford: Oxford University Press.

Zajonc, R. (1989). "Styles of Explanation in Social Psychology". *European Journal of Social Psychology,* 19, 345–368.

Developmental Tasks – Where Do They Come From?

August Flammer and Joannis Avramakis

One set of developmental processes consists of solving so-called developmental tasks. The concept of developmental tasks was introduced by Havighurst (1948; 1956; Havighurst & Taba, 1949; Schoeppe & Havighurst, 1952) and, according to Dreher & Dreher (1985b, 30), has antecedents in Tryon (1939), Zachry (1940), Blos (1941), and Frank (1944). It contends that persons must comply with certain requirements at specific, quite precisely defined stages in their life, requirements which, if solved successfully, contribute to the person's well-being and to the success with consecutive developmental tasks, whereas if failed, lead to misfortune of the individual, to disapproval by the society and to difficulties in the mastery of future tasks (Havighurst, 1972, 2).

Within the history of the theories of human development, the notion that development consists of solving developmental tasks may be considered as a substantial step further from the older stage models (see Flammer, 1988). For example, this concept allows for an interpretation of individual differences in developmental curves as due to the individual patterns of the solution of developmental tasks (cf. the related concept in Erikson, 1959) and to cultural differences with respect to the developmental tasks. The underlying concept of development appears to be a meaningful continuation of the emphasis on the culture-specificity of the development, as previously emphasized by Vygotsky (1934), Lewin (1946) and others.

By taking the term in a wider sense, there are developmental tasks to be solved at each age or developmental level. In a more limited sense, i. e., if the concept implies that a certain goal must be reached by means of strategic actions, developmental tasks are considerably more frequent in adolescence and in adulthood than at the school age or even in infancy.

In psychology, the concept of task generally implies that there is a clearly defined solution to be attained and that the solution can be attained by specific algorithms or sequences of actions, albeit that the solution of the task may require considerable effort. If talking about problems, there is generally not a clear conception of the goal state, of the path leading to it, of the starting position or of all three (Dörner, 1976). One could speculate whether it would be more appropriate to talk about developmental problems instead of developmental tasks. It is assumed here that both developmental tasks and developmental problems correspond to empirical facts. The constraint here is on developmental tasks, implicating that we are talking about developmental challenges, the solution of which is more or less clear, if not for the subjects who have to solve the task, then at least for some persons around him or her. Whether there are such persons and whether they have an interest in the solution of the developmental tasks by the subject is the main question of this paper.

Havighurst pointed out the fact that developmental tasks may have their roots in (1) a person's processes of physical maturation, (2) in social expectations or (3) in the individual's concerns and aspirations. Yet, for a physical state or a personal concern to become a (developmental) "task", there must be someone to "make" a task out of it, i. e., put up goals and oblige someone to act in order to reach the goals. In using the term "developmental task" in this sense, it is of interest to differentiate between different levels of generality of developmental tasks, different "authorities" or task givers having an interest in the solution, and different solution patterns. We assume that different solution patterns trigger different reactions by the task givers which again may be different according to types of developmental tasks. The aim of this paper is therefore to develop a conceptual framework of three types of developmental tasks, three classes of task givers and four solution patterns. The evaluative reactions by the task givers should allow to empirically consolidate the conceptual system.

1. Task givers

Irrespective of whether a developmental task has physiological roots or not, it can be given to an individual by the individual herself or himself (subjective developmental task) or by another person or persons (objective developmental task). Objective developmental tasks can be given either by specific persons or a group of persons (reference group) or by the culture, more specifically, the society as a whole which the individual belongs to (Table 1).

Table 1. Three classes of task givers

Developmental task		
subjective	objective	
the target individual by himself or herself	reference group (parents, teachers, friends, etc.)	society (public opinion, laws, institutions)

One may argue that no task is ever purposefully led to a solution if there is not a subject assuming the task as his or hers. But this is not meant by our distinguishing subjective from objective developmental tasks. According to our understanding, a subjective developmental task is one which originates from the subject, for instance if a person decides to become a famous musician or chooses a model person to be followed in life-style, performances etc. Most often, such subjective developmental tasks are not invented suddenly but are aligned to the individual's general life-goals on the basis of the subject's view of the circumstances and the actual conditions of the probable or planned biography (see Nurmi, 1987; 1989 a, b, c, d).

Reference groups as task givers represent a wide class of instances like parents, sometimes teachers, youth-group leaders, therapists, priests, bosses etc. More rarely they are friends, life-partners or one's own children. They may be one person or many. Probably, social groups as such do not give developmental tasks to an individual. Frequently, we would speak of social groups only if the members of a group agree explicitly on giving someone or all group members such a developmental task.

Of more interest here are developmental tasks put up by society. We are not so much concerned here with speakers of organizations, exponents of the society or specific prescriptions or laws, but with the more or less (mostly less) explicit truisms along whose lines a human biography has to run in a given culture. We may call them social representations in the sense of socially shared knowledge about what development ought to be. It has been argued that the society's care and participation in certain developmental task solutions amounts to a functional replacement of initiation rituals by developmental tasks (Flammer, 1991).

2. Generality of developmental tasks

There are developmental tasks which are valid for all persons in certain life conditions or for a subset of them or only for single individuals. Those developmental tasks which apply to all persons of a given culture, provided they have reached a certain level of development, are called normative. Normative developmental tasks are seldom given by single persons. They are mostly given implicitly, represented inherently in institutions such as the general school

Table 2. Three generality levels of developmental tasks

Generalization over		
all subjects at a given developmental level	a subset of persons at a given developmental level	valid only for single persons
normative developmental task	restricted normative developmental task	individual developmental task

system, in regulations of the old age pension, in marriage ceremonies, in military promotions, etc. (Table 2).

Restricted normative developmental tasks are those which apply only for a small subset of persons, like college students, the members of a ballet troup, the candidate believers within a certain church.

Finally, there are developmental tasks which hold only for single persons, be they given by the society, a reference group or the individual self, e. g., the personal goal to become a chess master in one's country (initiated personally or by one's father), or to become a public leader in an ecological movement. Most often such individual developmental tasks are given by the subject to himself or herself or by a single person close to the individual.

The literature on developmental tasks mainly makes reference to the normative developmental tasks (particularly Havighurst, 1948; Dreher & Dreher, 1985 a,b; Oerter, 1986; Siegfried, 1987; Rhyn, 1990; Schwaller, in prep.). Restricted normative objective developmental tasks appear in the literature implicitly under the heading of coping with restricted normative life-events (Riegel, 1975; Haan, 1977; Filipp, 1981; 1982; Seiffge-Krenke, 1986; Flammer, Grob, Lüthi & Kaiser, 1989).

Normative developmental tasks look so much like the normal course of development that there is no triviality in postulating that they are in fact tasks of development. How can the task character be proved? Our contention is the following: As the task-givers usually attempt to enforce a solution or at least try to enforce it and acknowledge either success or failure, it appears to be sensible to use the reactions of outsiders to failure or successful outcome of supposed developmental tasks as criteria. This is what we will elaborate in section 4.

3. Patterns of task solutions

The solution of a normative developmental task takes some time, usually years. Occasionally, it demands creative thinking, strategies suitable to a given situation and fairly often the solution demands much psychical, social and even physical resources. The task solving persons are usually quite aware of not

only being indebted to an existing task, but also that this task is in the process of being solved, has already been solved, or that it has not been solved yet.

Thus, Dreher & Dreher (1985a) were able to demonstrate with 15- and 16-year-old adolescents that their subjective judgement of their degree of mastery of a series of normative developmental tasks was increasing considerably over one year. This was particularly true for the tasks of knowing what career to choose and what must be learned to achieve it, of making friends, of developing ideas about what a life partner and a future family should be like, and of the development of an intimate relationship. There can be considerable differences between parents and the adolescents in the evaluation of the reached level of mastery, as Siegfried (1987) demonstrated with adolescents of 14 to 16 years of age. Urban students evaluated their level of mastery as being higher than did rural students, but urban parents rated the level of mastery by their children even lower than rural parents did. Throughout, the evaluation by the parents was lower than the one by the adolescents. Furthermore, urban parents believed they had more control over their adolescent children's development than did rural parents (Siegfried, 1987).

Interestingly enough, these analyses did not give any evidence that some persons felt that a given developmental task could not be solved. It is also striking that these adolescents indicated a multiplicity of developmental tasks actually being in the process of solution, quite in contrast to Coleman's focal theory (1978; 1979; 1980) which states that in any given moment there is typically only one crisis or conflict (or task) at its peak.

As the appearance of normative developmental tasks can fairly accurately be predicted by the concerned individual on the basis of his or her general social awareness (see Nurmi, 1987; 1989 a,b), it is possibile for him or her to be prepared for accepting the challenge when it arrives. There are other, mostly individual, developmental tasks which are not foreseeable, such as overcoming the loss of a loved one, coming to grips with a large lotto gain, or an unexpected pregnancy (Rossi, 1968).

Task givers apart from the concerned individual generally do not care too much about how a developmental task is solved, but are more interested in whether and when it is solved. It is their evaluative reaction to this aspect which we believe can help to empirically distinguish both task givers and task types. Developmental tasks can be solved correctly or incorrectly or not at all, on time, late or even early. Here we only take into account the solution as it is expected (correctly and on time), the late solution and the non-solution. Furthermore, we assume that late solutions and non-solutions are evaluated differently according to the causes the evaluators attribute to the delay or the non-solution. We distinguish between the causal attribution of unable and unwilling.

4. Sanctioning the solution of a developmental task

The giver of a task has an interest in its solution. He or she can be expected to acknowledge the solution, to urge a solution, to sanction an incorrect solution or a non-solution. If it is not clear who the task giver is, such responses may reveal him or her. We therefore propose to study peoples' reactions in response to the solution, non-solution, late solution, or early solution of a developmental task in order to find out the developmental task's giver. In Table 3 we sketch hypothetical response patterns. They have not been subject to systematic empirical tests yet. We expect at least three classes of developmental tasks (normative, restricted normative and individual; Table 2) to which people (the subject, the reference group or individuals there of, and "society"; Table 1) react in specific ways (Table 3) according to whether the task has been solved as expected, late or not at all, the last because the subject is either not willing or not capable of solving it (Table 3). The identification of such evaluative response patterns and the identification of developmental task types go hand in hand, i. e., are mutually supportive. They are either both successful or both unsuccessful.

Having solved a certain developmental task a person is generally satisfied with the solution and is pleased to have achieved one further step of development. If the developmental task

Table 3. Type of developmental task x solution x attribution (nested) and evaluation (su = subjective evaluation, gr = evaluation by reference group, so = evaluation by 'society').

| | Type of developmental task | | |
	normative	restricted	subjective
solved as expected	su:satisfaction gr:satisfaction so:unnoticeable	su:satisfaction, pride gr:pride so:respect	su:satisfaction pride gr:pride so:admiration
not solved ('refuses to solve')	su:(protest, disdain,neurot. reaction) gr:perplexity, shame, irrit. so:outlawing	su:(protest, disdain, neur.react.), gr:disappointment so:-	su:ignore, rationaliz., repression gr:- so:-
not solved ('cannot solve')	su:reduced self-esteem,sadness compensation gr:disappointment pity,sympathy, help, (shame) (help) so:pity, help	su:reduced s'-esteem,shame, compensation gr:disappoint-ment, pity, so:-	su:reduced self-esteem, sadness gr:- so:-
solved with delay	su:relief gr:relief so:(relief)	su:relief gr:relief so:-	su:relief gr:- so:-

is a restricted normative, one or if it is devised by the person herself or himself, the reaction includes pride as in typical cases of achieving individual tasks (Heckhausen, 1980).

Someone who has not (yet) solved a developmental task and believes to owe the public a solution, suffers in general due to this failure. This results in a lower self-esteem. If the developmental task is an individual one, the person's reaction may depend heavily on the importance he or she attributed to the task, on the "meaning" the task has, and on whether or not other people know of the failed task.

External task givers usually do not react conspicuously to the successful solution of normative developmental tasks (comparable to neglectful marriage partners who at least do not react in a negative way if given satisfaction to their expectations). In the case of failure to comply with developmental tasks, normative and possibly restricted normative, reactions from the social environment are to be expected. Probably in the majority of cases, the demand is made to solve the task without delay (especially by members of the reference group, for instance in the case of a uncompleted vocational training, or when a job has not been found yet). After repeated failure, the compliance with the demand may be considered as unrealistic, be it because the individual refuses to comply ("is lazy", "does not really try") or is unable (the task is "too hard" for him or her). The choice between these reactions depends on the precedent causal attributions of the failure.

By refusing to solve a normative developmental task, one risks social labelling and/or social rejection. If, for instance, out of real or supposed neglect, one does not complete a vocational training, he or she is considered lazy, a drop-out, in any case, it is his or her own fault and he or she will have to bear the negative consequences; or someone still living with his parents at the age of thirty, will merit no compassion for not having found a partner for life. Such labellings and social delimitations may become apparent in explicit verbal statements and also in social choices, in reduced contacts, in non-verbal forms of communication, and so on.

We have a different situation when according to the common view, a certain task cannot be solved by an individual, be it that his or her resources are too limited in relation to the task, or if the requirements of the task in relation to the resources of the individual are too high. This stimulates compassion by the people surrounding the individual and perhaps offers of help. Such people are considered disabled and deserve allowance and compensations. The evaluative reaction probably differs slightly when the developmental task is restricted normative instead of normative, especially if it was given by one of a few closely related persons (such as parents). The successful solving of such a task should fill the task givers with joy and pride, whereas a failure could entail pressure to eventually do the task and then often lead to disappointment of one's own aspirations.

As developmental tasks can often take years to be solved and the real progress is often not easily discerned, failure is often visible only in later stages. Students and parents must frequently rely on school records and promotions in class over years as indicators of progress in the preparation of a professional career (see Rossi, 1968). It is possible that the real situation is revealed too late.

5. Unreadiness and precocity

Reasonably, the sanctioning of unsolved tasks is only possible when compared with a normative time schedule. It is interesting to observe that for certain tasks a great flexibility exists (examples: finishing professional training, starting a family, leaving the parental home), and for others not (i. e. adequate social intercourse between the sexes, going to school, working out ideas for a future profession). There are other developmental tasks that may not have to be solved altogether (example: starting a family).

Developmental processes are generally desirable. Therefore it is not surprising that a quick and early solution of developmental tasks is usuaally considered as positive and is sanctioned with pride or admiration, but not in every instance. There is often a disparity of opinion among different individuals. An early display of adult-typical behaviour with boy-friends and girl-friends is usually rated as positive by the task solvers, but observed with ambiguity by parents.

The schedule for developmental tasks related with puberty is only partly given by the individual biological maturity (Peterson, 1988). Magnusson et al. (1981) established for instance that biologically precocious girls had boyfriends who were more frequently older, sooner than less mature girls. They also broke social rules (i. e., in the family or at school) more often and consumed drugs at an earlier age and on a more frequent basis. The breaking of rules did not carry less weight for them because they and their older friends were conforming to less strict norms than other adolescents, but these precocious girls, having broken a rule, could hope for milder, more tolerant sanctions from their friends than the less mature ones. Probably in the eyes of their friends, the development-specific evaluation was adapted to the special biological givings.

In the case of the developmental task of gradually untying the family bonds by taking a flat, for instance, precocity is considered quite differently. Excessive precocity will not be regarded positively either by adolescents or by parents, or by society. Why? One might think that the simple existence of a task implies the desirability of a solution to be found, but no condition as to a certain minimum time that must be respected before completion. We believe that in instances where a premature solution of developmental tasks is regretted, we have to search for further implicit tasks preceeding in the normal biography, which under these circumstances may not be solved in a satisfactory way.

In most cases, tasks that must be solved before another one can be tackled are so comprehensive that they are not easily definable. This becomes evident in the case of the premature departure from home. The previous complex task probably consists of accepting the protection and the guidance of the parents in the ongoing process of socialization, in going through the schools, maybe in learning a profession, in forming a personal world view and in becoming a mature, emotionally balanced and independent person. Our difficulty in formulating such a task must, however, motivate our further reflection on the very topic of developmental task; it could be that we take as developmental tasks, primarily, small developmental steps, which can easily be described and

the solution of which is relatively easily operationalized.

Sometimes prerequisite developmental tasks appear on seemingly unusual paths. Thus Russel (1974), in a research questionnaire on coping with parenthood, found that those who did not answer at the first invitation to participate in the research not only found parenting hard, but also were more often those who had had their child before being married. The common reactions to precocity and unreadiness cannot be reduced to a common denominator and are not included in Table 3.

6. Preliminary results

Within his master's thesis under the supervision of the first author, Heinz Rhyn (1990) has tested people's evaluative responses to various modes of completion of developmental tasks. He presented written scenarios to 123 adult Swiss subjects. The scenarios related to either one of two developmental tasks, i. e., becoming independent from parents (= autonomy task) and choosing a professional career (= professional task). The autonomy task a concerned taking one's own flat, the autonomy task b was about deciding oneself about one's leisure time and about going out at night. The professional task a contained a long-term career decision and starting to earn one's own money, the professional task b was about passing final exams of a vocational training. On the basis of a pretest about the "regular" age of fulfillment of the respective developmental task, the protagonist of each scenario was either too young, too old or at the regular age.

Precocious resolution of the autonomy task was generally rated as risky, while precocious resolution of the professional task was mostly not. Delayed resolution of both developmental tasks was evaluated differently according to the suggested causal attribution as to whether the protagonist was not able or whether he or she was unwilling.

Rhyn also asked his subjects for spontanous emotions they felt toward the described person (yes- or no-answers were to be given to a list of emotion words). The most frequent emotions are presented in Table 4.

Clearly, the emotional reactions were quite different according to the type of the task so-

Table 4. Most frequent emotional reactions to the types of developmental task solutions (data from Rhyn, 1990)

| | autonomy task | | professional task | |
	taking a flat	leisure time	career choice	vocational exams
precocious	rejection	being afraid	surprise	surprise
regular	respect	respect	respect	respect
delayed ("unable")	pity	pity	pity	pity
delayed ("unwilling")	pity	rejection	rejection	rejection

lution. In case of precocious resolution the feelings are more on the sceptical side (being afraid, rejection, surprise). The regular task solution was appreciated with respect throughout. While delay due to unableness provoced generally feelings of pity and sympathy, delay due to unwillingness was mostly rejected. To our surprise the variation between different developmental tasks was small.

7. Conclusion

Insofar as the (individual) development resides in the mastery of developmental tasks, individual and unique developmental processes are described easier with the concept of developmental tasks than by classical stage theories, and development appears to be more closely linked with social institutions, social representations and social transactions than is the case with most other theories. Therefore, such a point of view implies, to a large extent, an ecological view of development (Dittmann-Kohli, 1984; Oerter, 1986), and also requires that distinctions be made among developmental tasks, going beyond the area covered until now by the literature under this heading. We would like to suggest further focussed examinations of single developmental tasks, on the one hand taking into account the distinctions and criteria developed above, and on the other hand taking into account the various ecological conditions. These particular developmental tasks vary from one culture to another, according also to the economic conditions, and social norms subjected to changes in historic time. If, and to what extent the society, the parents and the concerned person are involved in developmental tasks should be discerned from the reactions of these persons to solutions and as well as to unreadiness or precocity. This is our methodological suggestion.

References

Blos, P. (1941) The adolescent personality. New York: Appleton-Century-Crofts.

Coleman, J. C. (1978) Current contradictions in adolescent theory. Journal of Youth and Adolescence, 7, 1–12.

Coleman, J. C. (1979) Current views of the adolescent process. In Coleman, J. C., Ed., The school years. London: Methuen, 1–23.

Coleman, J. C. (1980) The nature of adolescence. London: Methuen.

Dittmann-Kohli (1984) Die Bewältigung von Entwicklungsaufgaben bei Lehrlingen: Analyse- und Interventionsgesichtspunkte. In Olbrich, E., Todt, E., Hg., Probleme des Jugendalters. Berlin: Springer, 227–257

Dörner, D. (1976) Problemlösen als Informationsverarbeitung. Stuttgart: Kohlhammer.

Dreher, E. & Dreher, M. (1985a) Entwicklungsaufgaben im Jugendalter: Bedeutsamkeit und Bewältigungskonzepte. In Liepman, D., Stiksrud, A., Hg., Entwicklungsaufgaben und Bewältigungsprobleme in der Adoleszenz. Göttingen: Hogrefe.

Dreher, E., Dreher, M. (1985b) "Entwicklungsaufgabe" – theoretisches Konzept und Forschungsprogramm. In Oerter, R., Hg., Lebensbewältigung im Jugendalter. Weinheim: Edition Psychologie, 30–61.

Erikson, E. H. (1959) Identity and the life cycle. (dt. Identität und Lebenszyklus. Frankfurt: Suhrkamp, 1977).

Filipp, S. H., Hg. (1981) Kritische Lebensereignisse. München: Urban & Schwarzenberg.

Filipp, S. H. (1982) Kritische Lebensereignisse als Brennpunkte einer Angewandten Entwicklungspsychologie des mittleren und höheren Erwachsenenalters. In Oerter, R., Montada, L., Hg., Entwicklungspsychologie. München: Urban & Schwarzenberg, 769–790.

Flammer, A. (1988) Entwicklungstheorien. Bern: Huber.

Flammer, A., Grob, A., Lüthi, R., Kaiser, F. G. (1989) Kontrollattribution und Wohlbefinden von Schweizer Jugendlichen II. Forschungsbericht 1989–4. Bern: Psychologisches Institut.

Flammer, A. (1991) Entwicklungsaufgaben als Initiationsrituale? Entwicklungsaufgaben anstelle von Initiationsritualen? In Klosinski, G., Hg., Pubertätsriten – Aequivalente und Defizite in unserer Gesellschaft. Bern: Huber, in press.

Frank, L. (1944) Introduction: Adolescence as a period of transition. Forty-third Yearbook of the National Society for the Study of Education, Part I, Ch. 1. University of Chicago Press.

Haan, N. (1974) The adolescent's ego model of coping and defense and comparisons with Q-sorted ideal personlities. Genetic Psychology Monographs, 89, 273–306.

Haan, N. (1977) Coping and defending. Processes of self-environment organization. New York: Academic.

Havighurst, R. J. (1948) Developmental task and education. New York: McKay.

Havighurst, R. J. (1956) Research on the developmental-task concept. The School Review, 64, 215–223.

Havighurst, R. J. (1972) Developmental tasks and education. New York: McKay. 3rd ed.

Havighurst, R. J., Taba, H. (1949) Adolescent character and personality. New York: Wiley.

Heckhausen, H. (1980) Motivation und Handeln. Berlin: Springer.

Lewin, K. (1946) Verhalten und Entwicklung als eine Funktion der Gesamtsituation. In Lewin, K., Hg., Feldtheorie in den Sozialwissenschaften. Bern: Huber, 1963, 271–329.

Magnusson, D., Stattin, H., Allen, V. L. (1981) Differential maturation among girls and its relationship to social adjustment: A longitudinal perspective. In Baltes, P. B., Featherman, D. L., Lerner, R. M., Eds., Life-span development and behavior. New York: Academic, 136–172.

Nurmi, J.E. (1987) Age, sex, social class, and quality of family interaction as determinants of adolescents' future orientation: A developmental task interpretation. Adolescence, 22, 978–991.

Nurmi, J. E. (1989a) Development of orientation to the future during early adolescence: A four-year longitudinal study and two cross-sectional comparisons. International Journal of Psychology, 24, 195–214.

Nurmi, J. E. (1989b) Planning, motivation, and evaluation in orientation to the future: A latent structure analysis. Scandinavian Journal of Psychology, 30, 64–71.

Nurmi, J. E. (1989c) The changing parent-child relationship, self-esteem, and intelligence as determinants of orientation to the future during early adolescence. Research Report Nr. 10. University of Helsinki: Department of Psychology.

Nurmi, J. E. (1989d) How do adolescents see their future? A review of the development of future orientation and planning. Research Report Nr. 11. University of Helsinki: Department of Psychology.

Oerter, R., Montada, L., Hg. (1982) Entwicklungspsychologie. München: Urban & Schwarzenberg.

Oerter, R. (1986) Developmental task through the life-span: a new approach to an old concept. In Baltes, P. B., Featherman, D. L., Lerner, R. M., Eds., Life-span development and behavior. Hillsdale: N. J.: Erlbaum, 233–271.

Peterson, A. C. (1988) Adolescent development. Annual Review of Psychology, 39, 583–607.

Rhyn, H. (1990) Entwicklungsaufgaben und soziale Erwartungen. Lizentiatsarbeit. Bern: Psychologisches Institut der Universität.

Riegel, K. (1975) Adult life crises: a dialectic interpretation of development. In Datan, N., Ginsberg, L.H., Eds., Life-span developmental psychology. Normative life-crises. New York: Academic, 99–128.

Rossi, A.E. (1968) Transition to parenthood. Journal of Marriage and the Family, 30, 26–39.

Russel, C. S. (1974) Transition to parenthood: Problems and gratifications. Journal of Marriage and the Family, 36, 294–301.

Schoeppe, A. & Havighurst, R. J. (1952) A validation of development and adjustment hypotheses of adolescence. Journal of Educational Psychology, 43, 339–353.

Schwaller, C. (in prep.) Entwicklungsaufgaben in der Wahrnehmung von Sekundarschülern verschiedener Schulstufen und Schultypen. Dissertation. Universität Bern.

Seiffge-Krenke, I. (1986) Problembewältigung im Jugendalter. Zeitschrift für Entwicklungspsychologie und Pädagogische Psychologie, 18, 122–152.

Siegfried, G. (1987) Entwicklungsaufgaben in der frühen Adoleszenz: Ein regionaler Vergleich bei 14- bis 16-jährigen Sekundarschülern. Lizentiatsarbeit. Bern: Psychologisches Institut der Universität.

Tryon, C. M. (1939) Evaluations of adolescent personality by adolescents. Monograph of the Society for Research in Child Development, 4, 77–78.

Zachry, C. B. (1940) Emotion and conduct in adolescence. New York: Appleton-Century-Crofts.

Vygotsky, L. S. (1934, German 1977) Denken und Sprechen. Frankfurt: Fischer.

Knowledge in the Definition of Social Situations – Actualization of Subjective Theories about Trust in Counselling

Uwe Flick

1. Introduction

Subjective theories represent a model of social knowledge. Trust is a constitutive element of the social situation "counselling". In a research project, we tried to find out fifteen counsellors' subjective theories about trust, and how they translate this knowledge into professional actions. On one hand, examining the process of developing trust in counselling conversation shows how counsellors and clients interactively re-define the social situation of encounter in an institution like socio-psychiatric services ("Sozialpsychiatrische Dienste") in the sense of Thomas' theorem step-by-step into a situation of counselling. On the other hand, it becomes clear that this process and its essential stages are represented in counsellors' subjective theories about trust in different, identifiable submodels.

In the situation of counselling, the counsellor's knowledge about trust is actualized in two ways. First, it is formed in this situation in a process of sedimentation augmenting the stock of experience-based knowledge. Second, counsellors use this knowledge in the current interaction, in orientating in the situation, in classifying the situation and in deciding about alternatives of coping with it. By ways of evaluating this process, the present stock of knowledge is actualized again in the sense of modification and adaptation.

2. Theoretical Approaches to the Relation of Knowledge and Action

Sociologist W. Thomas (1928, p. 572) stated in the so-called "Thomas-theorem": "If men define situations as real, they are real in their consequences." For our discussion here, Ball (1972, p. 79) developed this theorem in one central aspect and pointed out: "To define a situation is to engage in social construction of reality; since this process involves knowledge,

it is the construction of social reality". As we shall see later, a process of constructing a certain kind of reality, or of defining a special situation, can be found in the analysis of counselling interaction. To explicate the role of knowledge Ball has outlined, subjective theories are reconstructed in this study.

How do people aquire subjective theories? Knowledge being part of subjective theories can be seen as a result of "sediments of formerly current situation-specific experience" (Schütz and Luckmann, 1975, p. 133). These experiences may result from a variety of different situations. As Schütz and Luckmann (1975, p. 157) further suggest, "the experiences are (...) modified, i. e. idealized, anonymized, typified when they enter the stock of knowledge. By this, the 'structural' signs of current experiences are 'neutralized' or overformed". If subjective theories are understood as a model of a "mundane stock of knowledge" (Schütz and Luckmann 1975, p. 157) or as a section of it, they don't contain experience with *concrete* persons and situations. They rather contain "typifications" (1975, p. 138) of experiences related to *types* of situations and in our case, to the "generalized client" (cf. Mead, 1934) or to a multitude of very different clients. Sedimentations of experience in the outlined sense lead to the consequence that experiences on different levels of abstraction become part of subjective theories, as their reconstruction will show.

One further aspect of the relation of knowledge and action and of the two empirical approaches this study is based on may finally be pointed out. Schütz and Luckmann again suggest: "Experiences build up polythetically, their sense can (...) be seized monothetically". While the analysis of actions (as counselling interaction) may explicate how experiences are made "polythetically, i. e. step-by-step" (Schütz, 1972, p. 143), the analysis of subjective theories (as a form of knowledge) may explicate monothetically "the conceptual meaning" of these experience as their result.

3. Empirical Approaches to Social Knowledge on Trust and its Realization

In this study two qualitative methods are used as empirical approaches and triangulated (see more generally Bergold and Flick, 1987, for further examples and methodological topics). Both methods will shortly be charactarized in the following sections.

3.1 Reconstruction of Subjective Theories

For reconstructing subjective theories, a method created by Scheele and Groeben (1988) is partly applied. The first step is a qualitative interview including open and hypothesis-directed questions in variable sequential order to explicate the contents of the subjective theory. In the second step, a graphic representation technique ("Struktur-Lege-Technik") is applied for the purpose of communicative validation of the interview's main results by the interviewee. This technique also shall explicate the structure of the subjective theory as seen by the interviewee (see Dann, this volume, for further explication of this research program). The last step of Scheele and Groeben's method, falsification or verification of reconstructed subjective theories in an observational experiment, has not been applied in this study for several reasons explained elsewhere (see Flick, 1987). One central argument pointed out by Bromme (1984, p. 53) against their strategy of verification of professionals' subjective theories as a kind of expert knowledge, stresses the fact that "the important feature of expert knowledge is not whether it can be verified, but whether it is functional for a certain activity (...) The functionality of knowledge, however, can be empirically analyzed in the context of the activities and of the demands which the actor has to cope with". For this purpose a different type of method was chosen for this study to analyze the functionality of subjective theories in context-sensitive ways.

3.2 Conversation Analysis of Counselling Interaction

Conversation analysis was developed as a central research program in ethnomethodology.

Besides mundane conversation, different forms of institutional interaction – such as counselling – became central topics of conversation analytic research (see Heritage, 1985, or Wolff, 1986, for recent developments). Main questions of conversation analysis are how and by which methods members of social interaction achieve order, how they establish, for example, counselling as a special type of social order. For this purpose, examples of mundane or institutional interaction are recorded, transcribed and interpreted.

4. An Example of the Relations between Knowledge and Action

In the following section an example of the interrelation of knowledge and action shall be demonstrated. First, a short excerpt of the beginning of a counselling interaction between a female social-worker (B) and a male client (K) will be presented (see Flick, 1989, for further examples of complete interpretations) to look afterwards for representations of the interactional problem the participants are negotiating here in B's subjective theory on trust.

4.1 Excerpt of Counselling as Professional Action

B: Hmm, well, your grandfather came to us (K: yes), well, he seemed to be very worried about you?

K: Yeah, I was feeling quite bad

B: Yes, what was the matter at that time?

K: In May, (.) you know, I drank too much a couple of days in a series and then I was feeling soo bad, because of the circulation (B: hmm), well everything, what you-, break out of sweat (B: hmm) raving of the heart, uuuh, burning eyes and everything, anyhow, and I didn't feel like laughing at all

B: And then your grandfather also said, uh, well (.) your family doctor had said, meanwhile you are in a very urgent danger of death. Do you have an urgent organic –

K: Well, well, danger of death –

B: complaints?

K: – not really, ne? (B: hmm) There's just my fear, if I carry on that way, that still might come, (B: hmm) and that must not really happen, you know, I don't lay any stress on this (B: hmm) and therefore it's kind of a thing about drinking in my case.

B: How did it begin?

As is clearly seen in other examples analyzed in our study (also generally shown by Wolff, 1986) a typical action of the counsellor at this point would be immediately to begin with the general exploration. In this example, she begins with the general exploration only after having ascertained step-by-step, whether there is an urgent situation in the client's case. This would imply an acute demand of action, such as referring the client to a physician in the team as B is a social worker. So, step-by-step, she discusses all the hints for an urgent situation – the fear of the grandfather and the reported statement of the family doctor. Only after successively clearing up these points, she can turn to the "normal" development of relationship and trust.

4.2 Representation of this Problem in the Counsellor's Subjective Theory

Her subjective theory "at one look – monothetically" (Schütz, 1972) reveals why the counsellor at this point, first communicatively – and that means in the sense of Schütz (1972, p. 150) "polythetically" – runs through the process of clearing, documented in the course of the interaction. In her subjective theory this process of experience is condensed in the conceptional relation "client comes in a situation of urgence (which hinders) development of trust" (see the excerpt illustrated below).

Schütz and Luckmann (1975, p. 154) point out that the relevance of the outlined relation between experience and knowledge is not just a process of storing experience, but also has implications for the constitution of subjective meaning in the current situation of action as follows: "Aquisition of knowledge is sedimentation of current experience in structures of sense according to relevance and typicality, that on their part influence the definition of current situations and the interpretation of current experience".

Our example can be used again to illustrate this relation. In the counsellor B's subjective theory on trust we find the following structure

of sense resulting from comparable experience. This part of the subjective theory becomes relevant in the above excerpt of counselling interaction:

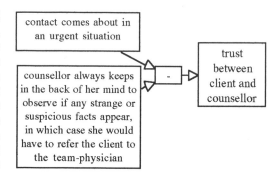

This part of B's knowledge has an influence on the definition of the situation by the participants insofar, as the need to answer the question of whether there really is an urgent situation in this case and whether the corresponding "imperative of action" (cf. Wagner et al., 1981) should be realized here (to refer the client to the physician), becomes the directive for the counsellor's actions in the first phase of the conversation in contrast to the 'normal' run of such sequences. Application of this stock of knowledge in the situation of action should not be understood as a deliberate and explicit application of those theories. In the situation of action, they rather become tacit knowledge (Polanyi, 1966), which is or can be activated by the actor.

Following this extremely micro-analytic approach based on only one example the next sections will deal in more general terms with some results of analyzing processes of situation-definition in counselling interaction (5.) and of analyzing their representation in subjective theories (6.).

5. (Re-)Definition of the Situation in Counselling Interaction

The institution of socio-psychiatric service is part of the public health departement. It not only has to help people, but also has to guarantee public order, and therefore has to exercise social control. So counselor and client meet in a context and under circumstances extremely different from those of typical counselling. Typical counselling can be characterized by the client's voluntary access, the orientation of the counsellor's actions only towards helping the client and without the frightening powers of intervention as a context. In contrast to that typical situation of counselling, most clients only come to the socio-psychiatric service because they were forced to by a citation initiated by other persons or institutions. These services are equipped with special powers to forcibly send people to a psychiatric ward or to put them under legal control etc. These powers have frightening effects on clients, which in most cases, add stress in the relationship between client and counsellor.

If counsellors here want to apply the instrument of "counselling" in "typical ways", they have to define the situation, as if it were a typical counselling situation. Therefore, they must cope with several demands: Because most counselling in this context results from other people's initiative, (relatives or neighbours of the client etc.), or institutions, the counsellors must establish a direct and dyadic interaction. For that purpose they have to explain the special premises of encounter and to give space to the client's point of view against perspectives and opinions of third persons or institutions concerning the client that hurry on ahead of the conversation. Our example shows how the counsellor step-by-step explains the information – and perhaps the prejudices – volunteered by the client's grandfather, and also how she gives the client a chance to correct them with his own point of view. Other examples show counsellors' attempts to form an alliance with clients against those persons or institutions that originally initiated the counselling.

Detailed analyses of the interaction process in counselling showed how counsellors as a first step open up and install a frame in the conversation (counselling as delimited space of freedom) mainly by "open starters" (for example: "And, what's the matter?") and by explaining how the counselling came about and its pre-defined problems. This frame is meant to help clients to explain their points of view and *their* problems, and to develop trust in the counsellor. Also, it helps making or defining a situation, as if it were a "typical" form of counselling, and not one in this special context of the public health departement. The second step is the reconstitution of the problem: first,

it is reconstituted as *the client's* problem instead of one pre-defined by others; then, like in any other counselling, it is reconstituted in a process of negotiation with the client into the peculiar problem, i.e. a problem that is more general, initiating or lying behind the problem presented by the client. This negotiation clears the counselor's ability and competence for the special case of the client and helps the client to develop trust in the counsellor. Finally, this problem interactively constituted in the situation of counselling is explored more profoundly. Towards the end of the conversation, counsellors complete the frame installed at the beginning by organizing the end of talk ("opening up closings" – Schegloff and Sacks, 1973) timely and if necessary, by arranging to continue at another date.

So here, counsellors have to deal with two types of situations: first, the real ones under the conditions of the public health departement and the prejudices about the client; second, the ideal ones of "typical counselling". If they want to gain the clients' trust, they have to redefine the first type of situation into the second one – or at least as far as possible. If they succeed in defining the situation "counselling" as real, the consequences of the defined situation become real and counselling as an instrument can work in this special context.

6. Submodels in Subjective Theories of Trust

The necessity of dealing with two types of situations and of redefining one into the other is represented in counsellors' subjective theories about trust. By comparatively analyzing the concepts contained in the subjective theories we can identify four submodels which we find in every subjective theory we analyzed. They structure and integrate the variety of concepts in the subjective theories. The first submodel represents the situation of encounter in the circumstances effected by the public health departement like the counsellors' special powers and duties, the clients' fear and demotivation, and their special, involuntary access. In this model, the hindering effects on trust and on the development of trust are central aspects. In addition to this model of starting situations we find a second model representing ideal conditions of typical counselling. This model features clients as motivated and voluntary, the counsellors' task as to help people (instead of forcing and controlling them), mutual trust and open-mindedness, little influence by the institution on counselling etc. In this model the description of trust as a state of mind, trusting behavior and institutional conditions supporting the development of trust are central aspects. A third model represents the process of redefining the situation and of developping trust. Here, actions of counsellors and clients supporting trust and sometimes the role of special competences given to the counsellor by the institution and the chance to use them *for* the client, are central topics. While the first model is used to identify and classify the given situation and its demands, the other models are used as a foil of orientation in producing a more or less typical situation of counselling. Finally, a fourth submodel represents other situations besides counselling, like visiting clients at home or sending them forcibly into hospitals, and their implications for trustful relations afterwards.

7. Perspectives

This contribution wanted to demonstrate the role of subjective theories in the process of (re-)definition of a social situation. They offer an applicable stock of knowledge for managing this process (actualization) and are also reactualized, i. e. supplemented, modified and adapted through this process of application. Further we wanted to show, how counselling can be conceived as a process of defining a social situation, and finally, which contributions phenomenological sociologists may offer for a theoretical foundation of this process and the role of knowledge in it. In micro-analyses, like the one presented here, we can come closer to understanding what is happening in complex social situations, and how the part of the actors' implicit knowledge in the definition of those situations can be seen. The triangulation of these two perspectives offers a way for mutual evaluation of those analyses.

References

Ball, D. W. (1972). The definition of situation: Some theoretical and methodological consequences of taking W. I. Thomas seriously. Journal for the Theory of Social Behaviour, 2, 61–82.

Bergold, J. B. & Flick, U. (eds.) (1987). Einsichten – Zugänge zur Sicht des Subjekts mittels qualitativer Forschung. Tübingen: DGVT-Verlag.

Bromme, R. (1984). On the limitation of the theory metaphor for the study of teachers' expert knowledge. In R. Halkes & J. K. Olson, (eds.). Teacher Thinking. A New Perspective on Persisting Problems in Education. Lisse: Swets and Zeitlinger.

Flick, U. (1987). Das Subjekt als Theoretiker – Zur Subjektivität Subjektiver Theorien. In J. B. Bergold & U. Flick (eds.) (1987). Einsichten – Zugänge zur Sicht des Subjekts mittels qualitativer Forschung (pp. 125–134). Tübingen: DGVT-Verlag.

Flick, U. (1989). Vertrauen, Verwalten, Einweisen. Subjektive Vertrauenstheorien in sozialpsychiatrischer Beratung. Wiesbaden: Deutscher Universitätsverlag.

Flick, U. (1990). Entzauberung der Intuition – Systematische Perspektiven-Triangulation als Strategie der Geltungsbegründung qualitativer Daten und Interpretationen. In J. Hoffmeyer-Zlotnik (ed.). Analyse qualitativer Daten, Opladen: Westdeutscher Verlag (in press).

Heritage, J. (1985). Recent developments in conversation analysis. Sociolinguistics, 15, 1–17.

Mead, G. H. (1934). Mind, Self and Society. University of Chicago.

Polanyi, M. (1966). The tacit dimension. Garden City.

Scheele, B. & Groeben, N. (1988). Dialog-Konsens-Methoden zur Rekonstruktion Subjektiver Theorien. Tübingen: Francke.

Schegloff, E. and Sacks, H. (1974). Opening up closings. In R. Turner (ed.). Ethnomethodology (pp. 233–264). Hammondsworth: Penguin. (originally: 1973).

Schütz, A. (1972). Gesammelte Aufsätze. Den Haag: Nijhoff.

Schütz, A. & Luckmann, T. (1975). Strukturen der Lebenswelt. Bd. I. Frankfurt: Suhrkamp, 1979 (originally: 1975).

Thomas, W. I. (1923). Situation analysis: The behavior pattern and the situation.

Thomas, W. I. (1928). The Child in America: Behavior Problems and Programs. New York: Knopf.

Wagner, A. C., Maier, S., Uttendorfer-Marek, I. & Weidle, R. (1981). Unterrichtspsychogramme. Reinbek: Rowohlt.

Wolff, S. (1986). Das Gespräch als Handlungsinstrument. Kölner Zeitschrift für Soziologie und Sozialpsychologie, 38, 55–84.

The Construction of Adult Child Intersubjectivity in Psychological Research and in School

Maria Luisa Schubauer-Leoni*, Anne-Nelly Perret-Clermont, Michèle Grossen

I. Introduction

Within the general theme of the present congress "social representations and the social bases of knowledge", we will concentrate on some aspects of the relationship between interpersonal communication and knowledge. We make the hypothesis that interpersonal relationships are very important both for the transmission of knowledge and the display of competence. In previous research (Perret-Clermont, 1980; Schubauer-Leoni, 1986a; Perret-Clermont & Schubauer-Leoni, 1989), we have had the opportunity to pay special attention to different modalities of social interactions and to their impact on cognitive development. We have also considered their impact on the aptitude to perform on psychological tests, and on the acquisition of elementary mathematical skills.

Obviously, the transmission of knowledge requires communication. Shared cognition can be accomplished only if both partners have common tools to display their cognition to each other. The common construction of understanding requires that, at some point, each partner makes the same assumptions about what is to be understood and the type of understanding that is to be developed.

In the case of the teaching situation, these processes are mysterious. Indeed, teaching requires from a "non-knower" that he comes to understand what the knower (in this case the teacher) is trying to say. By definition, there is something that he doesn't know yet. How can he then understand what the teacher refers to, if it is something he doesn't know? Of course the teacher accomodates his discourse in order to ensure the pupil grasps it. This accomodation often distorts the object of knowledge that the teacher is trying to transmit (Perret-Clermont et al., 1981). How is it possible, then, for the learner to really acquire the knowledge that he is meant to learn and not only a social representation of this knowledge?

When a psychologist wants to test the subject's competence, classically, he presents to him a test which is hoped to be "culture free" or even "school free" so as not to test memorized information but more complex cognitive functionings. It is difficult to imagine how a subject could understand in this case too, the tester's questions if they were completely culture free. If the one being tested (testee) wants to try to respond as adequately as possible to this test, he will certainly have to engage in some reflective activity in order to identify the meaning of the question and the expected possible answers (Light, 1986; Light & Perret-Clermont, 1989). This identification process relies on a series of cues whose meanings will be inferred from previous experience in similar settings. This means that the testee will refer to his previous cultural and social experience, particularly in the school situation, to decide how to behave (Elbers, 1986). Hence, the situation is not "culture free" and the tester is not only approaching the cognitive functioning of the subject, but also his capacity of generating answers as a function of his treatment of previous socio-cultural experience (Schubauer-Leoni et al., 1989).

Child psychologists have often considered that if a subject does not understand the other's discourse, it is simply because he is incompetent (e. g. because he lacks the prerequisite operative structures). This can be the case indeed, but it is not the only possible cause of failure. Communication might be failing between the adult and a competent child because they don't have the same frames of reference; they refer to different experiences; the meaning of the situation is different for one or the other; or, they are not involved in it for the

* We would like to thank the Swiss National Foundation for Scientific Research for its financial support (Grant no 1.738-0.83)

same purposes (Mercer & Edwards, 1981; Hundeide, 1985). Of course, we do observe that adults and children succeed at times in communicating about knowledge in testing situations as well as in school classrooms! How do they proceed to reach such a mutual understanding? This is the centre of our present question: how is an intersubjectivity between the partners constructed within an encounter, and how do they come to talk about the same object of knowledge and even to build together a common understanding of a new object of discourse?

Often it is not obvious whether psychological research in teaching and in cognition is concerned with "knowledge" or with "competence". Some authors have distinguished competence as a more profound structure that allows for the learning of knowledge. But is it really so, and can "competence" be tested as such? Our various attempts to test "competence" have made us quite aware now that we can never test competence independently of the meaning of the situation (e. g. the subject matter) through which this competence is revealing itself. Competence is always displayed within an event with different persons, specific tasks, objects and concepts. For instance, in the classical piagetian operatory test, the child is not required to reason in the vacuum but to reason about quantities. He is tested, therefore, on his knowledge (or on his present capacity to elaborate a common knowledge) about a given concept: conservation of quantity. Similarly, elementary school mathematics require reasoning from the pupils, but this reasoning is intricately subordinated to a terminology, to written conventions, to established definitions of concepts, and to given algorithms that previously have been culturally and pedagogically elaborated. Success in elementary mathematics requires not only cognitive functioning but, simultaneously, a proper acculturation to this type of activity (Schubauer-Leoni & Perret-Clermont 1980, 1985; Carraher, 1989).

Indeed all these subject matters are pre-existing to particular adult-child encounter: in books; in films; in museums; and also in school curricula, in the textbooks, and in the teacher's mind. Knowledge can be described as a socio-historical construction emerging from social interactions. In specific conditions individuals come to coordinate their actions and thoughts and regulate them according to different social traditions and experiences (Mugny, 1985; Wertsch, 1985; Rubtsov, 1989; Rogoff, 1990; see also Latour, 1979, 1987, for a consideration of this perspective in scientific life). Knowledge is constructed through social interactions not only on the societal level, but also on the individual level. These social interactions develop in conditions that are not always isomorphic to those that were prevailing at the time of the original construction of a given knowledge. The social conditions under which an understanding becomes established as "knowledge" (or more specifically as "scientific knowledge") are very specific and the child is not in the same social situation. It is quite unlikely that he will make the same "discoveries" in the same way again. What, then, are the social interactions that are likely to permit children to become competent in the objects of knowledge that adults want them to master? And, is the distortion between the previous socio-historical conditions in which this knowledge has been elaborated and the present social condition in which subjects learn, likely to result in the fact that the learners don't really acquire the expected knowledge, but only some sets of responses which they learn as fit to the school situation? Of course we hope that this last assertion is too restrictive a hypothesis, but it needs to be considered!

This brings us to modifications of our initial research paradigm. We will try to present these modifications on theoretical level and to illustrate them with empirical data. First, we will reconsider the classical *"peer interactions"* studies and wonder whether they are really *peer* interactions. Then we will turn to the *content* of the interactions and include the *object of discourse* in the model. This will bring us to abandon the claim that competence can be tested independently of the meaning that the context has for the interlocutors.

II. Theoretical Considerations

1. The nature of "peer" interactions

Most often peer interactions are presented like dyadic processes (or tryadic processes when three children are involved). To understand our data, we think that it is more useful to introduce in our model an understanding of the interaction situations in psychological research as situations that also involve *the adult*. Indeed, in nearly all the cases, the adult is the author of the setting in which the peers under observation interact. Of course, the modalities in which the adult's expectations affect the peers' interactions are likely to vary according to the way in which the adult-child and the child-child relationships are established. Figure 1 represents the case of symmetrical relationships between each partner.

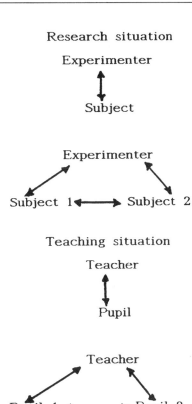

Research situation

Experimenter

Subject

Experimenter

Subject 1 ⟷ Subject 2

Teaching situation

Teacher

Pupil

Teacher

Pupil 1 ⟷ Pupil 2

Figure 4.

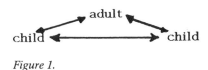

Figure 1.

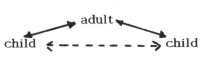

Figure 2.

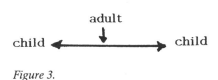

Figure 3.

Whereas in Figure 2 the strongest bounds are between the adult and the children who themselves interact only secondarily. In such a case, "peer" interaction is only a secondary event. Figure 3 represents another type of interaction in which the adult only tries to modify an interaction that takes place primarily between the children themselves. For most of our own studies, we have had experimenters who have tried to stimulate the dialogue between the peers and to keep out of their conversation in order to allow for a "horizontal" interaction between the children. Yet the adult is present and we might have underestimated his role.

If we consider more generally the context in which these interactions take place, it is possible to distinguish those that are in psychological settings (encounters between a psychologist and a child) from those in more explicitly socially regulated institutional settings such as schools (Figure 4). Obviously the implicitness of the communication process is different in the learning situation and in the testing situation. Not only are experimenters and teachers trained differently, but their intentions when they address the children are also different. The institutions to which they belong have norms for their behaviours. The "didactic contract" or the "experimental contract" that binds them to the children as partners have different presuppositions. Our hypothesis is that in both situations, but differently in each case, the adult patronizes the modalities of the interactions (between himself and the children but also among the children) because he is the initiator of the encounter and has a higher status.

The interlocutors do not always start their common discourse on the same premises and consequently misunderstandings do happen (Rommetveit, 1979). How are these misunderstandings dealt with? We have tried to transcribe detailed protocols of such interactions in order to follow the history of these misunderstandings and to observe how the children (who are from a status viewpoint in a "low" position) invent strategies to resolve these misunderstandings and how the adults (in the "high" position) react to expected, and also unforeseen behaviours. Obviously these social interactions are very rapid events and the interlocutors are not always conscious of the strategies that they develop in such conversational situations. When there is a communication breakdown it often looks like a "situation of emergency" and the partners immediately engage in "repair" transactions if they are aware of the breakdown. How is an intersubjectivity constructed between the partners in such circumstances?

2. What is the object of the common discourse in a testing or a learning situation? What is the status of the object of knowledge in these interactions?

Our model in figure 4 is bi-positional (the one asking and the one answering). When a teacher or an experimenter questions a child, the former is in the "high" position and this legitimizes the fact that he asks questions. The child is in the "low" social status and his role as a subject or as a pupil obliges him to answer. If he does not do so he will be declared incompetent, or uncapable to undergo the experiment. The adult questions the child about an *"object of knowledge"*. The introduction of this object into the model (Figure 5) makes its triangular. It then becomes evident that the partners of the interaction have to relate to one another but also to the object of discourse within which the object of knowledge is nested.

This object of knowledge pre-exists to the event of the encounter even if its reality is different for each partner. For instance, when a piagetian psychologist tests a child about an operatory notion, he conducts the interview according to his professional training, his epistemological concerns, and has in mind the colleagues to whom he will later address the description of his results. The child does not have the same reference points and his motivations to pursue the relationship with this strangely behaving adult are quite different!

In the school context the situation is slightly different. In this case the adult explicitly tries to transmit some knowledge to the child and in order to succeed, he transforms this knowledge to render it learnable by the pupil (Perret-Clermont et al., 1981). The "didactic contract" requires from the teacher that he introduces difficulties only progressively in his discourse, but in this case, the adult is not the author of the knowledge he transmits. His own relationship to this knowledge is marked by his previous cultural experiences and training. In the school situation, the pupil is generally conscious of the importance of this knowledge that he has to learn. In the testing situation, the object is likely to be less clear for him: "What is this psychologist trying to do when he invites me to play 'a little game'?" In the school situation, the child can refer to some scripts, but in the testing situation only the adult is trained to the script and the subject has to find his way without specific training for this peculiar relationship. Nevertheless, we observe in both cases

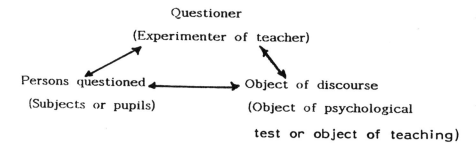

Questioner

(Experimenter of teacher)

Persons questioned ⟷ Object of discourse

(Subjects or pupils)   (Object of psychological

test or object of teaching)

Figure 5.

that children and adults are likely to proceed with more or less successful adjustments, to enter into the expectations of their partners, and to reach some type of intersubjectivity about the object of discourse. If this is not the case, then the dialogue breaks down and sometimes the relationship breaks down too. The maintenance of the relationship is quite dependent on the adult's and children's desire to maintain their point of view, to pursue the interaction, to defend their status, to reach an agreement, etc. and, in order to do so, it also depends on their capacity to operate with adequate cognitive and social strategies.

III. Empirical Illustrations

1. The effects of the experimental context

To illustrate this interdigitation between cognitive and relational processes we will present the results of two experiments concerned with the declared role of the experimenter or the institutional context of the testing.

a) Experimenter as "teacher" or "playmate"

In the first experiment we varied the role of the experimenter during a classical piagetian test of conservation of number. In the first experimental condition, the adult presented herself to the child "as a teacher who wants to understand what he knows". In the second experimental condition, the same person introduced herself as "a lady who wants to play with children".

In the second experiment we varied the institutional location of the testing of the child's capacity to formulate an additive problem. In the first experimental condition, the testing was done by the experimenter in the classroom and required a written reponse from each child. In the second experiment, the task was exactly the same and the experimenter rigorously gave the same instructions to each subject. The testing was done outside the classroom in a "psychological setting" within a one-to-one relationship.

Ninety-nine children underwent this experiment.* They were all tested individually; 49 belonged to the last form of the infant school (age range: 4,11 to 6 years) and 50 to the first year of primary school (age range: 5,11 to 7,9 years). The subjects were tested on the conservation of number in two different experimental conditions as described above. Social class and sex were controlled. Tables 1 and 2 show the results.

The data shows the interdependence between the cognitive and the social dimensions

Table 1. Pupils of infant school (age 5–6 years). Number conservation test.

	Non-conservers	Intermediate	Conservers	Total
Tester in role of "teacher"	18	1	5	24
	75%	4%	21%	100%
Tester in role of "playmate"	16	1	8	25
	64%	4%	32%	100%

($z = 0.7$; $p<.24$, Jonckheere test)

Table 2. Pupils of primary school (age 6–7 years). Number conservation test.

	Non-conservers	Intermediate	Conservers	Total
Tester in role of "teacher"	4	1	20	25
	16%	4%	80%	100%
Tester in role of "playmate"	10	3	12	25
	40%	12%	48%	100%

---

* This data was compiled in the italian speaking part of Switzerland, Ticino, by Romana Poncioni (1989) whom we would like to thank here. The "Scuola materna" places ludic activities as central in its curriculum. This is not the case in other areas of Switzerland, in which case we would not expect the same results as those presented here.

of the situation. Of course there is an age effect: the students of primary school perform better in this test than the younger children of the infant school, but more interesting is the difference found in these two schools according to the experimental condition. Children of infant school are slightly better in the "playmate" condition (but this does not reach statistical significance: it is only a small trend) whereas children of primary school perform much better in the "teacher" condition.

We understand these results as showing the structuring effects of the social roles attributed to the partners: if these roles are congruent with the institutional context, then they sustain the interaction and give the subject a better opportunity to display competence. If they are paradoxal for the situation (e. g.: the adult becoming a "playmate" within a primary school situation), then this dissonance between the expected and the actual role creates confusion and renders the child less likely to perform according to the adult's expectation and to the best of his cognitive competence.

b) Testing in or out of the classroom

This other research (Schubauer-Leoni, 1990) was conducted with seventy-three 8–9 year old pupils belonging to the second form of primary school in Geneva. These pupils were asked to write their solutions to addition problems on a sheet of paper. These subjects had been pretested in the ordinary classroom situation by another experimenter in order to assess their competence in elementary arithmetics. The pupils were then randomly divided into two experimental conditions: face-to-face testing out of the classroom or collective testing in the classroom.

The written productions of these pupils were analysed in order to classify them according to

the type of knowledge on which the pupils had relied. Three types appeared: the conventional arithmetical notation learned in the classroom, natural language, and drawings. Table 3 presents these results comparing the subjects who utilized the knowledge they had previously learned in school (conventional arithmetical notations) and the subjects who utilized non conventional means more idiosyncratically (language and drawing).

Obviously children do not "naturally" rely on the arithmetical writing that they learnt in the classroom. The data showed that the likelihood that they did rely on these pre-acquired symbolic tools was enhanced if they were tested in the classroom. They then used conventional writing more often, whereas only 3 out of 34 pupils did so when tested in a one-to-one situation out of the classroom.

Hence, the institutional location of the testing was not indifferent. The child developed an understanding of the meaning of the questions that were presented to him according to his understanding of the context. Even if the task seemed a classical scholastic task in the adult's opinion, it was not always considered as such by the child when he was interviewed by a stranger out of his usual school context.

2. The social construction and the object of discourse

In order to observe the progressive construction of a common object of discourse in these different contexts, we recorded and transcribed the adult's and child's discourses in different interactional settings. We varied the task and the role systems in which the interlocutors were placed: adult-child interaction in psychological settings (classical piagetian testing situations: Grossen, 1988; Grossen & Bell,

Table 3. Second form primary school pupils (age 8–9 years). Coding of additive operations.

	Conventional arithmetical notation	Drawing/natural language	Total
In the classroom	17	22	39
	44%	56%	100%
Ourside the classroom	3	31	34
	9%	91%	100%

(z = 3.04; p < .001) (reproduced from Schubauer-Leoni, 1990)

1988; assessments of elementary mathematical skills: Schubauer-Leoni, 1986b; teacher-pupils interactions in the usual classroom context: Schubauer-Leoni, 1986a, 1990.

Observations of adult-child interactions during piagetian tests showed that from the beginning the partners didn't always share the same presuppositions about the task and the nature of the encounter. For instance, in the three main items of this test (equalization of the quantity of juice in the two identical glasses; pouring from one of these glasses into a different one; adult opposing the child's assertions with a countersuggestion) children were likely to pay attention to aspects that were not relevant for the experimenter, e. g. sometimes they looked for perfection (almost obsessionaly!) in equalizing the quantities of juice in the identical glasses; or they considered practical consequences of the fact of drinking (how much juice would be left in drunken glasses!); or they inquired on who was the "other child" to whom the experimenter referred in his countersuggestion, etc. The analysis of the interactions revealed in a number of cases, how the child managed little by little, to modify his understanding of the task in order to join into the experimenter's intentions and to share with him a common definition of the situation. This construction of an intersubjectivity was achieved through a series of subtle indications (often implicit and non voluntary) that the experimenter gave to the child about the expected answers. At the same time, the child could be seen involved in a number of strategies (including silence!) that implicitly obliged the experimenter to give him more signs as to how he was meant to behave. All this occured as if the test situation which in the experimenter's opinion, was supposed to be an assessment of the child's *state* of cognitive development, were in fact, a *learning situation* in which he learned how to respond adequately to the adult's representation of a task yet unknown to him. To achieve this goal, the subject relied on a number of cognitive as well as social strategies. This understanding of the testing situation as a learning situation was well illustrated by the subjects of our research who were experimenters with novice peers. Indeed they did not usually maintain the expected "neutrality" of a proper experimenter questioning a subject; but instead they were inclined behave like "little

schoolmasters" in charge of teaching something to their mate in a classroom situation!

These observations clearly showed that the child's responses in a testing situation were not the direct expression of "competence" nor the direct result of a "micro-genesis" on the simple individual level, nor the "re-discovery" of a socio-historically constructed concept. His responses were the results of the construction of an intersubjectivity between himself and the experimenter. This joint understanding relied on cognitive as well as social skills within the present interaction between the partners.

In our research concerning a specific object of knowledge, mathematics, we have considered different interactions: a teacher who assessed his pupils' knowledge; or an experimenter who gave usual or unusual school exercises to children (Schubauer-Leoni, 1986a; Schubauer-Leoni & Perret-Clermont, 1988; Perret-Clermont et al., in preparation); or a child who had to role-play the teacher with another child. In all these cases we have observed that a tacit "didactic contract" ruled the teacher-child-mathematical knowledge interaction. But this tacit contract varied from one pupil to another according to the teacher's representations of his pupils and to the present history of this tripolar interaction. The teaching relationship appeared to be a very complex process, both cognitive and social, in which each interlocutor behaved according to his social position and status within the institutional setting, according also to his representations of what the knowledge was, and to his expectations of what his partner's representations were.

The role-playing experiments provided the opportunity to observe the children acting out their understanding of the pupil's and the teacher's roles and of the object of discourse. (They often had to go into a lot of trouble to enter into the debate or the task imposed by the experimenter). The role player in the teacher position often spent a lot of energy in strategies to consolidate his status: he chose a weak partner so as to make more evident his greater competence as a "teacher"; he asked the questions but answered them himself; he looked for support and approval from the adult even when the experimenter tried to keep out of the situation; and in some cases he abused the object of knowledge, teaching things that he did not really know in order to save his face and have the last word as a teacher! In this position, to be "the one who knows" seemed more important than transmitting some knowledge or even pretending to do so.

IV. Conclusion

Experimental and clinical data on tester-testee or teacher-pupil interactions show that the learning of specific objects of knowledge cannot be reduced to the simple acquisition of specific cognitive competence. Both knowledge and cognitive competence are dependent on each interactor's representations of the role of his partner, of what knowledge is about, of the common task, and of the setting in which the encounter takes place. The shared representations are organized in terms of a tacit *social contract* and constitute a system of reciprocal expectations that regulates the exchanges between the partners and that allows for the establishment of a common object of discourse. This object is always partly original because it is a fruit of the present encounter, and never totally isomorphic to the socio-historically constructed "established" object of knowledge that serves as a reference to the adult. This does not mean that the child only learns social representations of knowledge and never knowledge itself, but that each actualization of a competence, of an understanding or a knowledge takes a different meaning according to the setting. It appears then, that the child's endeavour is not only to acquire knowledge but also to understand its meaning in the interactional context in which it is embedded.

Still, knowledge per se, is not always a goal for the children. To display competence is also a matter of negotiating a social identity and a status within a structured social symbolic context in which he tries to situate himself.

Bibliography

Carraher, T. N. (1989). Negotiating the results of mathematical computations. *International Journal of Educational Research, 13*, 6, 637–646.

Elbers, E. (1986). Interaction and instruction in the conservation experiment. *European Journal of the Psychology of Education, 1*, 1, 77–89.

Grossen, M. (1988). *L'intersubjectivité en situation de test*. Cousset (Fribourg – CH): Delval.

Grossen, M. & Bell, N. (1988). Définition de la situation de test et élaboration d'une notion logique. In A. N. Perret-Clermont & M. Nicolet (Eds.), *Interagir et connaître*. Cousset (Fribourg – CH): Delval.

Hundeide, K. (1985). The tacit background of children's judgements. In J. V. Wertsch (Ed.), *Culture, communication and cognition*. Cambridge (Mass.): Cambridge University Press.

Latour, B. (1979). *Laboratory Life. Social construction of scientific facts*. London: Sage.

Latour, B. (1987). *Science in action: how to follow scientists and engineers through society*. Cambridge (Mass.): Harvard University Press.

Light, P. (1986). Context, conservation and conversation. In M. Richards & P. Light (Eds.), *Children of social worlds: Development in social context* (pp. 170–195). Cambridge (Mass.): Cambridge University Press.

Light, P. & Perret-Clermont, A.-N. (1989). Social context effects in learning and testing. In A. Gellatly, D. Rogers & J. A. Sloboda (Eds.), *Cognition and Social Worlds* (pp. 99–112). Oxford: Oxford Science Publication.

Mercer, N. & Edwards, D. (1981). Ground rules for mutual understanding. In N. Mercer (Ed.), *Language in school and community* (pp. 30–46). London: Edward Arnold.

Mugny, G. (Ed.). (1985). *Psychologie sociale du développement cognitif*. Bern: Peter Lang.

Perret-Clermont, A.-N. (1980). *Social interaction and cognitive development in children*. London: Academic Press.

Perret-Clermont, A.-N., Brun, J., Conne, F. & Schubauer-Leoni, M. L. (1981). Décontextualisation, recontextualisation du savoir dans l'enseignement des mathématiques à de jeunes élèves. *Interactions didactiques, 1*, Universities of Neuchâtel and of Geneva.

Perret-Clermont, A.-N., Grossen, M. & Schubauer-Leoni, M. L. (en préparation). La construction de l'intersubjectivité entre l'adulte et l'enfant dans des situations d'enseignement ou de recherche.

Perret-Clermont, A.-N. & Schubauer-Leoni, M. L. (1989). Social factors in learning and teaching: towards an integrative perspective. *International Journal of Educational Research, 13*, 6, 575–580.

Poncioni, R. (july 1989). *Il bambino e la matematica: un approcio psicosociologica del numero nell' ambito della scuola materna e della scuola elementare*. Mémoire de licence en Sciences de l'éducation, University of Geneva.

Rogoff, B. (1990). *Apprenticeship in thinking. Cognitive development in social context*. New York: Oxford University Press.

Rommetveit, R. (1979). On common codes and dynamic residuals in human communication. In R. M. Blakar & R. Rommetveit (Eds.), *Studies of language, thought and verbal communication*. London: Academic Press.

Rubtsov, V. V. (1989). Organization of joint actions as a factor of child psychological development. *International Journal of Educational Research*, *13*, 6, 623–636.

Schubauer-Leoni, M. L. (november 1986a). *Maître – élèves – savoir: Analyse psychosociale du jeu et des enjeux de la relation didactique*. Doctoral dissertation, University of Geneva.

Schubauer-Leoni, M. L. (1986b). Le contrat didactique dans l'élaboration d'écritures symboliques par les élèves de 8–9 ans. *Interactions didactiques*, 7, Universities of Neuchâtel and Geneva.

Schubauer-Leoni, M. L. (1990). Ecritures additives en classe ou en dehors de la classe: une affaire de contexte. *Résonances*, *6*, 16–18.

Schubauer-Leoni, M. L. & Perret-Clermont, A.-N. (1980). Interactions sociales et représentations symboliques dans le cadre de problèmes additifs. *Recherches en Didactique des Mathématiques*, *1–3*, 297–350.

Schubauer-Leoni, M. L. & Perret-Clermont, A.-N. (1985). Interactions sociales dans l'apprentissage de connaissances mathématiques chez l'enfant. In G. Mugny (Ed.), *Psychologie sociale du développement cognitif* (pp. 225–250). Bern: Peter Lang.

Schubauer-Leoni, M. L. & Perret-Clermont, A.-N. (1988). Représentations et significations de savoirs scolaires. *European Journal of the Psychology of Education*, special issue, 55–62.

Schubauer-Leoni, M. L., Bell, N., Grossen, M. & Perret-Clermont, A.-N. (1989). Problems in assessments of learning: the social construction of questions and answers in the scholastic context. *International Journal of Educational Research*, *13*, 6, 671–683.

Wertsch, J. V. (Ed.) (1985). *Culture, communication and Cognition: Vygotskian perspectives*, Cambridge (Mass.): University Press.

Social Markers in Written Action-Related Communication

Franziska Tschan

1. Introduction

Discussions of communication processes in organizations tend to equate written communication with the transmission of formal, factual information and oral communication with the transmission of social, contextual information. A careful analyis of letters and documents reveals, however, that they follow formal rules to a much smaller extent than one might expect. By demonstrating how such an analysis can be performed, this paper wants to hint to the existence of a clou of social representations refering to a code of social markers in written communication.

2. Social knowledge and individual action

As Moscovici (1964) has shown, social knowledge-systems can be found for many topics. Such knowledge-systems, called Social Representations, may be shared by an entire culture (Moscovici, 1984); sociological groups or by a special group only, e. g. professionals (Thommen, Ammann & von Cranach, 1987, Thommen, von Cranach & Ammann, 1991). Social Representations influence and co-determine individual action in a general way.

Thus, Thommen et al. (1987, 1991), have shown that therapists' cognitions, communications and interventions during a therapeutic session differ in accordance with their social representations which are supplied by the therapeutic school they feel closest to. Even though an individual assimilation of the social knowledge of a therapeutic school, the "Individual Social Representation", causes more variety in individual action, therapists with different background do act in accordance with their therapeutic school to a substantial degree.

3. Goal-directed behaviour of social systems and the processing of information

Going beyond action-theory approaches for individual action (Hacker, 1986; von Cranach et al., 1980; Oesterreich, 1981; Volpert, 1983),

von Cranach et al. (1986) propose a theory of goal-directed behaviour of social systems such as groups and organizations. A number of functional analogies can be found between the elaboration of action-related information of individuals and social systems (von Cranach et al., 1986; von Cranach, Ochsenbein, Tschan & Kohler, 1989; Ochsenbein, 1989).

Von Cranach proposes that any system has to be capable of elaborating certain information in order to set and reach goals and to perform actions in accordance with these goals, this elaboration of information relates to, among others: perception of the environment, self-monitoring, selection of goals, planning, execution control etc. An individual actor achieves this through cognition (von Cranach et al., 1986). When a group wants to reach a goal, the information normally is elaborated on two levels: On the individual level we can find action-related cognition whereas on the group-level the action-related information processing requires communication. We assume (Tschan, 1990) that not only individuals and groups, but also more complex systems, in our case an organization, can behave in a goal directed way. In this case, more system-levles will be involved. In organizations, one major part of goal-related communication will exist in a more or less formalized written form.

In the case of goal directed behaviour of an organization, all three system levels (individuals, groups or working teams, and the level of the organization itself) can participate in different compositions (Tschan, 1990): Individuals in a certain role (e.g. as leaders) can act for the whole organization and in another role as simple members of a team or as private persons. Groups can represent the whole organization or only communicate their team opinion without impact for the whole organization. Depending on the role the sender is assuming when issuing a given communication, its meaning may be quite different even though the content may be the same. In a goal directed process of an organization, we can find written communication from different system levels and with various importance for the process. But how can the participants in a goal directed process in a complex system distinguish the different meanings of a written communication? How can they decide in which role a sender or a sender system has acted and in which of their various roles as receiver they are addressed?

We assume that there is a system of social representations about written, action related communication in an organizational context. The knowledge about this system permits the identification of the communication to a system level and its relevance to the goal on the basis of social markers which convey the relevant information in such a way that insiders will be able to decode it.

4. Social markers as context-information

Our concepts of sender, receiver and information in social communications are based on Shannon and Weaver's communication model (1964). Different aspects of communication are described by Bühler (1934) and Watzlawick et al. (1980). They enlighten the social aspects of communication beyond the content-aspect. Following Bateson (1984), we use the term "context-information" for the non-content-aspects. Context information is meta-information which serves as an aid for decoding and interpreting the content.

A number of studies show that context-information in oral communication can be found in nonverbal or paraverbal cues (Watzlawick et al., 1980).

Scherer and Giles (1979) investigated certain cues of context information which they called "Social Markers". the functional description is as follows:

"The term 'social marker' should be taken in a fairly general sense to mean speech cues that potentially provide the receiver with information concerning the sender's biological, psychological and social characteristics. The term 'social marker' as a superordinate concept was chosen ... to highlight the fact that the markers with which we are concerned play an important role in social interaction" (Scherer & Giles, 1979, p. xii).

If one acknowledges functional analogies between cognition, oral communication and written communication in the action-related information-elaboration on different system levels, as we did above, and if, on the other hand, we agree that context-information is necessary to understand the full meaning of a communication, then we would expect to find context information, "social markers", in written communication as well.

5. System of social knowledge for written correspondence in formal contexts.

Guide books for writing in formal contexts can be found in every book store (Krist et al., 1982, Manekeller, 1984). According to Ettl (1984), the earliest guide-lines for written correspondence in business and administration known in the German culture date from the 16th century.

Two arguments speak against regarding such guidelines as conveying social representations, the knowledge of which enables us to convey context information by way of social markers: (1) from a historical point of view, Ettl argues that these "politeness-rules" are not very binding nowadays and are handeld with more freedom than they used to be. (2) It has been argued for a long time (e. g. Schmidlin, 1877 (!); Manekeller, 1984) that these rules have no function beside an exaggerated and out-moded politeness. If this were true, their violation would have no special significance beyond indication that one was not willing to obey these rules, that is, variations in style could not be used to convey specific information.

With regard to the first argument, it does indeed seem that the degrees of freedom have increased historically. However, the existence of formal norms ("DIN-norms" in Germany; "KV-instructions" in Switzerland) about correspondence clearly speak against the argument that there are no binding rules nowadays.

The second argument implies that variations in style do not systematically correspond to specific information about the social context. This is an empirical question, and it can be decided by examining the guidebooks with regard to the reasons they give for using different style, as well as by analyzing written communication in organizations to see if variations in appearance, style etc. contain cues about social information.

The guidebooks contain rules about length, style, and appearance of a document. Such directions are provided mainly for two reasons: the first is to save time and money during writing. This leads to recommendations such as using short sentences, avoiding old-fashioned spaces between lines, and avoiding indents. For example, it is now acceptable to begin the final greeting line without indentations on the left; unacceptable for many years. The second reason is based on the social relationship between the communicating systems. This concerns, for instance, honouring the receiver's social status and the self-representation of the sender (Ettl, 1984). This last function is comparable to the function of social markers mentioned above; it is also a context-information. Many rules about style, format, letter-heads, spacing, indents, positions of addresses, greeting notes etc. are related to this social function. So we have good reason to hypothezise that such functions can indeed be found in written communication. More specifically, we hypothesize that style serves as the most important cue for social information (Rafoth et al., 1988) but that the formal aspects mentioned can also be interpreted as social markers.

6. Social markers in written communication: an analysis of letters in the context of a change-process in an organization

Our analysis of social markers was carried out in the context of a case study of an organizational change process: "Contact Bern", a state agency dealing with drug prevention, caring for drug addicts etc. changed into a non-profit foundation. This "action of a social system" took five years, and we analyzed more than 250 written documents related to this process, as well as a number of interviews (Leimgruber, Stettler & Tschan, 1984; Tschan, 1990).

For the present context, we developed a coding system for social markers and analyzed 277 documents written in that organization to receivers both inside the organization and outside of it.

6.1 The categorial system

We distinguished four sending subsystems, three of them within our observed organization, Contact-Bern: staff of the organization as *individuals,* permanent *teams* or task-related *work groups,* and the *organization* itself. The fourth sending system is comprised of all "external" senders not belonging to Contact-Bern. These are mainly social welfare organizations. As these senders belong to the Bernese administration, we summarized them under the term *"external administration'.*

We developed a categorial system of social markers which classifies the written correspondance according to their formality. Our categories refer to (1) addresses, (2) formal roles, (3) presentation and (4) style.

Our first category of social markers concerns *addresses.* In a formal letter one can often distinguish the sender's "official", obvious address. It can be found in the letterheads or after the greeting note. But in a formal context the undersigned is often not the author or the writer of a document (e. g. an official person receives a completely prepared letter from his/her coworkers and signs it as his/her own). The author and the writer (e. g. secretary) are often marked with their logograms. These two markers are often found in formal letters and indicate wether the signing person is also the author/writer or not.

A second category concerns the apperance of formal *roles, titels,* and *functions* of the sender or receiver. More formal letters will contain more of these markers, whereas informal communication can do without them or with fewer of them.

Besides addresses and role naming, wich are *denotative* social markers, we can also distinguish *connotative* social markers. One of them we called the *presentation* of the whole letter. This category concerns issues such as using office stationary, printed letterheads, rubber stamps. These are signs of formality, whereas hand written letters or typed letters with handwritten supplements are rather informal. Therefore, we rated the appearance of the whole letter with regard to its correspondence with the official rules.

However, the general appearence of a document which causes its formal vs. informal character depends not only on the social markers used but equally if not stronger on its *style*. Therefore, documents were, in addition, classified as showing one of the following three styles: formal, personalized and mixed. "Mixed style" means that a document written in a rather formal style also contains some personal remarks or sentences.

Based on these ratings, the documents were separated into two main format categories: formal and rather informal.

As illustrations for the use and function of social markers in written documents we present a letter from our data (see also v. Cranach et al., 1987, p. 150). The content of this letter is rather common: It is a simple invitation for a meeting.

It is a formal letter which corresponds to the official rules for administrative letters in its general appearance: it contains a letterhead with a coat of arms. This designates the action level: it is an organization outside of Contact-Bern.

We find two types of recipients: "Main" participants, who are invited (as role and function namings show) as representatives for various social systems. The other ones invited (bottom of the page) have, whith regard to this invitation, a lower status, which is indicated by the fact that they are separated from the main recipients. The fact that we find all those invited on the same letter has two functions: it makes it easier and more economic for the sender (one letter for several recipients) and at the same time it informs the recipients about the other participants in the meeting.

In this letter the author is not identical with the official sender. The letter is signed by Mr. Riedi. However, the letters "Hä" at the top left corner of the letter indicate that "Hä" (short for "Hänni") has really written the letter (while "Pd" indicates the typing secretary). So the letter contains very clear and formal information about the hierarchy involved: Mr. Riedi is sending a letter, but writing is the task of his subordinate (Ms. Hänni), whereas typing it is the task of a secretary who is still further down in the hierarchy.

There is another interesting feature of this letter: Ms. Hänni is identifiable as the person who has written the letter, but at the same time she is one of the people who are invited (featuring among the (lower status) category of "further invited"). So, in a way, she has invited herself. For herself this might be redundant, but we see two reasons for this redundancy. As we know from an organizational analysis, Ms. Hänni has a lower status in the system "Jugendamt" (sender) than Mr. Riedi, who signed the letter. His signing, and also the stamp, the mention of his title and function (head of the "Jugendamt"), gives the letter more formal weight. On the other hand, the naming of Ms. Hänni as recipient informs the other recipients that she will participate in the meeting.

The style of this letter is polite, formal and impersonal.

Jugendamt
der Stadt Bern

Telefon 64 61 11
Postfach 3104
3000 Bern 7
Hä/Pd

Bern, den 20. März 1980
Predigergasse 6

- Herrn H. Dreyer, Kant. Fürsorge-
  direktion, Rathausgasse 1, 3011 Bern

- Herrn E. Ramseier, Kant. Fürsorge-
  direktion, Abt. Planung und Betrieb,
  Münsterplatz 3a, 3011 Bern

- Frau L. Kissling, Kant. Fürsorge-
  inspektorat, Herrengasse 22, 3011 Bern

- Herrn H. Ryser, Kant. Fürsorge-
  direktion, Rathausgasse 1, 3011 Bern

Neue Trägerschaft Contact-Bern

Sehr geehrte Damen und Herren,

Wir laden Sie hiermit ein zu einer Besprechung betreffend neue Trägerschaft der Beratungsstelle für Drogenabhängige Contact-Bern und zwar auf

Dienstag, 1.April 1980, um 14.00 Uhr, im Sitzungszimmer 407, 4. Stock, Prediger-gasse 5, 3011 Bern.

Die Unterlagen werden später noch zugestellt.

Mit freundlichen Grüssen

Städt. Jugendamt Bern
Der Vorsicher.

Dr. V. Riedi

Geht als Einladung auch an:
- Herrn A. Gasser, Fürsorgekommissär
- Herrn R. Stübi, Ressort Suchtgefahren
- Frau M. Hänni, Adjunktin, Jugendamt

6.2 Results: Correlates of formality

As the changing of the organizational structure of "Contact-Bern" occured in a rather formalized social context, we can generally expect a use of social markers which indicate a rather formal and distancing way of dealing with each other. However, it will be interesting to see if and under what circumstances indicators of informality can be found.

If Ettl (1984) is right and the social representation about social markers in written documents are not binding nowadays, we can expect to find no systematic differences which are related to the status of the sender system, to the receiver system or to the aim of communication. The only factor that could account for systematic differences would be preferences or habits of the sender.

If, however, we are correct in assuming that variations in formality are systematic and convey social information, we would expect that the preferred style of the sender is systematically related (1) to its formal status, (2) to the topic tht is dealt with, and (3) to the status of the receiver.

In our data, differences due to the general topic cannot account tor variations in social marking since all documents are related to the same topic.

Looking at the indicatior of formality as the use of social markers and style *by sender system* yields the results shown in Table 1.

If the use of social markers and style corresponds with its social standing, a system may develop a "writing-style" to present itself as more formal or more informal. This habit may

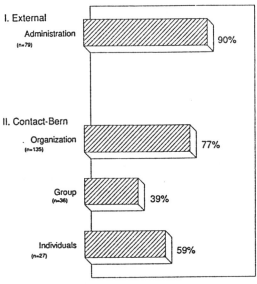

Table 1. Use of social markers according to sender-systems.

be used in every communication, independent of the receiver system.

From Table 1 and 2, it is obvious that the use of social markers and the choice of style indeed differ between the sender-systems. More formalized systems such as the *external administration* systems or the Contact-Bern on the *organizational level* use more formalized social markers than groups or individuals.

Referring to style, the differences between the documents written on the organizational or group level of Contact-Bern and the documents from the administration is evident. Most of the "system-internal" documents are written in mixed style. At the same time, the table

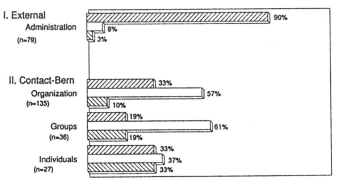

Table 2. Use of formal, mixed or personal style according to sender-systems.

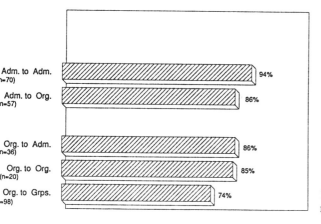

Table 3. Use of social markers by sender-receiver-combinations

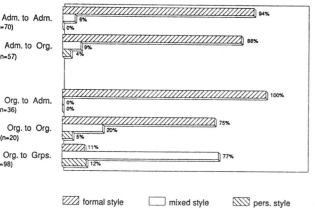

Table 4. Use of style by sender-receiver-combinations.

shows that individuals use more formal style and social markers than groups. It seems difficult to explain this by general characteristics of the senders since, in that case, one would expect more informality on the part of individuals. Other factors have, therefore, to be taken into account, such as the characteristics of the *receiver*.

And indeed, when we distinguish the results according to both sender *and* receiver we see that a sender system varies the formality of its correspondence according to the receiver system.

This is shown in Table 2 and 3: the differences for the most common sender-receiver-combinations.*

As Table 3 and 4 show, the more formalized systems (the organization as a whole and the external administrations) receive more formal-

ized documents than groups which are less formalized systems.

Even a very formalized system, such as public administration, adapts its correspondance to the receiver system in corresponding in a less formal manner with Contact-Bern, than with other administrative systems. As we know from the description of Contact-Bern, the self-image of this organization was a rather informal one; it seems that the administration systems adjust their written communication to this image. As sender, on the organizational level Contact-Bern sends letters in a formal style to the administration level and to the organizational level too, whereas the style becomes less formal, when the communication goes to the group level.

It is important to note that the characteristics of the receiver also resolve the puzzling

---

* Not all possible sender-receiver-combinations are shown. some are too infrequent to be interpreted.

finding that individuals write so often formal letters. About 50% of the papers written by individuals go to the organizational level or to the (outside) administration.

7. Discussion

Our analysis of the use of social markers and style in written action-related correspondence shows that the social systems analyzed seem to develop habits in using formal vs. informal correspondence. But at the same time they vary the appearance of their correspondence according to the receiver. Thus, contrary to the assertion of Ettl (1984), our results support the position that variations in appearance can systematically convey social cues and cannot be interpreted solely in terms of preferences or rule-braking.

The use of social markers and style in written (as well as in oral) communication presupposes social representation of a common code in administration culture. It yields much more information about the sender system and its view of the reciever system that we could analyze in this papier. At the same time, one has to keep in mind that social markers or style are not the only cues for detecting social relationships between systems, nore are they unambiguous. This is because written communication is often proceeded by oral communication which also contains social information, and often this information is necessary for the unambiguous interpretation of social markers in written communication. However, written communication does seem to contain much more context-information than is generally recognized, and it seems important to us that this should be pursued in research more than it has been so far.

Bibliography

Bateson, G. (1984). *Geist und Natur. Eine notwendige Einheit.* Frankfurt am Main: Suhrkamp.

Bühler, K. (1934). *Sprachtheorie. Die Darstellungsfunktion der Sprache.* Jena: Gustav Fischer.

Cranach, M. von, Kalbermatten, U., Indermühle, K. & Gugler, B. (1980). *Zielgerichtetes Handeln.* Bern: Huber.

Cranach, M. von, Ochsenbein, G., Tschan, F. & Kohler, H. (1989). Untersuchungen zum Handeln sozialer Systeme. Bericht über ein Froschungs-programm. *Schweizerische Zeitschrift für Psychologie 46,* 213–226.

Cranach, M. von, Ochsenbein, G. & Valach, L. (1986). The group as a self-active system. Outline of a theory of group action. *European Journal of Social Psychology, 16,* 193–229.

Ettl, S. (1984). *Anleitungen zu schriftlicher Kommunikation. Briefsteller von 1880-1980.* Tübingen: Max Niemeyer.

Farr, R.M. & Moscovici, S. (Eds.). (1984). *Social Representation.* Cambridge: University Press.

Hacker, W. (1986). *Arbeitspsychologie. Psychische Regulation von Arbeitstätigkeiten.* Berlin (DDR): Deutscher Verlag der Wissenschaften.

Hacker, W., Volpert, M. & von Cranach, M (Hrsg.). (1983). *Kognitive und motivationale Aspekte der Handlung.* Berlin (DDR): Deutscher Verlag der Wissenschaften.

Kirst, H. & Manekeller, W. (1982). *Moderne Korrespondenz.* Niederhausen: Falken.

Leimgruber, W., Stettler-Cottier, S.C. & Tschan, F. (1984). *Contact-Bern. Soziale Repräsentation, Organisation, Handlung Stiftungsgründung.* Unveröff. Lizentiatsarbeit, Universität Bern, Psychologisches Institut.

Manekeller, W. (1984). *Regeln der Geschäftskorrespondenz.* Bad Wörishofen: Hans Holzmann.

Moscovici, S. (1984). The phenomen of social representation. In R. Farr & S. Moscovici (Eds.), *Social Representation.* Cambridge: University Press.

Ochsenbein, G. (1989). Analoge Funktionen offener Informationsverarbeitung in menschlichen selbstaktiven Systemen. *Zeitschrift für Sozialpsychologie 20,* 27–37.

Oesterreich, R. (1981). *Handlungsregulation und Kontrolle.* München: Urban & Schwarzenberg.

Rafoth B.A. & Rubin, D.L. (1988). *The social construction of written communication.* New York: Academic Press.

Schmidlin, U. (1877). *Ueber die Deutsche Geschäfts-Sprache mit besonderer Berücksichtigung des kaufmännischen Briefstyls.* Zürich: Beitrag zum Programm des zürcherischen Technikums.

Scherer, K. & Giles, H. (Eds.). (1979). *Social markers in speech.* Cambrigde: University Press.

Shannon, E. & Weaver, W. (1984). *The mathematical theory of communication.* Urbana: University of Illinois Press.

Thommen, B., Amman, R. & Cranach, M. von (1988). *Handlungsorganisation durch soziale Repräsentationen.* Bern: Huber.

Thommen, B., Cranach, M. von & Ammann, R. (1991). The organization of individual action through social representations. A comparative study of two therapeutic schools. *This volume.*

Tschan, F. (1990). *Organisationen als sich zielgerichtet verhaltende Einheiten. Entwicklung eines theoriegeleiteten Beschreibungssystems im Rahmen einer Fallstudie.* Unveröffent. Dissertation, Universität Bern.

Volpert, W. (1983). Das Modell der hierarchischsequentiellen Handlungsorganisation. In W. Hacker, W. Volpert & M. von Cranach (Hrsg.), *Kognitive und motivationale Aspekte der Handlung* (S. 38–58). Berlin (DDR): Deutscher Verlag der Wissenschaften.

Watzlawick, P., Beavin, J. & Jackson, D.D. (1980). *Menschliche Kommunikation.* Bern: Huber.

Part III.

Knowledge and the
Social-Cultural Environment

Culture – Individual – Culture: The Cycle of Knowledge

Ernest E. Boesch

1. Introductory remarks

Action conveys information, both about contents of our environment, as well as about our abilities, skills, emotional attractions or repulsions, in short, our *action potential* (Boesch, 1980, 1991). Obviously, external and internal information are closely interrelated, always occurring jointly, yet leading to different kinds of "knowledge". This said, we will however, in the following pages, stress particularly the external origins of information, due to our specific problem, namely the cultural impact on the individual acquisition of knowledge.

Information on the environment, of course, is provided by *all* its contents. Thus, we derive knowledge not only from books or other storing media, but from nature and climate, streets, buildings, tools and implements, customs and habits, actions, gossip and rumours by social partners (Lang, 1990). Knowledge stored in verbal or pictorial form – as we generally understand it – constitutes, in fact, just a special case of messages; people in non-literate cultures will amass large amounts of knowledge without written sources, and so, indeed, do we all.

Information as such, however, is not yet knowledge. Many of our experiences do provide information, yet are simply forgotten. Knowledge results from the individual *assimilation of experience*. Genetic psychology, particulary the Geneva school, has demonstrated that even the fundamental qualities of our environment are actively structured during the ontogenetic development. It is obvious that the qualities studied by this school of psychology are far from exhausting all the aspects of the objectal world. Our object experience embraces more than weight, volume, number or physical causality of objects; objects have a price, they are beautiful or ugly, antique or modern, are toys, tools or trinkets, and such qualities, too, determine our handling of objects. Yet, being less general than the ones studied by Piaget and his colleagues, they would be likely to result from more idiosyncratic constructions.

Thus, my *first thesis* will be that the multiple information contained in, and offered by culture will become knowledge through individual assimilation, which entails selective perception, transformation and integration in order to fit the cultural messages into the action structures of the individual.

Of course, these action structures are determined to variable extents by the cultural molds, but these too may become transformed during the interaction: we are physically nourished by our environment, but our digestion, i.e. assimilation of food, transforms the environment in the process.

Mental assimilation too, changes both the individual and his environment, and since acquired knowlege tends to be socially transmitted, the successive individual assimilations would imply a risk of "distortion" (as, for instance, demonstrated already in Bartletts experiences on remembering, 1954), and thereby increase the dispersion of knowledge and threaten social coordination. Of course, the transmission of knowledge need not rely on verbal communication, but can as well result from actions.

My *second thesis*, therefore, would be that culture creates mechanisms of stabilization in order to contain such dispersion. Yet, let us not forget that mere stabilization would stultify culture. Culture also needs variation. A bureaucracy adhering rigidly to rules and regulations would not survive for long – inventiveness, adaptability, even daring are as necessary to culture as is stability. We would have to expect, therefore, that culture attempts in various ways to establish balances between stability and change. (The term of "culture" is used here as a contraction for a community and the structures of objects, institutions and ideas, conventions and rules which both result from its actions and in return shape and regulate them. [see Boesch, 1991])

These balances – and that would be my *third thesis* – will regulate the individual reception and transmission of information; Let us not forget, however, that these cultural rules for individual assimilation are themselves the result of individual action and may be transformed again in the course of the individual's acquisition of knowledge.

Thus, knowledge is constructed, starting from action experiences of various kinds, be they praxic, imaginative or conceptual. This "construction of knowledge" implies transformations which will be controlled by three interacting instances: first, the individual need for *consistency* over time and over action areas (both as to environmental orientation and to identity formation – see Boesch, 1991); second, the need for *coordination with others*, and third, the *cultural mechanisms of stabilisation and "change regulation"*. This implies that in spite of continuous controls, the cycle of knowledge is likely to entail progressive transformations of knowledge as well as of culture – which would less represent "progress" than adaptations to the needs of individuals, groups and generations.

Let us then consider these problems in more details, profiting from an event I recently observed.

2. The progressive integration of knowledge

The other day I saw a harvest dance of a Thai village group. There was a row of musicians playing to young women in traditional costumes imitating the movements of cutting rice and throwing the sheaves over their shoulders into the baskets carried on their backs. It all looked graceful, easily recognizable as a rhythmic rendering of harvesting.

We tend to take for granted that people all over the world perform harvest dances. Yet on second thought, is this not strange? Do we not all, after work, prefer doing something different – playing soccer, cards or chess, swimming, chatting or viewing television? Would the carpenter invent sawing or hammering dances, or the hairdresser plaiting games? Yet, harvesting dances do precisely that: repeat in the form of a play one's daily work. What then could be the purpose of such activity?

Let us first remember that adults, although not usually play working, still occasionally may introduce playful variations into their actual work. In his beautiful description of rice harvesting in an African village, Camara Laye speaks of the reapers going to the field, "marching to the rhythm of the tom-tom. The young men used to toss their glittering sickles high in the air and catch them as they fell, shouting aloud for the simple pleasure of hearing their own strong young voices, and sketching a dance step or two on the heels of the tom-tom players." "They would sing at work and even play during the periods of rest. And in the evening, they would go home contented, weary but happy. The good spirits had taken care of us; not one of us had been bitten by snakes that our trampling feet might have disturbed." (1954, p. 46–54).

Weary, but happy: the harvest had been brought in after so many months not only of labour, but also of anxiety. The experience would be one of triumph when the yield had been plenty and no accident had befallen the workers; but in other years, where the harvest was meager or accidents occured, it might also be felt as a defeat. So, each year, there was both hope and anxiety.

Thus, while the harvest dance would not reap a single stalk of rice, very likely it would relate directly to hope and anxiety. It might intend to express gratefulness to the spirits, or to invoke their kindness for the seasons to come. It might also, by the same token, satisfy that very human need to recall or conjure triumphs and successes, thereby reinforcing one's hope and confidence.

Obviously, playing at harvesting is an action different from the one of harvesting itself. In fact, the similarity is only superficial: while the movements performed may present some analogy, and while the dancing group may be composed in part by the workers in the field, differences certainly prevail over similarities. The participants might vary, the clothes would be different, but before all, the reaping movements would have become rhythmical, stylized, stimulated as well as regulated by music, in short, the dance would have become "merely" a symbol of the real performance. Such symbol, however, is not simply a sign, representing (for which purpose?) the "real" action, but it would have become a new action with its own intentions or purposes.

Dance is one of these. (We shall presently discover others.) Dancing provides an unusual experience of one's body: internal and external rhythms are optimally coordinated, and in the synchrony between movements and music the individual experiences, both, social harmony as well as his bodily action potential. Dance, therefore, is a peak experience – feeling onself functioning optimally and in a socially integrated way. Dancing, by its grace, symbolism and social approval, provides feelings of triumph, too (in Janet's sense).

Thus we move towards some deeper understanding of the action of playing at harvesting. Harvesting constitutes, for the individual, "praxical" knowledge. In playing at it, this knowledge is extended and integrated in new action situations. By being taken out of its pragmatic framework, it will be transformed: burdens or chores are translated into enjoyment and success. It may even be that the dance, for a girl or a boy, becomes a dominant goal, so that the cumbersome work in the field appears to be only the intrumentally necessary steps leading to it. Love and marriage may be hoped to come out of it rather than bags of rice. Thus, the dance, on the one hand, integrates harvesting into other areas of the villager's life, but will, on the other hand, affect in return the meaning of the work in the fields.

The harvesting dance, however, is just one event within a much broader process: the one of acquiring, assimilating and integrating cultural knowledge. Think of its antecedents: To start with, a young girl may simply have accompanied her mother to the field, then she would have imitated some of her movements, but soon she would also be charged with little chores, such as collecting left-over sheaves on the harvested field. She would playfully try to handle the sickle, and after a while start performing with it in earnest. All of that is practical construction of knowledge and competence, and it may go on until she is really skilled with her tool.

Note that this practical knowledge is already accompanied by extensions which integrate it into broader contexts of village life. Singing or, as in Camara Laye's example, tossing sickles into the air, are "coordinated actions" (Boesch, 1991), supporting the main action of harvesting, but by the same token serving other purposes, such as social communication and cohesion. Harvesting, however, will soon extend into other action areas. Thus, the child will learn about snakes and pests in the field, will be taken to the market for selling the rice, purchasing tools, bartering, and such activities will again be related to social interactions of a new kind, knowledge about other forms of agriculture, about prices, techniques of bargaining, rules of joking and politeness or of dealing with strangers, and so on. Harvesting thus progressively turns into a nucleus around which cluster quite a number of practical actions and domains.

Singing and dancing, however, lead to different integrations. While harvesting itself induces a progressive extension of mastery over the learner's environment, the transformation of instrumental movements into dance steps raises the level of consciousness, transforms the valence or emotional appeal ("Anmutung") of gestures, increases social approval, and through all this enhances the self-relevance of the praxis. Harvesting as a praxis, and the harvest dance as a ritual, are now two actions closely related, yet implying different criteria of success. In one, the number of rice-bundles reaped at the end of a day is of importance, in the other it will be the grace of one's movements, the charm of one's smiling, the qualities of the music, and we may easily imagine that a girl trained in the dance steps will afterwards also feel secretly guided by some rhythm or melody in her field work. Both actions are structured in different directions, but enrich each other.

Transforming one's work into a dance implies its own directions of extension. As a thanksgiving ritual to the spirits of the field, it relates the action to existential threats and anxieties as well as to the promised securities of religion. By exhibiting one's charm and beauty, it will connect the spheres of work with the ones of love, courting and social relationships, but also aesthetic enjoyment. Thus, while the field work would extend into the market and a network of economic concerns and knowledge, the dance would enhance subjective-functional qualities (Boesch, 1980), both in the experience of oneself and of one's surroundings. Real and symbolic action, while following their own courses of extension and integration, will complete each other and will jointly constitute an intricate knowledge of the individual's action field.

I said, "the individual's action field": of course, all these activities take place in social interaction; yet, in performing them it is the participating individuals who build up skill, consciousness, valences, meaning and action potential.

The example of the harvest dance has shown us the progressive assimilation of praxic knowledge, the rising of consciousness and reflection, and its extension and integration into other action areas. Even specific knowledge, like harvesting rice, forms complex practical as well as conceptual and symbolic networks, reaching out into different spheres of an individual's life. But this extension implies another aspect we have to consider now: the transformation, by assimilation, of knowledge itself.

3. The transformation of knowledge

I have learned psychology in Geneva and psychoanalysis in Zurich. However, few of my colleagues would consider me, today, to be a psychologist of the Genevan school: cultural psychology and action theory is no central Genevan concern. Similarly, few would consider me to be still a psychoanalyst as I have drifted too far away from its basic theoretical platform. Knowledge I had acquired became, in the course of life, amalgamated with personal experience and thinking, and thus the contents of my teaching would certainly have drifted, too. Would then my students have become action theorists and cultural psychologists? Only a handful. Most of them, too, would have acquired knowledge by transforming it in the process of assimilation.

Let us ask what knowledge means to us. Few people acquire knowledge purely for the sake of knowing. Much more than wanting to know, we want to feel *convinced*. Knowledge we look for should be experienced to be *true*, because only true knowledge can provide feelings of action potential. Knowledge should enhance and support our skills and capacity of orientation in a world we want to be "transparent".

If knowledge we consider to be "true" implies the feeling of conviction, knowledge we do not trust gives rise to the feeling of *doubt*.

Conviction does not necessarily correspond to correct, or to "objective" knowledge (here defined as knowledge which can efficiently control action). One can, as many examples demonstrate, be convinced of quite erroneous or unsubstantiated beliefs. Similarly, the feeling of doubt does not always imply deficient knowledge – some may doubt quite correct information. Yet both conviction and doubt can be very strong feelings, as experience shows again and again.

Conviction is closely related to the feeling of triumph, as Pierre Janet (1926/28) defined it: the self-enhancement due to successful action. As triumph regulates both the cessation of ongoing and the direction of future action, so conviction terminates the present search for knowledge and regulates the direction of future inquiry or interpretation. Feeling convinced of a thing, I believe to "understand" it and therefore tend to suspend further inquiry. Conviction, similar to triumph, is a strong self-reinforcing feeling. Yet, it can always be shaken by new experiences, and therefore, welcomes corroboration. Conviction, consequently, would be likely to foster two kinds of behavior: first, the openness towards confirming and reinforcing information, coupled with the rejection of contradicting one; second, the search for social approval and confirmation, implying selective social orientations. But there appears to be a third type of behavior related to conviction: *proselytism*. Conviction wants to convince, and this wish may go as far as eliminating – symbolically or even factually – those who refuse being persuaded. Indeed, doubt can be a nagging, self-diminishing emotion; infringements on our conviction threaten our action potential, and consequently our self. Proselytism, then, appears to be a self-protecting, defensive type of action.

It becomes understandable, thus, that we tend to defend our convictions as long as conflicting information can be avoided, refuted or repressed. There may, however, arise occasions where we no longer are able to shun contradictions – the "cognitive dissonance" has become too strong, or new action valences are imposed by situative changes. In such cases, often painful compromises and reorientations will take place, but occasionally we may also observe quite sudden "conversions": it seems as if people, wanting to conserve a *feeling* of conviction, would rather sacrifice its *content*.

Since, as I said, conviction need not be based on "objectively true" knowledge, we would have to ask what, then, determines our convictions or doubts. What we have seen so far suggests that the new information should appear to be, on the one hand, consistent with existing *systems of orientation and thought*, and, on the other hand, should be congruent with, or even support, *anticipated action*.

What, however, are these "existing systems of orientation and thought"? They imply, first, the environmental structures as known by the individual; second, they would (as far as the individual is aware of) include ideational systems according to which a cultural group explains, justifies and directs action (what I called "myths"); third, such systems of orientation would of course also comprise of subjective experience and anticipatory action structures (which I called "fantasms"). We often are not aware of the complex constellations involved in the perception and assimilation of information. Our concept of "storing information" induces the belief in a registration-recall concept of memory which is certainly at odds with the realities of behavior. Selections, eliminations and even distortions of information, rather than being deficiencies, result from action-related assimilation of experience – "action", here, not being limited to the pursuance of a single goal, but to the over-arching systems within which an individual places his or her goals (as to some perhaps less familiar terms used here, see Boesch, 1976, 1980, 1983, 1991).

Thus, new information has to fit present, individual as well as cultural, structures. Yet, it may also appeal not by its consistency with current frames of orientation, but by its divergence from them. Action also strives for newness, variation, alternatives instead of familiarity. Everyday culture may be perceived as a rigid structure and, hence, foster tendencies to escape, or at least to extend its limits. The emotional qualities related to this kind of orientation are "curiosity" and "daring" in their diverse forms.

In such cases, "*otherness*" rather than congruence will determine the appeal of new information, and again, this otherness will not necessarily have to offer "better" or "truer" knowledge, but will often simply attract by its newness. Much innovation and social change, rebellion and evasion will result from this appeal of the different, the deviant, the promise of improvements, enhancements, or simply excitement.

Knowledge, thus, is not simply "received", absorbed, but assimilated, thereby undergoing multiple processes of selection, transformation and integration into individual systems of action. We have to wonder then, why such idiosyncratic acquisitions of knowledge would not lead to ever greater divergences, ultimately producing chaotic cultural dissonance. We know that this may indeed occur occasionally, but on the whole it seems that cultures succeed in maintaining some sort of internal constancy. Let us therefore look at these processes of equilibration.

4. The feedback of knowledge

It seems that individuals in a cultural group, to a considerable extent, *share* knowledge of a congruent kind. The "subjectivation" just described, therefore has to imply additional processes leading to common structures of knowledge. These appear to be mainly twofold: first, social interaction induces mutual accommodation of knowledge. These "processual" accommodations would, however, produce common structures only within the frameworks of particular interactions. Therefore, we have to expect superordinate cultural "channelings" and "objectivations" of knowledge.

Social intercourse requires coordination of practical action and its cognitive reflection mainly in a denotative sense: for joining forces in a team we need agreement as to procedures, tools, timing, while each member may retain the private meanings he or she connects with the common action. In other words, homogenization of knowledge concerns praxic action and the "signal function" of concepts, but not subjective connotations or symbolism. People may, therefore, cooperate for very different motifs, may derive from the action different kinds of satisfaction or frustration, may integrate it into different superordinate action systems, yet all the aspects needed for sucessful common action would become coordinated; the meanings of an action for the participating individuals would overlap in their practical variance.

Yet, where practical coordination is less important, where meanings relate more strongly to individual systems of order and orientation than to actual praxis, major divergences may indeed occur: think of the cleavage between believers in the biblical Genesis and in Darwinist evolution in American society, or of the divergence between modern esoterical and scientific ideologies. But there are less extreme examples. Two professors of psychology would not lecture similarly on Piaget, and neither of them, presumably, would present a "true" picture of Piaget's thinking: They would have assimilated it through their own "mental lenses". Their divergence would be even greater were it not for cultural mechanisms of stabilisation.

Indeed, cultures introduce safeguards against too much distortion. These however, may vary considerably. Before being written down, the teachings of Buddha were transmitted orally for about five hundred years. During this incredibly long time, they were embroidered by many legends of the master's life, but there seem to be reasons for believing that the teaching as such was quite faithfully preserved. Similar records, although perhaps for shorter time-spans, exist for the conservation of myths, legends or historical records in non-literate cultures. If we think of Bartlett's experiments on the sequential oral communication of stories (1954), such faithfulness is astounding – but these experiments belong to a different culture. Faithful oral transmission, we might assume, is likely to go hand in hand with what Mary Douglas (1973) would call "strong grid and strong group", i.e. high coherence of a group's world view, as well as high pressure to conform to it. Such coherence of a cultural world view tends to entail a particular valuation of the teacher: the teacher would represent the ultimate authority, and therefore the disciples would strive at acquiring his knowledge as faithfully as possible. Self-realization by identification with models would, in such cultures, excel self-realization by originality.

Cultures may thus manage to preserve constancy over long periods of time; yet some changes will always occur: unforeseen situations may arise, young individuals will replace old ones, external imports may introduce new gadgets or new ideas, or culture itself, by its constraints and limitations, will induce strivings for change. Society has to be able to cope with such changes, in other words, it must achieve stabilization under conditions of variation. Somehow, a balance between conservation and change has to be found, and such balances may differ between cultures.

Let us look at a modern example of stabilization and change. Our scientific community tries to stabilize information by storing it in libraries and obliging the individual to refer to it. Our compulsory (and often compulsive) quotations and bibliographical references bear witness to this cultural stabilization mechanism. In a sense, we have replaced the single teacher's authority by the collected testimonies of experts.

Yet, we know that it only partly works: quotations are torn out of their context, selected arbitrarily, and inserted into new contexts which sometimes may considerably alter their meanings. Change finds its way in spite of cultural barriers. Individuals, we have seen, select and transform information for furthering their action tendencies, in our case, for buttressing one's own theories or interpretations of phenomena. Should the scientist be a person of high prestige, power or influence, his subjective views tend to become common parlance. Yet, even in such cases, his readers or listeners would operate their selections and assimilations of the information received.

Considering the balance between conservation and change, we become aware of a quasi natural connivance between the individual and his or her cultural group. The individual too, strives at constancy. His orientation system requires a consistent and therefore constant world; yet, by the same token, the individual tendency at optimizing the action potential calls for variation, change, innovation, and therefore the individual will also have to establish his or her personal balances between the two tendencies. Doubt, we have seen, is antagonistic to conviction; however, conviction, although providing security, may constrain, may also be contradicted by events or new information, hence breeding doubt and stimulating curiosity, exploration and adventurism. There appears to be a rhythmic alternation between the movements away from and back to stability.

Since cultures, as we have seen, need this balance too, we might now assume that an individual striving for change would meet a different reception in moments of cultural openness for change than in more conservative times. We sometimes say that "Time is ripe for a revolutionary or an innovator", implying that a synchrony has arisen between individual and cultural tendencies for transformation. In other situations or times, the same innovator would be doomed to failure. In the 1920s Pierre Janet published (in the framework of his theory of emotions) what we would call today a "cybernetic action theory". It took more than fifty years before his approach was followed, although not tied up with his name. In 1936 Robert Dottrens wrote his seminal book "L'enseignement individualisé"; educators took no note of it. Today, over half a century later, his theses appear to be rediscovered. These are only two of many examples of "untimely" innovators.

What does "timely" mean? In a rational frame of mind we sometimes tend to believe that the group encourages originality and change because existing knowledge has proven to be insufficient and needs improving. Change then, would equal progress. Yet, knowledge may be logically wanting, practically inadequate, and still not considered to be deficient; but knowledge may also be perceived to be unsatisfactory in spite of no logical or practical failings. Magical beliefs and practices have persisted over the ages, and even scientific ideologies and techniques, although outdated, might enjoy a long life. On the other hand, a tool or a car which functions satisfactorily will often be "improved" and changed, even against the "felt needs" of their users (who however, as experience shows, tend to follow course). Deficiency is not a necessary condition for change. Cultures often remained conservative simply by learning to live with inadequacies, while others turn towards progress for reasons often far from rational.

Change may be sought for practical and economic reasons, yet let us not forget that it is also an actional and often, even an aesthetic phenomenon. Change provides action opportunities more numerous and varied than constancy, and while it reduces security, it enhances individual worth. But change also provides excitement, thrill, surprise, novelty, in other words, leads to enjoyable action experiences. Thus, what may be hailed to be progress is in many cases simply due to individual, or generational, needs of variation. Such would obviously apply to fashion, but I often suspect that it would also be true for much of what we call progress in the areas of social scientific theories or political ideology.

Let me summarize: Although the "cycle of knowledge" would vary according to culture, information offered will always be selected and assimilated by its individual members, and they will in turn feed it back, by praxis as well as by ideation, as a transformed message. The amount of transformation occurring will be dependent upon both the cultural grids of constancy or change, and the individual's specific situation and aspirations. However, this process makes cultural change inavoidable; it may only be slowed down or accelerated, suspended (for a while) or fostered by historical circumstances. Thus, there would be good reasons for psychologists to be more interested in the transformations of knowledge in a cultural field. By studying the "cycle of knowledge", the destiny of information in its course from group to individual and back to the group, we would indeed gain important insights into the dynamics of action within a culture.

Quoted Literature

Bartlett, Sir F. (1954). Remembering. Cambridge: Cambridge University Press.

Boesch, E.E. (1976). Psychopathologie des Alltags. Bern: Huber.

Boesch, E.E. (1980). Kultur und Handlung. Bern: Huber.

Boesch, E. E. (1983). Das Magische und das Schöne. Stuttgart: Frommann-Holzboog.

Boesch, E. E. (1991). Symbolic action theory and cultural psychology. Heidelberg/New York: Springer.

Dottrens, R. (1936). L'enseignement individualisé. Neuchâtel: Delachaux et Niestlé.

Douglas, M. (1974). Natural symbols. London: Barrie and Jenkins.

Janet, P. (1926/1928). De l'angoisse à l'extase. Paris: Alcan, 2 vol.

Lang, A. (1990). The "concrete mind" heuristic – human identity and social compound from things and buildings (in print).

Laye, C. (1954). The African child. London: Collins.

Ecological Psychology's Trouble with Knowledge: One Terrible Example

Gerhard Kaminski

1. Ecological perspectives in psychology

Using the term "ecological" in psychology often means not more than referring, within a special domain, somehow or other to "everyday life" and transcending thereby laboratory experimentation. However, the attribute "ecological" may also indicate a much more fundamental and farreaching perspective. The only two approaches representing this kind of perspective in psychology are those of R. G. Barker and of J. J. Gibson (Kaminski 1989). Both of them are markedly influenced by biological ecology although in very different ways.

Gibson focuses mainly on the functional equipment of organisms which evolved in confrontation with their physical surroundings, especially on perceptual functions (Gibson 1979, Reed 1987, Munz 1989). He devotes but very little attention to concrete socio-cultural happenings in human everyday life on which Barker concentrated his research. Therefore, Gibson's ecological viewpoints will not be taken into consideration here any further.

Barker on the other hand takes over from biological ecology primarily a fundamental methodological principle: non-obtrusive observation of everyday life as it happens under natural surrounding conditions. He intends to establish within psychology a counterpart to experimental research which makes it possible to appraise experimental approaches with respect to their ecological adequacy or approximation (Barker & Wright 1949, Kaminski & Bellows 1982, Brinberg & McGrath 1985, Winkel 1987, Kaminski 1988b). Ecological perspective of this brand aspires to completeness, i. e., to obtaining, ideally, a complete picture of everyday life: how it is organized in natural units and how it functions in its natural dynamics and in all its natural variability which has to be taxonomized.

"Completeness", of course, can only be obtained within limited fields. At first, Barker confined himself to having single children observed minutely and continuously over whole days (Barker & Wright 1951). The child's "stream of behavior" appears to be segmented naturally in "episodes", i. e., macro-actions.

In a further period of research Barker strove for "completeness" with respect to the (publicly accessible) everyday life of a whole small town which was observed and described by a multifaceted but rather coarse-grained survey methodoloy. This undertaking presupposed the "discovery" of a fundamental kind of "natural" entity which was termed "behavior setting" and which achieved a central position in all of Barker's future work. Behavior settings are spatiotemporally concrete supraindividual happening systems of public life, such as a weekly farmers' market, a particular school lesson, a church service, a judicial trial, etc. (Barker 1968, Schoggen 1989). Inherent in behavior settings are dynamics of self-preservation and self-stabilization: If things are not progressing in accordance with the behavior setting "program", then the inhabitants care for corrections or for elimination of interferences. Barker developed a descriptive methodology which permits one to characterize all sorts of behavior settings in a uniform manner.

It is important to realize that Barker views the behavior setting not merely as one ecopsychological unit among others but simply as the fundamental ecopsychological unit at all. If he also operates with different units, either superordinated or subordinated to behavior settings, they all appear, in principle, to be derivable from the fundamental unit behavior setting.

If one adopts this point of view it appears rather plausible and attractive. For wherever in the world human everyday life occurs it always happens within concrete temporal limits and at distinct places, and it always happens then and there in a specifically regulated manner; in short: always in behavior setting format. Accordingly, the entirety of everyday life appears at first sight completely partitioned in behavior settings (Kaminski 1989). All agencies, structures and forces that might have a share in determining everyday life seem to exist merely as a secondary reality, insofar as they can only be traced within or through behavior settings as the primary givens.

What is going on within the individual participant of a behavior setting while participating has been articulated conceptually by Barker in a rather sketchy and coarse-grained manner (Barker 1968).

Thus, Barker, in order to develop a comprehensive ecological perspective for psychology, first focused on the individual's stream of behavior, he then shifted, however, to another fundamental unit, the very behavior setting, i. e., to a concrete supraindividual quasi-stationary system of social happenings; which rather amounts to a typically sociological way of analyzing human everyday life.

2. The theory probing function of the "terrible example"

The following section gives a very condensed and provisional report of a research project that aimed, right from its beginning, at putting to test ecopsychological conceptualizations which have been developed hitherto. This idea rose in the context of an, in many respects, exceptional event, the reactor catastrophy of Chernobyl and the reactions which it released in the population. This project was based on the following kind of considerations: Exceptional events of this scale ought to be taken by the ecological psychologist as a challenge to examine the conceptional tools at his/her disposal up to the present time. Would they suffice to describe and to interpret those exceptional events and reactions and would they be able to generate fruitful explanatory hypotheses?

It is obvious that, with respect to its primary objectives, this project differs fundamentally from other psychological investigations which were triggered and stimulated by the Chernobyl catastrophy (cf. Van der Pligt & Midden 1990, who edited a special issue of the Journal of Environmental Psychology on "Psychological fallout from the Chernobyl nuclear accident"). Our project happened to anticipate, in its general perspective and its methodology, an essential part of the recommendations for future research which are proposed in the final evaluating article of this issue (Earle & Cvetkovich 1990).

Answering the questions just mentioned before presupposes a comprehensive confrontation between this challenging realm of everyday life and the ecopsychological conceptualizations at hand. Which components of this realm can be subsumed under any of those conceptualizations, and which parts of this realm are not yet covered, i. e., not yet conceptualizable adequately (Kaminski 1983)?

About two weeks after the reactor accident we began collecting different kinds of data:

– Written messages that people had directed to governmental and administrative agencies or to broadcasting stations (questions, proposals, appeals, protests, etc.).
– Interviews (transcribed)with experts of different professional competence and responsibility in local and regional administrative agencies and in broadcasting stations who were charged with answering people's questions and giving advice on special telephone lines.
– Interviews (transcribed) with pregnant women, with mothers of infants and young children, with food store owners and with farmers, i. e., with people that were taxed by those events to an especially high extent.
– Issues of a local newspaper over a one-year period.

Since all co-workers of the project were, more or less, affected by those events themselves they could utilize their own personal experience in planning and preparing the investigation.

In all the verbal data collected, reference is made to various subprocesses and components of everyday life: Examples of observable everyday behavior are reported upon; diverse types of cognitive and emotional processes are described: perceptions, judgments, decision making, goal setting, planning of actions, emotional reactions, moods, and so forth. Also particulars about pertinent spatio-material surroundings are mentioned as well as particular objects and special aspects of them. The verbal data were primarily evaluated in a particular kind of "qualitative analysis" (Glaser & Strauss 1967) that cannot be extended here (cf. Witzel 1982, Jüttemann 1985, Silverman 1985, Strauss 1987).

Which, on the other hand, are the conceptualizations that are to be put to test by being confronted with this exceptional realm of everyday reality, as it is represented in all these "cognitive" data? The confrontation shall be confined here to the classical concepts offered by the ecopsychological or "ecobehavioral" perspective of the Barker school. Besides, diverse more or less solitary ecological concepts that are not embedded in an encompassing ecological perspective could, in principle, also be included in such a kind of "test by confrontation ", concepts like "place" (Moore, Tuttle et al. 1985), "stressor", "stress", "coping" (Lazarus & Cohen 1977, Lazarus & Launier 1978, Baum, Singer et al. 1982, Campbell 1983, Evans & Cohen 1987), "transition" (Wapner 1981, 1987), "trauma" (Vyner 1988), as well as action theories and their conceptual background (von Cranach 1982).

What comes to light if one attempts to project the descriptive and interpretative concepts of classical ecological psychology into this exceptional realm of everyday life? The question can only be answered here in a strongly condensed summary:

1. It appears possible, in principle, also to partition this particular realm of everyday reality primarily into behavior settings. However, this format of primary conceptual and factual systemic organization of everyday life was, right after the catastrophy, suddenly overwhelmed and superimposed by different kinds of structuring principles and forces. Countless behavior settings were at once penetrated by something that connected all of them, as dispersed and separate as they may have existed before. Let us call this connecting agent "the Theme Chernobyl". "Theme" is, so far, not more than a rather vague and ambiguous concept of everyday language. Even if we would try to exchange "Theme" by the notions "technological disaster" or "technological catastrophy" as they are used in environmental psychology (Baum, Fleming et al.1983) they would not really fit into this role because they are, as solitary concepts, not anchored

within an encompassing conceptual system of a psychological ecology. So, already this conspicuous, impressive complex of experiences which has been named and characterized by the term "Theme" reveals a severe conceptual deficit within ecological psychology.

2. What penetrates everyday life in such a sudden and massive manner, let us call it the "problem complex Chernobyl", seems to possess its own internal dynamics: it changed from day to day, even from hour to hour and it thereby seemed to effect that whatever people might say and do with reference to it, in all kinds of behavior settings, changed just as quickly. The entirety of these changes constitutes the history of this "problem complex". It must be admitted that the conceptualizations of classical ecological psychology do not provide for this kind of dynamics and historicity.

3. If one attends more closely to what happens within various behavior settings with reference to the "problem complex Chernobyl" it becomes evident that often something like "information" plays a central role: People search for pertinent information, they deal with relevant information that is offered in public, they exchange information. All this activity can be understood best by hypothesizing that the information is gathered and utilized by individuals to build up within themselves a cognitive representation, a knowledge system, a "mental model" (Johnson-Laird 1983) of the "problem complex Chernobyl".

The attempt of conceptualizing the formation of such kind of complex knowledge system overtaxes Barker's ecological perspective in a fundamental way. Since this perspective is dominated, nearly exclusively, by the supraindividual systemic unit "behavior setting" the individual him/herself appears in it mainly as a participant of behavior settings. Conceiving of the individual, beyond that, also as a systemic unit in its own is a complementary view which is merely sketched out by Barker (1978), but neither adequately elaborated nor consistently integrated into his ecological perspective (Boesch 1986, Kaminski 1988a). Thus, it turns out that an ecological personology (Little 1987, Singer & Kolligian 1987), the systematic ecopsychological conceptualization of the individual system, is still wanting.

4. In the classical Barkerian approach, psychological ecology and its fundamental unit "behavior setting" are nearly exclusively constituted through an observer's perspective. This view is more or less fixated, in a quasi-behavioristic manner, on the surface of what is immediately accessible by observation. "Knowledge" bases enabling and regulating the individual's behavior setting participation are referred to only incidentally. So the further development of the ecological perspective should also include conceptualizing the details of the individual's functioning while participating in a behavior setting (Kaminski 1987, Wicker 1987, Kaminski 1989, Fuhrer 1990).

This includes distinguishing between knowledge bases of different specificity; those which are specific for single behavior settings each, and knowledge systems that "bridge" and connect the individual's participation in more or less different behavior settings, sharing more or less commonalities (Schank 1982). Thus, the cognitive representation of the "problem complex Chernobyl" influenced the individual's participation in many diverse behavior settings, urging him/her, e.g., to search for pertinent information in all of them.

5. The synthesis and the elaboration of such kind of knowledge systems are not accomplished within proper behavior settings only, i.e., not merely within public life, but also within diverse fields of privat life. Once more it proves necessary to develop ecopsychological conceptualizations also for non-public compartments of everyday life.

6. Furthermore, the project data back the common view that in everyday reality various supraindividual social systems other than behavior settings are effective: couples, families, neighborhood, many kinds of organizations and associations, the population of a country, etc. The formation of a knowledge system of the "problem complex Chernobyl" may, in part, also be understood as a process whose subject is one of those social systems: a family develops its particular concept of this "problem complex Chernobyl" or a farmers' association theirs, etc. Within the single member of each of these social

systems the individual specific concept may well be differentiated from the family specific and from the association specific ones. Although social pschology and other social sciences have conceptualized and analyzed such kinds of social systems and processes abundantly they are not yet taken into account adequately in Barker's ecological perspective. Therefore, an integration, or at least a coordination, between the ecological perspective and those conceptualizations of pertinent social sciences, e.g., sociology of knowledge, appears necessary.

7. It is obvious that the formation of knowledge systems such as "the problem complex Chernobyl" is objectively enabled and induced essentially through the dissemination of verbal and iconic messages by media. Barker's ecological psychology allows for describing this whole system of information transfer but in a rather vague and unspecific manner.

8. If describing the formation of a complex knowledge system lies beyond ecological psychology's conceptual possibilities, less still it will suffice to deal with motivational aspects of this formation process and with its function in regulating actions.

3. An encounter of the ecological perspective and the research program "Social Representations"

Thus, the attempt to apply Barker's ecological perspective to this terrible complex of events makes obvious that this perspective is in want of a number of specific elaborations and extensions. At this point, it appears evident that it is just the research program "Social Representations" which suggests itself as a complement to the Barkerian way of approaching everyday life. Closer inspection reveals, however, that this kind of service could not leave this program untouched in itself.

What are the most essential commonalities of both approaches which render possible a certain mutual complementation? Like Barker, Moscovici (Farr & Moscovici 1984) focuses, in his research program, primarily on social aspects in everyday reality. As a social psychologist he too connects this priorization with aspirations and perspectives of fundamental research, with critical reflections on the limitations of the lab experimental research methodology, and with the view that psychology needs working off lots of deficits in description, where observational methodology had to play an important part. Thus, neighboring disciplines like sociology, ethnology, and cultural anthropology grow more interesting and relevant, and the boundaries to them become more permeable. In particular, both protagonists agree in stressing that humans and their behavior in everyday reality are, to a considerable extent, determined and governed by supraindividual structures. These are, in Barker's case, first and foremost behavior settings by whose determining structures the participant is guided in his/her observable behavior (Barker 1968, Barker & Schoggen 1973). In Moscovici's case, these are more or less general, historically shaped cognitive structures, just those "Social Representations", which function, so to speak, as a matrix for the formation of individual cognitions and their behavioral implications.

Which components of the conceptual equipment of the research program "Social Representaions" appear, in principle, appropriate for being integrated with Barker's ecological perspective and for compensating thereby its conceptual deficits?

1. In a more general view, the cognitivistic orientation of this research program could complement Barker's approach, which only advances sparsely behind the surface level of behavior description, in a rather fruitful way.

2. Characteristic examples of "Social Representations" which are referred to within this research program (e. g. ideologies, psychoanalysis as a theoretical system; cf. Thommen, Ammann et al. 1988) necessitate articulating everyday reality also by different, particularly by, in a certain sense, larger conceptual units as happens in Barker's ecological perspective with its strong, biased preference to the behavior setting unit.

3. Since this research program also enters into the relations between cognitive representations and language, it thereby challenges Barker's psychological ecology to treat and to assimilate the whole language domain, symbolic reality in general, much more thor-

oughly and specifically then it has done hitherto (Kruse 1986).

4. Moreover, the world of the mass media is taken into consideration by the research program "Social Representations" rather specifically, which is not the case in Barker's ecological psychology.

5. In Moscovici's research program, social and individual cognitive representations are taken serious also as regards their historical changeability. This raises genetic questions, again equally relevant for a psychological ecology, in different time perspectives: questions concerning short term acquisition and change of relatively specific cognitive structures (Fuhrer 1990), questions concerning the formation of social representations in ontogenesis, questions, after all, concerning their historical changes.

However, the attempt to transfer such kinds of conceptualizations from the research program "Social Representations" into Barker's psychological ecology meets, as has been announced before, with various difficulties. What are these difficulties like? And which consequences do they imply for the research program "Social Representations"?

1. Let us imagine we would turn to some piece of everyday happening, wherever, in the same manner as a Barkerian observer of behavior streams would do (Wright 1967). But we now would attempt continuously to find out where something like "shared knowledge" must be involved, i. e., knowledge which must exist in similar content in the heads of many or fewer people simultaneously, so that the happenings can function and appear just in the way to be observed. Probably, we would hardly succeed to separate "Social Representations", defined in Moscovici's sense as special kinds of "shared knowledge", from any other kinds of "shared knowledge". It follows that in view of an ecological psychology the research program should be recommended to give the concept of "Social Representations", as a fundamental concept, a most extensive interpretation instead of confining it right from the beginning by several specifications.

2. Suppose we would approach some particular piece of everyday reality in this ecopsycho-

logical manner, e.g., happenings in the course of a scientific congress: we then would probably be impressed and irritated by the multiplicity and the diversity of "shared knowledge" or "social representations" which we could unearth or infer. At this point, we would certainly hope for an "ecologyproof" taxonomy of social representations which would allow us to distinguish the many different variants of "shared knowledge" according to formal, to thematic, and to functional aspects, so that we could identify them, name them specifically, and, moreover, to understand them in their respective functions.

Within the research program "Social Representations", however, as far as I could see, merely single prototypical examples are selected and utilized for theory construction and for stimulating empirical investigations. Therefore, this research program should feel challenged by the ecological perspective to follow its own fundamental ideas and intentions much more consistently towards completeness of description and systematization.

3. How could a taxonomic systematization of the domain "Social Representations" in its entirety be approached? This question raises another fundamental problem: The most natural approach might seem to be gathering as many diverse, experienced and recollected, examples of "shared knowledge" as possible and to extract from them different taxonomic aspects. However, in an ecopsychological view this strategy would imply the risk of isolating "Social Representations" and systematizing them apart from their respective functional contexts. The ecological perspective originates in observation; hence, it is primarily confronted with behavior or actions within their respective surrounding conditions. Cognitions, also Social Representations, are but components of transactions and must be viewed and understood primarily according to their function within the transactions. Therefore, an "ecology-proof" taxonomization of Social Representations had to be evolved out of a taxonomy of transactional systems, as has been sketched, at least in principle, by von Cranach, Ochsenbein & Valach (1986; also

von Cranach, this volume) in constructing their theory of social actions.

4. By means of an "ecologization" and a respective taxonomization it would become possible to specify the concept of "Social Representations" in all its concrete applications. It would gain in precision and could be freed from ambiguities. This brings about heuristic benefit because thereby numerous new questions regarding the mutual relations between different kinds of Social Representations would be suggested. Besides, questions concerning the relations between Social Representations on the one hand and knowledge, knowledge acquisition, and knowledge application within individual systems on the other hand could be formulated much more precisely, which should help stimulating empirical research.

4. Summary

Although the classical ecological perspective had been initiated with the ideal of an "ecological completeness" in mind it nevertheless neglected largely the "knowledge" domain, included "Social Representations". Therefore, this ecological perspective could be fundamentally enriched by various suggestions offered by the research program "Social Representations".

On the other hand, the research program "Social Representations", which claims explicitly to refer primarily to everyday life, lacks sufficiently high aspirations to an extensive and thorough conceptual articulation of everyday reality. Therefore, it could profit essentially from a constructive dialogue with the classical ecological perspective and its recent further developments.

References

Barker, R.G. (1968). Ecological psychology: Concepts and methods for studying the environment of human behavior. Stanford, Ca.: Stanford University Press.

Barker, R.G. (1978). Behavior Settings: Human habitats and behavior machines. In R.G. Barker et Associates, Habitats, environments, and human behavior. Studies in Ecological Psychology and Eco-Behavioral Science from the Midwest Psychological Field Station (pp. 192–201). San Francisco: Jossey-Bass.

Barker, R. G. (1987). Prospecting in environmental psychology: Oskaloosa revisited. In D. Stokols & I. Altman (Eds.), Handbook of environmental psychology, Vol. 2 (pp. 1413–1432). New York: Wiley.

Barker, R. G., & Schoggen, P. (1973). Qualities of community life: Methods of measuring environment and behavior applied to an American and an English town. San Francisco: Jossey-Bass.

Barker, R. G., & Wright, H. F. (1949). Psychological ecology and the problem of psychosocial development. Child development, 20, 131–143.

Barker, R. G., & Wright, H. F. (1951). One boy's day. New York: Harper & Row.

Barker, R. G. et Associates. (1978). Habitats, environments, and human behavior. Studies in ecological psychology and eco-behavioral science from the Midwest Psychological Field Station, 1947–1972. San Francisco: Jossey-Bass.

Baum, A., Fleming, R., & Davidson, L. M. (1983). Natural disaster and technological catastrophy. Environment and Behavior, 15(3), 333–354.

Baum, A., Singer, J. E., & Baum, C. S. (1982). Stress and the environment. In G. W. Evans (Ed.), Environmental stress (pp. 15–44). Cambridge: Cambridge University Press.

Boesch, E. E. (1986). Verhaltensort und Handlungsbereich. In G. Kaminski (Hrsg.), Ordnung und Variabilität im Alltagsgeschehen (pp. 129–134). Göttingen: Hogrefe.

Brinberg, D., & McGrath, J. E. (1985). Validity and the research process. Beverly Hills: Sage.

Campbell, J. M. (1983). Ambient stressors. Environment and Behavior, 15(3), 355–380.

Cranach, M. von. (1982). The psychological study of goal-directed action: Basic issues. In M. von Cranach & R. Harré (Eds.), The analysis of action: Recent theoretical and empirical advances (pp. 35–73). Cambridge: Cambridge University Press.

Cranach, M. von. (1991). The multilevel organization of knowledge and actions. In M. von Cranach, W. Doise & G. Mugny (Eds.), Social representations and the social bases of knowledge. Proceedings of the 1st Congress of the Swiss Society of Psychology. Bern: Huber.

Cranach, M. von, Ochsenbein, G., & Valach, L. (1986). The group as a self-active system: outline of a theory of group action. European Journal of Social Psychology, 16, 193–229.

Earle, T. C., & Cvetkovich, G. (1990). What was the meaning of Chernobyl? Journal of Environmental Psychology, 10(2), 169–176.

Evans, G., & Cohen, S. (1987). Environmental stress. In D. Stokols & I. Altman (Eds.), Handbook of environmental psychology, Vol. 1 (pp. 571–610). New York: John Wiley & Sons.

Farr, R. M., & Moscovici, S. (Eds.). (1984). Social representations. Cambridge: Cambridge University Press.

Fuhrer, U. (1990). Handeln-Lernen im Alltag. Bern: Huber.

Gibson, J. J. (1979). The ecological approach to visual perception. Boston: Houghton Mifflin.

Glaser, B. G., & Strauss, A. L. (1967). The discovery of grounded theory. Strategies for qualitative research. New York: Aldine.

Johnson-Laird, P. N. (1983). Mental models. Towards a cognitive science of language, inference, and consciousness. Cambridge: Cambridge University Press.

Jüttemann, G. (Hrsg.). (1985). Qualitative Forschung in der Psychologie. Weinheim: Beltz.

Kaminski, G. (1983). Probleme einer ökopsychologischen Handlungstheorie. In L. Montada, K. Reusser, & G. Steiner (Hrsg.), Kognition und Handeln (pp. 35–53). Stuttgart: Klett.

Kaminski, G. (1987). Cognitive bases of situation processing and behavior setting-participation. In G. R. Semin & B. Krahé (Eds.), Issues in contemporary German social psychology. History, theories and applications (pp. 218–240). Beverly Hills, CA.: Sage.

Kaminski, G. (1988a). Problems of theory building in environmental psychology. In J. I. Aragones & J. A. Corraliza (Eds.), Comportamiento y medio ambiente. La psicología ambiental en Espana (pp. 121–131). Madrid: Comunidad de Madrid. Consejeria de Politica Territorial.

Kaminski, G. (1988b). The psychological experiment as a behavior setting genotype. In H. van Hoogdalem, N. L. Prak, Th. J. M. van der Voordt, & H. B. R. van Wegen (Eds.), Looking back to the future. IAPS 10/1988, Vol. 2 (pp. 98–105). Delft: Delft University Press.

Kaminski, G. (1989). The relevance of ecologically oriented theory building in environment and behavior research. In E. H. Zube & G. T. Moore (Eds.), Advances in environment, behavior, and design, Vol. 2 (pp. 3–36). New York: Plenum.

Kaminski, G., & Bellows, S. (1982). Feldforschung in der Ökologischen Psychologie. In J.-L. Patry (Ed.), Feldforschung. Methoden und Probleme sozialwissenschaftlicher Forschung unter natürlichen Bedingungen (pp. 87–116). Bern: Huber.

Kruse, L. (1986). Drehbücher für Verhaltensschauplätze oder: Scripts für Settings. In G. Kaminski (Ed.), Ordnung und Variabilität im Alltagsgeschehen (pp. 135–153). Göttingen: Hogrefe.

Lazarus, R. S., & Cohen, J. (1977). Environmental stress. In I. Altman & J. F. Wohlwill (Eds.), Human behavior and the environment: Current theory and research, Vol. 2. New York: Plenum.

Lazarus, R. S., & Launier, R. (1978). Stress-related transactions between person and environment. In L. A. Pervin & M. Lewis (Eds.), Perspectives in interactional psychology (pp. 287–327). New York: Plenum.

Little, B. R. (1987). Personality and the environment. In D. Stokols & I. Altman (Eds.), Handbook of environmental psychology, Vol. 1 (pp. 205–244). New York: Wiley.

Moore, G. T., Tuttle, D. P., & Howell, S. C. (1985). Environmental design research directions. Process and prospects. New York: Praeger.

Munz, C. (1989). Der ökologische Ansatz zur visuellen Wahrnehmung: Gibsons Theorie der Entnahme optischer Information. Psychologische Rundschau, 40, 63–75.

Pligt, J. van der, & Midden, C. J. H. (1990). Chernobyl: Four years later: Attitudes, risk management and communication. Journal of Environmental Psychology, 10(2), 91–99.

Reed, E. S. (1987). James Gibson's ecological approach to cognition. In A. Costall & A. Still (Eds.), Cognitive psychology in question (pp. 142–173). Brighton: The Harvester Press.

Schank, R. C. (1982). Dynamic memory. New York: Cambridge University Press.

Schoggen, P. (1989). Behavior settings: A revision and extension of Roger G. Barker's ecological psychology. Stanford, Ca.: Stanford University Press.

Silverman, D. (1985). Qualitative methodology and sociology. Describing the social world. Aldershot: Gower.

Singer, J. L., & Kolligian, J., Jr. (1987). Personality: Developments in the study of private experience. Annual Review of Psychology, 38, 533–574.

Strauss, A. (1987). Qualitative analysis for social scientists. Cambridge: Cambridge University Press.

Thommen, B., Ammann, R., & Cranach, M. von. (1988). Handlungsorganisation durch soziale Repräsentation. Welchen Einfluß haben therapeutische Schulen auf das Handeln ihrer Mitglieder? Bern: Huber.

Vyner, H. M. (1988). Invisible Trauma. The psychosocial effects of invisible environmental contaminants. Lexington, Mass.: D. C. Heath.

Wapner, S. (1981). Transactions of persons-in-environments: Some critical transitions. Journal of Environmental Psychology, 1, 223–239.

Wapner, S. (1987). A holistic, developmental, systems-oriented environmental psychology: some beginnings. In D. Stokols & I. Altman (Eds.), Handbook of environmental psychology, Vol. 2 (pp. 1433–1465). New York: Wiley.

Wicker, A. W. (1987). Behavior settings reconsidered: Temporal stages, resources, internal dynamics, context. In D. Stokols & I. Altman (Eds.), Handbook of environmental psychology (pp. 613–654). New York: Wiley.

Winkel, G. H. (1987). Implications of environmental context for validity assessments. In D. Stokols & I. Altman (Eds.), Handbook of environmental psychology, Vol 1 (pp. 71–97). New York: John Wiley & Sons.

Witzel, A. (1982). Verfahren der qualitativen Sozialforschung. Überblick und Alternativen. Frankfurt/Main: Campus.

Wright, H. F. (1967). Recording and analyzing child behavior. New York: Harper & Row.

Development According to Mothers: A Case of Social Representations

Luisa Molinari, Francesca Emiliani, Felice Carugati*

Introduction

The behaviour of the infant is so ambiguous that it is easy for the culture's beliefs about human nature to influence observers' interpretations of what they think they see (Kagan 1984). It is for this reason that one may find contrasting visions of infancy within the same cultural group, ranging from an image of the completely bewildered and confused infant to the one of the baby as thinker who knows, follows rules, has intentions and emotions.

In recent years, researchers from different domains have paid increasing attention to beliefs about the child in varying cultures and historical periods; however, only recently have developmental phsychologists begun to discuss scientists' visions of infancy and childhood. Bradley (1989) suggests that there can be no empirical observation of babies that does not imply an evaluative vision of infancy.

Gergen, Gloger-Tippelt, Berkowitz (1990) argue that the various investigations on beliefs about the child are important in a variety of respects. According to the authors, historical research about these conceptions fosters a reflexive self-consciousness about the way we were and the way we are. This should raise questions as to the tendency to view today's child as the universal child, an exemplar of the human nature.

The study of beliefs about childhood is also important because of their social implication, as they constitute a frame of reference for educational, religious as well as political institutions. Finally, the authors maintain that this kind of exploration is also interesting from a strictly scientific point of view because it is culture that defines the framework of inter-pretation of what a child is. As a consequence, common sense beliefs about the nature of the child furnish both the context for and the limits over scientific understanding. In such a way the authors touch on the topic of the relationship between scientific and common sense knowledge without linking it to the question of the origins of such conceptions. Questioning on the ontogenesis of these conceptions becomes crucial in order to differentiate the approach of social representations from the one of belief systems (Carugati, 1990).

Following suggestions put forward by Moscovici's theoretical conceptualisation on social representations (Moscovici, 1976; 1984), we have focussed on the dynamics of relative inexplicability on a given topic as one of the main origins of a discourse about this topic. Taking as examples intelligence and development, it has been shown (Mugny and Carugati 1989; Emiliani and Molinari, 1989a) that everyday explanations of children's development are originating by social groups as far as for them there are subjective different degrees of salience for the intriguing(and in some sense unexplicable) question about the origins of interindividual differences in intelligence and in timing of development.

Two main socio-psychological processes had been described: familiarization of the unfamiliar (interindividual differences) and conflicts of identification among adults. For example, parents have specific reasons for constructing and sharing representations of intelligence and development because they have to cope with (and have the responsibility of) the problem of interindividual differences between their children: these differences are by no means a matter of abstract explanation since parents are

* We are grateful to Professor Hans Schadee (University of Trento) and Professor Piergiorgio Corbetta (University of Bologna) for their precious help in the statistical analyses.
The support of the National Council of Research and the Italian Ministry of Education and University and Scientific Research is gratefully acknowledged. The work was funded by CNR award no. 88.01004.08 to the second author and by the Ministry to the second and third authors.

charged of responsibility and have to make everyday decisions. Furthermore they may feel themselves both lacking "scientific" knowledge and not doing "all that is needed" for improving intelligence and making development of their own children as best as possible; this concerns specifically mothers who are also working outside the family (teachers, office workers, etc.) and therefore may feel guilty for being less involved (at least as a matter of time spent) with their children. It is for this reason that the topic of development is closely linked with parental and professional identities as far as ambivalence for such experiences is concerned.

Lastly, we illustrated that social representations of development are a polysemous discourse assembling genetic and maturationist conceptions of abstract intelligence, environmentalist social intelligence, taking success at school as the best indicator of good development and arguing for the child with aptitude for mathematics as the prototype of a bright pupil, for whom no specific teaching methods are needed, insofar as intelligence is a gift unequally distributed among children.

Aim and Hypotheses

The aim of the present chapter is to go further on two crucial points in our approach to social representations of development. The first one refers to the origins: that is to say to the specific conditions under which adults are concerned with intelligence and development as a matter of gift and maturation or in a more interactive perspective.

The second point is concerned with the investigation of a possible relationship between different aspects of social representations. In particular, we intend to verify whether it is possible to outline a model which links more general aspects of representations such as conceptions of development, to more specific ones, such as ideas about learning processes and even more concretely to the images of child inferred by the degree of perceived influence, which are considered as mediators between representations and practices (cf. Molinari and Emiliani, 1990).

In this chapter we also intend to "throw a stone" in the sea of definitions used when talking about social representations, and try to define in a strict way the various steps of that approach. For this purpose, we call conceptions the systems of beliefs about a specific topic (i. e., the factors emerged from statistical analyses); theories are those topics which are linked together and comprise different conceptions, while social representations are the set of theories moulded by social dynamics and role conflicts.

The pattern of results presented here is derived from the data collected in a previous study (see Carugati, Emiliani and Molinari, 1990) with a questionnaire distributed to a sample of 622 women belonging to different social categories: mothers and non-mothers with various occupations (housewives, office workers and teachers).

The questionnaire included four main topics, namely: "Conceptions of development", "Learning processes", "Perceived influence on the child" and the "Contribution of scientific disciplines". On all answers to the first three topics of the questionnaire, three Factor Analyses were carried out, one for each topic.

In the present chapter, we outline a model of links among the factors which we intend to test with more sophisticated statistical analyses. Since the results of previous studies (cf. Emiliani and Molinari, 1989b) highlighted the role of the experience of motherhood in shaping social representations, we carried out these analyses only on the group of mothers (472 subjects); this allowed us to go beyond the question raised by several authors (cf. Potter and Litton, 1985; Hewstone, 1985) about the existence of one social representation for each specific social group. Our intent is to illustrate that it is not simply a matter of agreement, but that a group can construct and share a social representation about one specific object (the child and his development) which is constructed around different theories.

The model is articulated through three different steps. The first one is concerned with the origins of social representations. Two different sources are shown to be relevant for the construction of the "theory of gift" about development: the first source is the subjective lack of scientific models of explanations of development, while the second refers to the relative awareness of inexplicability of development (Mugny and Carugati, 1989).

In this study, we advance the hypothesis that two other sources may be added to the previous ones: i) sharing the idea that biology and mathematics are important for the explanation of children's development. It is assumed that subjects who share such an opinion agree with a "biological" perspective on development; ii) viewing psychology and social psychology as important disciplines, which will lead to sharing an interactionist view of development.

From a methodological point of view, we considered our subjects on the basis of their answers to specific items of the questionnaire: *"Mysterious"* are those mothers who agree on two items, that is, "The differences of character among children are a mysterious problem that science cannot explain" and "The differences among children as to learning skills are a mysterious problem that science cannot explain". *"Non-informed"* are mothers who answered "I do not know" to more than two items in the last part of the questionnaire, concerning the contribution of 12 scientific disciplines (from cultural anthropology to pediatrics) to the explanation of child development. Finally, we chose four of these disciplines, that is, *"Biology and mathematics"*, *"Psychology and social psychology"* to indicate those mothers who agree on the importance of such matters for the understanding of development.

These four topics are hypothesized as being significantly related to two general conceptions of children's development shared by our subjects, which were previously extracted from Factor Analyses; these are the "Character as a natural gift", which expresses the idea that nature unequally distributes several characteristics (in particular autonomy and firmness) among children, and "Social interaction", which takes into consideration the elements that concur in the socio-emotional development.*

In the second step, these two general conceptions are connected with those of learning processes, in particular to "Learning as spontaneous maturation" (in other words, a sort of non-learning), and to "Social interaction and learning", which stresses the importance of interpersonal relations inside the school setting. The conception of "Character as a natural gift" is assumed as related to that of "Learning as spontaneous maturation", while "Social interaction" is linked to the conception of learning as a result of relationships with teachers and schoolmates.

Finally, we attempt to verify whether the conception on learning processes are related to the degree of perceived influence on one's own child; this third step is considered as a crucial point for the understanding of the links between ideas and practices (in terms of perceived influence), in other words, between two different levels of articulation of social representations (Carugati, Emiliani and Molinari, 1990).

In particular, we focus on two images of perceived influence over one's own child, which emerged from our previous Factor Analyses, that is, the images of an "Autonomous child" and of an "Intelligent and sociable child". In this case, we hypothesize that those who agree with "Learning as spontaneous maturation" do not feel they can exert influence over the characteristics of intelligence and autonomy in their own children. On the contrary, those who agree on the importance of social interactions for learning also perceive a high degree of influence on the autonomy and intelligence of their own children.

Results

Statistical analyses

The theoretical model presented so far was submitted to empirical verification by a linear structural equations approach, known as the LISREL method (Joreskog and Sorbom, 1988). This model assumes: i) the existence of latent variables, for each of whom the "observed" variables were established "a priori"; ii) the existence of relations among such variables, which are not causal links, but simple correlations.

---

* The factors extracted by our previous Factor Analyses were composed by a greater number of items (see Molinari, 1991). However, to reduce the complexity of the model discussed in the present chapter, we refer only to 4 items per each factor, items which revealed to be highly significant for the definition of the factor itself.

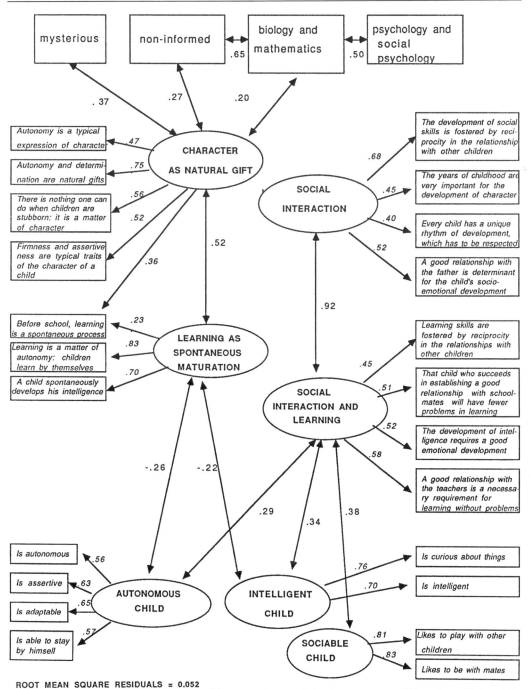

ROOT MEAN SQUARE RESIDUALS = 0.052
Note: to avoid more complexity of the pattern, we did not quote those correlations between sources of information and factors which
     were not necessary for the theoretical interpretation of the model (see Note 2).

Table 1. General pattern of results (χ^2 = 593 with 287 degrees of freedom).

With these characteristics, the model is intended in terms of a *confirmative factor analysis*, where the elements which are unknown in a traditional factor analysis (number of factors, correlations among factors) are theoretically predetermined. Being our "observed" variables measured on a ordinal scale, the initial correlation matrix was transformed into a polychoric correlation matrix (Program PRELIS).

The theoretical model described above was implemented in LISREL in two steps: first separately and secondly as a whole. The obtained measure of goodness of fit for the whole model seems satisfactory (Chi square = 593 with 287 degrees of freedom).

The whole model is presented in Table 1; the numbers in italics are standardized loadings of the Factor Analyses (unidirectional arrows), while the other numbers are correlation scores (bidirectional arrows) between the factors.*

A tentative model

The first set of arrows illustrates what we called the "origins" of social representations, that is, the nature of information available about the actual object of representation, in our case children's development.

The sources of information which we have hypothesized as being related to particular representations of childhood, are of a very specific kind, and refer to the importance attributed to some scientific matters for the explanation of development, or alternatively to the subjective feeling of not knowing the degree to which science can offer such explanations.

Our results show that in both cases our hypotheses were verified. In particular, the sense of inexplicability and the lack of a scientific model of explanation proved to be two sources which have an effect in moulding theories of development. The same can be said for the sharing of the idea that biology and mathematics are scientific disciplines which can contrib-

ute to the understanding of children's growth. In addition, our results show the existence of an apparently inconsistent linkage between the lack of information and the importance attributed to biology and mathematics; that is to say that those subjects who are not confident on the explicative power of several scientific disciplines seem to rely on exact sciences to understand children's development.

On the contrary, the link between sources and conceptions is not verified in the case of psychological information and "social interaction".

As far as the rest of the results is concerned, our hypotheses were verified, in the sense that two theories revealed to be present in the mothers' minds. As *theory of gift*, we intend the linkages between the conception of character, of learning in terms of maturation and the lack of perceived influence over children's intelligence and autonomy. The *theory of social interaction* views development and learning in terms of good relationships with social agents (at home and at school) and, consistently, mothers who share such view perceive themselves to be influential on their own children's autonomy, intelligence and sociability.

Discussion

The general pattern outlined in Table 1 allows some theoretical considerations. First of all, our results show the presence, inside the group of mothers, of two theories of children's development; these are structured along different steps and are consistently organized. The Theory of gift, however, is constructed in a more articulated way, since it is related to several sources of information, which did not prove to be linked to the Social interaction theory. This difference is illustrated by considering the specific content of the Theory of gift, which is concerned with the question of interindividual differences, a topic particularly

---

* The missing correlations are the following: "Non informed" and "Psychology and social psychology" (.43); "Mysterious" and "Learning as spontaneous maturation" (.30); "Mysterious" and "Autonomous child" (–.22); "Non informed" and "Autonomous child" (–.21); "Character as natural gift" and "Autonomous child" (–.48); "Character as natural gift" and "Intelligent child" (–.35); "Character as natural gift" and "Sociable child" (–.23); "Social interaction" and "Autonomous child" (.26); "Social interaction" and "Sociable child" (.20); "Autonomous child" and "Sociable child" (.58); "Autonomous child" and "Intelligent child" (.58); "Intelligent child" and "Sociable child" (.73).

salient for those categories of people who daily interact with children; those mothers who do not have any interpretation for interindividual differences or who refer to biological models (or both!) are prompt to consider "development" as a gift unequally distributed among children. In other words, when directly confronted with interindividual differences, people may feel a gap between the information at their disposal and the information necessary to account for this phenomenon.

Despite the fact that psychological models may indicate different perspectives which support the importance of early interactions for the child, our analyses did not confirm that such perspectives can be related to the idea that children develop through interactions with social agents. This brings us to a further consideration, that is, the existence, within the field of psychology, of highly individual and biological approaches; this alternative solution is a possible interpretation for the correlations found between the importance attributed to two sources, that is psychology (and social psychology) and biology (and mathematics).

In brief, our set of results supports the assumption that the sense of "unfamiliarity" of development is anchored, at the iconic level, to the image of "gift-character". On the other hand, we still do not know how an interactionist view of development is constructed by the mothers. Is this a matter of greater personal experience or of more complex and articulated sources of information? It is clear that further specific studies are necessary.

Finally, asking the mothers about the perceived influence on the characteristics of their own children, was a way of making the mother-child relationship salient at a representational level. The fairly high correlations obtained support the idea that general conceptions and images are consistently interrelated. This is illustrated by the systematic naturalizing effects of the theory of character and of spontaneous maturation on the lack of perceived influence over intelligence and autonomy of children. Conversely, mothers who are more inclined to the importance of early interactions are confident about their own participation in moulding both the cognitive and social traits of their children.

Concluding remarks

In discussing the results of wide-ranging reviews about parents' beliefs, Goodnow (1988) and Miller (1988) underline as a main limitation – and corresponding suggestion for future work – a lack of a comprehensive theory of how different beliefs may be interrelated, thus reflecting the generally atheoretical nature of much work on parental beliefs. Furthermore it is suggested that data collected on so many variables need techniques that serve to detect multiple bidirectional paths interrelating any two variables and extending to constitute self-modulating feedback (McGuire, 1986, p. 121).

Our work fits these suggestions insofar as it is concerned with the ontogenesis of social representations of cognitive development: by combining previous lines of research and proceeding further to account for the origins of representations, we illustrated the role of the shortage of information and of inferential pressure in specific categories of people, like mothers, who are constantly having to communicate, to take note of the assessment of their children, to make decisions; at the same time, mothers take the results of development of their own children as indicators of the success in the profession of "being mothers".

Thus, choosing a sample of mothers leads to a core of the ontogenesis of social representations. Their experience with children is partialled out: it is not a matter of contrasting groups, nor a matter of heavy sociological variables, like culture, socio-economic status, gender. In this sense we took a direction quite different from an account for the differences in parental experience, in terms of a kind of differential psychology of parents or teachers. This growing literature (e.g. Goodnow, 1988; Miller, 1988; Gergen, Gloger-Tippelt, Berkowitz, 1990; Dann, 1990) is of major importance for the genetic social psychology (Mugny and Carugati, 1989) which will have to take serious account of it. Our approach places particular emphasis on the socio-psychological dynamics which are at the origins of a discourse about a given topic, and which organize different contents of the discourse in significant structures (Duveen and Lloyd, 1989). These structures have functional necessity for particular groups (just as we have shown) and allow us to identify both groups which construct a representation and the content which is represented.

Following this line of thought, our theoretical model which combines different contents allowed us to make predictions about the feature of a significant structure for mothers. Putting together so many variables, we used as a technical tool a structural equation model to confirm the model.

The results seem to be clear: feeling the inexplicability or subjectively not being informed and having trust in biology and mathematics plays a central role in explaining development as a matter of gifted character and learning as spontaneous maturation. Furthermore mothers who are inclined towards an explanation in terms of character and maturation view themselves as little influencing autonomous and intelligent children. Conversely, the pattern which links an interactionist view on development, learning and the parents' influence is evident: sociable and intelligent children are seen as the "product" of good relationships with parents, other children and teachers.

It is also worth noting that autonomous and intelligent children are viewed by their mothers on the basis of the general conceptions they hold: in other words, autonomy and intelligence are by no means traits associated with a single "theory" of origins.

If, generally speaking, our results fit the model we put forward, further unresolved questions still remain: for instance the explanatory role played by scientific disciplines like psychology and social psychology as socially represented in everyday life. They seem marked (at least in the mothers' eyes) by an individualistic connotation which impedes their utilization in the understanding of the social construction of knowledge.

References

Bradley, B. (1989). *Visions of infancy*. Cambridge: Polity Press.

Carugati, F. (1990). Everyday ideas, theoretical models and social representations: the case of intelligence and its development. In G. R. Semin & K. J. Gergen (Eds.), *Everyday understanding* (pp.130–150). London: SAGE.

Carugati, F., Emiliani, F. & Molinari, L. (1990). Being a mother is not enough. Theories and images in the social representations of childhood. *Revue Internationale de Psychologie Sociale*, 3, 3, 289–306.

Dann, H. D. (1990). A new approach to psychological research and educational practice. In G. R. Semin & K. J. Gergen (Eds.), *Everyday understanding* (pp. 227–243). London: SAGE.

Duveen, G. & Lloyd, B. (1990). Introduction. In G. Duveen & B. Lloyd (Eds.), *Social representations and the development of knowledge* (pp. 1–10). Cambridge: Cambridge University Press.

Emiliani, F. & Molinari, L. (1989a). Il bambino nella mente. In F. Emiliani, M. Gelati & L. Molinari (Eds.), *Il bambino nella mente e nelle parole delle madri* (pp. 3–125). Firenze: La Nuova Italia.

Emiliani, F. & Molinari, L. (1989b). Mothers' social representations of their children's learning and development. *International Journal of Educational Research*, 13, 6, 657–670.

Gergen, K. J., Gloger-Tippelt, G. & Berkowitz, P. (1990). The cultural construction of the developing child. In G. R. Semin & K. J. Gergen (Eds.), *Everyday understanding* (pp.108– 129). London: SAGE.

Goodnow, J. J. (1988). Parents' ideas, actions, and feelings: models and method from developmental and social psychology. *Child Development*, 59, 286–320.

Herzlich, C. (1972). *Health and illness: a social psychology analysis*. London: Academic Press.

Hewstone, M. (1985). On common-sense and social representations: a reply to Potter and Litton. *British Journal of Social Psychology*, 24, 95–97.

Jodelet, D. (1983). *Civils et bredins: reprsentations sociales de la maladie mentale et rapport à la folie en milieu rural*. Paris: Doctoral dissertation.

Joreskog, K. G. & Sorbom, D.(1988). *Lisrel 7. A guide to the program and applications*. Chicago: Spss Inc.

Kagan, J. (1984). *The nature of the child*. New York: Basic Books.

McGuire, W. J. (1986). The vicissitudes of attitudes and similar emotional constructs in twentieth century psychology. *European Journal of Social Psychology*, 16, 89–130.

Miller, S. A. (1988). Parents' beliefs about children's cognitive development. *Child Development*, 59, 259–285.

Molinari, L. (1991). Identità sociale e conflitto di ruolo: principi organizzatori di rappresentazioni sociali dello sviluppo infantile. *Giornale Italiano di Psicologia*, 1, 97–118.

Molinari, L. & Emiliani, F. (1990). What is in an image? The structure of mothers' images of the child and their influence on conversational styles.

In G. Duveen & B. Lloyd (Eds.), *Social representations and the development of knowledge* (pp. 91–106). Cambridge: Cambridge University Press.

Moscovici, S. (1961). *La psychanalyse: son image et son public*. Paris: Presses Universitaire de France (2nd Edition, 1976).

Moscovici, S. (1984). *Psychologie sociale*. Paris: Presses Universitaire de France.

Mugny, G. & Carugati, F. (1989). *Social representations of intelligence*. Cambridge: Cambridge University Press.

Potter, J. & Litton, I. (1985). Some problems underlying the theory of social representations. *British Journal of Social Psychology*, 24, 81–90.

On the Knowledge in Things and Places

Alfred Lang

Why do we make things and places?

It is the contention of psychology in general that some dynamic structure *within* living beings is both the *resultant* as well as the *foundation* of any process or state called psychological. In particular, every instance of what an individual ever sees, hears, feels, thinks, acts, etc. has a potential of leaving some trace or becoming incorporated in its peculiar way into the psychological organization of that individual. And it is this psychological organization *within* the individual which in turn determines or codetermines both any further perception or action as well as further internal states or processes of that individual. In fact we all assume that nothing psychological ever happens *without* the (internal) psychological organization. We call it the psyche, the mind, the content of the psychological blackbox or the cognitive structure: strange indeed that psychologists have never found it worthwhile to agree on a single term in order to designate that most fundamental construct of their science.

However, most, if not all, of what people do also has a potential of leaving a trace in *the real surroundings of the actor* or of becoming incorporated in a peculiar way into *the (external) environment of the actor*. Be it in a more transient or in more durable way, many of our activities tend to change some aspect of the world, as it exists then independently of their originator.

In turn, this modified environment then has *a potential of influencing our further perceptions and actions*, those of the originator of the change as well as those of many other individuals. Again we are all inclined to agree that such transformations of the external world are in some way *the effects of* the psychological organization of the acting individual. And we also agree that behavior and experience of persons is in some way *influenced by* the situations and events thus created. In fact this is the central thesis of (trans-)action theories. However we do not usually combine the two principles of internal and of external organization into a single coherent construction.

Indeed, also the *external* environment functions *both as a resultant and as a foundation* of most processes or states called psychological. Yet effects of behavior, i.e. changes of the world brought about by behavior of persons, are considered not to be psychological in nature. They are generally taken to be objective facts and they do not interest psychologists in any other way than that they can be indicative of psychological processes (responses), or that some of them might eventually play a role as (co-)determinants of other psychological processes (stimuli). However, behavioral effects of the actions of many persons over time, taken in their totality as human culture, are an organized whole of meaning quite comparable to the mind in richness and differentiation and perhaps also in their power to incite and to control behavior.

The traditional separation of the world into the objective or material and the subjective or psychological is apparently self-evident; however, it is not a matter of fact but rather a particular conception or construction of the world. It should be pinpointed as Cartesian *dualism*, common in Western civilization of the last few centuries. The above examples of mutual effects between "the psychological" and "the material" call for an *interactive* dualism. Yet most modern psychologists confess to *epiphenomenalism* which is an asymmetric dualism that accepts body-to-mind sequels, such as from brain to conscious experience, but denies mind-to-body causation. The latter, however, obviously is factual when we think of the consequences on the material world of so many evaluations, plans or decisions which are undoubtedly mental. The preferred solution today is to retreat to monistic *materialism* which in turn disallows psychology a separate existence.

Psychologists, so it seems, have carefully avoided dealing with the outgoing branch of the mind-body-problem, although over the centuries a large body of speculation has been directed towards the assumed dependencies of the subjective on the objective. Fechner has posed the psychophysical problem in terms of the psychological being a function of the physical. The program has failed, although variants thereof are still pursued. And the *reactive image of man* proposed by psychophysics remains to reign over this science. It is obviously conterintuitive. It is incompatible with everybody's daily experience of being a subject, i. e. of being a person capable of deciding and acting, at least within certain restrictions, on the basis of one's own "free will". It is true that important portions of the world surrounding living beings have their characters independent of those subjects. Yet particularly for any human being, most entities, particularly the important ones in everyday life, are the result of human action, of action by the person in question as well as by others. It is human *culture*, evolved in many particular versions over many generations and supplemented and modified every moment, that is *the preeminent determinant of human existence.* No psychologist has ever formulated a program complementary to Fechner's psychophysics, i. e. to understand artifacts as a function of the mental. But the fact is that our civilization has simply acted that way: man as a measure for all things; and is on the verge of destroying living conditions.

Psychology, in a way then, has forbidden itself half of its potential subject matter. On becoming an empirical science, it has restricted its endeavor to a cause-effect way of looking at the world of people. Causes are assumed to be givens, they are thought to have effects on people. The business of psychology is understood to find out how these effects on people are brought about. Yet culture is not adequately described as an aggregation of stimuli. The *objective* is *not* simply the *material*, nor is the *subjective* well enough captured by subsuming it as the *mental*. Probably, the reverse type of psychophysics would be as much deemed to failure as the traditional one. What is needed is at least a bi-directional or transactional view of the ecological relation or, better still, a conception beyond Cartesian dualism. We live in a world of things and places, i. e. objects and spaces *that carry meaning*. And things and places form an ordered system which obeys both natural laws and psychosocial determinants.

In a related chapter entitled "The 'concrete mind' heuristic: human identity and social compound from things and buildings" (Lang, in press), I have proposed to give up the venerated separation of the world into the material and the immaterial. As much meaning is "stored" and is available for any individual being in her environment as in his brain. An action or a developmental change of an individual are often and vigorously incited by external structures or processes which have been built up or prepared by the actor himself or by other members of a smaller or larger cultural group. Actions can be controlled by external entities, as much as they are from within.

In fact, the mind as a complex and dynamic structure in continuous change is no less material in character than the totality of the cultural forms incorporated in the objects and spaces of our surrounds is mental, and vice versa, because *both incorporate or carry, by means of physical formations, an organization of meaning which is always both, objective and subjective.*

In addition, both of these structures, each considered in its own right, are genuine nonentities from a psychological point of view. The internal mind would be empty, if it could not represent the environment of the individual in question; and the cultural environment would be nil, if it were not produced and maintained by people. Human individuals of all societies, if deprived of their material belongings, from clothes to furniture or from tools to houses, would be at pains to acquire and maintain their personal identity. And a human society devoid of common material and symbolic structures from territories to signs of dominance or autonomy, from objects for exchange to cosmic myths, is simply incomprehensible. There must be *causes for animals and humans to turn spatio-temporal formations into carriers of meaning.* Common answers to this question are mostly precipitate and all too often of an arbitrary "for-this-and-that"-nature. Reasons are not enough. My contention is that the authentic preconditions for things and places are *of an essentially psychological nature* and that the answer is not completely different from that of explaining the evolution of the mind/brain.

External memory or *the "concrete mind"* is then a formula I have chosen as a catch phrase to point to the functional equivalence of the (internal) mind and the cultural environment. There is a large thesaurus of knowledge stored in the spaces and objects formed and cultivated by people. If we want to understand it, we have to study people in conjunction with these external structures. Men-environment-systems or *ecological units* are in my opinion the proper subject of investigation for psychology in an ecological perspective. Such systems are found on a scale ranging from the petty things of everyday settings to dwellings, neighborhoods, cities, institutional settings of all kinds to culture in its entirety.

Dialogue of a young man with things in his room

In the following section, a pilot study is briefly summarized which has been directed at understanding person-thing-relationships in the context of private rooms. Credit and thanks for the study go to Silvia Famos (1989) who did it under my direction as a *Diplomarbeit*. The method used combines a survey of (arti)facts and their topography in the present and in the former private room with a structured interview about the personal history of five important things in the rooms of four young men. Facts and transcripts have been grouped and interpreted in the form of parallel case studies. This method, of course, is a provisional one, because it is restricted to reflections on objects and people; it will have to be supplemented by methods directed at person-environment-systems in transactional development. Theoretical guidelines are gathered from the *symbolic action theory* of Ernst Boesch (1980, 1982, 1983, 1989), the psycho-sociological study on the *meaning of things* by Csikszentmihalyi & Rochberg-Halton (1981) and the author's *regulation theory of dwelling activity* (Lang 1987, 1988, in press).

The study illustrates that objects important for a person are placed at non-arbitrary points within a room and in relation to each other. Placement and the resulting thing-topography is only partially determined by the functions or the outside features of the objects, they are rather part and parcel of a complex ensemble

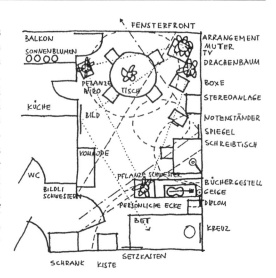

Figure 1a. Floor plan and important things in the present room of B. Dotted lines signify relations among the 5 special things, broken lines refer to ranges of meaning. The 5 "special things" are the *violin* (Geige, lower right), the *bed* (Bett, lower right), the *plants* (Pflanzen, lower center and upper left, center and right), the *picture* (Bild, middle left), and the *crucifix* (Kreuz, lower right).

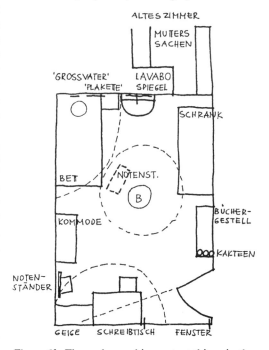

Figure 1b. Floor plan and important things in the former room of B. The "special things" are the *violin* (Geige, lower left), the *bed* (Bett, upper left), the *plants* (Kakteen, lower right); the *picture* and the *crucifix* are not yet present.

of meaning which is most readily made explicit in terms of *psychosocial identity of the person* involved. Although most of the things picked by the person as "special" are functionally passive objects, they enter a thing-person dialectic which can only be understood in a developmental perspective. The relative placements of the things is subject to subtle changes, and so does the relationship between the things and the person.

Although our material is, in the main, verbally communicated, it is apparent that much of the meaning of these things and their topography is not primarily of a planned character, nor is all of it spontaneously conscious. In the process of talking about these objects the persons involved are repeatedly surprised and amazed on the rich network of relations connecting their things with their room in a system of meaning. Indeed, much more is known to the person than they can and do talk about; but repeatedly new facets or new ways of understanding surface with the intensive engagement with these ordinary, everday, self-evident matters of course.

In an attempt to relate here some insights into the essence of the study, one of the cases (B) in Famos (1989) is briefly summarized and illustrated in Fig. 1.

B is a 25 year old machine construction engineer who also semi-professionally plays the violin in an orchestra and in a string quartet. After the recent death of his mother he moved from the parental home (Fig. 1b, former room) to a one-room apartment in another city, but in the vicinity of one of his two older sisters (Fig. 1a, present room). He is described as a good-natured and joyful person with an open mind, but socially well-mannered and rather cautious. A penchant for religious, naturistic or artistic experience dominates over social interests, although he can be an ardent debater of topics of interest to him.

The *five things chosen* to talk about by B are: the violin, the bed, his plants, a picture and a crucifix. In the following, in order to be brief, data and interpretation cannot be separated in a desirable manner. Obviously, in both rooms the *violin* takes a particular place near the bed in a most personal corner. While it has taken the central floor (note stand) in the former room, at present it seems more integrated, both with musical equipment and with other

professional and social items. Violin playing has been and is an important vehicle for finding personal identity for B; although not by family tradition a musical milieu, B's father induced and supported this interest. B has long considered a professional career but has recently settled for a high amateur level and sees his music in a complementary, rather than in the former competitive relation to his engineering talents and activities.

The *bed* is an important place in the room for B. As a slightly closed off space behind the entrance, it affords rest, regeneration, security; as an object with family history, it also reminds one of the continuity of generations. *Plants* have always fascinated B, but in his parental home, house plants were cared for by his mother, while B pursued his almost religious relation with nature preferably outdoors. After her death, and in his new room, he has developed his small set of cactuses to a rich collection of different plants spreading over large parts of the room. On the pretext of asking for her advice and help, the plants also help carry B's relation with his sister.

Both the picture and the crucifix are recent additions. The placement of the *crucifix* is an intentional and "displayed" effort to confess his spiritual engagement and, at the same time, somewhat paradoxically, to cultivate relations with religious family ancestors as well as to confirm religious attitude and find distance to the church as an institution. The *picture,* on the other hand, seems primarily to be a private dialogue of B with himself. Apart from the admission that the picture must have originated out of a mental constellation similar to his own, B only reluctantly and indirectly talked about details; from the facts that it is actually a photograf of a painting by an absent friend, showing a sleeping pair in a somehow spheric setting, and from the confession that B has selected it because of its content rather than its artistic value, one can conclude that B alludes to and reminds himself of his life situation as a somewhat solitary young man in search of personal relationship. An additional remark on the social functions of the rather big round table supports this line of interpretation.

Seen as carriers of meaning, each of the 5 things thus refers to one of the paramount *domains* of B's personal constitution and actual preoccupations: home base (bed) and fulfillment (violin) seem securely settled in the room, whereas the social (plants), partnership (picture) and spiritual (crucifix) yearnings for belonging each take their separate section of the room. In addition, these domains together form an *ensemble* of relationships which, especially when considered in their development, do not appear random nor entirely determined by functions or room architecture. While, for example, in the former room the home base (bed) was found at the far end, at present it is near the entrance; yet in both situations it is protected from immediate intrusion by the opening door. Items referring to personal and social relations, as good as absent in the parental home room, now nearly mushroom in the upper left half of the room; they appear to represent both factual and hopeful associations, the former mostly to kinspeople, the latter oriented towards deep and personal relations.

This short summary of one case cannot give more than a crude illustration of our contention that things are more than objects. Evidently, methodology and theory have to be elaborated in conjunction.

An eco-semiotic perspective on persons and their environment

The main purpose of the present pilot study was to help sharpen conceptual tools with the objective of an improved methodology. The last section therefore is a brief attempt to elaborate a conceptual perspective for dealing with ecological questions such as those in the above example.

Two markers can be used to characterize this approach: (a) it investigates men-environment-systems or *ecological units in evolution*; (b) it applies *triadic semiotics as a conceptual tool* for description and explanation of psychological process and structure.

Enough has been said in the first section on (a) and it should also be clear by now that our approach to persons in their environments is *neither materialistic nor mentalistic*. Psychology on the whole is no great success and probably cannot gain on one of the traditional platforms, be it behavioristic or cognitivistic. I propose semiotics in the tradition of Charles S. Peirce as a candidate for a new platform, because as *a general logic of representation* it perfectly fits the ecological problem. I hope to give more than the present sketchy impression elsewhere.

In semiosis, understood as a general *logic*, something stands for something to somebody. Semiosis, understood as a *process*, describes the encounter between two entities from which a third entity results. Semiotic terminology, and sometimes also conceptions, unfortunately are rather variable. Let me use the term *referent* (object, source etc.) for the first or originating entity, *interpretant* (subject, agent, etc.) for the second or mediating instance, and *representant* (sign proper or in the narrow sense, sign carrier etc.) for the third entity resulting from the process. The psychological interpretation of semiotics proposed here thus, in some way, deviates from the Peircean conceptions of interpretant and representant; here is not the place to give the reasons.

We have seen that a person selects and places furniture and related items in a particular ensemble. And we have tried to understand these actions as a result of a particular constellation of a given person and his social and cultural environment in a certain stage of joint evolution. In general then, we conceive of a system of separate but interrelated parts, some of them individual and social beings, some of them objects and spaces with certain physical, spatial, temporal, functional, formal etc. characteristics. In semiotics, every single entity that can be differentiated against others and that is also capable of entering a relationship with some other entity, can become a sign.

On the surface, *semiosis or the sign-process* is the process of using and producing such signs. Through semiosis sign-structures are created by some agent on the basis of sign-structures. Functionally, semiosis is a triadic *representational logic* that relates a referent to a representant by mediation of an interpretant.

In the present psychological context, the *interpretant* can be a person or any subsystem thereof. Seen from the outside by the researcher for instance, the person is of course the referent of the researchers semiosis and also a sign, viz. the representant of a highly complex and lengthy sign-process. *Signs* proper, i. e. representants, as well as referents are always *physical structures that carry meaning*. There is no meaning without a physical carrier; even the most abstract idea must be incorporated somewhere and sometime, be it in a brain structure or process or in a linguistic structure, spoken or written (see Lang, 1990). Otherwise it cannot become a component of semiosis and is without effect or nonexistent. Hardly any physical structure is without meaning as soon as it enters a semiotic relation and thus automatically produces a representant for that interpretant; but it has no meaning as such. *Signs are always incorporating aspects from both their referent and their interpretant.* To describe a sign, it is meaningless to give nothing but the specifics of its physical properties; you have to include its referent as well as its interpretant, because any given object can get various representants for different interpretants and thus also may incorporate different referents.

In a psychological interpretation of semiotics, *perception* as well as *action* are considered indeed *prototypical sign-processes.* Both build (sign-)structures that refer, for the particular perceiver or actor, to other (sign-)structures. Perceptions or intro-semioses build them in the brain, actions or extro-semioses in the world; perceptions have their referents in the world, actions in brain structures. And since any sign proper or representant can become the referent of another semiosis, a psychological interpretation of semiotics seems to fit the known facts about people in their environment particularly well.

We also might conceive of inner-brain neural or humoral processes in semiotic terms. Thinking or feeling, conscious or unconscious "mental" streams or states could in principle be understood as chains or nets of semioses. But we know nothing directly about the respective sign-structures used as referents and formed as representants in the brain/mind, except when some of them serve as referents in additional semioses resulting in external (verbal or behavioral) referents. I propose therefore to *concentrate on those sign processes that result particularly from encounters between persons and their surrounding world, i. e. the ecological semioses.* An eco-semiotic approach to person-environment-systems thus is an attempt to treat structure-formation processes within the person and some structure-formation processes outside in similar terms, and thus to emphasize the functional equivalence

of sign-processes originating in the mind with those based on things and places (Lang, in press, 1990).

An important advantage of a semiotic conception of the ecological relation is that there is no need to make any one of the two partners completely dependent on the other. One need not assume that an animal incorporates nothing but the natural laws that govern the surrounding world. Vice versa, man's rationality is not self-sufficient and limitless. In addition, *representants*, in semiotic parlance, are to be sharply distinguished from the common idea of (symbolic) *representations of something*, because the latter are dyadic, the former include a triadic relation. The question of whether a representant is a true or false representation of a referent is meaningless in a semiotic perspective, except when a particular interpretant is specified. This is not to say that sign systems would not vary in ecological efficiency or pragmatic value.

Of course, semioses occur in never ending chains or nets including circular references. Every representant which is a component of one semiosis can become the referent in another. Any given sign-structure stands at the apex of a double "pyramid" of semioses extendend in time. It has on the one hand a history of preceeding semioses, all of which have contributed in various ways to the coming into existence of the given sign. At the same time the sign-structure considered is also at the root of a similar tree of semioses spreading into the future; and this, of course pertains to any sign-structure.

It is meaningful then to investigate the chaining of semioses; the minimal target is a pair of succeeding semioses. Whereas psychology has interested itself in certain aspects of the chaining of a *perceptive* or *intro*-semiosis followed by an *extro-* or *behavioral* semiosis, it has, except in some fields of social psychology, neglected the pairing of an extro-semiosis followed by an intro-semiosis. One could say that in the former case, the world "speaks" to itself by mediation of a living agent. In the second case, a person "speaks" to themself or to other persons by external channels and using messages carried by objects with their potential of representants to become referents. The latter then points to the fact that communicative acts in a very general sense presuppose two chained semioses.

Such considerations lead to the feasibility of *semiotically understanding a person's intercourse with places and things* and thus going beyond the specific material, formal or functional features of a given object or space. As a part of a sign-process a representant turned referent might carry a general *communicative function*. In a study by Daniel Slongo (1990) it has proven useful to interpret things and places in the home in terms of *six general sign-functions*; they have been defined in reference to Karl Bühler and Roman Jakobson and are briefly described in the following paragraphs.

Relatively few things in a room, so it seems in a certain contrast to linguistic communication, become a component of a sign process exclusively by their *notative* or referential function as pointed out by Bühler. Nevertheless, in many rooms we could identify things that in a way stand for or symbolically represent some other persons to the inhabitant or to some of her visitors. Much more prevalent are *appellative* and *expressive* functions of things: chairs invite one to sit down, plants or pets call for regular attention etc.; and many items including decorations, pictures, trinkets, plants etc. placed in neat or sloppy arrangements tell something about their owner.

Preliminary evaluations of the data in the study by Slongo in addition reveal a rather important role of what Jakobson called the *phatic* function of things and places. It is common-sense that things and their arrangements contribute to create atmosphere; but it is an open task to understand how this is brought about, under what circumstances it works, and how recipients of these messages are affected. Furthermore, a *reflexive* (or metacommunicative) and an *autonomous* (or esthetic, poetic) sign function could be distinguished.

In fact no systematic surveys of these functions of household items are available. Csikszentmihalyi & Rochberg-Halton (1981) have sampled the field and also placed the *cultivation of things* in the context of personal and social identity. Although they interpret their social meaning, they have classified things mostly by their use rather than by their communicative function. Investigations into the *psychological process of interacting with and by things and places* are wanting.

References

This chapter is a major rewrite of the paper presented at the congress in September 1989. Some of the theoretical considerations presented at the meeting have been elaborated in Lang (in press), the empirical material has been enhanced, and a sketch of an outlook into further developments of the approach has been added. The author gratefully acknowledges the active cooperation of Daniel Slongo who is actually engaged in elaborating the conception of things as "concrete mind" in his thesis work.

References to Peirce, Bühler and Jakobson have been omitted, since they can be found in major reference books, e. g. in Nöth 1985.

Boesch, Ernst E. (1980) *Kultur und Handlung: Einführung in die Kulturpsychologie.* Bern: Huber. (270 pp.)

Boesch, Ernst E. (1982) Das persönliche Objekt. In: E. D. Lantermann (Ed.) *Wechselwirkungen: Psychologische Analysen der Mensch-Umwelt-Beziehung.* Göttingen: Hogrefe

Boesch, Ernst E. (1983) *Das Magische und das Schöne: zur Symbolik von Objekten und Handlungen.* Stuttgart-BadCannstatt: Frommann-Holzboog. (335 pp.)

Boesch, Ernst E. (1989/90) *Symbolic action theory for cultural psychology* (Provisional Draft 1989/90). Saarbrücken, by the author (to be published 1991 by Springer in Berlin).

Csikszentmihalyi, Mihalyi & Rochberg-Halton, Eugene (1981) *The meaning of things – domestic symbols and the self.* Cambridge: Cambridge Univ. Press

Famos, Sylvia (1989) Dialog junger Menschen mit Dingen im Zimmer: Bedeutung und Topographie wichtiger Objekte im Lebenszusammenhang. Diplomarbeit, Seminar für Angewandte Psychologie Zürich.

Lang, Alfred; Bühlmann, Kilian & Oberli, Eric (1987) Gemeinschaft und Vereinsamung im strukturierten Raum: psychologische Architekturkritik am Beispiel Altersheim. *Schweizerische Zeitschrift für Psychologie 46* (3/4) 277–289.

Lang, Alfred (1988) Die kopernikanische Wende steht in der Psychologie noch aus! – Hinweise auf eine ökologische Entwicklungspsychologie. *Schweizerische Zeitschrift für Psychologie 47* (2/3) 93–108.

Lang, Alfred (1990) Was ich von Kurt Lewin gelernt habe. In: K. Grawe et al. (Eds.) *Über die richtige Art, Psychologie zu betreiben.* Göttingen: Hogrefe, pp. 121–135.

Lang, Alfred (in press) The "concrete mind" heuristic – human identity and social compound from things and buildings. pp. Chapter in: C. Jaeger; M. Nauser & D. Steiner (Eds.) *Human ecology: an integrative approach to environmental problems*. London: Routledge.

Nöth, Winfried (1985) *Handbuch der Semiotik*. Stuttgart: Metzler.

Slongo, Daniel (1990) Zeige mir, wie du wohnst … – eine Begrifflichkeit über externe psychologische Strukturen anhand von Gesprächen über Dinge im Wohnbereich. Diplomarbeit, Psychologisches Institut der Universität Bern.

Thematic Perspectives and Epistemic Principles in Developmental Social Cognition and Social Representation

The Meaning of a Developmental Approach to the Investigation of Social Representations

Annamaria Silvana de Rosa*

Introduction

More than a quarter of a century has passed since the publication of Moscovici's book on the social representation (S. R.) of psycho-analysis (1961) which represents a U-turn in the investigation of the social foundations of knowledge. S-R-inspired literature has developed so widely that it has become a "European paradigm" for the investigation of social world knowledge. It places its emphasis on a *constructive* and *interactionist* perspective, which regards the belief systems and theories that guide the social behaviour of individuals as being not merely cognitive but also the outcome of social processes; it is recognised as an alternative to the *social cognition* model predominant in the United States. The latter, in fact, adopts a fundamentally individualist perspective and attributes the genesis of social behaviour to individual cognitive processes or to an internal mechanism, as in the case of "prototypes" or "cognitive schemata"; these remain in a sense, pre-social, even when the object of investigation is peculiarly social (Forgas, 1981).

Recent attempts to identify significant, plausible interconnections between these two ways of attaining knowledge of the social world (de Paolis, 1986; Augoustinos & Innes, 1987) seem to neglect the *different heuristic horizon of the concept of society* which inspires American social cognition (attribution theory, human information processing) and the European social representation approach. The former is based on a concept of society as a sum of dyadic interpersonal relations (Ugazio, 1988) while the latter refers the genesis of S. R.

back again to the re-elaborative dynamic processes of knowledge activated in social exchange; these are contextualised within an *"organised society"* (Amerio, 1982) as a complex set of class, group and sub-group strata which have various ideological orientations and share different symbolic social meanings and cultural values. However all this only serves to illustrate the need to stimulate an integration between cognitive aspects oriented on the one hand towards the contents and on the other hand towards the processes which guide knowledge of the social world.

Over the last ten years there has been an opening at an interdisciplinary level towards heuristic horizons which have been traditionally held to belong to specific disciplinary areas. Social psychology has discovered "cognition" (Eiser, 1980; Hamilton, 1981; Hastorf & Isen, 1982), or rather rediscovered it, if the historical-epistemological studies of authors who have revised the cognitive roots of social psychology are taken into due account (Zajonc, 1980; Taylor, 1981; Forgas, 1983; Moscovici, 1986; Palmonari, 1987, 1989).

The emphasis placed on the social aspect in developmental psychology (McGurck, 1978; Doise & Palmonari, 1984, 1988; Goodnow, 1988) has echoed this discovery/rediscovery; it was already present, though with a greater socio-determinist outlook, in various theoretical and research approaches: for example, in socio-ethological studies (Bowlby, 1969; Schaffer, 1977; Hinde, 1978; Trevarthen, 1979), social learning studies (Bandura, 1977), social behaviourist work (Staats, 1975) and psycho-linguistic studies of interaction processes in

* Dipartimento di Psicologia dei Processi di Sviluppo e Socializzazione, Università degli Studi "La Sapienza"; via dei Marsi, 78 – 00185 ROMA – ITALIA – tel. 0039-6-446.28.02 electronic mail: derosa@itcaspur.earn

language construction (Bruner & Sherwood, 1981).

Recognition of the importance of the so-cially-connected meanings which individuals and groups give to social situations has led child psychologists to question the nature of children's social knowledge and the way it is constructed; this has also produced research trends which vary in terms of historical origin and theoretical background such as:

1) the trend derived from the Piagetian model, which has shifted its focus of attention from the study of the logical-formal structures of thought to the understanding of situations and social phenomena (Furth, 1978, 1979, 1980; Damon, 1977; Waller, 1978; Berti & Bombi, 1981); for some authors the latter are particularly relevant for moral develop-ment (Kohlberg, 1976). Reviews by Shantz (1975), Barker & Newson (1980), Flavell & Ross (eds. 1981) and Butterworth and Light (eds. 1982) provide a complete picture of the varied Anglo-Saxon literature that follows this line; Ecksenberger and Silbereisen (eds. 1980) do the same for German studies.

2) the line of research dealing with the devel-opment of social competence in the child, such as the ability to perceive/comprehend others whether they be normal (Livesley and Bromley, 1973; Glick & Clarke-Stewart, 1978) or deviant (Coie & Pennington, 1976; Marsden & Kalter, 1977; Dollinger, Thelen & Walsh, 1980).

3) the line of research derived from the exten-sion of cognitive models from general psy-chology, usually adopting an experimental laboratory approach. This trend is made up of:

a) research which looks to "human informa-tion processing theory" (Klahr, 1980; Sie-gler, 1983) and various cognitive models like prototypes, social schemata, scripts etc. (Solso, 1979; Nelson, 1981, 1986; Schank and Abelson, 1977; Abelson, 1981; Siegler, 1983; Mandler, 1983; Arcuri, De Negri Trentin, Job and Salmaso, 1988).

The concept of "script", which is derived from the concept of "social schemata", is defined as the conceptual representation of stereotyped sequences of events which are applicable to frequent conventional situations whose level of generalisation is relatively limited. From this theoretical perspective no distinction is made be-tween social and non social knowledge since the objective is to provide a unifying explanatory picture of comprehension, memory and reasoning. Comprehension and interpretation of an event (social and non-social) are regarded as being the re-sult of the activation of an organised struc-ture in the form of "schema" or "script" i.e. a structure which involves the tem-poral and causal connections between events, including elements relative to in-tentions, aims, rules etc. From the devel-opmental point of view two types of pro-blem are posed: 1) the modes of develop-ment of the scripts; 2) the role of cognitive processes and the gradual increase in so-cial experience in the comprehension and representation of routine episodes through the scripts.

b) research derived from attribution theory examined from a developmental point of view (Kassin, 1981; Lalljee, Watson & White, 1983). Although in much recent research the processes of attribution no longer only refer to inductive types of operation but also involve the influence of pre-existing factors in the conscious sub-ject (anticipation, hypothesis, intuitive theories), it should be noted that the analysis of the way in which the "naive" subject explains, and explains to himself, social and non-social events through a category system is once more dealt with by resorting to inter-individual mechanisms as if the explanation of daily life events was taking place in a "social vacuum" (Tajfel, 1972; Semin, 1980; De Grada & Mannetti, 1988).

4) the line of research into the socio-genesis of intelligence (Doise & Mugny, 1981; Mugny & Carugati, 1985; Mugny, De Paolis & Caru-gati, 1988) and into the role of social inter-action in cognitive development (Perret-Clermont, 1980); within this trend the social world is regarded more as a fundamental element which takes part in the construction of cognitive processes than as an object of knowledge.

The emergence in Europe of a valid social psychology of development (as set out in the

Table 1.

SOCIAL OBJECTS STUDIED	
DEVELOPMENTAL PSYCHOLOGY	SOCIAL PSYCHOLOGY
Social Cognition	*Social Representation*
Inter-individual relations and inter-group comparisons	
moral judgement, rules and conventions, 'role taking'	
Kohlberg, 1963,1969,1971, 1976, et Al. 1983; Hoffman, 1976; Damon, 1977; Furth, 1980; Turiel, 1975, 1978; Feffer & Gourevitch, 1960; Flavell,1968;Higgins,1981; Panier-Bagat, 1982; Barbieri, Legrenzi & Starc, 1986	Emler,1987 *
interpersonal perception and comprehension	
Livesley & Bromley, 1973; Peevers & Secord, 1973; Feffer, 1974; Flavell, 1974; Brooks-Gunn & Lewis, 1975; Selman,1976,1980;Barenboim,1981; Rogers, 1984; French,1984; Dunn, 1988; Miller & Aloise, 1989; Gavin & Furman, 1989	Farr & Moscovici, 1984
interpersonal relations: (concepts of friendship, authority, obedience, cooperation, conflict, power)	
Bigelow, 1977; Damon, 1977; Mannarino,1980 Youniss, 1980; Selman, 1981; Berndt, 1981; Hartup, 1984; Bombi, Celegato & Cristiante, 1985; Fabbri Montesano & Panier Bagat, 1988 a, b	Abric, Faucheux, Moscovici & Plon, 1967; Flament,1967,1971; Codol, 1969; Abric, 1970, 1987; Codol & Flament, 1971; Di Giacomo,1985; Catellani & Quadrio,1988; Catellani, Quadrio & Saitta, 1989*
intelligence and its social definitions	
Wellman & Estes, 1986; Astington, Harris & Olson, 1988; Estes , Wellman & Woolley , in print	Mugny & Carugati, 1985 *; Poeschl, Doise, Mugny, 1985 *; Schurmans, Dasen, Vouilloz, 1989; Carugati, 1990a, 1990b
health, illness and death	
Campbell, 1975; Bibace & Walsh, 1981; Brewster, 1982; Eiser, Patterson & Eiser, 1983; Speece & Brent, 1985 ; Bush, 1987; Burbach & Peterson, 1986; Del Barrio, 1988	Herzlich,1969, 1984; D'Houtaud, 1976 ; 1978; Leventhal, Meyer & Nerenz, 1980; Herzlich & Pierret , 1984; Markova & Wilkie, 1987, et Al. 1989; Laplantine,1989; Mannetti & Pierro, 1989;Aebischer, 1991
mental illness, deviance and handicap	
Marsden , Kalter, et al 1977; Hoffman, Marsden, Kalter, 1977; Mauer, 1979; Dollinger, Thelen & Walsh, 1980 Coie & Pennington, 1976; Gottlieb & Gottlieb, 1977; Voeltz, 1980; Tallandini, 1982; Dobert & Nunner-Winkler1985; Weiss, 1986; Younger, Schwartzman & Ledingham, 1986	Paicheler & Edrei, 1980; Jodelet, 1983, 1987, 1989b; de Rosa, 1985*, 1987a*,1987b,1988a , 1988b, 1988d, 1991a, 1991b, 1991c*,1991d*; Buendia,1985; Deconchy,1985; Ayestaran, 1985; Ayestaran & Paez, 1986; Ayestaran, de Rosa, Paez, 1987*; Schurmans, 1988; de Rosa & Iaculo, 1988*;Bellelli, 1987, 1991; Paez, 1987; Zani, 1987;Morvan, 1988; De Roten, 1989; D'Alessio, 1989*; Duruz, 1989; Becchi, E., Bondioli, A.Mazzoleni,M., 1990; de Rosa & Schurmans,1990a*,1990b*
sexuality, socio-sexual rules and gender	
Bernstein & Cowan, 1975; Goldman & Goldman, 1982; Hutt, 1984; Jagstaidt -Janet, 1984; Amman-Gainotti & Sellardi,1989	Doise & Weinberger, 1972; Deschamps & Doise, 1975*; Giami et al., 1983 ; Aebischer, 1985; Lloyd & Smith, 1985*; Duveen & Lloyd, 1986*; Lloyd, 1986*; Lloyd, Duveen, Smith, 1988*; Lorenzi-Cioldi, 1988
body	
Munari et. al. 1976; Crider, 1981 Amann-Gainotti, 1987, 1988	Jodelet, 1984a

Table 1 continued

Social Cognition	Social Representation
_____Social organisation and institutions_____	
economics: (concepts of work, wealth, property, distribution, social class etc.)	
Jahoda, 1979, 1981; Webley, 1983; Berti, & Bombi, 1981; Ajello, 1984, 1989	Vergès, 1984, 1987; De Polo & Sarchielli, 1983, 1987;Bellelli,Morelli, Petrillo, Serino, 1983*; Silem, 1981 *; Ripon, 1983; Abric, 1984; Emler & Dickinson, 1985*; Duveen & Shields, 1985*; Mannetti & Tanucci, 1988 *; Grize, Vergès, & Silem, 1988; Burgard, Cheyne & Jahoda, 1989*
politics: (concepts of government, law, penal system, country, foreigner etc.)	
Piaget & Weil, 1951; Danziger, 1958; Jahoda, 1964; Adelson & 0'Neil, 1966; Adelson, Green & O'Neil, 1969; Greenstein, 1969, 1974, 1975; Tapp & Kohlberg, 1971; Connell,1970,1971; Furth,1978; Ajello,1984; Amann-Gainotti, 1984	Percheron, 1974*; Percheron, Bonnal, & Boy, Dehan, Grunberg, Subileau, 1978*; Robert P. & Faugeron C. ,1978; Vala, 1981; Louis-Guerin & Brillon,1984; Pierre-Puységur & Corroyer,1986*,1987* Almodovar, 1988*;Pogliani & Quadrio,1988 Quadrio & Venini, 1988; Nigro & Galli, 1988*; Quadrio, Catellani & Sala, 1988; Quadrio & Magrin, 1988
institutions and institutional roles, social services : (family and its transformations, childhood as social category, school, hospital, transport..)	
Bredzinsky , Singer & Braff, 1985; Furth 1976, 1980; Scabini, 1984; Goodnow 1988; Goodnow et al., 1985; Arcuri, De Negri Trentin e Salmaso, 1988; D'Alessio, 1988; D'Alessio & Venini, 1988;	Gilly, 1980, 1986; Mollo,1974,1986 Emiliani, 1982; Emiliani, Zani, Carugati , 1982 ; Emler, Ohana & Moscovici, 1987*; Chombart de Lawve, 1979, 1986; Audigier et. al. , 1986; Palmonari & Zani, 1989; Petrillo, 1990* Corsaro, 1990*; D'Alessio, 1990; Molinari & Emiliani, 1990
city, urban and rural environment	
Sfondrini, 1982; Gaetti e Venini, 1982; Axia, 1986	Ledrut, 1973; Milgran & Jodelet, 1976; Bonnes, 1980; Jodelet 1982; Milgran, 1984; Chombart de Lauwe, 1987 *; de Rosa, Ardone, Bonnes, 1988; de Rosa, 1988c
technology: (electrical circuits, computers, radioactivity etc...)	
Turkle, 1984; Singery- Mason & Varisco, 1987	Tiberghien, Delacotte, 1976*; Bensaid,1984a, 1984b; De Grada, Ercolani, Areni, Sensales, 1987*; Elejabarrieta, 1987; Galli, Nigro, 1987; Nigro, Galli,Poderico, 1988*; Desautels J., Avadon M., Larochelle, M. 1988; Schiele & Boucher, 1989; Vergès, 1991

positions taken by authors such as Doise, Mugny, Palmonari, Carugati, Emler, Duveen amongst others) has highlighted the risk of how in some cases these interdisciplinary changes have merely "borrowed" objects of study rather than brought about real integration of explanatory models.

Objectives

This paper draws upon a more general theoretical model as a result of empirical research carried out over the last ten years (de Rosa, 1984, 1987a, 1987b, 1988a, 1988b, 1988d, 1991a, 1991c) and the recent critical debate on social representation (Farr 1977, 1984, 1987; Bau-bion-Broy, Lapeyr & Malrie, 1977; Ramognino, 1984; Harré, 1984; Le Bouedec, 1979, 1986; Litton & Potter, 1985; Potter & Litton, 1985, 1987; Semin, 1985, 1989; Hewstone, 1985; Doise, 1985a, 1988, 1990; Doise & Palmonari, 1986; Betocchi Villone, 1986; Potter & Wetherell, 1987; McKinlay & Potter, 1987; Parker, 1987; Jahoda, 1988; Moscovici, 1982, 1985, 1988, 1989, 1991a, 1991b; Jodelet, 1984b, 1989a, 1991; Breakwell & Canter, eds. 1989; Beauvois 1988, 1990; Trognon & Larrue 1988; Palmonari, 1980, 1989; Wagner, 1989; de Rosa, 1990a, 1990b, 1990c, 1990d, 1990e, 1991b; Fraser & Gaskell, 1990; Aebischer, Lipiansky & Deconchy 1991).

This article will attempt to set out some notes; its twin objective is:

a) to make a critical comparison between developmental social cognition and social representation;

b) to underline the importance of a developmental approach to the study of social representation.

A. Towards a critical comparison between developmental social cognition and social representation: thematic perspectives and epistemic principles

The table set out above shows the thematic perspectives which developmental and social psychology have followed when identifying common "social" objects of investigation. The table uses a purely thematic criterion for matching and attempts to analyse a large quantity of what might be termed "social cognition" research; this research is oriented from the developmental (including all the above noted trends) and the social representation perspective.

It is clear that the table is necessarily selective and therefore partial and incomplete; it does not claim to provide an exhaustive panorama of the literature on the subject or a critical review of it. The only aim of the table is to underline certain thematic links which can be found in the vast amount of research which uses the two perspectives in question.

The social cognition/social representation subdivision which is attributed to developmental psychology/social psychology is more of a response to the criterion of graphically illustrating the perspectives than to that of definitive bipolarisation: in fact, as is well known, there are both social cognition-inspired research trends in social psychology and social representation-inspired trends in developmental psychology.

The contents of the "social representation" section includes studies carried out on both adults and children: those carried out on children and/or adolescents have been marked with an asterisk.

As table 1 shows there is no doubt that many broad connections can be identified at the "content" level between studies which, though using different perspectives, investigate the same areas of social world knowledge construction and organisation.

Comparative analysis of methodology and

results are essential for further investigation and would be interesting to carry out, but it would not be possible to carry out such a large scale review here. The aim of this article is not a thematic analysis but a comparison between the models and theoretical perspectives of social cognition and social representation.

The first observation to be made is this: as well as the parallelism between objects of study in both the social representation and social schemata approach, prototypes and scripts, the informative elements which organise content through the subjects' active selection processes, are regarded as being hierarchically organised around a central nucleus, though with a different emphasis on social meanings for the former and on logical-formal ones for the latter;

Moreover if the same importance is attached to the study of "content" as is attached to it in the social representation model (Moscovici 1986), researchers will surely be able to benefit from knowledge of investigations which have the same object of study, despite the fact that these investigations have their own theoretical-methodological instruments that are of different epistemological orientation and are used within disciplinary areas like social and developmental psychology which are close but not identical in their historical-heuristic perspectives.

It should be noted however that in social representation the content of representation is a vitally important element in the dynamics of representation (*social representation is always a representation of something (the object) by someone (the subject), whose respective characteristics always affect the representation*).

"It is not the nature of the object which differentaites the social from the non-social but the relationship that is established with it. There are sacred cats and sacred houses while there are human beings regarded as less than objects, for example by their doctors. By blurring the distinction between social elements and interpersonal elements, doubt is cast on a great deal of the work done in the area of social cognition" (Moscovici, 1986: 36 – my translation).

Social representation research tends to stress socially significant variables through which the objects of social knowledge are structured and give form to representations which are shared by individuals and groups.

In a specific reference to research on moral judgement, Emler recently criticised Lickona's claim that:

"Content tells us *what* a person believes, which is obviously dependent on culturally variable experiences, whereas structure tells us how a person *thinks about* the content of his belief; this reasoning, so the theory goes, is universal." (Lickona, 1976).

Emler's criticism is explicit:

"Constructivists use the content-form distinction more generally as a way of handling cultural influences on thought; culture may affect the content but not the form of social knowledge" (Emler 1987: 378).

Apart from similarity in content and their differing relevance for knowledge of the social world, the literature also shows, albeit in an unsystematic way, other elements of convergence and divergence between the American social cognition model and the European social representation one.

Attempts to identify epistemologically significant *transversality* between the two models have been identified:

a) in wide-ranging theoretical analyses which compare large trends – all under the social cognition heading, with the aim of tracing the structural principles which characterise their similarities and differences (Forgas, 1981; Palmonari, 1987, 1989; Ugazio, 1988; Jodelet, 1989a);
b) in more detailed analyses which focus on individual concepts (like schema, script, prototype, representational field etc.: Augostinous & Innes, 1987, 1990; Semin, 1989) or theoretical models (like attribution theory: Hewstone, 1989) or thematic fields (e. g. moral development, Emler, 1987).

In this paper it is not possible to trace the paths these various discussions take. It is sufficient to underline that, although authors have different ideas as to possible integration of the above theoretical approaches, they are all in agreement in recognising a common *"constructivist"* approach to the social knowledge models of American and European social cognition.

In fact these authors recognise that both trends emphasise the *"active structuring of knowledge by the subject"*, both as "naive scientist" and "vehicle of common sense and pre-existing knowledge". However they also stress' *the different acceptance of the concept of "social"* present in the two approaches – the one regarding it purely as a criterion of inter-individual and collective knowledge sharing, and the other as an element which generates that knowledge.

The concept of "social" has often had various ambiguous or generic interpretations made of it in the literature when placed alongside the term "representation" or the even vaguer term "cognition". Moscovici has recently clarified this point:

"By recognising that representations are at the same time both generated and acquired, the prestabilised static nature which representations used to have in the classic interpretation can be avoided. *It is no longer the substrata but the interaction which counts.*

There follows the correct observation that:

"what enables us to call representations "social" is not so much their individual or group supports as the fact that they are elaborated *during processes of exchange and interaction*" (Codol, 1982: 2)". (Moscovici, 1989: 82 – my translation).

Thus it is not the criterion of the common object or of sharing which legitimises the social nature of representations but the logic of the social exchanges which produce them.

Ugazio (1988) rightly identifies integration between constructivism and interactionism as the epistemic element which characterises the European approach to social representations compared to the American approach which,

"by adopting a strictly individual type of contructivism which regards cognitive structures as invariant, ends up with a definition of social psychology as a simple extension of general cognitivist psychology for the study of social stimuli" (Ugazio, 1988: 44)

Similar criticisms have been made by Semin about the making of a distinction between the concepts of prototype and social representation, although they are recognised as being similar in their reality categorising function:

"while the social representation approach emphasises the indispensable aspect of the social element, above all in its treatment of categorisation processes as irreducible to the individual subjective dimension, the prototype approach is based on precisely the opposite. Despite its claim to be working on social categories its objective is to examine the organisation and representation of categories in the mind of the individual ... the essential difference between the two approaches derives from the fact that in the case of the prototype approach the problem is with "internal" mechanisms while in the case of social representations the emphasis is on factors which affect the way in which we order our environment" (Semin, 1989: 245–247 my translation).

Hewstone discusses the possible integration of attribution theory and the social representation model; he recognises that the social representation approach is different from the social cognition one in that it stresses the bases,

Table 2.

SOCIAL COGNITION	SOCIAL REPRESENTATION
constructivist perspective	integration between constructivist and interactionist perspective
individualist perspective (social behaviour explained through individual processes)	interactionist conception based on the dynamics of interpersonal and social exchanges
metaphor of the subject as 'naive scientist' and 'economiser' of cognitive resources	metaphor of the subject as 'actor' of daily life
simplified and non-historical conception of society as collection of individuals linked only by interpersonal relations	conception of 'organised society' (society not as a collection of social atoms, but articulated and stratified in classes, groups, sub-groups)
social world treated in the same way as the natural world, as an object of cognitive operations and categorisation (superiority of the unvarying form over varying contents)	social world treated on the basis of the complexity of its contents and its normative, ideological and value implications (integration between form and content)
social concepts as acquisition within a universal sequence of stages, not socially determined. Social influence is only recognised as facilitating logical operations within problem-solving strategies available in own cultural context (e.g. Piaget's cross-cultural studies)	social concepts as socially trasmitted sets of information, re-elaborated through interaction between individuals and groups and reconstructed by the social actors on the basis of social experience. Importance given to the symbolic order of own culture.
focus on the 'how' and 'why' of knowledge	focus on 'what kind' of representation and 'of what'
cognition as formal and logical structures	representations as set of rational/ non-rational, logical / emotional, normative and evaluative components, with action-guiding value.

contents and social origins of knowledge; it is from these that attributions are forged (Hewstone, 1989: 261).

Thus social representations contribute to clarification of the genesis of attribution processes and the widely shared nature of explanatory causal processes. This view sees social representations not only as the product of cultural determinants, but also the origin of cognitive processes and their inter-individual consensus, the socio-normative background within which the meanings of the explanatory mechanisms used by people to interpret reality are codified.

The distinctive positions of the two approaches to social knowledge construction in the child can thus be summed up as shown in Table 2.

B. Towards a developmental approach to the study of Social Representations

An examination of the functions attributed to social representations (*familiarisation of material and social reality* and *intergroup communication*) will clearly reveal the meaning of proposal oriented in the direction of a developmental and genetic approach.

Anyone with experience of a relationship with a child is aware of their increasing demands for explanations about the world (whether it be social or material) at every unknown word, new figurative element, ambiguous perception or image of unfamiliar situations; they are attempting to find a meaning or a meaningful connection between their infinitely small already-known universe and the infinitely large unknown universe opening up in front of them. How they construct their representational maps day by day, moment by moment, interaction by interaction and experience by experience is a fascinating question for any researcher into social representation, whether they be social psychologist, developmental psychologist or anthropologist.

The part played by "the construction of language-mediated social meanings" (Gumperz, 1982; Rommetveit, 1984; Semin, 1987; Trognon & Larrue) in this process has still to be investigated by means of an integration which would combine the approach of the developmental/interactionsist/psycholinguistic school

with the approach of social psychologists interested in the genesis of social representations and in social representations as generators of socially shared cognitive mechanisms.

If we take up Doise's recent expectation (1988) ("A particularly interesting way of studying the nature of "social world images" must be the study of their genesis in children ..." – my translation), which has often been repeated by Moscovici (1984, 1986, 1990), the importance of a developmental approach to the study of social representations can be summarised as follows:

a) the importance of carrying out research on populations (like classes in various institutional environments or the sibling subsystem in the nuclear family etc.); these provide an ideal opportunity for studying the degree of sharing of representational systems because of their nature as *groups with a history* (see inter alia: Cook-Gumperz, Corsaro & Streck eds., 1986; Corsaro, 1990).

b) the importance of studying the *processes of social consensus construction* i. e. the communicative-interactive means by which a piece of social representation data is transmitted and re-elaborated in relation to the various primary and secondary child socialisation contexts; the reasons for this are the following:

– on the one hand the importance of *symbolic mediations* which intervene in *asymetric exchanges* between the cognitive and representational world of adults and of children and between the universes of children of different ages (see inter alia: Emiliani, 1982; Chombart de Lauwe, 1986; Molinari & Emiliani, 1990; Semin & Papadopoulou, 1990).

– on the other hand the *negotiation of polysemous models of consensual or alternative definition of reality* during adult/child and child/child interaction of social categories which are different in terms of age, sex, socio-economic cultural level) (see e. g.: Emler & Dickinson, 1985; Emler, Ohana & Dickinson, 1990).

In this sense, a developmental approach to the study of social representations provides a good opportunity for examining the *dynamics between S-R development and social influence theory* in a bi-directional perspective of social exchanges, given that:

"children make up a socio-genetic category which is dominated but emotionally tied at an inter-individual level to members of the corrispondingly dominant category – the adults (Chombart de Lauwe, 1986: 101 – my translation)

The micro-ethnographic study (Corsaro, 1990) on children's secondary adjustment to adult social rules in American and Italian nursery schools is an interesting illustrative investigation on the development of social representations as a collective process involving children's interaction with peers and adults.

"First, the analysis of children's secondary adjustments provides evidence that the children share a basic understanding of adult social rules. Secondly, secondary adjustments provide a forum in which children are able to elaborate their own set of social representations. In the process of acquiring a sense of adult social structure, children simultaneously come to produce their own unique peer culture. ... Knowledge of the content of a rule is never sufficient for its application; rules must be applied and intepreted in social context. In this sense children's social representation of adult rules does not involve simply thinking (or cognition) about social life; rather it involves children's psychological activities in their social lives. Children's social representation of adult rules and culture is initially, in line with Vygotsky (1978), always a collective process. Social representations become psychologically active for individual children as a result of their reconstruction of prior shared cultural experiences with adults and peers. To understand fully children's ontogenesis of social representations it is necessary for researchers to be willing to enter children's worlds and peer cultures" (Corsaro, 1990: 14, 25).

c) the importance of studying at a young age the processes of *anchoring* and *objectifying* through which children begin to construct their symbolic order of reality by organising new information into a mosaic of elementary representational maps whose *Gestalten* acquire values which are increasingly more significant at a social level over time (e. g.: the investigations on S. R. of mental illness from childhood to adulthood: de Rosa, 1987b, 1990a; or on S. R. of radioactivity, in statu nascenti, immediately after Chernobyl accident: Nigro, Galli & Poderico, 1988).
Unlike traditional social cognition-inspired research, SR research emphasises not so much cognitive aspects as symbolic aspects or those dealing with integration between conscious and unconscious rational and non-rational aspects. Moscovici has written about this that:

". the concept of social cognition implies a conscious logical process. This is not true for social representations. These are based on conventions and symbols and include conscious, unconscious, rational and irrational aspects. The result of this is that the term "cognitive" is not precise when it is applied to social phenomena. It would be more appropriate to use the word "symbolic", which is not the same thing. It is thus wrong to say that social representations are cognitive representations. Psychosociologists tend to confuse cognitive and symbolic. If, as is claimed, the cognitive revolution is behind them, the symbolic revolution has still to arrive and this also involves general psychologists. Without this revolution, social representations can only provide a small contribution" (Moscovici 1986: 73 – my translation);

d) the importance of studying by longitudinal and cross-cultural research the *consistency over time* (stability versus variability) and *across cultures* (urban/rural, western and non-western etc.) of concepts relative to deteminate social objects from childhood to adulthood. This is particularly important from a transcultural point of view, so that the "comparative by definition" nature of social representations (Moscovici, 1986: 76) can be taken into due account (e. g.: de Rosa, 1984, 1987; Ayesteran, de Rosa, Paez, 1987; Emler, Ohana & Moscovici, 1987; de Rosa & Schurmans, 1990a, 1990b);

e) the importance of studying social knowledge construction processes in relation to variables such as (individual and social) experiential *proximity to/distance from* the objects being studied. This point is well supported by considerations suggested by Markova & Wilkie, 1987; et al. 1989 as regard the powerful source of influence of social representations of people with

HIV/AIDS and haemophilia in parents and close friends;

f) the importance of investigating "ab origine" the social genesis of ties between *representational systems and behavioural strategies* (von Cranach, 1982, 1989; Amerio, 1991) regarding socially relevant aspects such as the processes of inter-group stereotyping and category discrimination etc.

g) the importance of using *open methodologies* which integrate studies based on semi-directed interviews, unstructured material or conversational analysis with studies using observational techniques for the analysis of the interrelations between verbal and non-verbal, thought strategies and plans of action (see: de Rosa, 1990a; Bellelli, 1990; Mannetti, 1990).

Conclusions

The notes contained in this article, which has the twin aim of providing a critical comparison between develomental social cognition and social representation and of underlining the importance of a developmental approach to the study of social representations, does not claim to be exhaustive or original. In fact there are several contributions which have anticipated aspects of the above objectives.

As regards the critical comparison between cognitivist approaches – albeit in socio-psychological terms rather than developmental ones – it was the specific subject of a paper delivered by Moscovici to students at the Université d'Eté in Aix-en-Provence (1981) and published in English (1982) and French (1986); in it the representational model was conceived as the third phase in the cognitive revolution (or reform?) in social psychology, following on from the attitude era and the social cognition era.

However, although a few firm contacts have been made in this comparison (Forgas, 1981; Moscovici, 1982, 1986, 1988, 1989; Palmonari, 1987, 1989; Emler, 1987; Ugazio, 1988; Jodelet, 1989a; Semin, 1989; Hewstone, 1989), it has not prevented ambiguity and blurring of the confines between the two fields.

Editorial work has produced a kind of epistemic confusion: for example, in social representation "readings" or "bibliographiesø,

contributions can be found which are directly inspired by different cognitive psychology models (prototypes, schemata etc.) and where no attention has been paid at a theoretical level to their connection with social representation.

This article has attempted to mark out the thematic horizons and epistemic principles which make up the ground for meeting and differentiation between social cognition in its various expressions and social representation.

As regards the objective of defining the meaning of a developmental approach to the study of social representation, empirical work has been appearing for some years and a few readings specifically oriented in this direction have started to appear recently (Duveen & Lloyd, 1990).

Studies which combine a developmental perspective with an intercultural one (in terms we have already suggested: de Rosa, 1984) aimed at studying the variations in the social representations of specific objects over time and across cultures (such as in the investigations of Ayesteran, de Rosa, Paez, 1987; Emler, Ohana & Moscovici, 1987; de Rosa, Schurmans, 1990a, 1990b) are being usually completely disregarded (see: 'Bibliographie générale sur les représentations sociales' edited by Denise Jodelet & Jocelyne Ohana (Jodelet, 1989a) and bibliography edited by Wolfgang Wagner in periodical newsletter distributed to the participants of 'Social Representations' Communication Network).

We hope that in future an increasing number of studies oriented towards integration of contributions from social psychology, develomental psychology and anthropology, can contribute to the development of the *tridimensional nature* of social representation, defined by Denise Jodelet (1989) as *vitality*, *transversality* and *complexity*.

We conclude with Doise's note:

"Only by explicitly studying the articulation between system and meta-system, between cognitive and social, and providing them with a more elaborate theoretical platform will studies of the development of social cognition be turned into authentic studies of social cogniton" (Doise, 1988: 103 – my translation)

Note

A preliminary version of this paper has been presented – with M. Amman-Gainotti – in the *Sammelband der Zusammenfassungen der Referate, 1. Kongress der Schweizerischen Gesellschaft fur Psychologie – Soziale Vorstellungen und die sozialen Grundlagen des Wissens* (Bern, 31 August–2 September 1989).

The French version of this article was published in *Les Cahiers Internationa ux de Psychologie Sociale*, 1990, 5: 69–109.

Bibliography

N.B. = The following bibliography is too large for an article, but it lists the vast amount of literature whose thematic paths and explanatory principles this article has attempted to set out.

Abelson, R.P. (1981) Psychological status of script concept, *American Psychologist*, vol. 36, 7, 715–729.

Abric, J.C., (1970) Image de la tâche, image du partenaire et coopération en situation de jeu, *Cahiers de Psychologie*, 13, 71–82.

Abric, J.C., Faucheux, C., Moscovici, S. & Plon, H. (1967) Rôle de l'image du partenaire sur la coopérations en situation de jeu, *Psychologie française*, 12, 267–275.

Abric, J.C. (1984) L'artisan et l'artisanat: analyse du contenu et de la structure d'une représentation sociale, *Bulletin de Psychologie*, 37, 861–875.

Abric, J.C. (1987) *Coopération, compétition et représentations sociales*, Fribourg: DelVal.

Adelson, J. O'Neil, R. (1966) Growth of political ideas in adolescence: the sense of comunity, *Journal of Personality and Social Psychology*, 4, 295–306.

Adelson, J, Green, B. O'Neil, R. (1969) Growth of the idea of law in adolescence, *Developmental Psychology*, 1, 327L–32.

Aebischer, V. (1985) *Les femmes et le langage. Les représentations sociales d'une différence*, Paris: P.U.F.

Aebischer, V. Deconchy, J.P. Lipiansky, R. eds. (1991) *Idéologies et répresentations sociales*, Del-Val: Fribourg.

Aebischer, V. (1991) Vers une anthropologie des médicines naturelles, in Aebischer, V., Deconchy, J.P. Lipiansky, R. eds. *Idéologies et répresentations sociales*, DelVal: Fribourg: 183–204.

Ajello, A.M. (1984) Conoscenze sociali e intervento educativo, in C. Pontecorvo ed. *Regole e socializzazione*, Torino: Loescher, 233–300

Ajello, A.M. (1989) Children's informal reasoning in economics: when information is not enough, *Paper presented at Third European Conference for Research on Learning and Instruction* (Madrid, September 4–7 1989)

Almodovar M.J. (1984) L'enfant enjeu de savoirs. A propos de la description psychologique des effets du divorce, *Dialogues*, 86, 59–67.

Almodovar M.J. (1988) Le psy, le juge et l'enfant. La mobilisation des savoirs psychologiques dans l'intervention judiciaire, *Cahiers du CRIV*, 4, 62–72.

Amann-Gainotti, M. (1984) Quelque données sur l'évolution de la représentation du monde social chez des enfants de différents milieux socio-culturels, *Archives de Psychologie*, 52, 17–29

Amann-Gainotti, M. (1987) Pubertà e rappresentazioni dell'evento mestruale, *Psichiatria dell'infanzia e dell'adolescenza*, 54, 3, 261–270

Amann-Gainotti, M. (1988) La rappresentazione dell'interno del corpo. Uno studio evolutivo, *Archivio di Psicologia, Neurologia e Psichiatria*, 4, 480–496.

Amann-Gainbotti, M. & Sellardi, T.(1989) Immagini della gravidanza in soggetti maschi e femmine in età scolare, *Rivista di Scienze Sessuologiche*, 2, 2, 95–104.

Amerio, P. (1980) Alcuni aspetti di articolazione tra lo psichico e il sociale: motivazione, decisione, azione, in P. Amerio, G.P. Quaglino eds. *Mente e società nella ricerca psicologica*, Torino: Book Store.

Amerio, P. (1982) *Teorie in psicologia sociale*, Bologna: Il Mulino.

Amerio, P. (1987) Groupes, représentation et identité sociale, in J.L. Beauvois, R.Joule, J.-M. Monteil eds. *Perspectives cognitives et conduites sociales*, Cousset: Del Val.

Amerio, P. (1991). Idées, sujets et conditions sociales d'existence. in V. Aebischer, J.P. Deconchy, R. Lipiansky (eds) *Idéologies et répresentations sociales*, DelVal: Fribourg: 99–116.

Ayestaran, S. ed. (1985) *Psicologia de la enfermedad mental: ideologia y representacion social de la enfermedad mental*, III Cursos de verano en San Sebastian. Bilbao: Imprenta Boan.

Ayestaran, S. & Paez, D. (1986) Representaciones sociales de la enfermedad mental, *Revista de la Asociacion Espanola de Neuropsiquiatria*, 6: 95–128.

Ayestaran, S., de Rosa A.S., Paez, D. (1987), Representatcion social, processos cognitivos y desarrollo de la cognicion social, in D. Paez ed.

Pensamento, individuo y sociedad. Cognicion y representacion social, Madrid: Editorial Funadamentos, 16–66.

Arcuri, L. (1985) *Conoscenza sociale e processi psicologici,* Bologna: Il Mulino.

Arcuri, L. De Negri Trentin, R. Job, R. & Salmaso, P. (1988) Linee di tendenza nell'organizzazione delle conoscenze sociali. Uno studio evolutivo. in W. Doise & A. Palmonari, *Interazione sociale e sviluppo della persona,* Bologna: Il Mulino, 141–154

Astington, J.W., Harris, P.L. & Olson, D.R. eds. (1988) *Developing theories of mind.* New York: Cambridge University Press.

Audigier et. al. (1986) Représentations des élèves et einsegnement, Paris: INRP, coll. *Rapports de recherche,* 12.

Augoustinos, M. (1990) The mediating role of representations on causal attribution in the social world. *Social behaviour,* 5, 49–62.

Augoustinos, M. & Innes, J.M.(1987) Individual and shared representations of society: social schemata or social representations? *Paper presented at the 16th Annual meeting of Australian Social Psychology,* Canberra, ACT.

Augoustinos, M. & Innes, J.M. (1990). Towards integration of social representations and social schema theory. *British Journal of Social Psychology,* 29: 213–231.

Axia, G. (1986) *La mente ecologica. La conoscenza dell'ambiente nel bambino,* Firenze: Giunti Barbèra.

Bandura, A. (1977) *Social learning theory* Englewood Cliffs, N.J: Prentice-Hall.

Barbieri, M.S., Legrenzi, P. & Starc, R. (1986) Trasgredire: aspetti psicologici delle regole sociali nei bambini, *Giornale Italiano di Psicologia,* XIII, 4: 569–585.

Barker, W.D.L. & Newson, L.J. (1980). The development of cognition sociale: definition and location. In S., & C. Mogdil (eds.), *Towards a Theory of Psychological Development.* Windsor: NFER: 233–67.

Barenboim, C. (1981) The development of person perception in childhood and adolescence: from behavioral comparison to psychological constructs to psychological comparison, *Child Development,* 52, 129–144.

Baubion-Broy, A., Lapeyr, M. & Malrie, P. (1977) Remarques sur la notion de représentation sociale, *Psychologie et Education,* 3: 37–56.

Beauvois, J.L. (1988). *Editorial:* Les représentations sociales, *Connexions,* 51: 5–8.

Beauvois, J.L. (1991). *Processus cognitifs, sociocognitifs, représentationnels et idéologies.* in V. Aebischer, J.P. Deconchy, R. Lipiansky (eds.)

Idéologies et répresentations sociales, DelVal: Fribourg.

Becchi, E., Bondioli, A., & Mazzoleni, M. (1990) Parlare di handicap coi maestri: rappresentazioni e ruoli semantici, *Atti del Convegno 'Le rappresentazioni sociali dell'infanzia: modelli teorici e teorie ingenue' Università degli Studi 'La Sapienza'* (Roma, 16–17 Marzo, 1989). *Rassegna di Psicologia,* 3: 31–63.

Bellelli, G. ed. (1987), *La représentation sociale de la maladie mentale,* Atti del Convegno Internazionale: Le rappresentazioni sociali della malattia mentale (Napoli-S.Maria di Castellabate, SA., 7–10 October 1986). Napoli: Liguori: 29–45.

Bellelli, G. (1990) La tecnica delle associazioni libere nello studio delle rappresentazioni sociali. Aspetti cognitivi e linguistici. *Rassegna di Psicologia,* 3: 17–30.

Bellelli, G. ed. (1991) *L'altra malattia,* Napoli, Liguori (in print)

Bellelli, G. Morelli, M., Petrillo G., Serino, C. (1983) La rappresentazione dei rapporti economici e lo sviluppo degli orientamenti di azioni: una ricerca a partire dal lavoro minorile, *Psicologia e Società,* 3–4, 17–27.

Berndt, T.J. (1981) *Relations between cognition sociale, non-cognition sociale and social behaviour: the case of friendship* in J.H. Flavell & L. Ross eds. *Social cognitive development,* Cambridge: Cambridge University Press, 176–99

Bernstein A.C. & Cowan P.A. (1975) Children's concepts of how people get babies. *Child Development,* 46, 1, 77–91.

Berti A.E. & Bombi, A.S. (1981) *Il mondo economico nel bambino,* Firenze: La Nuova Italia.

Betocchi Villone, G. ed. (1986) Problemi di metodologia di studio delle rappresentazioni sociali, *Psicologia e Società,* Numero speciale

Bigelow, B.J. (1977) Children's friendship expectations: a cognitive-developmental study, *Child Development,* 48, 246–253.

Bilbace, R. & Walsh, M. (1981) Children's conceptions of illness. in R. Bilbace, & M. Walsh, eds. *Children's conceptions of health, illness and body functions. New Directions for Child Development,* 14, San Francisco: Jossey Bass, 34–42.

Bombi, A.S, Celegato, R. & Cristiante, F. (1985) Children's representations of friends and enemies, *Proceedings of the Eight Biennal Meeting of ISSBD* (Tours, 6–10 July 1985)

Bonnes, M. (1980) La rappresentazione dello spazio ambientale come possibile concetto-cerniera tra lo psichico ed il sociale, in P. Amerio, G.P. Quaglino eds. *Mente e società nella ricerca psicologica,* Torino: Book Store.

Bowlby, J. (1969) *Attachment and loss,* vol. 1 Attachment, New York: Basic Books.

Breackwell G. & Canter, D. eds (1989) *Empirical approaches to social representations*, Oxford: Oxford University Press.

Bredzinsky D., Singer L.M. & Braff A.M. (1984) Children's understanding of adoption. *Child Development,* 55, 869–878.

Brewster, A.B. (1982) Cronically ill children's concept of their illness, *Pediatrics*, 69, 3, 355–362.

Brooks-Gunn, J. & Lewis, M. (1975) Person perception and verbal labelling: the development of social labels, Paper presented at the *Congress of the Eastern Psychological Association*, New York.

Bruner, J. & Sherwood, V. (1981) Thought, language and interaction in infancy. In P. Forgas ed. *Cognition sociale*. London: Academic Press, 27–52.

Buendia, J.M. (1985) El tratamiento de la enfermedad mental. Su representacion social en la poblacion murciana, *Psiquis*, 3–85.

Burbach, D.J. & Peterson, L. (1986) Children's concepts of physical illness: a review of the cognitive-developmental literature, *Health Psychology*, 5, 3, 307–325.

Burgard, P., Cheyne, W.M. & Jahoda, G. (1989) Children's representations of economic inequality: a replication, *British Journal of Developmental Psychology*, 7: 275–287.

Bush, J.P. (1987) Pain in children. A review of the literature from a developmental perspective, *Psychology and health*, 1, 215–236.

Butterworth, G. & Light, P. eds. (1982) *Cognition sociale*. Chicago: The University of Chicago Press.

Campbell, L. (1975) Illness is a point of view: the development of children's concepts of illness, *Child development*, 46, 92–100.

Carugati, F. (1990a) From social cognition to social representation in the study of intelligence. In Duveen, G.& Lloyd, B eds. *Social representations and the development of knowledge*, Cambridge: Cambridge University Press: 126–143.

Carugati, F. (1990b) Everyday ideas, theoretical models and social representations: the case of intelligence and its development, in G. Semin & K.H. Gergen, *Everyday understanding . Social and scientific implications*, London: Sage.

Catellani, P. & Quadrio, A. (1988) La rappresentazione sociale del nemico pubblico e del nemico privato, *Giornale Italiano di Psicologia*, 4.

Catellani, P. Quadrio, A., Saitta E. (1989) Livello iconico e livello verbale nella rappresentazione sociale del nemico in età evolutiva. *Contributi del Dipartimento di Psicologia*, I.S.U. Università Cattolica di Milano: 71–85.

Chandler, M.J. (1977) Cognition sociale: a selective review of current research. in Overton, *Knowledge and development*, New York: Pergamon Press.

Chombart de Lauwe, M.J. (1979) *Un monde autre: l'enfance. De ses représentations à son mythe,* Paris: Payot.

Chombart de Lauwe, M.J. (1987) *Espaces d'enfants,* Cousset: DelVal.

Chombart de Lauwe, M.J. (1986) Liens entre les représentations véhiculées sur l'enfant et les représentations intériorisées par les enfants. In W. Doise & A. Palmonari, *L'étude des Représentations sociales*, Delachaux et Niestlé: Lausanne.

Chombart de Lauwe, M.J. & Nelly Feuerhahn (1989) La représentation sociale dans le domaine de l'enfance in D. Jodelet (1989) *Les représentations sociales*, Paris: P.U.F.

Codol, J.P. (1969) Représentation de soi, d'autrui et de la tâche dans une situaztion sociale, *Psychologie française,* 14, 217–228.

Codol, J.P. & Flament C. (1971) Représentations de structures sociales simples dans lesquelles le sujet est impliqué, *Cahiers de Psychologie,* 14, 203–218.

Coie J.D. & Pennington B.F. (1976) *Children's perceptions of deviance and disorder*, Child Development, 1976, 47, 4O7–413.

Connell, R.W. (1970) Class consciousness in childhood. in *Australian and New Zeland Journal of Sociology*, 6, 87–99.

Connell, R.W. (1971) *The child's construction of politics,* Carlton: Melbourne University Press.

Cook-Gumperz J., Corsaro W. & Streeck eds. (1986) *Children's Worlds and Children's Language*. Berlin: Mouton.

Corsaro, W.A. (1990) The underlife of the nursery school: young children's social representations of adult rules. In Duveen, G.& Lloyd, B (1990) *Social representations and the development of knowledge*, Cambridge: Cambridge University Press: 11–26.

Crider, C. (1981) Children's conceptions of the body interior, *New directions for child development,* 14, 49–66.

D'Alessio M. (1988) La rappresentazione del neonato tra natura e cultura,in M. D'Alessio ed. *Psicologia neonatale*, Firenze: Nuova Italia Scientifica, 205–217.

D'Alessio, M. (1989) La rappresentazione del matto in età evolutiva, *Marginalità e società*, 6, 86–130.

D'Alessio, M. (1990) Childhood representation: an implicit theory of develoment, in B. Lloyd & G. Duveen, *Social representation and the development of knowledge*, Cambridge: Cambridge University Press: 70–90.

D'Alessio M. & Venini L. (1988) Modelli e tipologie

familiari nelle rappresentazioni infantili, *Psicologia e Società*, 3–4, 35–52.

D'Alessio, M. & Venini, L. (1989) La rappresentazione delle emozioni infantili in un campione di bambini, adolescenti e giovani. *Contributi del Dipartimento di Psicologia*, Università Cattolica di Milano, vol. 3, 99–114.

Damon, W. (1977) *The social world of the child*, San Francisco: Jossey-Bass Publishers.

Damon, W. (1979) Why study social-cognitive development?, *Human Development*, 22, 206–211.

Damon, W. (1981) Exploring children's cognition sociale on two fronts, in J. Flavell & L. Ross eds. *Social cognitive development*, Cambridge: Cambridge University Press, 154–175.

Danziger, K. (1958) Children's earliest conceptions of economic relations (Australia), *The Journal of Social Psychology*, 47, 231–240.

Dasen P. & Heron A.(1981) Cross-cultural tests of Piaget's theory. In H. Triandis & A. Heron eds. *Handbook of cross-cultural psychology*, vol. 4 Developmental psychology, Boston: Alyn & Bacon.

Deconchy, J. P. (1984) Systèmes de croyance et représentations idéologiques. in S. Moscovici, *Psychologie Sociale,* Paris: P.U.F.: 331–355.

Deconchy, J. P., (1985) *La représentation du' malade mentale et évaluations morales*. Colloque "Handicapés et Université" (Paris-Nanterre, 18–2O giugno 1985).

Deconchy, J. P. (1991) Mécanismes idéologieques et représentations idéographiques. Essai de recherche expérimentale. in V. Aebischer, J. P. Deconchy,R. Lipiansky (eds.) *Idéologies et répresentations sociales,* DelVal: Fribourg: 205–234.

De Grada, E. Ercolani, A. P., Areni, A. & Sensales, G. (1987) La rappresentazione del computer in gruppi diversi della popolazione, *Rassegna di Psicologia*, 2/3, 5–24.

De Grada, E. & Mannetti, L. (1988) *L'attribuzione causale. Teorie classiche e sviluppi recenti*, Bologna: Il Mulino.

D'Houtaud A. (1976) Les représentations sociales de la santé. *Revue internationale de l'education pour la santé*, 19, 99–118 et 173–190.

D'Houtaud A. (1978) L'image de la santé dans une population lorraine: approche psychologique des représentations de la santé, *Revue d'Epidémiologie et de Santé publique*, 26, 299–320.

Del Barrio C. (1988) El desarrollo de la explicacion de processos biologicos: como entienden los ninos la causa de una enfermedad y su curacion. *Infancia y Apprendizaje*, 42, 81–95.

Del Val, J. (1981) La representacion infantil del mundo social, *Infancia y Aprendizaje*, 13: 35–67.

De Polo, M. & Sarchielli, G. (1983) Le rappresentazioni sociali del lavoro, *Giornale Italiano di Psicologia*, 3: 501–519.

De Polo, M. & Sarchielli G. (1987) *Psicologia della disoccupazione*, Bologna: Il Mulino.

de Rosa, A. S. (1984) Psychogenetic Aspects in Social Representations of 'Mad Person' and 'Madness'. In S. Ayestaran Etxeberria (ed.), *Psicosociologia de la Enfermedad Mental: Ideologia y Representacion Social de la Enfermedad Mental.* III Cursos de Verano en San Sebastian. Bilbao: Imprenta Boan: 219–84.

de Rosa, A. S. (1987a.) Différents niveaux d'analyse du concept de représentation sociale en relation aux méthodes utilisées. in Bellelli G. ed. *La représentation social de la maladie mentale,* Napoli: Liguori: 47–63.

de Rosa, A. S. (1987b) The social representations of mental illness in children and adults. In Doise W. e Moscovici S. (eds.) *Current Issues in Social Psychology,* Cambridge: Cambridge University Press: 47–138.

de Rosa, A. S. (1988a.) Il folle e la follia nelle rappresentazioni sociali 'naives' e 'scientifiche' in *Gravità della psichiatria,*a cura della Società di Psichiatria Democratica Centro Italia, Bulzoni: Roma: 265–277.

de Rosa, A. S. (1988b.) Sur l'usage des associations libres dans l'étude des représentations sociales de la maladie mentale, *Connexions*, 51: 27–50.

de Rosa, A. S.(1988c) 'Place-identity' et évaluation de l'environment urbain, *Acts du Colloque Europeen: 'Contenu et fonctionnement de l'identité'* (Aix-en-Provence, March 10–12 1988): 37–46.

de Rosa, A.S. (1988d.) Aspetti strutturali e di contenuto nelle rappresentazioni sociali della malattia mentale in gruppi naïves e di 'esperti'. in V. Mayer & R. Meran (eds.) *Il Laboratorio e la città*, Milano: Guerini & Associati, I: 799–809.

de Rosa, A.S. (1990a) Per un approccio multi-metodo allo studio delle Rappresentazioni Sociali, *Rassegna di Psicologia*, 3: 101–152.

de Rosa, A.S. (1990b) Dalla teoria alla meta-teoria sulle cognizioni sociali: linee emergenti di un dibattito critico, *V Congresso Nazionale della Divisione di Psicologia Sociale, Società Italiana di Psicologia (*Milan, March 27–29 1990).

de Rosa, A.S. (1990c) Contents, methods and levels of explanation in social cognition and social representation approaches, *General meeting of European Association of Experimental Social Psychology* (Budapest, June, 19–23 1990).

de Rosa, A.S. (1990d) Social Cognition and Social Representations: two ways towards knowledge of the social world?, *First European Meeting on Social Cognition, Max-Planck-Institut für Psycholo-*

gische Forschung (München, September 10–15 1990).

de Rosa, A.S. (1990e.) Considérations pour une comparaison critique entre les R.S. et la Social Cognition. Sur la signification d'une approche psychogénetique à l'étude des représentations sociales, *Cahiers Internationaux de Psychologie Sociale*, 5: 69–109.

de Rosa, A.S. (1991a) Idéologie médicale et non-médicale et son rapport avec les répresentations sociales de la maladie mentale. In V. Aebischer, J.P. Dechonchy R. Lipiansky (eds.), *Idéologies et représentations sociales*, Fribourg: Delval: 235–272 .

de Rosa, A.S. (1991b) La società e il malato mentale: opinioni, atteggiamenti, stigmatizzazioni e pregiudizi. in Bellelli, G. ed. *L'altra malattia*, Napoli: Liguori (in print).

de Rosa, A.S. (1991c) Agenzie di socializzazione e rappresentazioni della malattia mentale in età evolutiva . in Bellelli, G. ed. *L'altra malattia*, Napoli, Liguori (in print).

de Rosa, A.S. ed. (1991d) *Se per la strada incontri un matto. Sviluppo dei sistemi di credenze e risposta sociale alla devianza in bambini e adolescenti*, Milano: F. Angeli (in print).

de Rosa, A.S. (1991e). *Atteggiamenti emotivi e rappresentazione del sistema familiare*, Firenze, O.S. (in print).

de Rosa, A.S. (1991f) Social cognition e Rappresentazioni Sociali in prospettiva evolutiva: una doppia via alla conoscenza del mondo sociale? *Rassegna di Psicologia*, 3 (in print).

de Rosa, A.S., Ardone R.G. & Bonnes M. (1988) Rappresentazione dell'ambiente urbano e 'place-identity', in V. Mayer & R. Meran, a cura di, *Il Laboratorio e la città*, Milano: Guerini & Associati, I: 519–527.

de Rosa, A.S. & Iaculo, G. (1988) Struttura e contenuti della rappresentazione sociale del 'malato mentale' in bambini, genitori ed insegnanti. *Rassegna di Psicologia*, V., 1: 21–54.

de Rosa, A.S. & Schurmans, M.N. (1990a) Madness imagery across two countries, *Rassegna di Psicologia*, 3: 177–193.

de Rosa, A.S. & Schurmans, M.N. (1990b). Immaginario e follia nelle rappresentazioni sociali di bambini e adolescenti di due Paesi Europei, *Psicologia Clinica*, 3: 297–340.

De Roten, Y. (1989) Représentations sociales de la pathologie mentale mesurées à l'aide du différenciateur sémantique d'Osgood. Comparison entre des professionnels du monde psychiatrique et des non-professionnels, *Recueil des résumés des exposés, 1er Congrès de la Société Suisse de Psychologie Représentations sociales et fondaments sociaux du savoir*, 82.

Desautels J., Avadon, M., Larochelle, M. (1988) La représentattion de la science véhiculée par les programmes d'enseignement des sciences du ministère de l'Education au secondaire. *Collection du Laboratoire de Recherche sociologique de l'Université Laval*.

Deschamps, J.C. (1973–74) L'attribution, la catégorisation sociale, et les représentations inter-groupes. *Bulletin de Psychologie*, 27, 710–721.

Deschamps, J. C. & Doise, W. (1975) Evolution des représentations inter-sexes entre 7 et 13 ans, *Revue Suisse de Sociologie*, 1, 107–128.

Di Giacomo, J. P.(1981) Aspects méthodologiques de l'analyse des représentations sociales. *Cahiers de Psychologie Cognitive*. 1: 397–422.

Di Giacomo, J. P. (1985) *Rappresentazioni sociali e movimenti collettivi*. Napoli: Liguori.

Dobert R., Nunner-Winkler G. (1985) Interplay of formal and material role-taking in the understanding of suicide among adolescents and young adults. *Human Development*, 28, 225–239.

Doise W.(1982). *L'explication en psychologie sociale*, P. U. F.: Paris.

Doise W. (1984) Levels of analysis in the experimental study of intergroup relations. in Moscovici S. & Farr R. (eds.) *Social representations*, Cambridge University Press: Cambridge: 255–268.

Doise W.(1985a.) Les représentations sociales: definition d'un concept, *Connexions,*45: 243–253.

Doise W.(1985b) Psychologie sociale et constructivisme cognitif. *Archives de psychologie*, 53: 127–140.

Doise, W. (1985c.) Représentations sociales chez des élèves: effets du statut scolaire et de l'origine sociale, *Revue Suisse de Psychologie*, 44, 67–78.

Doise W. (1987a.) Le social et l'individuel: théories générales et recherches intergroupes. *Psychologie et éducation*, 11: 57–74.

Doise W. (1987b.) Pratiques scientifiques et représentations sociales: que faire de la psychologie de Piaget? . *Cahiers du centre de recherche interdisciplinaire de Vaucresson*, 3: 89–108.

Doise, W. (1988) Les représentations sociales: un label de qualité, *Connexions,* n.51: 99–113.

Doise, W. (1989) Cognitions et représentations sociales: l'approche génétique in D. Jodelet ed. *Les représentations sociales*. Paris: P.U.F., 341–362.

Doise, W. (1990) Les représentations sociales. In C. Bonnet, R. Ghiglione & T.F. Richard eds. *Traité de Psychologie Cognitive*, Paris: Dunod.

Doise, W. & Lorenzi-Cioldi, F. (1991) L'identité comme représentation sociale. in V. Aebischer, J.P. Deconchy, R. Lipiansky, *Idéologies et répresentations sociales*, DelVal: Fribourg: 273–286.

Doise, W. & Mugny, G. (1981) *La costruzione sociale dell'intelligenza,* Bologna: Il Mulino.

Doise, W. & Palmonari, A. (1984) Introduction: *The sociopsychological study of individual development* in W. Doise & A. Palmonari eds. *Social interaction in individual development* Cambridge/Paris: Cambridge University Press/ Editions de la Maison des Sciences de l'Homme: 2–22.

Doise, W. & Palmonari, A. eds. (1986) *L'étude des représentations sociales,* Paris: Delachaux & Niestlé.

Doise, W. & Palmonari, A.(1988), *Lo studio sociopsicologico dello sviluppo individuale* in W. Doise & A. Palmonari eds.*Interazione sociale e sviluppo della persona*, Bologna: Il Mulino, 11–30.

Doise, W. & Papastamou, S.(1987) Représentations sociales des causes de la délinquance: croyances générales et cas concrets. *Déviance et Société*, 11, 153–162.

Doise, W. & Weinberger, M. (1972–73) Représentations masculines dans différentes situations de rencontres mixtes, *Bulletin de Psychologie*, 26, 649–657.

Doise, W., Meyer, G. & Perret-Clermont, A.N. (1976) Etude psychosociologique des représentations d'élèves en fin de scolarité obligatoire. *Cahiers de la Section des Sciences de l'Education*, 11, 15–27.

Dollinger S.J., Thelen M.H. & Walsh M.L. (1980) *Children's conceptions of psychological problems*, Journal of Clinical Child Psychology, vol. 9 (3), 191–194.

Dunn, J. (1988) *The beginnings of social undesrtanding,* Cambridge: Harvard University Press.

Duruz, N. (1989) Discours d'experts, discours populaire concernant la pathologie mentale,*Recueil des résumés des exposés, 1er Congrès de la Société Suisse de Psychologie Représentations sociales et fondaments sociaux du savoir,* 83–84.

Duveen, G. & Lloyd, B. (1986) The significance of social identities, *British Journal of Social Psychology*, 25, 219–230.

Duveen, G. & Lloyd, B. (1990) *Social representations and the development of knowledge*, Cambridge: Cambridge University Press .

Duveen G., Shields M. (1985) Children's ideas about work, wages and social rank. *Cahiers de Psychologie Cognitive*, 5, 411–412.

Eckensberger, L.H. & Silbereisen, R.K. eds. (1980) *Entwicklung sozialer kognitionen*, Stuttgart: Klett-Cotta.

Eiser, J.R. (1980) *Cognitive social psychology,* Maidenhead: McGraw-Hill.

Eiser, C. Patterson, D. & Eiser, R. (1983) Children's knowledge of health and illness: implications for health education, *Child, care, health and development,* 9, 285–292.

Elejabarrieta, F.J. (1987) La teoria de las representaciones sociales y su aplicacion en el estudio del conocimiento social de la informatica, *Boletin de Psicologia*, 1987, 15, 7–31.

Emiliani, F. (1982) Azione concreta e rappresentazione sociale: uno studio su operatrici di asilo nido. *Giornale Italiano di Psicologia*, 1, 143–151.

Emiliani, F. Zani, B. & Carugati F. (1982) Il bambino e l'asilo nido. Immagini a confronto. *Giornale Italiano di Psicologia*, 3, 455–468.

Emler, N. (1987) Socio-moral development from the perspective of social representations, *Journal for the theory of Social Behaviour* 17 4, 371–388.

Emler N. & Dickinson J. (1985) Children's representation of economic inequalities: the effect of social class, *British Journal of developmental Psychology*, 3, 191–198.

Emler, N. Ohana J. & Dickinson, J. (1990) Children's representations of social relations. in Duveen, G. & Lloyd, B. (1990) *Social representations and the development of knowledge*, Cambridge: Cambridge University Press: 47–69.

Emler N., Ohana J. & Moscovici (1987) Children's beliefs about institutional roles: a cross-national study of representations of the teacher's role, *British Journal of Educational Psychology*, 57, 28–36.

Estes, D. Wellman, H.M. & Wolley, J.D. (in press) Children's understanding of mental phenomena. *Advances in Child Development*.

Fabbri Montesano D. & Panier Bagat M. (1988a) Normes et valeurs: le concept d'obéissance chez l'enfant. *Archives de Psychologie,* 56, 23–39.

Fabbri Montesano D. & Panier Bagat M. (1988b) Lo sviluppo del concetto di potere: analisi di relazioni interpersonali efettuate da bambini di età compresa fra i 5 e gli 11 anni, *Attualità in Psicologia*, 3, 3, 9–19.

Farr, R. M.(1977). Heider, Harré and Herzlich, on health and illness: Some observation on the structure of 'représentations collectives', *European Journal of Social Psychology,* 7: 491–504.

Farr, R. M. (1984) Les représentations sociales in S. Moscovici ed. *Psychologie sociale*, Paris: P.U.F., 379–389.

Farr, R.M. (1987) *Social representations. Special Issue. Journal for the theory of social behavior,* 17, 4.

Farr, R.M. & Moscovici, S. eds. (1984a). *Social Representations.* Cambridge: Cambridge University Press.

Farr, R.M. & Moscovici, S. (1984b) On the nature and role of representations in self's understanding of others and of self, in M. Cook ed.

Progress in Person Perception, London: Methuen.

Faugeron, C. & Robert, P. (1976) Les représentations sociales de la justice pénale, *Cahiers internationaux de Sociologie*, 61, 341–366.

Feffer M.(1974) A development of inference about other in T. Mishel, *Understanding other persons*, Oxford England: Blackwell.

Feffer, M.H. & Gourevitch, V. (1960) Cognitive aspects of role taking in children, *Journal of Personality*, 28, 383–96.

Feuerhahn, N (1985) Approche des représentations sociales de l'image de soi dans l'expression graphique, *Bulletin de Psychologie,* 38, 267–273.

Fincham, F. D. (1983) Developmental dimensions of attribution theory. in J. Jaspars, F.D. Fincham & M. Hewstone eds. *Attribution theory and research: conceptual, developmental and social dimensions*, London: Academic Press: 117–164.

Fiske, S.T. & Taylor, S.E. (1984) *Cognition sociale*, Reading: Addison Wesley.

Flament, C. (1967) Représentations dans une situation conflictuelle: une étude interculturelle, *Psychologie Française*, 12, 207–304.

Flament, C. (1871) Image des relations amicales dans les groupes hiérarchisés, *Année psychologique*, 71, 117–126.

Flament C. (1986). L'analyse de similitude: une technique pour les recherches sur les R.S. in Doise W et Palmonari A. *L'étude des R.S.,* Delachaux et Nestlé, Paris.

Flavell, J.H. (1968) *The development of role-taking and communication skills in children*, New York: Wiley.

Flavell, J.H. (1974) The development of inference about others. in T. Mishel, *Understanding other persons*, New Jersey: Rowman & Littlefield.

Flavell, J.H. & Ross, L. eds. (1981) *Social cognitive development*, Cambridge: Cambridge University Press.

Forgas, J.P. ed. (1981) *Cognition sociale. Perspectives on Everyday Understanding.* London: Academic Press: .

Forgas (1983) What is social about cognition sociale?, *British Journal of Social Psychology*, 22, 129–144.

Fraser, C. & Gaskell, G. eds. (1990) *The social psychological study of widespread beliefs*, Oxford: Oxford University Press.

French D.C. (1984) Children's knowledge of the social functions of younger, older and same age peers . *Child Development,* 55, 1429–1433.

Furth, H.G. (1978) *Young children's understanding of society*, H. McGurk ed. *Issues in childhood social development*, London: Methuen.

Furth, H.G. (1979) *How do children understand so-*

cial institutions, F. Murray ed. *The impact of piagetian theory,* Baltimore: University Park Press.

Furth, H.G. (1980) *The world of grown-ups*, New York: Elsevier.

Gaetti A., Venini L. (1982) L'incidenza della zona di residenza urbana sull'elaborazione cognitiva dell'immagine di città. Ricerca su un campione di bambini milanesi. *Ricerche di Psicologia*, VI, 22–23, 187–201.

Galli, I, Nigro, G. (1987) The social representation of radioactivity among italian children, *Social science information*, 25, 535–549.

Gavin, L.A. & Furman, W. (1989) Age differences in adolescents' percpetions of their groups, *Developmental Psychology*, 25, 5: 827–834.

Giami A., Humbert-Viverat C., Laval D. (1983) *L'ange et la bête. Représentation de la sexualité des handicapés mentaux*, Paris: Ed du CTNERHI.

Gilly M. (1980) *Maître-élèves: rôles institutionnels et représentations*. Paris: P.U.F.

Gilly M.(1986) Institutional roles, partner's representations and attitudes in educational interactions, in J.M. De Corte, J.G.L.C. Lodewijks, P.Parmentier, P. Span eds. *Learning and instruction*, Oxford Leuven: Pergamon Books.

Giust-Desprairies F. (1988) Le sujet dans la représentation sociale, *Connexions*, n.51; 83–98.

Glick, J. & Clarke-Stewart, K.A. (1978) *The development of social understanding*, New York: Gardner Press.

Goodnow, J. (1988) Parents' ideas, action and feelings: models and methods from development and social psychology, *Child Development*, 59, 286–320.

Goodnow, J., Knight, R. & Cashmore, J. (1985) *Adult cognition sociale: implications of parents' ideas for approaches to development.* in M. Perlmutter ed. *Cognition sociale*, Hillsdale, N.J.: Erlbaum.

Goldmann R. & Goldmann Y. (1982) *Children's sexual thinking.* Routledge and Kagan, London.

Gottlieb J. & Gottlieb, B.W. (1977) Stereotypic attitudes and behavioral intentions towards handicapped children, *American Journal of mental deficency*, vol 82, 1, 65–71.

Green, J. & Wallat, C. eds. (1981) *Ethnography and Language in Educational Settings*. Norwood, N.J.: Ablex.

Greenstein, F.I. (1969) *Children and politics,* New Haven: Yale University Press.

Greenstein, F.I. (1974) The king leader: a child's view of the President, *New York Society*, 19, 751–53.

Greenstein, F.I. (1975) The benevolent leader revisited: children's images of political leaders in three democracies, *American Political Science Review*, 69, 1371–99.

Grize, J.B., Vergès, P. & Silem, A. (1988) *Les salariés face aux nouvelles technologies. Vers un approche socio-logique des représentations sociales*, Paris: CNRS.

Gumperz, J. (1982) *Language and Social Identity*. Cambridge: Cambridge University Press.

Hamilton, M. (1981) *Cognitive processes in stereotyping and intergroup behaviour*, Hillsdale: Erlbaum.

Harré, R. (1984). Some reflections on the concept of 'social representation' *Social research*, 51: 927–938.

Hartup, W.W. (1984) I bambini e i loro amici, In H. McGurck ed., *Lo sviluppo sociale del bambino*, Torino: Boringhieri.

Hastorf A., & Isen A.M. (1982) *Cognitive social psychology*, New York: Elservier.

Herzlich, C. (1969) *Santé et maladie. Analyse d'une représentation sociale*. Prais: Mouton.

Herzlich, C.(1984) La problématique de la représentation sociale et son utilité dans le champ de la maladie. *Sciences Sociales et Santé*. 2 (2): 71–84.

Herzlich, C. & Pierret, J. (1984) *Malades d'hier, Malades d'aujourd'hui. De la mort collective au devoir de guérison*. Paris: Payot.

Hewstone M. ed. (1983) *Attribution Theory: Social and Functional Extensions*. Oxford: Basil Blackwell.

Hewstone, M. (1985) On common-sense and social representations: a reply to Potter & Litton.*British Journal of Social Psychology*. 24: 95–97.

Hewstone, M. (1989) Represéntations sociales et causalité in D. Jodelet ed. *Les représentations sociales*. Paris: P.U.F., 252–276.

Higgins, E.T. (1981) Role taking and social judgment: alternative developmental perspectives and processes, in J. Flavell & L. Ross eds. *Social cognitive development*, Cambridge: Cambridge University Press, 119–153.

Higgins, E.T., Herman, C.P., Zanna, M.P. eds. (1981) *Social Cognition: The Ontario Symposium*, Hillsdale: Erlbaum.

Higgins E.T. & Parson, W. (1983) Cognition sociale and the social life of the child: stage as subcultures. in E.T. Higgins, D.N. Ruble & W.W. Hartup eds. *Cognition sociale and social development*, Cambridge: Cambridge University Press.

Hinde, R. A. (1978) Social development: a biographical approach. in J. Bruner & A. Garton eds., *Human growth and development*. Oxford: Clarendon Press.

Hoffman, E., Marsden, G. & Kalter, N. (1977) Children's undesrstanding of their emotionally disturbed peers: a replication, *Journal of Clinical Psychology*, 33, 4: 949–953.

Hoffman, M.L. (1976) Empathy, role-taking, guilt and the development of altruistic motives, in T. Lickona ed. *Moral development and behavior*, New York: Holt, Rinehart and Winston.

Hoffman, M.L. (1981) Perspectives on the difference between understanding people and understanding things: the role of affect. in J. Flavell & L. Ross eds. *Social cognitive development*, Cambridge: Cambridge University Press, 67–81.

Hutt, C. (1984) La differenziazione dei ruoli sessuali nello sviluppo (1984) McGurck ed., *Lo sviluppo sociale del bambino*, Torino: Boringhieri.

Ibanez Gracia, T. (1988) *Ideologias de la vida cotidiana*, Barcellona: Sendai.

Jagstaidt-Janet, V. (1984) *La sexualité et l'enfant*, Neuchàtel: Delachaux et Niestlè.

Jahoda, G. (1964) Children's concepts of nationality: a critical study of Piaget's stages, *Child Development*, 35, 1081–92.

Jahoda, G. (1979) The construction of economic reality by some glaswegian children, *European Journal of Social Psychology*, 9, 115–27.

Jahoda, G. (1981) The development of thinking about economic institutions: the bank, *Cahiers de Psychologie Cognitive*, 1, 55–73.

Jahoda G.(1988) Critical notes and reflections on 'social representations' *European Journal of Social Psychology*, 18: 195–209.

Jahoda, G. & Lewis, I.M. eds. (1988) *Acquiring culture: cross-cultural studies in child development*, London: Croom Helm.

Jaspars, J., Fincham, F. & Hewstone eds. (1983) *Attribution theory and research: conceptual, developmental and social dimensions*, London: Academic Press.

Jaspars, J. & Hewstone, M. (1984) La théorie de l'attribution, in S. Moscovici ed. *Psychologie sociale*, Paris: P.U.F.310–329.

Jodelet, D. (1982) Les représentations socio-spatiales de la ville, in P.H. Derycke ed. *Conceptions de l'espace*. Paris: Université de Paris X.

Jodelet, D. (1983) *Civis et bredins: représentations sociales de la maladie mentale et rapport à la folie en milieu rural*. Thèse de doctorat d'Etat. Paris.

Jodelet, D.(1984a.) The representation of the body and its transformations in R. Farr & S. Moscovici (eds.) *Social Representations*. Cambridge: Cambridge University Press: 211–238.

Jodelet, D. (1984b.) Représentation sociale: phénomènes, concept et théorie. In S. Moscovici (ed.) *Psychologie sociale*. Paris: P.U.F.: 357–78.

Jodelet, D. (1987) Malades de cerveau, malades de nerfs. Construction et corrélates d'un savoir sur la folie. in G. Bellelli (ed.), *La représentation sociale de la maladie mentale*, Atti del Convegno Internazionale: 'Le rappresentazioni sociali della malattia mentale' (Napoli-S.Maria di Castellabate, SA., 7–10 October 1986). Napoli: Liguori: 181– 194.

Jodelet, D. ed. (1989a) *Les représentations sociales.* Paris: P.U.F.

Jodelet, D. (1989b) *Folie et représentations sociales,* Paris: P.U.F.

Jodelet, D. (1991) L'idéologie dans l'étude des représentations sociales. in V. Aebischer, J.P. Deconchy, R. Lipiansky, *Idéologies et répresentations sociales,* DelVal: Fribourg: 15–34.

Kassin, S.M. (1981) From the lay-child to lay-man: developmental causal attribution in S. Brehm, S.M. Kassin & F.X. Gibbons eds. *Developmental social psychology*, New York: Oxford University Press.

Kister, M.C. & Patterson, C.J. (1980) Children's conceptions of the causes of illness: understanding of contagion and use of immanent justice, *Child Development,* 51, 839–846.

Klahr, D. (1980) Information processing models in intellectual development, in R.H. Kluwe, H. Spada eds. *Developmental models of thinking,* New York: Academic Press.

Kohlberg, L. (1963) The development of childrens orientations toward a moral order: sequence in the development of moral thought. *Vita Humana,* 6: 11–33.

Kohlberg, L. (1969) *Stage and sequence: the cognitive approach to socialisation* in D. Goslin ed. *Handbook of socialisation theory and research,* Chicago: Rond McNally.

Kohlberg, L. (1971) From is to ought: how to commit the naturalistic fallacy and get away with it in the study of moral development in . T. Mischel ed. *Cognition development and epistemology*, New York: Academic Press.

Kohlberg, L. (1976) Moral stage and moralisation: the cognitive-developmental approach in T. Lickona ed. *Moral development and behaviour*, New York: Holt, Rinehart & Winston.

Kohlberg, L., Levine, C. & Hewer, A. (1983) *Moral stage: a current formulation and a response to critics.* Basel: S. Karger.

Lalljee, M., Watson M. & White, P. (1983) Some aspects of the explanations of young children. in J. Jaspars, F. Fincham & M. Hewstone eds. (1983) *Attribution theory and research: conceptual, developmental and social dimensions*, London: Academic Press: 165–192.

Laplantine, F. (1989) Antropologie des systèmes de représentations de la maladie: de quelques recherches menées dans la France contemporaine réxaminées à la lumière d'une expérience brésil-

ienne, in. D. Jodelet ed.(1989) *Les représentations sociales.* Paris: P.U.F.: 277–298.

Leahy R. L. (1981) The development of the conception of economic inequality: descriptions and comparison of rich and poor people, *Child Development,* 52, 523–532.

Le Bouedec, G. (1979) *Contribution à la méthodologie d'étude des représentations sociales.* Thèse de doctarat . Univ. Catholique de Louvain.

Le Bouedec, G. (1986) Implicazioni metodologiche degli studi sulle rappresentazioni sociali, *Psicologia e società,* 1: 8–19.

Ledrut, R. (1973) *Les images de la ville,* Paris: Anthropos.

Leventhal H., Meyer, D. & Nerenz, D. (1980) The common sense representations of illness danger, in S. Rachman ed. *Medical Psychology*, Oxford: Pergamon Press.

Lickona T. ed. (1976) *Moral development and behaviour.* New York: Holt, Rinehart and Winston.

Lipiansky, M.E. (1991) Représentations sociales et idéologies. Analyse conceptuelle. in V. Aebischer, J.P. Deconchy, R. Lipiansky, *Idéologies et répresentations sociales,* DelVal: Fribourg: 35–64.

Litton I. & Potter J. (1985) Social representations in the ordinary explanation of a 'riot'. *European Journal of Social Psychology*, 15: 371–388.

Livesley W.J. & Bromley D.B. (1973) *Person Perception in childhood and adolescence,* Wiley J. & Sons LTD, London.

Lloyd, B. (1986) The social representation of gender, in J. Bruner, H. Weinreich-Haste eds. *Making sense: the child's construction of the world.* London: Methuen.

Lloyd, B., Duveen, G. (1990) A semeiotic analysis of the development of social representations of gender. In Duveen, G.& Lloyd, B eds. (1990) *Social representations and the development of knowledge,* Cambridge: Cambridge University Press: 27–46.

Lloyd, B., Duveen, G. & Smith C.M. (1988), Social representations of gender and young children's play: A replication, *British Journal of Developmental Psychology,* 6: 83–88.

Lloyd, B. & Smith, C.M. (1985) The social representation of young children's play, *British Journal of Developmental Psychology,* 3: 65–73.

Lorenzi-Cioldi, F. (1988) *Individus dominants et groupes dominés. Images masculines et féminines.* Grenoble: Presse Universitaire de Grenoble.

Lorenzi-Cioldi, F. & Joye, D. (1988) Représentations sociales de catégories socio-professionnelles: aspects méthodologiques, *Bulletin de Psychologie,* 61, 377–390.

Louis-Guérin C. & Brillon Y. (1984) Les attitudes du public canadien envers le crime et le droit pénal, *Revue Internationale de Criminologie*, 1, 51–59.

Mannarino, A. P. (1980) The development of children's friendship. in H. Foot, A. Chapman, J. Smith eds. *Friendship and social relations in children*, New York: Wiley.

Mandler, J.M. (1978) A code in the mode. The use of story schema in retrieval, *Discourse Processes*, 1, 14–35.

Mandler, J.M. (1983) Représentation, in J.H. Flavell, E.M. Markeman eds. *Cognitive development*, vol. 3 of P. Mussen ed. *Manual of Child Psychology*, New York: Wiley.

Mannetti L. 1990 Rappresentazioni sociali: un 'fenomeno' in cerca di una metodologia adeguata, *Giornale Italiano di Psicologia*, XVII, 1: 121–143.

Mannetti L. & Pierro A. 1989 I giovani e l'AIDS, *Rassegna di Psicologia*, 3, 35–55.

Mannetti L. & Tanucci G. (1988) The meaning of work for young people, *Rassegna di Psicologia*, V, 3: 5–21.

Markova, I. & Wilkie, P. (1987) Representations, Concepts and Social Change: The phenomenon of AIDS, *Journal for the Theory of Social Behaviour*, 17: 4: 389–409.

Markova, I, Wilkie, P., Naji, S.A. & Forbes, C.D. (1989) Knowledge of HIV/AIDS and behavioural change of people with haemophilia, *Psychology and health* .

Marsden G., Kalter N., Plunkett J.W. & Barr-Grossman T. (1977),*Children's Social Judgments Concerning Emotionally Disturbed Peers*, Journal of Consulting and Clinical Psychology.

Marsden, G. & Kalter, N. (1977) Children's understanding of their emotionally disturbed peers. I. The concept of emotional disturbance, *Psychiatry*, 29, 227–238.

Mason, L. & Varisco, B.M. (1987) Bambini e informatica: la rappresentazione del computer, *Rassegna di Psicologia*, vol. 4, 2/3/, 59–68.

Mauer, R.A. (1979) Young children's responses to a physically disabled storybook hero, *Exceptional children*, 45: 326–330.

McGuire W.J. (1986) The vicissitudes of attitudes and similar representational constructs in twentieth century psychology. *European Journal of Social Psychology* 16: 89–130.

McGurk ed. (1978) *Issues in childhood social development*, London: Methuen.

McKinlay A. & Potter J. (1987) Social representations: A conceptual critique, *Journal for the theory of social behaviour*, 17: 471–487.

Milgram, S. (1984) Cities as social representation, in R. Farr & S. Moscovici, eds. *Social representations*, Cambridge: Cambridge University Press.

Milgram, S. Jodelet, D.(1976) Psychological maps of Paris. in H.M. Proshansky, W.H. Ittelson, L.G. Rivlin eds. Environmental Psychology: people and their physical settings, New York: Holt, Rinehart & Winston (2 ed.).

Miller, H. P. & Aloise, P.A. (1989) Young Children's Understanding of the Psychological Causes of Behaviour: a review, *Child Development*, 60: 257–285.

Molinari, L. & Emiliani, F. (1990) What i s an image? The structure of mothers'images of the child and their influence on conversational styles. In G. Duveen & B. Lloyd eds. *Social representations and the development of knowledge*, Cambridge: Cambridge University Press: 91–106.

Mollo S. (1974) Représentations et images respectives que se font des deux autres partnaires: les enfants, les parents, les maîtres, in M. Debesse, G. Mialaret, *Traité des sciences pédagogiques*, 6, Paris: P.U.F.

Mollo, S. (1986) *La sélection implicite à l'école*, Paris: P.U.F.

Morvan, J.S. (1988) *Représentations des situations de handicap et d'inadaptation chez les éducateurs spécialisés, les assistants de service social et les enseignants spécialisés en formation*, 2 vol., Paris: Publications du CTNERHI: P.U.F.

Moscovici, S. (1961.1ed.) (1976 2ed.) *La psychanalyse, son image et son public*. Paris: P.U.F.

Moscovici, S.(1981). On Social Representations. In J.P. Forgas (ed.), *Cognition sociale. Perspectives on Everyday Understanding*. London: Academic Press: 181–209.

Moscovici, S. (1982) The coming era of social representations, in J.P. Codol & J.P. Leyens eds. *Cognitive analysis of social behavior*, The Hague: Nijhoff.

Moscovici, S.(ed.) (1984a). *Psychologie sociale*. Paris: P.U.F.

Moscovici, S.(1984b). The phenomenon of social representations. In R.M. Farr & S. Moscovici (eds.), *Social Representations*. Cambridge/Paris: Cambridge University Press and Editions de la Maison des Sciences de l'Homme: 3–69.

Moscovici, S. (1985). Comment on Potter & Litton, *British Journal of Social Psychology*, 24: 91–91.

Moscovici, S. (1986) L'ère des représentations sociales. in W. Doise & A. Palmonari, *L'étude des R.S.*, Paris: Delachaux et Nestlé: 34–80.

Moscovici, S. (1988). Notes towards a description of Social Representations. *European Journal of Social Psychology*, 18, 211–250.

Moscovici, S. (1989) Des représentations collectives aux représentations sociales in D. Jodelet ed. *Les représentations sociales*, Paris: P.U.F., 62–86.

Moscovici, S.(1990) Social psychology and developmental psychology: extending the conversation. In B. Lloyd & G. Duveen eds. *Social representations and the development of knowledge*, Cambridge: Cambridge University Press: 164–185.

Moscovici, S. (1991a). La fin des reorésentations sociales? in V. Aebischer, J.P. Deconchy, R. Lipiansky, *Idéologies et réprésentations sociales,* Del-Val: Fribourg: 65–84.

Moscovici, S. (1991b) Die prälogische Mentalität der Zivilisierten. in U. Flick ed. *Alltagswissen über Gesundheit un Krankheit,* Heidelberg: Asanger Vlg.

Moscovici, S. & Hewstone, M. (1983). Social representations and social explanations: from the 'naive' to the 'amateur' scientist. In M. Hewstone (ed.). *Attribution Theory: Social and Functional Extensions.* Oxford: Basil Blackwell.

Mugny, G. & Carugati, F. (1985) *L'intelligence au pluriel. Les représentations sociales de l'intelligence et de son développement.* Cousset: DelVal.

Mugny G., de Paolis, P. & Carugati, F. (1988) *Regolazioni sociali e sviluppo cognitivo,* in W. Doise & A. Palmonari eds. *Interazione sociale e sviluppo della persona,* Bologna: Il Mulino, 111–130.

Munari, A. et Al. (1976), L'anatomie de l'enfant: étude génétique des conceptions anatomiques spontanées, *Archives de psychologie,* 44, 171, 103–114.

Nelson, K . (1981) Cognition sociale in a 'script' framework J. Flavell & L. Ross eds. *Social cognitive development*, Cambridge: Cambridge University Press, 97–118.

Nelson, K. ed. (1986) *Event knowledge: structure and function in development,* Hillsdale N.J.: Erlbaum.

Newson, J. (1974) Towards a theory of infant understanding, *Bulletin of the British Psychological Society,*, 27, 251–57.

Nigro, G. & Galli, I. (1988) *La rappresentazione sociale del potere.* in Quadrio, A. & Venini, L. eds. *Potere e relazioni sociali e politiche,* Milano: Vita e Pensiero, 53–71.

Nigro, G., Galli, I. & Poderico, C. (1988) *I bambini e il nucleare. Genesi ed evoluzione di una rappresentazione sociale,* Milano: Giuffré.

Paez, D. ed. (1987) *Pensamento, individuo y sociedad. Cognicion y representacion social* Madrid: Editorial Fundamentos.

Paicheler H. & Edrei, C. (1980) Réflexions critiques sur la notion de 'représentations social' des handicapés physiques, *Médias et handicapés,* Paris: ADEP-Documentation.

Paillard M. & Gilly, M. (1972) Représentation des finalités de l'école primaire par des pères de famille: première contribution, *Cahiers de Psychologie,* 15, 227–246.

Palmonari, A. (1980) Le rappresentazioni sociali., *Giornale Italiano di Psicologia* 7 (2): 225–246.

Palmonari, A. (1987) La psicologia sociale di fronte ai comportamenti collettivi: verso nuovi paradigmi di ricerca, *Rassegna Italiana di Sociologia,* a. XXVIII, 1, 55–78.

Palmonari, A. (1989) *Processi simbolici e dinamiche sociali,* Bologna: Il Mulino.

Palmonari, A. Zani, B. (1989) Les représentations sociales dans le champ des professions psychologiques in D. Jodelet ed. *Les représentations sociales.* Paris: P.U.F. 299–320.

Panier Bagat, M. (1982) *Verso l'autonomia morale,* Firenze: Giunti.

Parker, I. (1987) Social representations: Social Psychology's (Mis)use of sociology, *Journal for the theory of Social Behaviour,* 17: 447–470.

Peevers, H. & Secord, P.F. (1973) Developmental change in attribution of descriptive concepts to persons, *Journal of personality and social psychology,* 26: 120–28.

Percheron, A. (1974) *L'univers politique des enfants,* Paris: Presse de la Fondation nationale des Sciences Politiques.

Percheron, A. Bonnal, F. Boy D., Dehan N.,Grunberg G., Subileau F.(1978) *Les 10–16 ans et la politique,* Paris: Presse de la Fondation nationale des Sciences politiques.

Perret-Clermont, A.N. (1980) *Social interaction and cognitive development in children*, London: Academic Press.

Petrillo, G. (1990) Le rappresentazioni sociali dell'infanzia nei modelli ingenui della socializzazione, *Rassegna di Psicologia,* 3: 153–176.

Piaget, J. Weil, A.M. (1951) Le développement, chez l'enfant, de l'idée de patrie et des relations avec l'entranger, *Bulletin International des sciences Sociales,* Paris: UNESCO, 605–21.

Pierre-Puysegur, M.A. & Corroyer, D. (1986) L'enfant et son environnement social: ce que les enfants français de 6 à 10 ans savent du système pénal, *Revue canadienne de Psycho-Education,* 15, 2: 164–186.

Pierre-Puysegur, M.A. & Corroyer, D. (1987) Les représentations du système pénal chez les enfants de six à dix ans, *Enfance,* 3: 215–229.

Poeschl G., Doise, W. & Mugny, G. (1985) Les représentations sociales de l'intelligence et de son développement chez les jeunes de 15 à 22 ans, *Education et recherche,* 3, 75–94.

Pogliani, A. & Quadrio, A. (1988) La rappresentazione del potere giudiziario in Italia, in V. Ugazio ed. *La costruzione della conoscenza,* Milano: F. Angeli.

Potter, J. & Litton, J. (1985) Some problems underlying the theory of social representations. *British Journal of Social Psychology*, 24: 81–90.

Potter, J. & Wetherell, M. (1987) *Discourse and social psychology,* London: Sage .

Quadrio, A., Catellani, P. & Sala, V. (1988), The social representation of politics, *Archivio di psicologi, neurologia e psichiatria* 1, 5–27.

Quadrio, A. & Magrin, M.E. (1988) L'immagine dello Stato nei giovani, in Quadrio, A.& Venini, L. eds. *Potere e relazioni sociali e politiche,* Milano: Vita e Pensiero, 72–81.

Quadrio, A.& Venini, L. eds. (1988) *Potere e relazioni sociali e politiche,* Milano: Vita e Pensiero.

Ramognino, N. (1984). Questions sur l'usage de la notion de représentations en sociologie. in C. Belisle & B. Schiele (éds). *Les savoirs dans les pratiques quotidiennes*, Editions du CNRS, Lyon.

Ripon A. (1983) L'étude des représentations en psychologie du travail, *Psychologie du travail,* 15, 33–39.

Robert P. & Faugeron C. (1978) *La justice et son public. Les représentations sociales du système pénal.* Paris: Masson.

Roberts M.C., Beidleman W.B. & Wurtele S.K. (1981), *Children's perceptions of medical and psychological disorders in their peers,* Journal of Clinical Child Psychology, vol .10 (2), 76–78.

Rogers, C. (1984) La percezione che il bambino ha degli altri. in McGurck ed. *Lo sviluppo sociale del bambino*, Torino: Boringhieri.

Rommetveit, R. (1984) The role of language in the creation and transmission of social representations. in R.M. Farr & S. Moscovici (eds.), *Social Representations.* Cambridge/Paris: Cambridge University Press and Editions de la Maison des Sciences de l'Homme: 331–359.

Ross, L. (1981) The 'intuitive scientist' formulation and its developmental implications, in J. Flavell & L. Ross eds. *Social cognitive development*, Cambridge: Cambridge University Press, 1–42.

Rothenbergh, B.B. (1970) Children's sensitivity and the relationship to interpersonal competence, intrapersonal comfort,a nd intellectual level, *Developmental Psychology,* 2: 335–350.

Scabini, E. (1984) Famiglia e rappresentazione dell'infanzia. in M. Groppo ed. *Psicologia dell'educazione* vol. II. Milano: Unicopli,23–37.

Schaffer, H.R. ed. (1977) *Studies in mother-infant interaction*, London: Academic Press.

Schank, R.C. & Abelson, R.P.(1977) *Scripts, plan, goals and understandfng,* Hillsdale: Erlbaum.

Schiele, B. & Boucher, L. (1989) L'exposition scientifique: une manière de représenter la science, in D. Jodelet, *Les représentations sociales,* Paris: P.U.F., 406–424.

Schurmans, M.N. (1988) *Les représentations sociales de la maladie mentale: une étude de sociologie de la connaissance.* Thèse de doctorat, FSES, Université de Genève.

Schurmans, M.N., Dasen, P. & Vouilloz, M.F. (1989) *Representations sociales de l'intelligence: Cote d'Ivoire et Suisse, Second regional European Conference of the International Association for Cross-Cultural Psychology* (IACCP), (Amsterdam, Juin 1989).

Selman, R.L. (1976) Social-Cognitive understanding. A guide to educational and clinical pratice, in T. Lickona ed. *Moral development and behavior*, New York: Holt, Rinehart and Winston.

Selman, R.L. (1980) *The growth of interpersonal understanding. Developmental and clinical analyses,* New York: Academic Press.

Selman, R.L. (1981) The child as a friendship philosopher, in S.R. Asher, J.M. Gottman eds. *The development of friendships*, New York: Cambridge University Press.

Semin, G.R. (1980) A gloss on attribution theory, *British Journal of Social and Clinical Psychology,* 19, 291–300.

Semin, G. (1985). The 'phenomenon of social representation': a comment on Potter & Litton. *British Journal of Social Psychology*. 24: 93–94.

Semin, G. (1987) On the relationship between theories in psychology and ordinary language, in W. Doise & S. Moscovici eds. *Current issues in european social psychology*, Cambridge: Cambridge University Press.

Semin, G. (1989) Prototypes et représentations sociales, in D. Jodelet ed. *Les représentations sociales.* Paris: P.U.F., 239–251 .

Semin G. & Gergen, K.H. (1989) *Everyday understanding . Social and scientific implications,* London: Sage.

Semin, G. & Papadopoulou, K. (1990) The acquisition of reflexive social emotions: the transmisssion and reproduction of social control through joint action. In G. Duveen & B. Lloyd eds. *Social representations and the development of knowledge*, Cambridge: Cambridge University Press: 107–125.

Sensales, G. & Areni, A. (1988) Studenti e Università (I parte): aspetti costitutivi della rappresentazione dell'Università in studenti romani di 'La Sapienza', *Rassegna di Psicologia*, 3: 23–54.

Sfrondini, M. (1982) La percezione della città nel bambino. Il caso di Oxford. *Ricerche di psicologia*, 22–23, 203–222.

Shantz, C.U. (1975) The development of cognition sociale, in E.M. Hetherington, *Review of child development research*, vol 5. Chicago: The University Press of Chicago, 257–323.

Shantz, C.U. (1983) Cognition sociale, in P.H. Mussen ed. *Handbook of Child Psychology*, vol. III: Cognitive development, New York: Wiley.

Shweder, R., Mahapatra, M. & Miller J. (1987) Culture and moral development In J. Kagan & S. Lamb eds. *The emergence of Morality in Young Children*, Chicago: University of Chicago Press.

Siegler, R.S. (1983) Information processing approaches to development. in P.H. Mussen ed. *Handbook of child development*. vol. 1.: History, Theory and Method., New York: J. Wiley .

Sigel, I.E. ed. (1985) *Parental Beliefs Systems*. Hillsdale, N.J.: Erlbaum.

Silem, A. (1981) Le statut des représentations sociales dans l'initiation économique des adolescents, *Cahiers de Sociologie économique*, 415, 75–93.

Singery J. (1984) L'impact de l'informatique sur les représentation sociales et les comportements des employés, *Bulletin de Psychologie*, 37, 843–860.

Singery-Bensaid J. (1984) La représentation d'objet sociaux multidimensionnels: l'ensemble des organismes de la protection sociale, *Bulletin de Psychologie*, 37, 833–842.

Solso, R.L. (1979) *Cognitive Psychology*, New York: Harcourt Brace Jovanovich.

Speece M.W., Brent S.B. (1985) Children's understanding of death: a review of three components of a death concept. *Child development*, 55, 1671–1686.

Sperber, D. 1974. *Le symbolisme en général* Paris: Hermann.

Staats, A.W. (1975) *Social behaviorism*, Homewood, III: Dorsey Press.

Tajfel, H. (1972) Experiments in a vacuum. in J. Israel & H. Tajfel eds. *The context of social psychology: a critical assessment*, London: Academic Press.

Tallandini, M. (1982) *Cosa pensano i bambini della droga ?*, Milano: F. Angeli.

Tapp, J. Kohlberg, L.(1971) *Developing senses of law and legal justice*, Journal of Social Issues, 27, 32.

Taylor, S.E. (1981) The interface of cognitive and social psychology, in J.H. Harvey ed. *Cognition, Social Behavior and the Environment*, Hillsdale: Erlbaum.

Thommen, B., Amman, R. & von Cranach, M. (I982) Handlungsorganisation durch soziale Repräsentationen, *Forschunsberichte aus dem Psychologischen Institut der Universitat Bern*, 6.

Thommen, B., Amman, R. & von Cranach, M. (I988) Handlungsorganisation durch soziale Repräsentationen, Bern: Huber.

Tiberghien, A. & Delacotte G. (1976) Manipulations et représentations de circuits électriques simples par des enfants de 7 à 12 ans, *Revue française de Pédagogie*, 34, 32–44.

Trevarthen, C. (1979) Instincts for human understanding and for cultural cooperation: their development in infancy. in M. Von Cranach, K. Foppa, W. Lepenies & D. Ploog eds. *Human ethology*. Cambridge: Cambridge University Press: 530–571.

Trevarthen, C. (1982) The primary motives for cooperative understanding in G. Butterworth & P. Light eds. *Cognition sociale*. Chicago: The University of Chicago Press, 77–109.

Trognon A. & Larrue J. (1988) Les représentations sociales dans la conversation, *Connexions*, n.51: 51–70.

Turiel, E. (1975) The development of social concepts: mores, customs and conventions, in D.J. De Palma, J.M. Foley eds. *Moral development. Current theory and research.* Hillsdale: Erlbaum.

Turiel, E. (1978) The development of concepts of social structure: social convention, in J. Glick, K.A. Clarke-Stewart eds. *The development of social understanding,* New York: Gardner Press.

Turkle, S. (1984) *The second self: computers and the human spirit*, New York: Simon and Schuster.

Ugazio,V. (1988) I processi cognitivi: da una propsettiva intraindividuale ad un approccio sociale . in V. Ugazio ed. *La costruzione della conoscenza*, Milano: F. Angeli.

Vala, J. (1981) Grupos sociais e representaçao social da violencia, *Psicologia*, 2: 329–342.

Vergès, P. (1984) Une possible méthodologie pour l'approche des représentations économiques, *Comunication, Information,* 6, 2–3: 375–96, Montréal: Université de Laval.

Vergès, P. (1987) A social and cognitive approach to economic representations in W. Doise & S. Moscovici eds. *Current Issues in European Social Psychology*, II, Cambridge: Cambridge University Press: 271–304.

Vergès, P. (1991) Représentation des technologies nouvelles et détermination idéologique, in in V. Aebischer, J.P. Deconchy, R. Lipiansky, *Idéologies et répresentations sociales*, DelVal: Fribourg: 159–174.

Villone Betocchi, G. ed. (1986) Problemi di metodologia di studio delle rappresentazioni sociali, *Psicologia e Società*, numéro special, 1.

Voeltz, L.M. (1980) Children's attitudes towards handicapped peers, *American Journal of mental deficency*, vol. 84,5, 455–464.

von Cranach, M. (1989) The multi-level organisation of knowledge and action. In *Sammelband der Zusammenfassungen der Referate 1. Kongress Schweizerische Gesellschaft für Psychologie* (Bern, 31 August–2 September 1989): 42–56.

von Cranach, M. & Harré, R. (eds). 1982. *The analysis of action: recent theoretical and empirical advances.* Cambridge: Cambridge University Press.

Wagner, W. (1989) Social Representation and Habitus. Some problems in relating psychological with sociological concepts. *Paper presented at the 1st European Congress of Psychology,* Amsterdam.

Waller, M. (1978) *Soziales Lernen und Interaktionskompetenz.* Stuttgart: Klett-Cotta.

Webley P., Wrigley V. (1983) The development of conceptions of unemployement among adolescents. *Journal of Adolescence,* 6, 317–328.

Weiss, M.F. (1986). Children's attitudes toward the mentally ill: a developmental analysis, *Psychological Reports,* 58: 11–20.

Wellman, H.M. & Estes, D. (1986) Early understanfing of mental entities: a reexamination of childhood realism. *Child Development,* 57, 910–923.

Wyer, R.S. & Srull, T.H. (1984) *Handbook of cognition sociale,* Hillsdale: Erlbaum.

Younger, A. J., Schwartzman, A.E. & Ledingham, J.E. (1986) Age-related differences in children's perceptions of social deviance: changes in behavior or in perspective, *Developmental Psychology,* 22, 4, 531–542.

Youniss Y.(1980) *Parents and peers in social development.* University Chicago Press, Chicago.

Youniss Y.& Smollar Y. (1985) *Adolescent relations with mothers, fathers and friends.* University Chicago Press, Chicago.

Zajonc, R.B. (1980), Cognition and cognition sociale: a historical perspective. in L. Festinger ed. *Retrospections on social psychology.* New York: Oxford University Press.

Zani, B. (1987) Stratégies therapeutiques et représentations sociale de la maladie mentale. in G. Bellelli ed. *La représentation sociale de la maladie mentale,* Napoli: Liguori: 107–120.

Social Representations of Intelligence: Côte d'Ivoire and Switzerland

Marie-Noelle Schurmans & Pierre R. Dasen*

1. Introduction

In cross-cultural psychology, research that attempts to define a concept according to criteria from within the society under study (what some authors call the "emic" approach), is still a goal that is not often achieved. The only topic that has given rise to research with coherent results is the study of how different societies define, each in their particular language, the concept that would be translated, in English or French, as "intelligence". Berry (1984) and Dasen et al. (1985) have reviewed these studies: those carried out in African societies have all found a predominance of a "social" definition of intelligence, or rather, to follow Mundy-Castle's (1975) wording, an integration between the "technological" and the "social" components of intelligence, with a clear predominance of the latter. Technological (i. e., intellectual, cognitive) skills are only part of intelligence if they are used for the welfare of the social group and not for individual promotion. This social definition of intelligence seems to be widespread in Africa South of the Sahara.

A study that was carried out in a Baoulé village (Kpouebo) in Côte d'Ivoire (Dasen et al., 1985) on the semantic space of the concept of n'glouèlê, confirmed the clear predominance of "social" components (such as the willingness to do chores for the family, respect for elders and wisdom) over "technological" components (such as attention, observation, speed of learning, school intelligence and manual dexterity).

When discussing this study with colleagues, we often encountered the following two critical comments.

1) Concepts such as n'glouèlê have a semantic space that is much wider than the dictionary definition of the word intelligence; it is therefore not possible to translate one for the other. In fact, in the true spirit of an emic approach, the two are not to be compared. Of course there is no metric equivalence between these concepts, but there certainly is functional equivalence: in both societies, the concepts can be viewed "as consisting of *purposive selection and shaping of and adaptation to real-world environments relevant to one's life*" (Sternberg, 1984, p. 312).

2) While the first criticism shuns any comparison, the second one amounts to postulating a conceptual equivalence between the two terms: the social components of intelligence, it is argued, are not specific to Africa, but would also be found in mundane definitions in Western societies, especially in rural areas where the children are still actively contributing to the family economy through performing chores.

In the studies of mundane definitions of intelligence in Western societies, social components do indeed occur, but they are much less important and are hardly taken into account in the construction of so-called intelligence tests. For example, American students, studied by Bruner, Shapiro & Tagiuri (1958), included terms such as "honest, responsible, sociable, sincere and warm" in their definition of intelligence. Mugny & Carugati (1985), in an important study using factor analysis on the answers to questionnaires with teachers, teacher trainees, parents and other subjects, have found a social factor defined as adaptation to the dominant social norms: intelligence is to

* This research was carried out with the help of M.-F. Vouilloz, ORDP, Sion. We wish to thank the authorities and population of Evolène for their hospitality, and the following students for taking part in this study: A. Akkari, N. Brütsch, D. Castillo, F. Cattafi, M. Clavien, M. Donoso, J. Ferreira, M. Gast, C. Guye, A. Maurer, F. Maurer, J. Momberg, A. Oliveira, P. Rojas Espana, C. Schlar, E. Verheecke and D. Zinetti, who also contributed to the data analysis. Thanks are also due to A. Mundy-Castle who was helpful in revising an earlier version of this paper.

conform to the norms of a bureaucratic society, particularly in school. If this is indeed a social dimension of intelligence, it refers to individual success attained through the efficient manipulation of social relationships, while the social dimension found in all of the studies in Africa refers to collective rather than individual success.

Furthermore, the studies of social representations of intelligence in Western societies have been carried out mainly with urban samples and with techniques different from the ones chosen by Dasen et al. (1985), who used semi-directive interviews with parents. It therefore seemed interesting to carry out a similar study in a Western rural environment.

2. The research in Evolène

A. The general hypothesis

Based upon the conceptual distinction between technological and social components of intelligence, our general hypothesis is that the former are more valued in Western industrial societies, while the latter are more prized in traditional African contexts. This means that in the social construction of the concept of intelligence in the Western world, behaviour leading to the control over the physical environment is highly valued, while the recognition of a collective being is less legitimate; social skills promoting a harmonious communal life and close social links do not form a part of what is called "intelligence" but are in the realm of moral philosophy. The components of present day Western definitions of intelligence are congruent with a rational positivist logic: these are the capacity to acquire knowledge, observational skills and logico-deductive reasoning. This acception of intelligence, reinforced by the educational establishment and spread through the media, has been legitimized to various degrees in the different social groups within Western society; hence, "intelligence" refers to the skills that allow a cognitive appraisal of a reality accessible to science and logic, rather than to the management of social relationships and group cohesion. Within Western society, then, we expect to find social representations of intelligence centered primarily on individual learning skills, and on

the use of cognitive processes. This dominant centration is likely to hide more specific conceptual dimensions elaborated by the different social groups according to their particular place in the social structure.

Studying the social representations of mental illness, Schurmans (1990) found a clear distinction between dimensions at the level of the society and others at the level of social groups. Within the spontaneous theories that social groups elaborate in response to the questions raised by their social, symbolic and material environments, there coexist two levels of analysis. On the one hand, there are, at the level of the whole society, those materials that have been shaped by history and have acquired the status of collective representations through their insertion into the dominant value system; on the other hand, within the various social groups that make up a society, more specific value systems exist that reflect the relationships and the explicit or implicit conflicts between these groups, and shape the meaning of the various social reconstructions of reality.

We therefore posit the following hypothesis: cognitive components form the societal dimensions of Western social representations of intelligence, while other dimensions coexist at the level of social groups that reflect particularities of their means of production and life goals.

B. Population

Our medium term research goal is to compare the social representations of intelligence in different social groups. In the first part of the project reported here, we have decided to work in a community characterized by its rural lifestyle, a history of isolation and the importance of social links, in order to attempt a first comparison with the previous study in Côte d'Ivoire. Evolène, in one of the side valleys of the Rhone River (Val d'Hérens, Canton of Valais) in the Swiss Alps, corresponds well to these criteria. Situated at an altitude of between 1,100 and 4,357 meters, at a distance of 25 km from the main town of Sion, it consists of three villages and three hamlets spread over an area of 22'118 hectares, with a population of 1,550 inhabitants. Until the turn of the century, the people of Evolène have lived in isolation from the larger Rhone valley; their contacts were rather turned towards the Aosta Valley that could be reached during the summer months on a foot-path over a mountain pass, where the same patois is still spoken and the same breed of cows are raised. Their activities were exclusively rural, and were centered around semi-nomadic cattle raising, using different ecological zones according to the season, and some subsistence agriculture; they were thus virtually self-sufficient. Endogamous practices are still visible in the social setup, as reflected in the small number of family names. The people all know each other, not only through their first names but according to their descent, and until very recently cooperative work, community evenings and religious rituals marked the rhythms of collective time in work, leisure and worship. Thus Evolène presents the characteristics of the communal type of society that we were looking for.

However tourism has started to make an impact on this community since the beginning of this century, World War II opened it even more to external influences, the nearby construction of a large hydro-electric dam in the fifties provided many new jobs, the increased importance of schooling and television exposed it to the images of the outside world ... This penetration of outside influences encountered the resistance of the peasantry, religious traditions and a strong regional identity, but since the fifties, more and more of the families are giving up agricultural work in favour of activities linked to the tourist trade and many of the men commute to Sion in the Rhone Valley for their jobs. In the last half-century, the community has been subjected to accelerated social change that has lead to the coexistence of two types of societies (Preiswerk & Crettaz, 1986) that are at the same time cohesive and conflictual:

– a society of mountain farmers, more and more threatened in its existence, that shares the values of "being together", and for which the cow serves the double function (pragmatic and symbolic) of social reproduction;

self-centered, it resists to change, it is tradition itself;
– a changing society, characterized by the development of the secondary and tertiary sectors; it accepts the presence of outsiders, incorporates the urban ideas of individual success, professions and careers, while still remaining linked to the group and to the locality; it tends to turn the elements of tradition into a useful folklore within the new goals of modernization.

In Evolène we thus find ourselves confronted with a complex social situation, marked by the recent modernization: the dynamics of acculturation and resistance to change bring about divergent life goals for the Evolène people. The coexistence of the traditional and the changing societies delimit two conflicting orientations, one that attempts to close itself off from threatening outside influences, in order to save the cohesion and permanence of the group, and the other open to outside influences and valuing change, but at the same time protecting itself from the takeover by the urban society.

We have attempted to take this situation into account in the design of our study by selecting two sub-samples within the Evolène community: those families who practice agriculture and cattle raising at least on a part-time basis (A) and those who derive their income from the modern sector (NA). We selected thirty-four families, seventeen in each group, approximately matched on demographic data (age of parents and number and age of children).

C. Methods

Semi-directive interviews were carried out by two students, one acting as interviewer and the other as observer, whenever possible in the presence of both parents;* these lasted about two hours, and in most cases consent was given to record the interviews on tape. The interviews dealt with various aspects of family life and daily routines, educational practices and

---

* For the sake of consistency with our previous research in West Africa, where individual interviews would have been culturally inappropriate, our "subjects" are therefore the thirty-four "families"; disagreements between the two parents were usually resolved during the interview.

principles, and included at the end the following two separate parts on the social representations of intelligence.

1) Spontaneous definitions. The parents were asked: "How does one recognize, according to you, whether a child of about nine years is intelligent?"

2) Card selection. The parents were presented with a set of thirty-four cards, each containing an adjective or a phrase derived from the study in Côte d'Ivoire, from the first interviews with group A, and some of our own production. The parents were requested to select those items that they considered to be characteristics of intelligent behaviour, and then to make a second selection of the five most important items, and finally to place these in order of importance.

The interviews were later transcribed, and two successive data-condensations were performed (Miles & Hubermann, 1984).*

3. Results

A. The spontaneous definitions of intelligence

The results of the content analysis of the spontaneous definitions of intelligence are reported in Table 1. This contains the categories used in the study in Côte d'Ivoire (social components = S, technological components = T) as well as a few new categories that had to be introduced as a function of the new material collected in Evolène (cf. S5 and T5). These refer particularly to sociability (to be sociable, communicative, to make contacts easily), reasoning (the ability to think, logical reasoning) and a use of language that seemed to us different from the Baoulé "O si hidjo", for example "how to ask questions". A few components that were difficult to classify as either social or technological were put into a mixed category (S/T), for example "knowing how to make decisions".

The Baoulé parents spontaneously mentioned many more social (S) than technological (T) components: 63% of the items are so-cial. The reverse is true for the parents of our Evolène samples: only 25% of the items are clearly social. This demonstrates that, if the social components found in the previous research are not totally absent, the technological ones predominate strongly. This is true of the parents in both groups (A and NA), in fact the differences between the two groups are negligible: the parents of group A refer more to sociability and include manual dexterity (as do the Baoulé), while the parents in group NA refer more to language and independence (for example, "to do things alone"), but these differences are small compared to the overall similarity.

If, for the people interviewed in Evolène for this study, intelligence is mainly technological, it is certainly not linked to schooling. Twenty-four parental couples (twelve in each of the samples) spoke very clearly on this topic: instruction is not to be equated with intelligence. To be intelligent is not to be successful in school, but on the contrary, to have out-of-school knowledge available; also, social success does not come automatically from success in school, and several examples are quoted of people who failed in school and were later successful in life.

B. The choice of cards

In Table 2, we present the frequencies with which each item on the cards was chosen in the two sub-samples. The items are listed according to the categories used for the analysis in the previous section.

In the choice of cards, there is a confirmation of the predominance of technological items, but on the other hand a slight increase in the choice of social items (38%, excluding the mixed categories) when compared to the spontaneous definitions. This increase is especially noticeable in group A (43%, compared to 32% in group NA), and comes from category S1: the item "to work hard" is chosen only by members of group A, who also chose twice as often as those of group NA the items "to be helpful", "to be honest", and, in S2, "respectful". This

---

* The details of the data condensation procedures, as well as results that could not be reported here in full, can be obtained by writing to the authors.

Table 1: The spontaneous definitions of intelligence among Baoulé (Kpouebo) and Swiss (Evolène) parents: Frequencies of the occurrence of each category in the content analysis of the interviews.

Components mentioned (in Baoulé)	Kpouebo	Evolène A	NA	Tot
SOCIAL INTELLIGENCE (S)				
S1 (O ti kpa) Helpful, responsible honest	51	4	5	9
S2 (Agnyhiè) Polite, obeying, honest	24	1	0	1
S3 (O si hidjô) Social use of language	16	1	1	2
S4 (Angundan) Wisdom	11	1	5	6
S5 Various social:				
Sociability		4	0	4
Imitation of adults		1	0	1
Modest (to remain simple)		1	1	2
Total S	102	13	12	25
TECHNOLOGICAL INTELLIGENCE (T)				
T1 (I gni ti klè klè) Observation, attention, to learn fast	22	17	21	8
T2 (O si floua) Instruction, school intelligence	6	5	3	8
T3 (I sa si n'goulèlê) Manual dexterity	12	8	0	8
T4 (I ti ti kpa) Good memory	19	2	2	4
T5 Various T:				
Langage		2	7	9
Independance		0	3	3
Logical reasoning		2	3	5
Total T	59	36	39	75
Total S and T	161	49	51	100
S/T (mixed social/technological)			4	4

difference between the two groups (on category S1) is statistically significant (chi square = 15.18, d. f.=1, p<.01). The members of group A also chose more frequently than those of NA the items: "to have a good memory", "persevering", "orderly" and "courageous".

A principal component analysis (PCA) performed on this material confirms the appropriateness in this new setting of the opposition between some social dimensions and some technological components as they were first defined in the research in Côte d'Ivoire: the typical S1 items are opposed on the same factor to T1 items.

The analysis of the results thus confirms, in the dimensions given by the spontaneous defi-

nitions of intelligence, the preponderance of technological characteristics, in direct opposition to the definition of the Baoulé's nglouèlê. This reflects, however, a socially expected, normative answer. If one suggests (through the technique of choosing cards) the possible appropriateness of other dimensions, the members of group A take advantage of the situation to reveal a more social definition, coherent with their mode of production that relies on hard work and the sharing of responsibilities in the family enterprise, to which the children often contribute to a large extent. Our interpretation is that the spontaneous definition first given when faced with urban, intellectual interviewers is rooted in society level norms, in

Table 2. Choice of cards. Frequencies of choices of items in groups A and NA.

Code	Item	A	NA	Total
S1				
PRE	Taking responsibility*	14	7	21
HON	Honest*	9	4	13
SER	Helpful*	7	3	10
TRV	Hard working*	7	0	7
S2				
RES	Respectful*	10	5	15
POL	Polite*	6	4	10
TRD	Respectful of tradition*	3	3	6
OBE	Obeying*	2	1	3
S4				
REF	Wise, thoughtful*	11	9	20
S5				
SIM	Modest (to remain simple)	10	9	19
INT	Intuitive, sensitive	5	6	11
NAT	To be close to nature	4	3	7
FIE	Proud	0	0	0
Total S		88	54	142
T1				
COM	To understand quickly*	14	14	28
OBS	Good observer*	12	12	24
DEB	Resourceful*	8	11	19
APP	To learn fast*	8	10	18
MAL	Clever	6	7	13
VIF	Alert	3	7	10
T2				
ELE	A good pupil*	6	4	10
T3				
SAV	To have practical know-how	7	11	18
MAN	Manual skills*	4	2	6
T4				
MEM	Good memory*	13	7	20
T5				
LOG	Logical reasoning	15	15	30
ADA	Adaptable to change	10	9	19
PAR	To speak well	7	5	12
Total T		113	114	227
S/T				
DEC	To take decisions	14	11	25
INI	To show initiative	10	14	24
Total T/S		24	25	49
OTHERS				
BOU	Persevering	11	6	17
ORD	Orderly	8	2	10
COU	Courageus	6	2	8
TEN	Tenacious	4	2	6
CAR	Good character	1	3	4
REN	Withholding	0	0	0
Total Other		30	15	45

*Items derived from previous research in Côte d'Ivoire.

this case the exogenous dimensions carried by the school and the media. On the other hand, the wider choice given by the second technique, allows more endogenous definitions to appear, reflecting group dimensions of social representations and illustrating the potentially conflicting goals of the two groups (A and NA).

C. Semi-directive interviews with parents

While the first results show that the opposition between the parents living from agriculture and those in the modern sector is a discriminating variable in the relation to the social representations of intelligence at the group level, the two sub-samples are not really homogenous. An analysis of variance was carried out on the factor scores of the 12 PCA factors, using group membership (A/NA) as the independent variable; the latter was statistically significant ($p = .02$) on the first factor only, explaining only 16% of the variance. This prompted us to search for finer distinctions. In a second stage of this research project, we therefore subdivided the two groups further by using data provided by parts of the interview, namely family history and socio-professional data, the organization of daily and yearly rhythms, cooperation within the family, participation of the children in domestic chores, educational principles and practices, and the respect for and persistence of local traditions. These themes have allowed us to determine indicators of "family goals", and to construct two complementary dimensions, the relationship to the environment and the attitude towards tradition, that allowed us in the next stage of data analysis to draw finer distinctions than that between groups A and NA.

From the double condensation of the transcripts of the interviews and observations we have derived twenty-seven variables that have been subjected to a correspondance analysis (AFC), following Benzecri (1973). The first factor (explaining 21% of the information) represents the opposition between A and NA: at one end we find the families who own land, who live in traditional houses, whose organization of time and activities are marked by agricultural work and seasonal rythms, a family history continuously linked to cattle raising,

and who value and still use the patois. The other end of the dimension represents the families who have sold or rented out their land, whose family history shows a (long standing or recent) departure from agricultural life, who live in more modern dwellings, whose children no longer speak patois, and practise non-traditional hobbies (such as taking music or dance lessons).

The second factor (10% of the information) seems to reflect the "family project", which corresponds on the one hand to the traditional social project of the village community, and on the other to the process of individualization. One end of the dimension seems to represent the acceptance of those aspects of tradition that create the cohesion of a social group that is conscious of its particularity, while the other end could represent the breaking away from the group. The variables that define this dimension can also be considered as markers of modernization, i.e. secularization, differentiation and mobility. The families can no doubt be distinguished through their professional choices, but also according to the meanings they establish around them. Thus, the A/NA distinction should be considered as only one indicator among others of the families' participation in the modernization process.

Figure 1 shows the clusters of families that are produced when they are situated in the space defined by the first two factors. Six clusters can be distinguished:

– the A's which are engaged in the process of individuation in relation to the community (A–I);
– those NA's who share with the first group these centrifugal attitudes (NA–I);
– the A's which are centrally located on the cohesion/individuation dimension (A–M);
– the NA's in the same median position (NA–M);
– the A's that share the value of social cohesion (A–C);
– the NA's who share these centripetal attitudes (NA–C).

Another AFC analysis was carried out on the data concerning the choice of cards, adding the information of the families' cluster groups as defined above. The results of the factorial projection of these items appear in Figure 2.

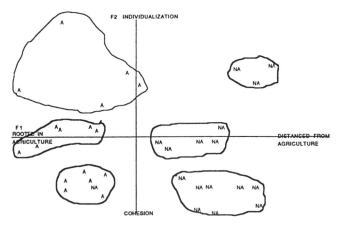

Figure 1: Correspondance analysis (AFC) on variables derived from the semi-directive interviews.

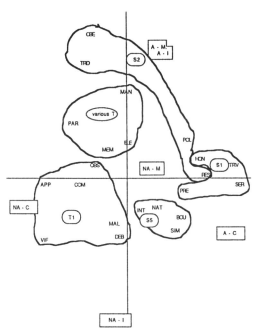

Figure 2: Correspondance analysis (AFC) on the choice of cards.

The choice of technological items (T1) versus social items (S1, S5) now clearly appears to be linked to the groups defined by the mode of production and the position on the dimension of cohesion vs. individuation. A clear opposition appears between group A–C which tends to choose items from S1 and S5, and group NA–C which selects T1 items. Note that both groups have a family project that fosters the traditional values of religion, solidarity and mutual aid, being together and keeping a specific community identity. On the other hand,

the NA–I group tends to choose both T1 and S5 items, while the A–I and A–M groups tend to choose some S2 items.

Contrary to what could have been expected, the technological items are not chosen preferentially by the group intuitively most engaged in the modernization process (NA–I), but by group NA–C. It seems that these families, while they do not give up the local specificity, tend to foster an alternative model that includes the values linked to the dominant definition of intelligence in the society. These societal dimensions seem to be, in a way, adopted by the NA–C group and proposed as alternatives to the traditional group-level dimensions. This pressure comes only from the NA group that values cohesion, the NA–I and NA–M groups choosing a more diversified selection of items.

The appropriateness in this context of our initial distinction between social and technological items appears to be well established by these data. The construction of the meanings of intelligence according to this distinction seems to be part of the confrontation between two competing social projects, that of the continuity of a community identity distinct from the urban model, and that of the integration of a world-view that we hypothesize to have come recently from the outside. Our first distinction between A and NA appears to be even more meaningful if we add to it the concept of social project: the social agents who share the will to keep the community cohesion and specificity are divided into two sub-groups. The first sub-group, composed of families living from agriculture, shows a representation of intelligence that expresses a resistance to social change, and the second sub-group, consisting of families in the non-agricultural sector of the economy, is attempting an integration that combines social change with group cohesion. Around the various opinions on the definitions of intelligence, two social projects emerge: one of community withdrawal and one of social innovation, but both integrated in the overarching project of community cohesion.

For the continuation of our research, the theoretical line suggested by these first observations could be that, in the analysis of the ongoing social change, exogenous stimuli do not appear to be the only and sufficient cause of change, since the community seems to have the capacity to reinterpret external constraints and to construct an original, socially oriented response. The next step in our research project will be to extend our design to elderly people in order to study in more detail the impact of social change on the social representations of child development and education.

References

Benzecri, J. P. (1973). *Analyse des données*. Paris: Dunod.

Berry, J. W. (1984). Toward a universal psychology of cognitive competence. *International Journal of Psychology, 19*, 335–361.

Bruner, J. S., Shapiro, D., & Tagiuri, R. (1959). The meaning of traits in isolation and in combination. In R. Tagiuri & L. Petrullo (Eds.), *Person perception and interpersonal behavior*. Stanford, Ca: Stanford University Press.

Dasen, P. R., Dembélé, B., Ettien, K., Kabran, K., Kamagaté, D., Koffi, K. A., & N'guessan, A. (1985). N'glouèlê, l'intelligence chez les Baoulé. *Archives de Psychologie, 53*, 293–324.

Miles, M., & Huberman, M. (1984). *Qualitative data analysis*. Newbury Park, CA: Sage.

Mugny, G., & Carugati, F. (1985). *L'intelligence au pluriel. Les représentations sociales de l'intelligence et de son développement*. Cousset, FR: Delval.

Mundy-Castle, A. C. (1975). Social and technological intelligence in Western and non-Western cultures. In S. Pilowsky (Ed.). *Cultures in Collision*. Adelaide: Australian National Association for Mental Health.

Preiswerk, Y., & Crettaz, B. (Eds.). (1986). *Le pays où les vaches sont reines*. Sierre: Monografic.

Schurmans, M.-N. (1990). *Maladie mentale et sens commun. Une étude de sociologie de la connaissance*. Neuchâtel: Delachaux & Niestlé.

Sternberg, R. J. (1984). A contextualist view of the nature of intelligence. *International Journal of Psychology, 19*, 307–334.

One Man's Meat, Another Man's Poison?
Stressors And Their Cultural Background

Norbert Semmer

As an industrial and organizational psychologist, I am interested in guidelines for designing work in such a way as to prevent people from being overly stressed. Turning to recent psychological stress research and theory, I learn, however, that general principles of the design of work under the aspect of stress reduction are in vain, since "one man's meat is another man's poison". The perception of events and their evaluation depends on values, goals, norms, perceptual styles, coping skills, resources, etc. Therefore, a normative approach which looks for general guidelines is not warranted, since all these factors are subject to vast individual differences. Looking for general guidelines, therefore, reflects nothing but the naive and simplistic conceptions of the past.

This may be exemplified with a few citations from a recent programmatic paper by Vossel (1987). He writes:

"The assumption ... that different individuals react in the same way to identical situations can hardly be maintained. ... It follows that it is not appropriate to define stress solely on the basis of stimulus properties, ... " (p. 130).

He accuses normative approaches as being "characterized by a situation-based concept of stress that denies psychological processes of mediation" (p. 134), and concludes that it "is not simply the occurrence of a life event that defines its stressfulness, but the subjective evaluation of an event's impact. Consequently, the use of individual weights acknowledges the central role of appraisal processes."

Based on such an approach (which is widely shared) a concept like "stressor" makes, indeed, no sense, since it *a priori* assumes certain psychological characteristics of an event or a situation. In this line of thinking, the search for more general guidelines would indeed be in vain.

There are, however, some important questions to be asked in light of such an argument.

Does the – undeniable – fact that there are individual differences really imply that stress is a phenomenon which can be accounted for exclusively by individual idiosyncracies? Does the psychological mediation of the stress process really imply that there are no properties of events that have a shared meaning in a given culture?

This paper concentrates on the role of culturally shared beliefs in determining stress emotions, coping, and the like. Its main thesis is that those shared elements tend to be overlooked in current stress research which is dominated by an overly individualistic perspective.

Culturally shared aspects of emotional experiences

Consider the case of a student who comes to a therapist asking for advice because he or she was "nervous" in face of an important exam coming up the following week. In all likelihood, the therapist would send the student home, remarking that "being nervous" was perfectly normal in that situation, and unless he or she had more serious problems, no therapy was needed. On the other hand, if the student had asked for help because he or she was nervous whenever entering a bus, tram or train, the therapist would be much more likely to offer help.

This may be a trivial example. But it illustrates that we have quite clear – and culturally shared – notions of what constitutes a "legitimate" emotional reaction to an exam, or a train-ride, etc. There are, as Averill (1982, 1986) puts it, "rules of appraisal" which govern how events are perceived and interpreted and under what circumstances they constitute a legitimate reason for a certain emotion.

That emotions are "socially constituted syndromes" or "transitory social roles" (Averill, 1986, 100) is further illustrated by the fact that some emotional experiences seem to be confined to certain cultures, such as the Japanese "amae" (cf. Morsbach & Tyler, 1986)* while supposedly identical emotional experiences actually may be experienced quite differently in different cultures (cf. Heelas, 1986).

It should be added that the same applies to coping. Within limits, alcohol is considered a legitimate means to relieve minor tension in certain (sub)cultures. Many societies have highly ritualized ways of dealing with humiliations or other stressful events – a duel among European aristocrats could be conceived in this way, as can mourning rituals, etc.

Communalities in stress appraisal

The examples given above illustrate the point but do not constitute serious empirical arguments. That there are communalities in stress appraisal is, however, reflected empirically in findings of substantial agreement between raters who are asked to rate the "stressfulness" of events (cf. Cohen, 1988).

Of course, this argument is only partially convincing for two reasons: first, the determination of such an agreement requires that the values of several groups are averaged before they are correlated. By that procedure, differences within the groups, which may be substantial, are eliminated. Second, despite substantial similarity, there are also important differences when one compares different social or ethnic groups, people with and without experience of events, etc. (cf. Filipp, 1981; Perkins, 1982; Vossel, 1987).

What seems more important, therefore, is to compare the relationship between life event scores based on individual weights, on weights assigned by external raters, and on unit weights, i.e. simple sums. Furthermore, these different scores should be related to dependent variables such as symptom scales. If the strong emphasis on individual processes is correct, then scores based on individual weights should yield substantially better results than standard weights or unit weighting.

As it turns out, correlations between various forms of weighting are usually above .90 (e.g. Newcomb, Huba & Bentler, 1981; Skinner & Lei, 1980; Vinokur & Selzer, 1975; Zimmerman, 1983). Of course, even with correlations of that magnitude, the two scores may theoretically show different relationships to other variables such as symptoms of impaired physical and/or psychological well-being. However, if differences of this kind are found, they tend not to be very large. Thus, Vinokur & Selzer (1975) report correlations with symptoms which are, on the average, higher by .04 for individually weighted scores as compared to unit weighting.

Results like this apply not only to the original concept of life events in terms of change *per se*. Concentrating only on those life events that have been shown to be responsible for the relationship with symptoms, that is, *undesirable* life events, individual weights are not appreciably better than a simple sum (Newcomb, Huba, & Bentler, 1981).

This is also corroborated by our own findings in a study with adolescents ("Berlin-Bremen-Study: Semmer, Lippert, Fuchs, Rieger-Ndakorerwa, Dwyer, & Knoke, in press; cf. Semmer, Dwyer, Lippert, Fuchs, Cleary, & Schindler, 1987). The project was concerned with health behaviors, their determinants and correlates, and among the variables we assessed were daily hassles, a minor form of life events (cf. Kanner, Coyne, Schaefer, & Lazarus, 1981). Examples for the events we asked for are "You were bored", "Your parents got angry at you for being home late", "You lost something", etc. The answering format was: (1) "Did not happen", (2) "happened but did not bother me", and (3) "happened and bothered me".

This answering format allows a number of different weighting schemes. One can argue (a) that only events that were scored as "bothering" should count. On a normative basis, one could also argue (b) that all events which happened should count. And one could argue (c) that all events which happened should count but events which were scored as "bothering" should be weighted more strongly.

---

* "The Japanese consider *amae* to be a very basic emotion (…). Yet, there is no equivalent emotion within Western societies. Roughly translated, *amae* can be described as a wish to be loved or a need for dependency. Unlike the English concept of love, however, amae does not have a sexual connotation. (…) And unlike the English concept of dependency, *amae* has a positive rather than a negative connotation." (Averill, 1979, p. 348)

In line with the above-mentioned results, the three versions correlate extremely high with one another, with coefficients in the total sample of 1250 adolescents as well as in various subsamples being all higher than .90 (this and the following results from Zimmermann, 1986).

More important, however, is the relationship between the various hassles-scores and the experience of distress. The simple sum of all hassles which have happened correlates r = .33 with a distress-scale. The coefficient for the weighted sum in which those hassles that have explicitly been judged as bothering, is .34 and thus practically identical.

Thus, our results are in agreement with the above-mentioned examples, and all this is in line with the conclusions reached by Cohen (1988) in a recent review article: "...(c) event desirability can be determined either by judges or by the subjects themselves because agreement between these two methods is usually high; ... and (d) unit and weighted scores of undesirable events are equally predictive of psychological problems." (Cohen, 1988, 20).

Thus, while individual weighting may explain some additional variance, the bulk of it is explained by simple sums.

That weighted and unweighted scores yield equivalent or at least next-to-equivalent results may, of course, be due to several reasons. Most importantly, whether or not a certain event is remembered and mentioned in an interview or questionnaire may be influenced by the stressful nature of the event for the individual. This has, indeed, been found to influence the reporting of events (cf. Perkins, 1982), especially when questionnaires are used (Paykel & Dowlatshahi, 1988). On the other hand, there is evidence for high agreement between subjects' reporting of events and relatives' confirmations in careful research (e.g. Brown, 1974).

Although not concerned with single events but with chronic stressors, our own results in the area of stress at work show that contamination of measures with factors such as individual recall, preferences, social desirability or symptom status does add method variance but cannot account for the relationships found. Expert ratings of the stressfulness of jobs and the median of group ratings which are not contaminated with these individual factors do yield important and significant relationships between stressors and psychosomatic complaints (cf. Greif, Bamberg, & Semmer, 1991; Semmer & Zapf, 1989; Zapf, 1989).

Thus, while such factors may add spurious variance, it seems highly unlikely that they can explain all the effects found. Commonly shared meaning of stressors, therefore, must play an important role in explaining both the high correlations between various methods of scoring and the very similar relationships of these different scores to dependent variables.

Incidentally, it is interesting to note that the behavior of stress researchers actually takes account of this situation. Looking at the themes which are being investigated makes this immediatedly clear. In stress experiments we find independent variables such as shock, noise, feedback about alleged failure, strange or aggressive behavior of other "subjects"; in field studies, people investigate the impact of disasters, exams, job loss, death and illness of close people, crowding, time pressure, etc. etc. All of this corresponds to what most people would a priori consider stressful. Lists of life events and hassles as well as the chapters of numerous books provide further examples.

Thus, in spite of many verbal attacks against working with "stressors", stress researchers actually draw upon the social knowlegde concerning "stressful" situations and stimuli in selecting their concrete area of research. Folkman & Lazarus (1985, 168) even write: "What is needed is further investigation of these appraisal and coping variables in other stressful contexts, particularly those that are more stressful than a mid-term exam."

Stressors as social phenomena

In predicting reactions to "stressful" situations, much is already gained if we know something about the social situation of individuals who react differently to the same situation. Of course, failing an exam means something different depending on whether we deal with the only qualification for a certain professsion or with just some additional education, whether one has a solid financial background or not, whether one has experienced redundancy or not, whether one is supporting a family or not, etc. Its impact depends on the conditions for repeating the exam, on the character of the labor market, etc. But once we know this, our judgment of the severity of this stressor can be considerably improved – without knowing the individual's reaction! Similarly, our guess about the annoying character of aircraft noise might be considerably improved if we know that the individual in question is making his or her living in a company which produces aircraft and which, in addition, is the only big employer in the area.

Of course, this does not apply equally to all situations and events. They differ in the extent to which they depend on "purely individual" (as opposed to socially shared) preferences. The evaluation of aircraft noise might, in general, be easier than the evaluation of a defeat of the local soccer team (although even here we might improve our prediction considerably if we know that a certain individual has been living in the area for a long time, is male and a blue collar worker!). And the evaluation of aircraft noise may, in turn, be more difficult than that of, say, a big flood or fire. However, to reduce the situations which may legitimately regarded as "common stressors" to severe threats, as is often done, ignores the vast amount of social beliefs regarding many situations which are quite common.

Misunderstandings surrounding the concept of "stressor"

In contrast to Vossels (1987) assertion, the perspective advocated here does not imply that a *psychological* approach is abandonded, leaving a sociological/epidemiological approach which may be fruitful but does not say anything about psychological processes. When, to take up the above example of aircraft noise, we learn that someone is making a living at the local aircraft company, we also learn something about the importance of airplanes for these people's attainment of important goals; we learn something about their likely role requirements, about the the dissonance they might experience, about the social norms they might be exposed to in their community, etc. etc. Activity, goals, norms, roles – concepts such as these certainly help one to understand the psychological processes involved.

Perhaps some of the misunderstanding sur-

rounding this issue stems from the assumption that defining a stimulus or a situation as a stressor implies relying upon its *physical* properties and not upon its *social* quality. Defined socially, the term "environmentally induced stress" is not, as Lazarus & Folkman (1986, 75) assert, useless. Rather, it is an important part of understanding stress processes.

The work of Brown and his associates illustrates this very convincingly. They ask for *"contextual"* information which allows them some social understanding of the situation, and then use their own social knowlege for judgment. "Therefore, after taking into account that, say, a woman is unmarried, is a practicing Catholic, and is in the middle of studying for a medical degree in which she has done well, we ask *ourselves, as investigators*, the degree of threat *most women* would feel on discovering an unexpected pregnancy in such circumstances." (Brown and Andrews, 1986, p. 258, emphasis added).

This certainly is not to deny the importance of individual processes in the experience of stress. Rather, the dichotomy between "general" and "individual" processes should be overcome, and we should realize more strongly that *both* are going on, that individual processes do contain *general* features and cannot be reduced to idiosyncratic processes.

In addition, there are different levels of "generality". Group norms, local cultures, regional differences, national differences, differences of social class, education, profession, social status, etc., can be taken into account, and *should* be taken into account, otherwise important and valuable information might be lost.

There is a second misunderstanding concerning the concept of "stressors". Often, this concept is dismissed on the ground that something cannot be regarded a stressor unless each and every individual experiences stress when it occurs. This assumption is, however, unnecessary. Rather, stressors may be defined in terms of *risk*, implying an increased probability of stress experiences in a certain population. Defined in these terms, a traffic jam may very fruitfully be regarded as a stressor, even though it may or may not be stressful to any given individual.

In line with the above argument, such a definition of stressors may be confined to different levels of generality. Thus, the threat of losing one's life may be defined as a stressor for mankind, losing $ 500.– may be seen as a stressor for people who are not rich, the lack of an elevator in a public building may be seen as a stressor for handicapped and elderly people, etc.

Reconciling idiographic and nomothetic perspectives

This approach of embedding personal stress experiences in their cultural background can, I believe, help to overcome the unnecessary fight between "nomothetic" and "idiographic" perspectives. Stress will in the end always be an individual experience but the individual processes involved are co-determined by the historical situation of a given cohort, relate to socially defined roles, and reflect socially shared beliefs and values (cf. Laux & Weber, 1987; Thomae, 1987; see also the concept of "social representation", e. g. Farr & Moscovici, 1984).

This way of thinking certainly leaves room for an idiographic approach to the study of stress. But it also leaves room for the concept of stressors and for its implication that there *can* be guidelines for designing our environment, our working life, our educational institutions, etc. in such a way as to minimize stressors, that is, high risks of stress.

At the same time, such a way of thinking implies an important qualification for each of these approaches. Those who work with the idiographic approach must keep in mind that not all differences between people can be seen as based on idiosyncratic processes but must be interpreted in light of the *social situation* of these individuals. And those working with a more nomothetic approach, looking for common stressors, must keep in mind that guidelines for the design of our surroundings must allow for the possibility of indivuals to adjust things to their individual needs and desires (cf. Ulich, 1990).

References

Averill, J. R. (1979). The functions of grief. In C. Izard (ed.), *Emotions in personality and psychopathology* (pp. 339–368). New York: Plenum.

Averill, J. R. (1982). *Anger and aggression: An essay on emotion.* New York: Springer.

Averill, J. R. (1986). The acquisition of emotions during adulthood. In R. Harré (ed.), *The social construction of emotions* (98–118). Oxford: Basil Blackwell.

Brown, G. W. (1974). Meaning, measurement, and stress of life events. In B. Snell Dohrenwend & B. P. Dohrenwend (eds.), *Stressful life events: their nature and effects* (pp. 217–243). New York: Wiley.

Brown, G. W. & Andrews, B. (1986). Social support and depression. In M. Appley & R. Trumbull (eds.), *Dynamics of stress* (pp. 257–282). New York: Plenum.

Cohen, L. H. (1988). Measurement of life events. In L. H. Cohen (ed.), *Life events and psychological functioning* (pp. 11–30). London: Sage.

Farr, R. M. & Moscovici, S. (Eds.).(1984). *Social representation.* Cambridge: Cambridge University Press.

Filipp, S.-H. (1981). Ein allgmeines Modell für die Analyse kritischer Lebensereignisse. In S.-H. Filipp (Hrsg.), *Kritische Lebensereignisse* (S. 3–52). München: Urban & Schwarzenberg.

Folkman, S. & Lazarus, R. S. (1985). If it changes it must be a process: Study of emotion and coping during three stages of a college examination. *Journal of Personality and Social Psychology, 48,* 150–170.

Greif, S., Bamberg, E. & Semmer, N. (eds.) (1991). *Psychischer Stress am Arbeitsplatz.* Göttingen: Hogrefe.

Hacker, W. (1986). *Arbeitspsychologie. Psychische Regulation von Arbeitstätigkeiten.*Schriften zur Arbeitspsychologie (hrsg. v. E. Ulich) Nr. 41. Bern: Huber

Heelas, P. (1986). Emotion talk across cultures. In R. Harré (ed.), *The social construction of emotions* (pp. 234–266). Oxford: Basil Blackwell.

Kanner, A. D., Coyne, J. C., Schaefer, C., & Lazarus, R. S. (1981). Comparison of two modes of stress measurement: Daily hassles and uplifts versus major life events. *Journal of Behavioral Medicine, 4,* 1–39.

Lazarus, R. S. & Folkman, S. (1986). Cognitive theories of stress and the issue of circularity. In M. Appley & R. Trumbull (eds.), *Dynamics of stress* (pp. 63–80). New York: Plenum.

Laux, L. & Weber, H. (1987). Person-centred coping research. *European Journal of Personality, 1,* 193–214.

Morsbach, H. & Tyler, W. J. (1986). A Japanese emotion: *Amae.* In R. Harré (ed.), *The social construction of emotions* (pp. 289–307). Oxford: Basil Blackwell.

Newcomb, M. D., Huba, C. J., & Bentler, P. M. (1981). A multidimensional assessment of stressful life events among adolescents: Derivations and correlates. *Journal of Health and Social Behavior, 22,* 400–415.

Paykel, E. S. & Dowlatshahi, D. (1988). Life events and mental disorder. In S. Fisher & J. Reason (eds.), *Handbook of life stress, cognition and health* (pp. 241–263). Chichester: Wiley.

Perkins, D. V. (1982). The assessment of stress using life events scales. In L. Goldberger & S. Breznitz (eds.), *Handbook of stress. Theoretical and clinical aspects* (pp. 320–331). New York: The Free Press.

Semmer, N. K., Dwyer, J. H., Lippert, P., Fuchs, R., Cleary, P. D., & Schindler, A. (1987). Adolescent smoking from a functional perspective: The Berlin-Bremen Study. *European Journal of Psychology of Education, 2,* 387–402.

Semmer, N., Lippert, P.; Fuchs, R.; Rieger-Ndakorerwa, G.; Dwyer, J. H. & Knoke, E. A. (in press). *Gesundheitsverhalten im Kindes- und Jugendalter. Ausgewählte Ergebnisse der Berlin-Bremen Studie.* Stuttgart: Kohlhammer.

Semmer, N. & Zapf, D. (1989). Validity of various methods of measurement in job analysis. In K. Landau & W. Rohmert (eds.), *Recent developments in job analysis* (pp. 67–78). London: Taylor & Francis.

Skinner, H. A. & Lei, H. (1980). Differential weights in life change research: useful or irrelevant? *Psychosomatic Medicine, 42,* 367–370.

Vinokur, A. & Selzer, M. L. (1975). Desirable versus undesirable life events: Their relationship to stress and mental distress. *Journal of Personality and Social Psychology, 32,* 329–337.

Vossel, G. (1987). Stress conceptions in life event research: Towards a person-centred perspective. *European Journal of Personality, 1,* 123–140.

Thomae, H. (1987). Conceptualizations of responses to stress. *European Journal of Personality, 1,* 171–192.

Ulich, E. (1983). Humanisierung der Arbeit – Konzepte, Mögichkeiten und Probleme. In H. Siegwart & G. J.B. Probst (Hrsg.), *Mitarbeiterführung und gesellschaftlicher Wandel* (S. 271–286). Bern: Haupt.

Ulich, E. (1990). Individualisierung und differentielle Arbeitsgestaltung. In C. Graf Hoyos & B. Zimolong (Hrsg.), *Ingenieurpsychologie* (Enzyklopädie der Psychologie, Themenbereich D, Serie III, Bd. 2, S. 511–535). Göttingen: Hogrefe.

Zapf, D. (1989). *Selbst- und Fremdbeobachtung in der psychologischen Arbeitsanalyse.* Göttingen: Hogrefe.

Zimmerman, M. (1983). Weighted versus unweighted life event scores: Is there a difference? *Journal of Human Stress, 9,* 30–35.

Zimmermann, I. (1986). *Life Events, Daily Hassles und psychisches Wohlbefinden im Jugendalter.* Unpublished Master's Thesis, Technical University of Berlin, Berlin.

Part IV.

Social Practices and the Dynamics of Social Representations

Subjective Theories and Their Social Foundation in Education

Hanns-Dietrich Dann

During the fifties, social scientists explicitly took into account that the ordinary person also has psychological concepts and uses them in his or her everyday life (Heider, 1958; Kelly, 1955; Schütz, 1953/54). Since Uwe Laucken (1974) published his "Naive Behaviour Theory", intensive research has begun especially in German speaking countries, and during recent years, in the Anglo-American area too (e.g. Shavelson, 1988). Although different headings are prefered, e.g. professional or lay theories; implicit or tacit theories; everyday understanding; everyday psychology; common-sense-psychology or subjective theories; central assumptions are formulated with considerable agreement, which characterize the underlying conception of man, i.e., the autonomous and responsible person who performs goal-directed actions, who actively and cognitively structures his or her scope of action, and in doing so uses a complex knowledge system which he or she has acquired during the life span.

1. A working definition of "subjective theories" and main research questions

With regard to formal aspects, not all kinds of knowledge can be described as subjective theories. Only the most complex forms of knowledge systems are subsumed under this topic. A majority of authors presumably would agree with the following components of a working definition (Dann, 1990):

1. Subjective theories are relatively stable cognitive (or mental) representations of "reality", which nonetheless may be altered through experience. As such, they have to be distinguished from momentary and conscious cognitions, which of course may be manifestations or actualizations of subjective theories, as well as of other elements of knowledge.
2. Subjective theories are often implicit (as unreflected belief systems), yet in part they may be accessible to the actor's consciousness, so that he or she is able to report about them. This may be the case at least under some specific conditions (e.g. if they are concerned with salient and frequent events, were recently activated during intentional behaviour, and if reasonable support for explication is offered).
3. Subjective theories have similar structural properties as scientific theories. Specifically, they can be adequately represented as having an argumentative structure (e.g. if-then statements), which allows conclusions to be drawn or inferences to be made. By that, subjective theories are separated from single cognitions or isolated knowledge elements.
4. Analogous to "objective theories" in science, subjective theories in principle, fulfill the functions of (a) defining situations, i.e. constituting personal reality; (b) explaining (and often justifying) past events; (c) predicting or mere expecting further events; and (d) generating suggestions for attaining desired or avoiding undesired events.
5. Moreover, subjective theories are important factors in organizing, regulating and controlling actions. At least certain subjective-theoretical structures constitute an important part of the knowledge base of actions; under certain conditions they are activated in the course of actions. Together with other factors, e.g. emotional processes, they influence the kind of observable behaviour within the context of goal-directed action.

This latter statement seems especially important. Much of the theoretical attractiveness of the concept is apparently due to this basic assumption.

No doubt, this working definition is not without problems, e.g. the notion of analogy between subjective theories on the one hand and objective (scientific) theories on the other. A discussion of these and other questions has been conducted by several authors (e.g. Laucken, 1982; Dann, 1983; Dann & Wahl,

1985), and in an especially sound manner by Groeben, Wahl, Schlee and Scheele (1988). They also clear up several misunderstandings. One of them is the suggestion that using the concept of subjective theories presupposes the fiction of complete rationality. Instead, human beings are conceived as having potential, but not absolute rationality, under all conditions and for all possible reactions. How far-reaching human behaviour may be reconstructed in this way, is at last an empirical question, as well as the kinds of rationality which are used in everyday-life.

However, Groeben et al. (1988) argue for a definition of "subjective theories" which is narrower than the one explicated above. They propose to use the term for those complex cognitions "... which may be actualized and reconstructed in dialogue consensus ..." (p. 22) between an interviewer and his or her interviewee. Other assessment techniques are said not to be in correspondence with the epistemological conception of human beings. According to this proposal, all kinds of reconstructions which are not subjected to "communicative validation" are considered as subjective theories in a broader sense, and as "a mere preliminary approach" (p. 23). As a consequence, the majority of empirical research conducted so far misses the narrow definition of subjective theories. There is also no sense of speaking about implicit subjective-theoretical structures in this case, because a consensus between researcher and subject about implicit structures is not attainable. It seems questionable, if such a methodological restriction is appropriate or agreeable. We should better point to the innovative potential of dialogue consensus techniques and strive for a methodological enrichment in this direction. So far as such methods lead to better results, they will be prefered more frequently.

Considering subjective theories as important co-determinants of actions, the following questions have to be answered by research:

1. The *structure* of subjective theories (knowledge organization): How is subjective-theoretical knowledge about several topics composed and organized? Which kinds, forms or prototypes of knowledge have to be distinguished? How is it possible to assess subjective theories? What kinds of methods for reconstruction and representation have to be developed?

2. The *function* of subjective theories (knowledge application): How is subjective-theoretical knowledge actually used in everyday life? What are the different functions which have to be fulfilled in detail? How are subjective theories normally used in the regulation and justification of actions? Which conditions influence these applications? Under which conditions do subjective theories loose their action-regulating function?

3. The *development* of subjective theories (knowledge acquisition): How is subjective-theoretical knowledge acquired, built up and developed in the long run? Which conditions influence these acquisition processes? How can subjective theories and related actions be modified in order to improve the actor's problem solving capacities?

These research questions have also to be answered under differential aspects, because interindividual differences have to be expected. Anyway, the starting point in this area is always individual theories. Only after that, generalizations across several persons are possible through aggregative procedures, which may lead to overindividual social representations. First empirical results are available for all the above mentioned questions. Most of the research has been conducted in the field of education, learning and instruction, and especially on teachers' cognitions.

2. Analysis of teachers' subjective theories

As an example of research in this area I will report some of the results which have been yielded during a research project on "Aggression at School". Our main question was: What are the cognitive representations and processes used by teachers in their conflict management with students during instruction? The project's starting point was the subjective theories teachers hold concerning aggressive and disruptive student actions and their own actions regarding these students. Knowing more about the structure and functioning of teachers' everyday understanding of aggressive interactions is assumed to provide a framework for improving their problem solving capacities in this respect.

In an endeavour to specifically identify those aspects of teachers' aggression-related subjective theories which have an action-regulating function, we developed a set of assessment methods. These methods include more traditional questionnaire techniques as well as innovative tests and reconstruction strategies (Dann & Humpert, 1987; Humpert, Tennstädt & Dann, 1987; Krause & Dann, 1986).

One of the instruments was a pool of concrete causes, or factors to which aggressive behaviour could possibly be attributed (e. g. the weather, the class composition, the teacher-student relationship, etc.). Teachers had to indicate on a five-point scale how important they considered each factor to be for the occurence of student aggression. Four scales were derived from this item pool according to Weiner's matrix for causal attributions: external and stable (unchangeable) explanations; external and variable (changeable) explanations etc. To test the relationship between the teachers' explanatory dimensions and their conflict-related actions they were systematically observed during classroom hours. For this purpose we developed a special observational system, which contained 10 categories for disruptive student behaviours and 11 categories for the teacher's reactions (Humpert & Dann, 1988).

In particular, external variable explanations are linked to overt behaviour, that is, classwork organization, educational climate, teacher-student relationship, etc., factors which substantially depend on the teacher's own influence. The more a teacher considers these factors as important causes of students' aggression, the more he reacts with neutral behaviour and the less he relies on punitive reactions (Dann, 1990). Moreover we found that teachers who adhere to these external variable explanations were also more successful in conflict management during classroom hours. Successful teaching in this respect was assessed from data of systematic observation, as well as expert ratings and teachers' self statements (Dann, Tennstädt, Humpert & Krause, 1987). Finally, it could be demonstrated that teachers who are high on the external-variable scale have a better educational climate in their classroom. They perceive their students as being less ag-

gressive, more cooperative, and more emotionally involved (Kohler, 1987).

High external-variable explanations for aggressive student behaviour include, in all likelihood, two aspects: namely (1) teachers feel more responsible for their students and do not shift responsibility to other factors; and (2) they see themselves as having more influence on their students and do not feel powerless. In line with this interpretation, teacher training which proved to be effective for conflict management techniques gave rise to an increase in external-variable explanations and teachers' perceived influence on aggressive students (Tennstädt & Dann, 1987).

The method for assessing subjective theories outlined so far is concerned with *functional knowledge*, that is, knowledge about the possible causes of behaviour. Another kind of knowledge could be called *action knowledge*, that is, knowledge about what to do in certain situations in order to obtain a specific goal. Moreover, most of the results reported so far rely on correlational evidence; they don't allow any statement about the direction of influence between cognitions and behaviour. Is interactive behaviour at least partially dependent on subjective theories? Or are subjective theories only justifications of otherwise guided behaviour? Last but not least, one could ask: Do subjective theories assessed by paper-and-pencil tests really represent the perspective of the teachers themselves? The single teacher in answering the final questionnaire has no chance of expressing his individual perspective independently from the categories provided. The study reported now addresses these issues.

A postactional interview and graphic representation technique was developed (Krause & Dann, 1986). This reconstruction process is realized in three steps. (1) Aggressive interactions are observed during classwork. (2) Immediately after the lesson, an interview is carried out focussing on a specific episode which in the teacher's opinion, contained aggressive behaviour. Basically the teacher is encouraged to explicate thoughts and feelings which he or she had experienced at that very moment as well as assumptions which have been important to him or her. (3) Finally, by an intensive dialogue between interviewer and teacher, the interview data is arranged in a graphic display. The basic formal structure of the graphic representation

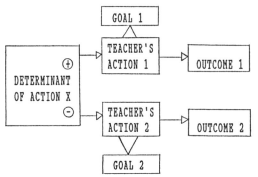

Figure 1. Basic formal structure of the graphic representation of teachers' action knowledge.

is shown in Figure 1. The teachers' thinking about their own actions normally refers to four concepts: determinants of the action; the action itself; the action's goal; and the action's outcome which might be a determinant for the next action. These determinants are of special interest here. If one asks a teacher "What do you normally do in this situation?", his or her answer will often be "it depends on …", and then he or she mentions certain conditions, which, in his or her view, are possibly crucial determinants of his or her actions. For a given teacher's thinking the real graphic structures are much more complex.

The three steps, (observation during classwork, interview, and graphic reconstruction), are repeated on different episodes over several days. Thereby, a first proposal of the graph is revised until the teacher can fully agree with its content. This procedure is referred to as "communicative validation" of subjective theories; the ultimate criterion for a correct reconstruction being the "dialogue consensus" between the two interview partners.

Of course, dialogue consensus does not guarantee that the cognitions are really relevant for actions. We therefore visited our teachers during classhours for a second time (Dann & Krause, 1988). Over a period of several days, new aggression-relevant episodes were observed. From the graphic representations, predictions can be made concerning the teachers' new actions in comparable situations. The question to be answered is: Does the teacher under specified conditions, behave in the same manner as predictable from the graph?

Correct predictions of systematically observed behaviour turned out to be much more frequent than could be expected by chance. The degree of consistency between predicted and realized actions, ranging between 0 and 1, was about .70. Even 43% of the predictions reached a degree of consistency-value of 1.0. Wahl, Schlee, Krauth & Mureck (1983) in a similar study, using only yes-no decisions instead of degrees of consistency, found 38 % correct predictions, which was significantly higher than chance findings. These results seem to indicate that postactional interview and graphic representation techniques with communicative validation, may have a substantial degree of validity in assessing action-relevant subjective theories. Again, the prediction studies do not prove in a strict sense that subjective theories may fulfil an action-regulating function. But the evidence that subjective theories do not only serve a justifying function for otherwise guided behaviour, is now much better than on the basis of the correlational studies alone.

As a consequence, subjective theories of teachers may be considered as important parts of their professional knowledge base, which guides their actions at school. As has been elaborated in research on "teachers' cognitions", teachers are experts in their field and have acquired a body of expert knowledge (e.g. Bromme, 1987; Calderhead, 1987). This is not simply knowledge of a particular subject (e.g. maths, foreign languages etc). It also consists of knowledge of learners and learning processes, of students' mistakes and instruction methods, of disruptive student behaviour, appropriate measures and a lot of other aspects of school life. Teachers use this expert knowledge in their daily practice, i.e. in interpreting situations, in generating plans of action, in steering actions and in evaluating their outcome.

From a developmental point of view we probably have to assume an interdependent relationship: During a continuous interchange certain constellations are built up with specific subjective theories and corresponding action patterns within a cultural context. In this continuing sozialization process, cultural and subcultural influences as well as actions and their experienced consequences lead to certain subjective theories, which in turn regulate actions

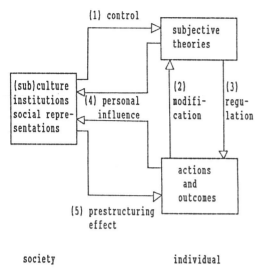

(1) control

subjective
theories

(sub)culture
institutions
social repre-
sentations

(4) personal
influence

(2)
modifi-
cation

(3)
regu-
lation

actions
and
outcomes

(5) prestructuring
effect

society   individual

Figure 2. Functional relationships between subjective theories and actions within a cultural context.

and exert their influence on (sub)cultural conditions. In accordance with this position, subjective theories can be considered as individually modified social representations in which societal knowledge is organized (v. Cranach, Mächler & Steiner, 1983). The individual professional knowledge is hence of social origin, as it contains overindividual societal aspects. The link between social representations and subjective theories is established, above all, by communicative processes. Moreover, (sub)cultural and institutional conditions exert a prestructuring effect on possible actions and their outcomes, which in turn give rise to modifications of subjective theories. These arguments show that in this area, the issue of simple causality is not one which can easily be applied. From a developmental point of view we should better assume a dialectic relation between subjective theories and actions.

Subjective theories and actions of teachers are of course, especially influenced by school. This institution with its societal structures and functions, determines not only the objective, but also the subjective conditions of teachers' actions to a considerable degree (Thommen, 1985). It is probable that subjective theories of teachers are partially acquired during the formal teacher education, but also during their years as students at school and especially during the years as practising teachers. Hence, the college system, the school system and the in-

dividual institutions the single teacher has shared in, with its special norms and conventions, are of relevance here. Up until now, there is nearly no empirical research on the socialization processes during the ontogenesis of subjective theories (Groeben et al., 1988).

According to these theoretical assumptions on the relationship between subjective theories and action, one should expect that teachers who differ for instance, in their conflict management capabilities, have also different subjective theories. This was exactly what we found in our teaching success study (Dann et al., 1987; Dann 1989a). More successful teachers turned out to be quite different from less successful teachers: The subjective theories of successful teachers are more complex, more efficiently organized and more consistent with overt behaviour.

Certainly subjective theories are not always used in the regulation of actions. There are conditions under which they lose their action-regulating function. From action theory, (especially Tomaszewski, 1978), it can be expected that this is the case when the person is in an unusual emotional state. In the previously mentioned prediction study, (Dann & Krause, 1988), we found the degree of consistency between subjective theories and behaviour to be especially low if teachers were very angry and felt hindered in pursuing their goals. It can be shown that hostile goals within an aggression motive are activated in such situations (Kornadt, 1982). Under certain conditions, this leads to aggression motivated actions; in this case to more punitive and escalating measures towards disruptive students. It seems important to note that even such cases of inconsistency between subjective theory and action can easily be explained in action theoretical terms.

3. Modification of teachers' subjective theories and actions

If subjective theories together with emotional processes fulfil important action-regulating functions within a cultural context, and if, from a developmental point of view, we have to assume a dialectic relation between subjective theories and actions, then a modification of subjective theories under certain conditions should result in corresponding changes of behaviour. This is the basic idea for intervention programs which take the teachers' subjective theories as a starting point and try to transform them as far as necessary and possible into more appropriate kinds of knowledge in order to improve the teachers' problem solving capacities. Three principles seem to be important to achieve this goal (Dann, 1989b; Dann, 1991):

1. The already existing knowledge and problem solving capacity has to be activated. This can be realized by reconstructing teachers' subjective theories about their problems and their corresponding actions in these problem situations. The initially implicit or tacit theories have to be made explicit and accessible for change.
2. The individual subjective theories have to be confronted with new knowledge, which may be offered by teaching colleagues as well as by educational research. To become effective for action, the new knowledge has to be integrated into the existing knowledge system. The existing knowledge shall be enriched and dysfunctional components eliminated during this process.
3. To guarantee that the newly generated knowledge becomes better than the old one, it has to be used within the relevant context. Practical action is necessary and allows the successful application of the newly emerging knowledge to problem situations. Thus, teachers are able to develop new and better action strategies for handling problem situations, to really learn from their educational practice and, in the long run, to establish more efficient routines of interactive teaching.

These principles might be relevant for different contexts of learning and instruction, especially where the goal is not only to augment the learner's knowledge, but also to modify some aspects of his or her modes of action. How these principles can be realized has already been demonstrated for teacher education (Born, Kuster, Flückiger & Füglister, 1983; Müller-Fohrbrodt, 1988) and for in-service training of teachers (Huber et al., 1982; Schlee & Wahl, 1987; Tennstädt, Krause, Humpert & Dann, 1987).

The target group for our "Konstanzer Trainingsmodell (KTM)" (Tennstädt et al., 1987) are teachers who, in their own opinion, have special problems with aggressive and disruptive students, as well as teachers who generally want to strengthen their educational impact. The KTM is designed as a self-help programme with two teachers working together in tandem, i.e. mutually visiting each others lessons, discussing their respective problems, and working out possible solutions according to selected parts of the programme.

According to our action theoretical approach, a teacher action may be split up into several components or sub-processes, especially the understanding of the situation, the development of an action programme, the processing of the programme and the evaluation of the action's outcome. Ten training elements are assigned to these sub-processes (Tennstädt, 1987). According to the individual nature of his problems, every teacher makes his selection of these training elements. For this purpose the training begins with diagnostic steps consisting of the interview and graphic representation technique, (Krause & Dann, 1986), and the observational system, (Humpert & Dann, 1988), which have been described above.

A central training element contains several proposals of action strategies with a number of concrete measures which are described in detail and which may be adapted to the trainee's special needs. These strategies and measures are grounded on communication theory, as well as on principles of group dynamics and social-cognitive learning. Other training elements are concerned with, for example, strategies of social perception, attribution patterns, action goals and situational pressures. Special attention is given to emotional processes which may disturb cooperative forms of dealing with aggressive and disruptive students. Altogether the KTM is intended to support more professional conflict resolution and management in classes. First empirical evaluations show a number of positive changes during the training process in observable behaviour as well as in self-perception of students and teachers (Tennstädt, 1987; Tennstädt & Dann, 1987).

Conclusions

Teachers' subjective theories are obviously, as our studies show, subject to change within a cultural context. Such changes influence the type of actions teachers engage in, that is, they effect a change in teaching activities. As a consequence, subjective theories do not only serve a justifying function for otherwise guided behaviour; together with emotional processes they also fulfil important action-regulating functions. However, teachers' actions and their consequences will introduce changes in subjective theories as well.

Because of these interdependent relations it is impossible to make simple causal statements in this domain. Moreover, "scientific" theorizing without taking into account subjective theories in this area of educational psychology is a vacuous undertaking. Last, but not least, our results yielded so far seem to show that using subjective theories as a central concept allows the performance of psychological research and educational practice according to the same principles and to a certain extent, even with the same methods.

Literature

Born, R., Kuster, H., Flückiger, V., & Füglister, P. (1983). Teilnehmendes Lehren – mitgestaltendes Lernen. In L. Montada, K. Reusser, & G. Steiner (Hrsg.), *Kognition und Handeln* (S. 240–252). Stuttgart: Klett-Cotta.

Bromme, R. (1987). Der Lehrer als Experte – Entwurf eines Forschungsansatzes. Denken und Wissen von Lehrern aus der Perspektive neuerer Forschung zum Problemlösen. In H. Neber (Hrsg.), *Angewandte Problemlösepsychologie* (S. 127–151). Münster: Aschendorff.

Calderhead, J. (Ed.). (1987). *Exploring teachers' thinking*. London: Cassell.

Cranach, M. v., Mächler, E., & Steiner, V. (1983). *Die Organisation zielgerichteter Handlungen: ein Forschungsbericht*. Bern: Universität, Psychologisches Institut.

Dann, H.-D. (1983). Subjektive Theorien: Irrweg oder Forschungsprogramm? Zwischenbilanz eines kognitiven Konstrukts. In L. Montada, K. Reusser, & G. Steiner (Hrsg.), *Kognition und Handeln* (S. 77–92). Stuttgart: Klett-Cotta.

Dann, H.-D. (1989a). Was geht im Kopf des Lehrers vor? Lehrerkognitionen und erfolgreiches pädagogisches Handeln. *Psychologie in Erziehung und Unterricht, 36*, 81–90.

Dann, H.-D. (1989b). Subjektive Theorien als Basis erfolgreichen Handelns von Lehrkräften. *Beiträge zur Lehrerbildung. Zeitschrift zu theoretischen und praktischen Fragen der Didaktik der Lehrerbildung, 7*, 247–254.

Dann, H.-D. (1990). Subjective theories: a new approach to psychological research and educational practice. In G. R. Semin, & K. J. Gergen (Eds.), *Everyday understanding: social and scientific implications* (pp. 227–243). London: Sage.

Dann, H.-D. (1991). Pädagogisches Verstehen: Subjektive Theorien und erfolgreiches Handeln von Lehrkräften. In K. Reusser, & M. Reusser (Hrsg.), *Verstehen lernen – Verstehen lehren. Verstehen als psychologischer Prozeß und als didaktische Aufgabe*. Bern: Huber (im Druck).

Dann, H.-D., & Humpert, W. (1987). Eine empirische Analyse der Handlungswirksamkeit subjektiver Theorien von Lehrern in aggressionshaltigen Unterrichtssituationen. *Zeitschrift für Sozialpsychologie, 18*, 40–49.

Dann, H.-D., & Krause, F. (1988). Subjektive Theorien: Begleitphänomen oder Wissensbasis des Lehrerhandelns bei Unterrichtsstörungen? *Psychologische Beiträge, 30*, 269–291.

Dann, H.-D., & Wahl, D. (1985). Subjektive Theorien als Gegenstand und Forschungsprogramm der Psychologie. In D. Albert (Hrsg.), *Bericht über den 34. Kongreß der Deutschen Gesellschaft für Psychologie in Wien 1984* (S. 739–742). Göttingen: Verlag für Psychologie Dr. C. J. Hogrefe.

Dann, H.-D., Tennstädt, K.-Ch., Humpert, W., & Krause, F. (1987). Subjektive Theorien und erfolgreiches Handeln von Lehrern/-innen bei Unterrichtskonflikten. *Unterrichtswissenschaft, 15*, 306–320.

Groeben, N., Wahl, D., Schlee, J., & Scheele, B. (1988). *Das Forschungsprogramm Subjektive Theorien. Eine Einführung in die Psychologie des reflexiven Subjekts*. Tübingen: Francke.

Heider, F. (1958). *The psychology of interpersonal relations*. New York: Wiley. Dt. Übers. 1977. *Psychologie der interpersonalen Beziehungen*. Stuttgart: Klett.

Huber, G. L u. .a. (Hrsg.) (1982). *Fernsehkolleg Lehrerprobleme – Schülerprobleme. Ein Programm zur Verbesserung pädagogischer Handlungsmöglichkeiten*. Tübingen: Deutsches Institut für Fernstudien an der Universität.

Humpert, W., & Dann, H.-D. (unter Mitarbeit von T. v. Kügelgen und W. Rimele) (1988). *Das Beobachtungssystem BAVIS. Ein Beobachtungsverfahren zur Analyse von aggressionsbezogenen*

Interaktionen im Schulunterricht. Göttingen: Verlag für Psychologie Dr. C. J. Hogrefe.

Humpert, W., Tennstädt, K.-Ch., & Dann, H.-D. (1987). *Erfassung subjektiver Theorien von Hauptschullehrern, des Unterrichtsklimas sowie berufsbezogener Einstellungen. Dokumentation und Beschreibung der von der Forschungsgruppe "Sozialpsychologie der Schule" entwickelten Skalen* (Projekt "Aggression in der Schule", Arbeitsbericht 12). Konstanz: Universität, Sozialwissenschaftliche Fakultät.

Kelly, G. A. (1955). *The psychology of personal constructs*. New York: Norton. Dt. Übers. 1986. *Die Psychologie der persönlichen Konstrukte*. Paderborn: Junfermann.

Kohler, J. (1987). *Das Konstanzer Trainingsmodell (KTM). Überprüfung der impliziten Annahmen.* Unveröff. Dipl.-Arbeit, Universität Konstanz.

Kornadt, H.-J. (1982). *Aggressionsmotiv und Aggressionshemmung. Bd. 1, Empirische und theoretische Untersuchungen zu einer Motivationstheorie der Aggression und zur Konstruktvalidierung eines Aggressions-TAT*. Bern: Huber.

Krause, F., & Dann, H.-D. (1986). *Die Interview- und Legetechnik zur Rekonstruktion kognitiver Handlungsstrukturen ILKHA. Ein unterrichtsnahes Verfahren zur Erfassung potentiell handlungswirksamer subjektiver Theorien von Lehrern* (Projekt "Aggression in der Schule", Arbeitsbericht 9). Konstanz: Universität, Sozialwissenschaftliche Fakultät.

Laucken, U. (1974). *Naive Verhaltenstheorie*. Stuttgart: Klett.

Laucken, U. (1982). Aspekte der Auffassung und Untersuchung von Umgangswissen. *Schweizerische Zeitschrift für Psychologie, 41*, 87–113.

Müller-Fohrbrodt, G. (1988). *Einführung in die konstruktive Bearbeitung von Problemsituationen. Ein Ansatz zur erfahrungsbezogenen Ausbildung von Pädagogen* (Berichte und Studien Nr. 24). Trier: Universität, Abt. Pädagogik.

Schlee, J., & Wahl, D. (Hrsg.) (1987). *Veränderung*

Subjektiver Theorien von Lehrern. Oldenburg: Universität, Zentrum für pädagogische Berufspraxis.

Schütz, A. (1953/54). Common sense and scientific interpretation of human action. *Philosophy and Phenomenological Research, 16*, 1–37.

Shavelson, R. J. (1988). Contributions of educational research to policy and practice: constructing, challenging, changing cognition. *Educational Researcher, 17* (10), 4–11, 22.

Tennstädt, K.-Ch. (1987). *Das Konstanzer Trainingsmodell (KTM). Ein integratives Selbsthilfeprogramm für Lehrkräfte zur Bewältigung von Aggressionen und Störungen im Unterricht. Bd. 2: Theoretische Grundlagen, Beschreibung der Trainingsinhalte und erste empirische Überprüfung*. Bern: Huber.

Tennstädt, K.-Ch., & Dann, H.-D. (1987). *Das Konstanzer Trainingsmodell (KTM). Ein integratives Selbsthilfeprogramm für Lehrkräfte zur Bewältigung von Aggressionen und Störungen im Unterricht. Bd. 3: Evaluation des Trainingserfolgs im empirischen Vergleich*. Bern: Huber.

Tennstädt, K.-Ch., Krause, F., Humpert, W., & Dann, H.-D. (1987). *Das Konstanzer Trainingsmodell (KTM). Neue Wege im Schulalltag: Ein zeitgemäßes Selbsthilfeprogramm für Unterrichten und Erziehen. Einführung: Kurzinformation* (Nachdruck 1991). *Bd. 1: Trainingshandbuch* (2. korrig. und erweit. Aufl. 1990). Bern: Huber.

Thommen, B. (1985). *Alltagspsychologie von Lehrern über verhaltensauffällige Schüler*. Bern: Huber.

Tomaszewski, T. (1978). *Tätigkeit und Bewußtsein. Beiträge zur Einführung in die polnische Tätigkeitspsychologie*. Weinheim: Beltz.

Wahl, D., Schlee, J., Krauth, J., & Mureck, J. (1983). *Naive Verhaltenstheorie von Lehrern. Abschlußbericht eines Forschungsvorhabens zur Rekonstruktion und Validierung subjektiver psychologischer Theorien*. Oldenburg: Universität, Zentrum für pädagogische Berufspraxis.

Management and Leadership as Relational Phenomena

H. Peter Dachler

The social-psychological phenomena implied by leadership and management in work organizations have gained a special significance with respect to practical consequences of a rapidly changing environmental context of organizations, and the exponential increase in the complexity and ambiguity of problematic issues with which organizations are confronted and will increasingly be confronted in the future (e. g. Schön, 1982). Leadership and management within the context of modern organizations also pose some fundamental challenges to psychological theory and research with respect to understanding the interplay between *individual* attributes and behaviors and those of *organizations as a whole* (e. g. Dachler, 1988; von Cranach & Tschan, 1990; Graumann & Moscovici, 1986). The central theme of this paper argues that the *social foundations of knowledge* and the *relational construction of reality* are fundamentally ignored aspects in the efforts to understand the issues we subsume under the concept of leadership. Moreover, these overlooked and constituting aspects of leadership contribute to seeing leadership as an individually based, causal set of factors in the design and development of social, government and economic institutions rather than making it possible to explore leadership as a fundamentally collective, *social-relational process* of organizational design and change. Thus, it is the main thesis of this paper that not individual attributes and behaviors represent the crucial focus for understanding and explaining leadership. Rather it is precisely the issue of *social-interpretative processes* as the bases for constructing the conceptualizations of "leadership" realities, that represent the precondition for integrating the concepts of leadership and management into theories of organizing in general (cf. Hosking, 1989).

Similar issues have been raised by theorists, such as Moscovici (1972) and Tajfel (1972, 1981) who have lamented the fact that we do not yet possess a satisfactory account of the nature of *socio-psychological* processes through which collective phenomena or "collective individuality" can be understood. Knorr-Cetina (1987) has recently addressed these issues very directly by challenging the traditional juxtaposition of individual action and social structures. The theoretical and practice-oriented debate regarding the underlying conceptions and methods used in understanding and explaining leadership and management in work organizations should begin to address and struggle with precisely this traditional juxtaposition of individual and collective identity (Dachler, 1990a; 1989; 1988; Smircich & Morgan, 1982).

Since we see leadership and management theory as an opportunity to move toward a more adequate account of social-psychological processes through which the collective "identity" of organizations could be more meaningfully understood, I would like to briefly outline some of the major issues that need to be addressed in leadership and management research. This might help in providing an initial basis for re-thinking some *programmatic* questions for leadership and management research and its constituting role in the understanding and in the practical managing of today's complex organizational world.

Management, leadership and organization theory as epistemological phenomena

Let me start with the problem of management, leadership and organization theory as basically epistemological phenomena. To the extent that epistemology has played a role at all in the area of leadership, management and organizational research, the concern has been primarily with the philosophical and methodological processes of generating and validating collected data as well as with the way, we as scientists derive understanding and explanations *about* these phenomena.

This focus is a consequence of the predominating scientific tradition of distinguishing between the observing *subject* and the *"contents"* (i. e. attributes and behavior) of the *"objects"* to be investigated. Furthermore, this distinction is an integral part of the basic idea that acquisition of knowledge and understanding is fundamentally an attempt to match private representations of the world with contours of the world itself (Gergen, 1982). Critique of this central idea (e.g. Gadamer, 1986; v. Glasersfeld, 1981; Gergen, 1982; Schmidt, 1987), however, has opened up new perspectives in epistemology, bringing central ideas of the work of people like Berger & Luckmann, (1966); Neisser, (1976); Piaget (1937; 1970); and Weick, (1979), more directly into the domain of leadership and management theory and research. For example, there has emerged an increasing interest in researching the *processes* of knowing, understanding, and interpreting organizational realities within the context of the fundamental relatedness of participating organizational actors (cf. Berger & Luckmann, 1966; Dachler, 1988; 1990b; Gergen, 1982; Hosking, in press; 1989; Kruse, 1987; Moscovici, 1976; Smith, 1982; Weick, 1979). Furthermore, the role of communication within relational settings for the way collective realities are interpreted has received increasing attention (e. g. Palazzoli et al., 1984; Watzlawick et al., 1967).

These initial steps towards an alternative perspective of epistemology in general are developing the basic idea, that understanding, i.e. the way some "text" is known as reality, involves ongoing, circular processes between "pre-existing" and usually implicit conceptual frameworks and what is thereby selected out of the essentially unlimited potential that is knowable in the "world out there". Understanding and knowing is therefore not a relatedness between subject-object but between subject-subject. In creating the reality of the world of which one is a constituting part, one recreates at the same time one's own reality.

Within such a perspective of knowing, the dominating concern of social science to reduce, if not eliminate the subjectivity of the researcher, as well as of the investigated social actor (the object of research) as mistakes or as inaccuracies based upon the assumption that subjectivity misinforms our knowledge about the objective nature of the individual and so-cial world we want to know, becomes a myth or at least a perspective whose meaning and usefulness has become rather ambiguous. The reason for this is the fact that if our knowledge is to be as close a reproduction of some objective state of affairs as possible, it must be possible to know this objective state of affairs independently of our evolved means of knowing in order to be able to assess the degree of correspondence between our representations of the world and its objective manifestations. As is becoming increasingly clear, however, we can only know the world through the sensory and mental processes with which we have evolved and through the history driven, socially derived conceptual frameworks which we impose on the infinite potential options available in the world.

While these issues are certainly not new, there is relatively little work done on the *consequences* of such epistemological considerations for the social scientific process of inquiry in general and, more to the topic of this paper, for the *programmatic research agendas* in the areas of leadership, management, and social-organizational systems in general. Dominant research traditions still take collected data at face value and simply worry that their objectivity or validity is threatened by measurement error and other subjective processes, which we attempt to reduce as well as possible with our tool kit of methodological instruments and control procedures. What is hardly recognized as a crucial problem of knowing and understanding is the *joint* production of data by the researcher *together* with the investigated individual or social actors. Such a jointly accomplished production of data must be understood as a *social process* between researcher and human subjects, as well as, of course, between the observed social actors themselves *in the context* of their relationships with the investigators (cf. Dachler, 1989; Gergen, 1982; Knorr-Cetina, 1987).

It is the fundamental subjectiveness, or if you wish, the social interpretation of "observed" facts as well as the embeddedness of the interpretation processes in the social and cultural context that we must begin to understand. More importantly, these epistemological processes have to become an explicitly reflected aspect of our leadership and management theories and methodologies since, as people like Benson (1983) and others have pointed out, our scientific knowledge depends upon epistemological processes we do not theorize.

In summary, the main focus of leadership, management and organization research might better be directed at the socially based epistemological processes rather than at specific content issues, such as behavioral patterns of successful leaders, optimal structures and strategies, contents of employee motivation, etc., since such content issues, while important, are not "facts of an objective organizational reality", but an emergent reflection of socially constructed realities in constant change. It is these processes of collectively understood realities that are at the heart of leadership and management. And in this sense they become an integral part of the processes of organizing in general.

For the study of leadership, management and organization theory, the consequences of the above epistemological perspectives pertain to a rather different set of questions to be asked. Contrary to the traditional search for traits, behavior styles or types of individual leaders, the main questions relate to how the processes of leadership and management in organizations emerge, how realities of leadership are interpreted within the network of relations, how organizations are designed, directed, controlled and developed on the bases of collectively generated knowledge about organizational realities, and how decisions and actions are embedded in collective interpretation, sense-making, and attribution processes from which structures of social interdependencies emerge and in turn reframe the collectively generated organizational realities. Within such a perspective, the traditional distinction between leadership of people and management of organizations is no longer very useful.

We have far too long sliced up organizations into separate content areas of study, each being studied by separate specialists, with the result that we have had little success in giving accounts of organizational realities as a whole, as is shown, for example, by the current confusion inherent in research and theory regarding organizational culture. Another informing example of such an approach are the many attempts at humanizing the *immediate* work environ-

ment, without taking into consideration what basic new organizational realities would have to emerge in order to support, maintain, and give meaning to the job redesign efforts carried out in isolation. The many disappointing results are certainly in good part a consequence of such an "isolationist" approach to humanizing work (cf. Dachler & Enderle, 1989, S. 99).

The consequences of methodological individualism for integrating conceptions of leadership and management into organization theory

I would like to briefly point out the extent to which methodological individualism as a paradigm sets boundaries on the extent to which leadership and management can be understood as basically an issue of *organizing* in general.

If one proceeds from the currently still dominating structural/functional perspective of organizations, the questions *that make sense* within that framework must focus on issues such as division of labor, hierarchy of authority, on the fundamental distinction between the active subject and the passive object, with its implicit model of domination and separation in relationships in general. Out of this perspective it also makes sense to focus on dealing with problems such as designing positions whose tasks and competencies are rationally defined only within the principles of division of labor and hierarchy, or defining goals and objectives that only follow the functionalist logic, etc. More specifically, in a functional perspective of organizations, the idea of organizational effectiveness and efficiency is rationally based upon *a priori*-defined objectives and goals, on the basis of which the success of specific, logically interrelated organizational positions is established.

Interestingly, within such a perspective of organizations, an individualistic focus on leadership and management makes sense. Within such a framework it is sensible to focus on individuals who, by their position in organizations, are defined as leaders or managers, and about whom we want to know what individual skills, dispositions, attributes, and behavioral patterns or styles lead to what has already been logically defined as success in a given managerial position. If questions about the organization *as a whole* are posed, the logical starting point is to think about some aggregation of individual attributes, behaviors, or other individual output. Furthermore, even the management of an organization as a whole is individualized to the attributes and behaviors of a given chief executive or to the aggregated individual outputs of some monocentric coalition of powerholders.

The point of critique which needs to be underlined is not one of truth or falsity regarding methodological individualism, but the fact that within such a tradition of thinking, it becomes nearly impossible to take seriously in our research and theorizing, the fundamental collective or social nature of organizing. More specifically, within the logic of methodological individualism, it appears to make little explanatory sense and seems rather impractical to ask whether we would gain new insights if we thought of leadership and management as a social process, as phenomena embedded in social relationships defined by socially derived or constructed knowledge. Thus, it is our *implicit* preconceptions and assumptions which have a very strong bearing on what are considered to be meaningful, or useful questions and toward what kind of answers or solutions we strive as being practical, or in line with our implicit values and goals.

Consequently, the current crisis in leadership and management (e.g. McCall & Lombardo, 1978; Neuberger, 1984) must in fact be located in the *contextual metaperspective* regarding the nature of organizations as a whole. To keep looking for new variables in leadership situations, or additional traits, skills, personality variables, values, etc. which successful leaders or managers should have is singularly unproductive, as our recent research history in this area has clearly shown. This is so because we usually neglect to critically question the implicit preconceptions, assumptions, and naive theories about the nature of organizations which give meaning to the specific hypotheses derived for leadership and management research. To the extent that we finally can see the importance of other kinds of images of organizations, for instance, the inherent social political processes by which the experienced realities and problems are socially generated in organizations, or the various self-referential

and self-organizing processes on the basis of which structural forms appear and change, it becomes possible, useful and sensible to start asking very different kinds of questions regarding leadership and management.

Furthermore, related issues such as the idea of management success, appear as a rather different problem issue. Traditional approaches start from the point of view of commonly used management diagnostic and selection procedures, where success is seen as a consequence of the systematic analyses of predefined job and task requirements and their assumed contributions to the overall success of organizations. But within a social-relational view of organizations, it becomes meaningful to ask, to what extent management success and its implied objectives are in good part a *reflection* of constantly renegotiated social construction processes, based upon different implicit theories, beliefs, prejudices and dominant values and interests, that are constructed and reconstructed in the changing social and political dynamics within organizations and their societal, cultural, technical, and economic environment (Dachler, 1990c). Success is not a God-given, objective outcome.

Whether such different questions and the corresponding differences in the insights generated about leadership and management turn out to be in fact more useful from an explanatory, as well as from a practical point of view, depends upon their meaning and significance within the context of *what* issues, and *how* organizations seem to interpret as problems in need of solutions. Note, however, that the criterion for good research is no longer one of correspondence with some objective reality that is known independently of our process of inquiry. Instead, such criteria refer to the extent to which certain conceptual frameworks and the kind of results that are generated in that context are understandable, meaningful and heuristically useful within the context of socially constructed problem situations that organizations within their complex interdependencies have created for themselves. If, therefore, modern organizations are increasingly faced with a growing complexity and a resulting increase of problem ambiguity, the question can no longer be one of seeking more sophisticated organizational structures and selecting or training personnel in new required attributes, such as holistic thinking (Ulrich & Probst, 1988), flexibility, creativity, independent entrepreneurship and cooperative skills in team situations, as if one had to adapt the internal mechanisms of a machine to new requirements of the environment. The search must focus on the *social processes* on the basis of which new interpretations of realities can emerge that seem to be more meaningful and useful in understanding and dealing with the new state of affairs and the changed goals and values they usually imply.

Toward relationship as the basic unit of analysis in leadership and management research

Based upon the previous considerations, I would like to propose that the fundamental issues for understanding leadership and management lie in the complex interrelatedness of organizational actors and that therefore, our basic unit of analysis ought to be relationships, not individuals.

By relationships we do not refer to the still dominating paradigmatic conception of basically instrumental and influence-based notions of interpersonal, intra-group, inter-group and other forms of relationships that are still for the most part implied in current theories and practice of relational phenomena. Above all, relationships are inherently communicative. One can therefore think of them as "thick-layered" texts which are in principle equivocal and in need of interpretation. Texts are thick-layered and subject to multi-meanings since they are produced and heard by others within a multitude of interdependent contexts, such as societal, organizational, functional, task and various other meaning frameworks. In addition, they are produced and interpreted by others in the context of *embeddedness* in complex multiple and simultaneously activated relational networks. Texts produced by a manager, for example, reflect not only the context of the ongoing relationships but implicitly or explicitly also his or her relationships to other constituents or "partners" within and outside the organization. Therefore, both the content of what is communicated in relationships as well as the meaning of that content, i.e. the implicit metalevel communication of how

the content of the communication is to be understood, is always a reflection of the relational contexts. (cf. Bateson, 1972; 1979; Palazzoli et al., 1984 Watzlawick et al., 1967; Weick, 1979).

That leadership and management are social constructions which have emerged out of history from complex relationships and continue to be supported and cemented by the resulting social structures and the kind of relationships these imply, is in part a function of a nearly completely overlooked dynamic, namely that of the interplay between the masculine and feminine representation of reality. This dynamic refers to the implications of *how* the relations between the two halves of humanity are constructed for the *totality* of a social system (Eisler, 1990). She cogently observes, that "... the way we structure the most fundamental of all human relations (without which our species could not go on) has a profound effect on every one of our institutions, on our values, and ... on the direction of our cultural evolution, particularly whether it will be peaceful or warlike (Eisler, 1990, p. xix)". Based upon the division of labor which social evolution imposes upon the social structures and the corresponding relationships between the sexes since prehistoric times, the masculine world view has focussed on history making and, as Dinnerstein (1976) puts it, on world-structuring projects, whereas the feminine representation of reality is committed not only to the fundamental concerns of preserving the human species, but also to embracing the subjective and the emotional aspects of our world as well as the preservation of relationships to what is natural and to what it is to be human in general (cf. Gilligan, 1982).

Of particular concern with respect to leadership, management and organization theory is the increasing realization, that the dominant perspectives are nearly a total reflection of the masculine way of thinking. Gilligan (1982), for example, shows with impressive evidence, that the story of human development in general, and of the development of morality and responsibility in particular has only been told out of the masculine framework of thinking about reality. Interesting in this connection, is the fact that within the dominant masculine representation of reality, the story told by the feminine voice *cannot* be understood or is *misunderstood* because it does not appear to *fit* the projects and root objectives of the patriarchal model of reality and therefore is experienced (or socially constructed) as weak, irrational, ambivalent and lacking in persuasiveness and ability to get one's point of view accepted and adhered to by others (cf. Dachler, 1990b).

The issue I want to raise for this paper is not the problem of women in leadership or management positions, as crucial as that topic is, of course. I simply want to point out to what extent certain fundamental messages whose *meaning* is derived from the context of the feminine world view cannot be understood or are misinterpreted within the very different context of the masculine understanding of reality. Thus, taking the masculine representation of reality as self-evident and in that sense as the objective reality, is not only a myth, but it is, more importantly, a *dangerous assumption* about what knowledge and reality means. The self evidence of the masculine culture literally prevents the realization that its reality is *only one possible option*. As long as that option however is constructed as being objective, all the alternative possible options, for instance, those that could be derived from the feminine model of reality, are ignored or put off as meaningless, weak or not fitting the major world construction projects of the masculine understanding of reality.

Within the masculine framework of thinking about reality one can also show quite clearly a strong and worrisome pattern of implicit and deep rooted assumptions regarding the *nature and meaning of relationships* (e.g. Baker-Miller, 1986; Dinnerstein, 1976; Eisler, 1990; Gilligan, 1982). Generally speaking, the masculine perception of relationships emphasizes distance and delimitation. Contest and competition, to positively distinguish oneself from others by means of achievement and success, to mark a standpoint relative to others – these are all fundamental masculine *identity scripts* (Dachler & Dyllick, 1988; Müller, 1988). There are innumerable investigations which either directly or indirectly indicate that embeddedness in close relationships or in wide ranging, complex relational networks is experienced and feared as creating dependency, as threatening autonomy, as restricting self-reliance and above all, as undermining the fundamental masculine identity (e.g. Gilligan, 1982).

Similarly, studies on leaders and managers show consistent patterns of concerns that are symptomatic for a separation of one's own ego from the outside world, with the result that relationships to the outer social and natural world undergo a fundamental restriction and thereby develop the appearance of being objective and rational. Themes such as marking one's position, locating oneself relative to others, seeing oneself as the origin of the impetus to action, acting as role models who jump ahead in order to show the direction for others to follow, and being superior relative to followers on some crucial task relevant dimensions in order to be accepted as a leader, are all implicit assumptions within the self understanding of (mostly masculine, but often also feminine) leaders and managers (cf. Kruse, 1987; Müller, Biedermann, Alioth, Vaassen, Dachler, Dyllick, Feldmann and Hill, 1988).

If we look at the now popular leadership and management themes, that call for team spirit, cooperation, working with one another instead of against each other, providing visions, creating more independence for employees as a means of fostering creativity and motivation, designing participative systems, and so on, one has to recognize that such normative demands, despite their admirable goals and impressive scientific, moral and ethical substantiation cannot but remain "words". Alternatively, one could perceive them as social political actions that simply attempt to reduce the "negative" consequences of the masculine perspective of relationships, which in its self-evidence is *not* fundamentally questioned as only one option, and an option which in today's circumstances perhaps has reached its limits in its ability to fit our fundamental societal and organizational concerns.

The reason for this lies in neglecting to actively confront the concealed paradox that in the dominant masculine perspective, the capability for relationships and its corresponding very broadly understood capability for communication is restricted and crippled, comprising only an insignificant part of what *could potentially be possible in human interactions*. Such an evaluation of relationships within the masculine world view makes sense only within the context of the strongly relationship-oriented feminine representation of reality. To the extent that the feminine voice is not only heard, but also active attempts are made to understand and learn from its stories, a social reality can emerge, in whose context the *relational world* of the masculine construction of reality naturally appears impoverished, far removed from the basics of life and from what is in its natural roots. By being able to actually experience such an evaluation of the meaning of relationships in the context of the masculine framework of understanding reality, the basis is laid for a fundamental re- examination of the basic tenets that make up the masculine perspective as well as the social "order" that has evolved within that cultural context. Through such reconstruction processes, the limits of the knowledge base inherent in the masculine culture can become increasingly exposed (Dachler, 1990b).

The above arguments point to similar principles as are applicable to other organizational settings in which, for instance, marketing and production managers have to agree on some common understanding of and approach to some problem. The implicit social reality of a marketing manager is in crucial ways different from that of a production manager. These different realities are not personal differences but differences in the meaning of marketing and production problems as they have historically evolved and as they have acquired an ever-changing meaning within basic economic, technical, social, ecological and ideological contexts in society and within the organization itself. Thus, the crucial issue is not who has the most power to force through a given decision. Instead, the crucial issue relates to the implicit assumptions, prejudices and naive theories that guide the interpretation of the relational reality in this decision context and how these implicit assumptions can be changed in light of slowly *reframing* the social context for the mutual decision making situation.

Thus, rather than understand and decide the traditional marketing-production conflicts and misunderstandings observed in many organizations from a pre-conception of "right or wrong" or of one-dominating-the-other within the organizational context, one could also focus on a) the fundamental relational processes between the two functional departments and b) try to make explicit the implicit "cultures" inherent in the two functions, so that they can become accessible to critical analysis and the

necessary dialogue. Only from such a dialogue can a common understanding of the relational reality emerge. Instead of arguing about which function is more central or more dominant within the history and overall objectives of a given organization, a focus on the relationship between the two functional departments is likely to teach us a great deal about a) the differently understood realities inherent in the two functions and b) the *meaning* of the relationship between the two functions that emerges from the two different world views and the various processes of *negotiating* (Hosking & Morley, 1988) a common understanding of the reality both functions create for each other.

Within a relational approach to leadership and management, it might also become more apparent that the personal attributes of individual actors in relationships are not something objective that they bring with them to their relationships as they do their physical characteristics. Instead, we might begin to understand psychological characteristics of individual actors as a consequence of their relatedness. In other words, the attributes experienced ourselves and attributed to us by others serve as an additional process by which actors in relational networks struggle to interpret and make sense of the social reality they are in the process of experiencing (cf. Dachler, 1989; 1990C; Gergen & Davis, 1985).

Some summarizing comments on the usefulness of a relational approach to leadership and management

Several theoretical consequences with respect to allowing management and leadership theory to become a constituting aspect of the processes of organizing in general, and the ability to *ask different kinds of questions* that are not seen as meaningful, useful or practical within the traditional structural/functional approach to organization theory, have already been discussed. I would therefore like to summarize some of the main themes and practical consequences which seem to me, very important. Most of these refer to re-interpretations of basic problems in management and organizational settings in general.

Modern organizations increasingly face a

growing complexity, which in turn also makes problems to be solved less structured and more ambiguous in meaning. Moreover, an increasing internationalization among organizations is taking place. These developments require a fundamental rethinking of management and organization theory. Among the most crucial consequences of these developments are the increasing limits put on what is knowable and what can be accomplished with the traditional means – ends, deterministic, and analytical-reductionist thinking so deeply embedded in current management approaches (cf. Schön, 1982). As a consequence, the traditional doer-fixer image of leader-managers and the imagined controllability of structure and process in organizations is seen as increasingly problematic. Instead, a slowly emerging recognition is taking place that *interdependence* presents new challenges and that a great deal more "reconstruction" must take place which allows alternative ideas and approaches to emerge that are forged together in complex relational networks.

Thus, leadership and management are *not* individual issues but fundamentally relational processes in the construction of organizational realities. Leaders and managers form within their relational networks two closely interdependent realities: one with respect to the so-called objective reality, such as rules and regulations, technology, products, formal structures, etc; the other, and more fundamental reality concerns the meaning, the understanding, the conceptual frameworks and their implied values and goals, only on the basis of which the so-called objective reality can even be constructed and understood. Instead of the implicit assumption that the manager as intentional, active subject forms the reality of the passive object who does not participate in the intended values and goals of what reality is to be created, a relational perspective implies a subject-subject relationship of managerial reality construction. Managers are thereby an integral part of the *complex process of reality formation*. In socially constructing reality they simultaneously construct themselves and their reality in relation to others.

Such a perspective allows us to move away from the idea that managers are managers by virtue of their superiority over their subordinates which has greatly contributed to the perpetuation of immaturity among employees (Sievers, 1989). It also allows a recognition to what extent historically grown conceptions of organization in the context of the masculine perspective has made it extremely difficult for females to be effective without being required to "emancipate" themselves toward the masculine point of view. Furthermore, we can begin to understand the extent to which a dominant perspective has prevented the integration of the central themes of the feminine representation of reality into the processes of organizing, processes that seem more appropriate to the complexity and ambiguity faced by modern organization than seems to be the case with the traditional masculine model of how to understand and manage organizations (Dachler, 1990c). Finally, the focus on epistemological processes rather than on content issues in leadership and management phenomena may finally allow a full and direct inquiry into the social, subjective, political processes governing organizations as a basis for a broader understanding of the interplay between socially constructed realities (knowledge) and structural properties of organizations. All of this also implies *not* a positivistic assessment of knowledge on the basis of right or wrong, true or false. Rather, the issue becomes one of asking to what extent possible alternative options for framing problems, for finding approaches, for developing solutions are being ignored or overlooked as a consequence of being misunderstood within a dominant representation of reality which is taken as self- evident, as part of the natural order of things.

References

Baker Miller, J. (1986). *Toward a new psychology of women* (2nd ed.). Boston, MA: Beacon.

Bateson, G. (1972). *Steps to an ecology of mind.* New York: Bantam Books.

Bateson, G. (1979). *Mind and nature.* New York: Bantam Books.

Berger, P. L. & Luckmann, T. (1966). *The social construction of reality.* Garden City, N. Y.: Doubleday.

Dachler, H. P. (1990a) Führung und Organisation im Kontext von kultureller und sprachlicher Vielfalt in zukünftigen Organisationen [Leadership and organization in the context of cultural and liguistic variety of future organizations]. In K. Bleicher und P. Gomez (Hrsg.), *Zukunftsperspektiven der Organisation* (S. 45–66). Bern: Stämpfli.

Dachler, H. P. (1990b, Mai). *Oekologisches Denken als Beziehungsphänomen: Zur Integration widersprüchlicher Kulturen der Geschlechter* [Ecological thinking as a relational phenomenon: Integrating the contradictory cultures of the sexes]. Vorlesung im öffentlichen Vorlesungszyklus der Hochschule St. Gallen "Mensch-Umwelt-Wertvorstellungen: Das technisch-patriarchalische Denken und seine Auswirkungen.

Dachler, H. P. (1990c). Managementdiagnostik aus systemischer Sicht [Management diagnostics from a systemic perspective]. In W. Sarges (Hrsg.) *Management-Diagnostik* (S. 1–9). Göttingen: Hogrefe.

Dachler, H. P. (1989). Selection and the organizational context. In P. Herriot (Ed.), *Handbook of assessment in organizations* (pp. 45-69). Chichester: Wiley.

Dachler, H. P. (1988). Constraints on the emergence of new vistas in leadership and management research: An epistemological overview. In J. G. Hunt, J. R. Baliga, H. P. Dachler, and C. A. Schriesheim (Eds.), *Emerging leadership vistas*, Vol. 8, Leadership Series (pp. 261–285). Boston, MA: Lexington.

Dachler, H. P. & Dyllick, T. (1988). "Machen" und "Kultivieren": Zwei Grundperspektiven der Führung ["Doing" and "cultivating": Two basic perspectives of leadership]. *Die Unternehmung*, 4, 283–295.

Dachler, H. P. & Enderle, G. (1989). Epistemological and ethical considerations in conceptualizing and implementing human resource management. *Journal of Business Ethics*, 8, 597–606.

Dinnerstein, D. (1976). *The mermaid and the minotaur; Sexual arrangements and the human malaise.* New York: Harper & Row.

Eisler, R. (1990). *The chalice and the blade.* London: Unwin Paperbacks.

Gadamer, H. G. (1986). *Wahrheit und Methode. Grundzüge einer philosophischen Hermeneutik*, 5. Aufl. [Truth and method. Foundations of a philosophical hermeneutic]. Tübingen: Mohr-Siebeck.

Gergen, K. (1982). *Toward transformation in social knowledge.* New York: Springer.

Gergen, K. & Davis, K. E. (1985) *The social construction of the person.* New York/Heidelberg: Springer.

Gilligan, C. (1982). *In a different voice: Psychological theory and women's development.* Cambridge, MA: Harvard University Press.

Graumann, C. F. & Moscovici, S. (Eds.) (1986). *Changing conceptions of leadership.* New York: Springer.

Hosking, D. M. (in press). The organizing skills of chief executives: A strategic decision making perspective. *Revue de psychologie appliquée.*

Hosking, D. M. (1987). Führungsprozesse [Leadership processes]. In S. Greif, H. Holling & N. Nichelson (Hrsg.), *Arbeits- und Organisationspsychologie* (S. 235–239). München: Psychologie Verlags Union.

Hosking, D. M. & Morley, I. E. (1988). The skills of leadership. In J. G. Hunt, B. R. Baliga, H. P. Dachler & C. A. Schriesheim (Eds.), *Emerging leadership Vistas*, Vol. 8, Leadership Series (pp. 89–106). Lexington, MA: D. C. Heath/Lexington Books.

Knorr-Cetina, K. D. (1987). The micro-sociological challenge of macro sociology: Toward a reconstruction of social theory and methodology. In K. D. Knorr-Cetina and A. V. Cicourel (Eds.), *Advances in social theory and methodology; Toward an integration of micro- and macro-sociologies.* Boston/ London: Routledge & Kegan Paul.

Kruse, L. (1987). Führung ist männlich: Der Geschlechtsrollen- Bias in der psychologischen Forschung [Leadership is masculine: The sexrole bias in psychological research]. *Gruppendynamik, 18,* 251–267.

McCall, M. W. Jr. & Lombardo, M. M. (Eds.) (1978). *Leadership: Where else can we go?* Durham, N. C.: Duke University Press.

Moscovici, S. (1972). Society and theory in social psychology. In J. Israel and H. Tajfel (Eds.), *The context of social psychology*, pp. 17–68 . London: Academic Press.

Moscovici, S. (1976). *Social influence and social change.* London: Academic Press.

Müller, W., Biedermann, C., Alioth, A., Vaassen, B., Dachler, P., Feldmann J. & Hill, W. (1988). Führungslandschaft Schweiz [The landscape of leadership in Switzerland]. *Die Unternehmung*, 4, (whole issue).

Neisser, U. (1976). *Cognition and reality.* San Francisco: Freeman.

Neuberger, O. (1984). *Führung [Leadership].* Stuttgart: Enke.

Palazzoli, M. S., Anolli, L., di Blasio, P., Giossi, L., Pisano, I., Ricci, C., Sacchi, M. & Ugazio, V. (1984). *Hinter den Kulissen der Organisation [Behind the stageset of the organization].* Stuttgart: Klett-Cotta.

Piaget, J. (1937). *La construction du réel chez l'enfant* [The construction of reality in the child]. Neuchâtel: Delachaux et Niestlé.

Piaget, J. [1970]. *Genetic epistemology*. New York: Columbia University Press.

Schön, D. A. (1982). *The reflective practitioner*. New York: Basic Books.

Schmidt, S. J. (Hrsg.) (1987). *Der Diskurs des radikalen Konstruktivismus* [The discourse of radical constructionism]. Frankfurt: Suhrkamp.

Sievers, B. (1989). Leadership as a perpetuation of immaturity. Personal communication based upon a first draft of a working paper.

Smircich, L. & Morgan, G. (1982). Leadership: The management of meaning. *Journal of Applied Behavioral Science, 18,* 257–273.

Smith, K. K. (1982). *Groups in conflict – Prisons in disguise*. Dubuque, Iowa: Kendall/Hunt.

Tajfel, H. (1972). Experiments in a vacuum. In J. Israel and H. Tajfel (Eds.), *The context of social psychology* (pp. 69-122). London: Academic Press.

Tajfel, H. (1981). *Human groups and social categories: Studies in social psychology*. Cambridge: Cambridge University Press.

Ulrich, H. & Probst, G. J.B. (1988). *Anleitung zum ganzheitlichen Danken und Handeln* [An introduction to holistic thinking and action]. Bern/Stuttgart: Huber.

von Cranach, M. & Tschan, F. (1990). Mehrstufigkeit im zielgerichteten Verhalten von Organisationen [Multisteps in goal-oriented behavior of organizations]. In F. Frei und I. Udris (Hrsg.), *Das Bild der Arbeit* (S. 208–226). Bern/Stuttgart: Huber.

von Glasersfeld, E. (1981). Einführung in den radikalen Konstruktivismus [Introduction to radical constructionism]. In P. Watzlawick (Hrsg.), *Die erfundene Wirklichkeit* (S. 16–38). München: Piper.

Watzlawick, P., Beavin, J. H., & Jackson, D. D. (1967). *Pragmatics of human communication. A study of interactional patterns, pathologies, and paradoxes*. New York: Norton.

Weick, K. E. (1979). *The social psychology of organizing*. Reading, MA: Addison-Wesley.

Scientific and Public Knowledge of AIDS: The Problem of Their Integration

Ivana Marková

1. Scientific and public knowledge

In a very broad sense one can talk about two kinds of knowledge: scientific and public or social representational. Scientific knowledge is general understood to be concerned with the "reified universe" (Moscovici, 1984) and to be based on intellectual precision and empirical evidence. Its purpose is to understand the natures of objects and events existing independently of human individuals. Scientific knowledge is characterised by impartiality and is not supposed to be affected by societal values. In contrast, public or social representational knowledge is concerned with the "consensual universe". In this universe objects and events are made accessible to public awareness by focussing on their social, historical and cultural relevance, on values and on what is understood as common sense (Moscovici, 1984).

One could thus assume that the universes of scientific and of public knowledge have independent lives of their own, each within its own frame of reference. It is even possible to argue that one and the same person could operate within these two frameworks while keeping them separate from each other. When engaged in his or her scientific endeavour, the person would use the former framework, while in other contexts, the latter could be applied. I shall not be concerned here with whether such separation of *reified* and consensual universes is possible and, if it were, under what conditions it could happen. Rather, it is important for my purpose that the public is often faced with a problem of integrating scientific knowledge with social representational knowledge. Such integration is necessary not only for coherent mental functioning but also for the actualization of knowledge in a variety of daily and special activities.

2. From scientific theories to social representations

On the basis of his research, Moscovici (1984) has proposed a model according to which scientific theories, through their circulation in society, become transformed into social representations. He has stated that the evolution of social representations undergoes three phases. In the first, a theory of a scientific discipline is elaborated. In the second or "representative" phase, the scientific theory is diffused within a society through societal images, language and concepts. In the final phase, the social representation becomes appropriated by educational, political and cultural institutions or by the state, and it transforms itself into an ideology that is publicly enforced in the name of science. The public diffusion of Freud's theory, of the comprehension of medical techniques, and of concepts of health and illness in recent years in France, are all examples of social representations that can be understood according to Moscovici's three phase theory. Within this model, social representations are formed by the *anchoring* of unfamiliar scientific phenomena and theories into something already known, and by objectification, i. e. by the transformation of abstract scientific concepts into concrete and generally accessible images or representations.

3. Social representation of sexual pollution and taboo and scientific knowledge of HIV/AIDS

Although the transformation of scientific into social representational knowledge has been documented many times, it is only one of several possible relationships between these two kinds of knowledge. In this paper I shall focus on a situation in which social representation actually precedes the existence of a scientific theory. The beginning of the AIDS epidemic in the early eighties was characterized by a phase with virtually no scientific theory or at least with a very incomplete medical account concerning the cause, epidemiology, infectiousness, diagnosis and prognosis of AIDS. Yet, while medical science puzzled over the "new disease", the public responded to AIDS immediately by applying available social representations that have existed in western culture for centuries. AIDS was identified as a sexually transmitted disease, so it was the existing social representations of sex pollution, immorality, the punishment of sinners, and of public danger by outcasts (Douglas, 1966; Brandt, 1985) that were immediately applied. As Douglas (1966) has suggested, external danger that threatens the community fosters solidarity from within and against those who are seen as responsible. Pollutors become doubly incriminated. First, they are reprobated because they have crossed the line between the moral and sacred on the one hand, and the immoral and profane on the other. Second, by their immoral behaviour, they endanger others (Douglas, 1966, pp. 138–9). The public and general press focussed their attention on those "in the fast lane", i. e. those who had sex with many different partners. AIDS was publicly labelled a "gay plague".

Scientific accounts of natural phenomena aim at *explicit statements* of facts and at explanations that can be justified by rational arguments and by empirical research. The formalization of such clear and unambiguous statements is the ideal of science. Social representations are characterised both by explicit statements and implicit meanings. In the case of AIDS, social consciousness has been constantly raised by explicit and vivid images of AIDS and its victims. The public and the mass media made explicit connections between plague, immoral behaviour and sexually transmitted diseases (Sontag, 1989; Brandt, 1985, 1988). Thus, newspaper headlines plainly stated that virus victims were "swirling in a cesspit of their own making" and that the spread of AIDS was to be blamed on degenerate conduct, to give but a few examples (Markova and Wilkie, 1987). In addition, social representations of sex pollution and immoral behaviour live through their implicit meanings. Certain kinds of images are never spelled out by society and certain words are rarely expressed so as not to bring about calamity (Douglas, 1966; Sontag, 1978). Social representations thrive on implicit meanings circulating in society in their semi-conscious and unconscious forms. The less people are aware of them, the more powerful their effect (Moscovici, 1984). With the gradual development of scientific knowledge, and in their effort to combat the spread of HIV and AIDS, health campaigns have adopted a knowledge-based scientific approach to educate the public. Thus the recent governmental campaign in the UK ran the slogan "don't die of ignorance" and it focussed on the presentation of fear-arousing images and on the provision of information about HIV/AIDS. In this campaign, in educational leaflets, films and packages, the HIV virus was presented as a valueless, odourless and colourless object moving in spatio-temporal configurations with respect to the white blood cells. It was shown penetrating white cells, destroying them and eventually suppressing and extinguishing human immunity. In addition, patients' wounds that would not heal, cancers that would not improve and wasted bodies that further deteriorated were shown in the hope that the viewers would adopt safe sex practices.

4. Knowledge of HIV/AIDS and behavioural changes of people with haemophilia

As early as 1982 HIV was identified in factor concentrates used for the treatment of haemophilia, and by that time a great number of people with haemophilia worldwide were already infected by HIV. In a longitudinal study based on interviews, counselling and questionnaires conducted in the West of Scotland in 1986–87, the responses of patients with haemophilia, and of their families, to information about HIV infection and AIDS were explored. Participants were patients with haemophilia and their families who attended the Haemophilia Regional Centre in the Glasgow Royal Infirmary and the staff in the hospital. By 1986 blood donors were being screened for the presence of HIV infection, and blood products, i. e. concentrates of clotting factors used for the treatment of bleeds, were being heat treated to destroy any HIV that might have slipped through the screening process. Although many patients with severe haemophilia were already known to be HIV antibody positive, the general belief amongst professionals at that time was that only about 5–10 per cent of those who were HIV antibody positive would go on to develop full-blown AIDS.

It was found that the participants were very well informed about HIV, AIDS and the risks of infection to themselves and others (Wilkie et al. 1990). However, many patients were very reluctant to tell certain categories of people, such as employers, insurance companies and strangers, about their haemophilia. A number of people said that they had confided information about their haemophilia only to their closest friends, and they used the term "stigma" to express their worries with respect to telling others. Of the 59 patients who participated in this study, 27 (46%) said that after the emergence of the AIDS epidemic they had become more reluctant to reveal their haemophilia. This group included 11 of the 13 HIV antibody positive patients. Forty five patients (76%) implied or explicitly stated that they were concerned about the stigmatising effect of HIV infection and AIDS. It was worrying that 13 of the 59 patients (22%) said that they would not reveal their HIV antibody status, whether positive or negative, even to their sexual partners (Marková et al., 1990 b).

Of the 59 patients, 40 were sexually active and of these, 15 (38%) reported using condoms. Most of those who did not wear a condom were single patients. Five of the single non-users were HIV antibody positive.

The failure to apply safe sex practices was not due to the patients not knowing the risk to their partners. Rather, they found it extremely difficult to cope with their situation. Comments of patients during interviews made it clear that safe sex practices presented problems for both those who had and those who did not have stable relationships with their partners. A frequent comment from these respondents was that using a condom made them feel "dirty" and that it was a constant reminder of their contamination and of their association with AIDS. Difficulties with using a condom were also envisaged by those who had never had a sexual partner, such as 16–20 year olds. These patients assumed that most girls were on the pill and therefore would question the patient's use of a condom. These patients tended

not to form any long-term relationships that would commit them to explaining their HIV antibody status to their partners; tended to drift and satisfied themselves with one-night stands which did not require an explanation to the girl. In stable relationships the use of a condom was also found to be "offensive". Some patients said that they had not told their wives explicitly that they were HIV antibody positive or that they were at risk of infection. The wives, however, implicitly understood and did not ask questions. The use of the condom would have meant that this unspoken contract between husband and wife would have been broken. Thus, it would have been seen as an "offence" (Marková et al. 1990 a).

In spite of the fact that most patients gave correct answers concerning the risk to household contacts, they associated HIV and AIDS with uncleanliness and several parents expressed great concern about the control of infection following the diagnosis of HIV in their sons. One mother said that she had "spent a small fortune on bleach since she knew about HIV". She was very concerned that nobody should get infected from her household and she did not want anyone to think that she kept a "dirty house". Indeed, the word "dirty" was raised on many occasions. Another mother admitted that she poured disinfectant down the toilet after her son had been there. Of course, she did this without his knowledge. Interestingly, these sons commented on their mothers' behaviour, one, for example, saying that "mun had got a bit too fussy. She was always cleaning up and the house stank of disinfectant".

Patients were asked to rate on a five-point scale, 1–5, from very low to very high, how they thought others perceived the seriousness of HIV infection. These ratings were correlated with the patients' responses concerning their own perceptions of the risk of HIV to themselves and to others. No relationships between the two sets of data were found for patients who were HIV antibody positive. However, in the case of HIV antibody negative patients several correlations between their beliefs about others' perceptions and their own perceptions were found. In particular, if an HIV antibody negative haemophilic patient believed that others perceived HIV infection as serious he tended: to reduce his treatment by factor VIII (this was in spite of the fact that in

1986–87, when this research was carried out, factor VIII was no longer contaminated by HIV); to wish not to have children; to be certain about his own risk of AIDS; to be concerned about AIDS; to perceive family members to be at risk of HIV; to perceive his partners to be at risk of HIV; to feel no control over AIDS.

All 104 members of hospital staff who were involved in the study (doctors, nurses and clerical staff) gave correct answers about the transmission of HIV infection and they knew that HIV was transmitted by blood and semen. However, in spite of knowing how HIV is transmitted, 42 (40%) of them, including 3 doctors, thought that persons with HIV should be barred from working in food industry and from professions in which handling of food is required.

The perceived risk of HIV/AIDS to non-sexual contacts by a proportion of the patients, and the associations of patients and their families of HIV/AIDS with dirt, is reminiscent of the study by Jodelet (1986). In this revealing research Jodelet has identified very effective strategies by which villagers isolated themselves from mentally ill ex-patients. In a similar vein, Sontag (1989) refers to the perceived contagiousness of illnesses and to irrational and implicit beliefs with respect to AIDS.

5. The problem of integration of scientific and social representational knowledge

For the individual, the term "knowledge of HIV/AIDS" can have different meanings. These range from "neutral", "objective" and "scientific" information that is written down in books, leaflets, and policy documents, to knowledge based on a person's life experience. While the former kinds of meaning are impersonal and detached from the person, the latter kind of knowledge of HIV/AIDS is intimately related to the person's self. This kind of knowledge may be threatening to the individual's physical and mental condition and to his or her social identity. It involves not only the individual's own belief about HIV/AIDS but also his or her awareness of others' beliefs and of social representations of HIV/AIDS.

Health education campaigns, focusing on the presentation of scientific knowledge of HIV/AIDS to the general public, have failed to address the problem of the integration of scientific and social representational knowledge. They even have not acknowledged that there is any problem to be solved. The integration of the two kinds of knowledge is difficult for the following reason. Scientific knowledge of HIV/AIDS calls for "responsible behaviour" so that the disease is not transmitted to others. It uses scientific and rational arguments in order to direct people to appropriate actions. Social representational knowledge, on the other hand, focuses the individual's attention on the threat of their being stigmatised and rejected by others if they were to reveal their HIV antibody status or the fact that they belonged to one of the high risk groups. Thus, while scientific knowledge calls for a particular kind of action, social representational action calls for the exact opposite.

6. Implications of the case of AIDS for the theory of social representations

The case of AIDS clearly shows that even before a scientific theory concerning the disease had begun to develop, there was a ready-made social representation, incorporating images of sex pollution and of taboo subjects, available to respond spontaneously and instantaneously to AIDS. Only as the scientific theory took shape and became more specific, did the social representation of HIV/AIDS start to differentiate itself from its original form. Thus, while the original representation existed as vaguely familiar and undifferentiated images of sex pollution, punishment and taboo subjects, the present representation has been developed through *differentiation and specification* of the originally undifferentiated images. The process of differentiation appears to have been due to several factors. First, as the science progressed, it interacted with the original social representation. Second, organised groups of people at risk of HIV/AIDS, e. g. homosexuals and people with haemophilia, actively raised public awareness of HIV/AIDS. They did so by pointing to differences between HIV/AIDS and other diseases, questioning existing morality, drawing attention to different kinds of sexual practices and changing the terminology concerning HIV/AIDS. Finally, these active groups together with the mass media have provided the public with explicit statements about sexuality and HIV/AIDS. Thus they have diminished the power of the original social representation by depriving it of its implicit meanings.

In conclusion, the two issues discussed in this paper, namely the mode of actualization of knowledge within the two kinds of universe, i. e. *reified* and consensual, and *differentiation* as a means of formation of social representations, should become incorporated into the theory of social representations.

References

Brandt, A. M. (1985), *No Magic Bullet*. New York and Oxford: Oxford University Press.

Brandt, A. M. (1988), AIDS in historical perspective: Four lessons from the history of sexually transmitted diseases, *American Journal of Public Health*, 78, pp .

Douglas, M. (1966), *Purity and Danger*. London: Routledge and Kegan Paul.

Jodelet, D., (1986), *Civils et Bredins*. Thèse pour le Doctorate d'Etat. Paris: Ecole des Hautes Etudes en Sciences Sociales.

Marková, I. and Wilkie, P. A. (1987), Representations, concepts and social change: The phenomenon of AIDS. *Journal for the Theory of Social Behaviour*, 17.

Marková, I., Wilkie, P. A., Forbes, C. D. (1989), Coping strategies of haemophilic patients who are at risk from acquired immunity deficiency syndrome (AIDS) and implications for counselling. Unpublished Final Report to the Scottish Home and Health Department.

Marková, I., Wilkie, P. A., Naji, S. A., and Forbes, C. D. (1990 a), Knowledge of HIV/AIDS and behavioural changes of people with haemophilia. *Psychology and Health*, 4, 125–133.

Marková, I., Wilkie, P. A., Naji, S. A., and Forbes, C. D. (1990 b), Self- and other-awareness of the risk of HIV/AIDS in people with haemophilia and implication for behavioural change. *Social Science and Medicine*, 31, 73–79.

Moscovici, S. (1984), The phenomenon of social representations. In: R. M. Farr and S. Moscovici (eds.) *Social Representations*. Cambridge and New York: Cambridge University Press; and Paris: Editions de la Maison des Sciences de l'Homme.

Sontag, S. (1989), *AIDS and its Metaphor*. London: Allen Lane, Harmondsworth: Penguin Books.

Wilkie, P. A., Marková, i., Naji, S. A., and Forbes, C. D., (1990), Daily living problems of people with haemophilia and HIV infection: implications for counselling. *International Journal of Rehabilitation Research*, 13, 13–21.

Social Impact of Experts and Minorities, and Smoking Cessation*

Juan Antonio Pérez and Gabriel Mugny

The routes of persuasion

Recent studies on persuasion argue that two routes of attitude change are possible: one more "peripheral", the other more "central" (cf. Petty and Cacioppo, 1986; Zanna, Olson and Herman, 1987). In the same vein, our model of the process of social influence (Mugny and Pérez, 1991) presupposes two distinct processes in attitudinal or behaviourial changes. One, more typical of high psychosocial status sources (majority, experts, etc. . . .) is based on *social comparison*, either on the psychosocial resources respective to the source and the target, or on social identification, and accounts for the phenomena of uniformity and conformity. The other, more typical of minorities and less credible sources, is founded on a socio-cognitive *validation* (Moscovici, 1980), that, starting from a decentration relative to the dominent normative point of view and taking into account divergent points of view, leads to the constructive elaboration of a new attitude or behaviour. In this contribution, we will develop the articulation of these two processes relevant to an issue of which the social, or even individual importance is obvious: smoking.

Our recent studies in the field of persuasion and communication research are concerned with how individuals generate specific persuasive appeals and how these appeals influence other people. We started this line of research with the observation that the antismoking campaigns (since the purpose, from a social influence perspective, is to change the behaviour of smokers) resort mainly to messages from expert sources. They probably do that as they rest on the "naive psychology" or beliefs, i. e. on social representations, about the most effective tactics for persuading others (Rule and Bisanz, 1987). One of the dominant beliefs is that the efficiency of influence strategies is based on expertise; specifically, the legitimacy of scientific competence. This seems to be based on a more general social representation according to which individuals belonging to higher social positions have the privilege of disposing of the initiation of truth, as largely developed in the scientific psychology of persuasion (McGuire, 1985). Under the concept of the human being as a rational player, one can suppose in reality that "true" information would, under this concept, be considered serious and as a behavioural guideline. Through our research we would like to determine if the degree of legitimacy of persuasive information of the source (classically studied under the cover of the notion of credibility) really constitutes a factor for changing the attitudes of the smoker. This would lead back to the idea that changes are possible via the process of social comparison that would be present here in the form of informational and normative dependence of the smoker (Deutsch and Gerard, 1955). To evaluate this closer, a counter-hypothesis can just as well be stated, according to recent studies on innovation (Moscovici, 1980; Nemeth, 1986): the more competence or expertise a source enjoys, the more its point of view has a chance of imposing itself as obvious, the targets having to think less about its content. Briefly, the smoker would often be impervious (see Alcalay, 1983) to a repetitive argument (for example: health), like a truism that one considers as vested without having to think about its foundations or its implications. Further, one must admit that smokers, considering the continuous attacks aimed at them, develop most probably a sociocognitive immunisation that allows them to resist and preserves their smoking habits. They will even further develop this immunity in front of experts, who are the symbols of these threats. In front of them, the smoker could be more preoccupied protecting his identity rather than validating the opposite point of view. Even from a social comparison

* The studies presented in this contribution were supported by the Fonds National suisse de la Recherche Scientifique.

point of view, it is not sure whether expertise has a guaranteed social impact.

Our idea approaching this problem from the validation process point of view, from which we know that it is initiated by conflicts of an optimum intensity, was that a change could stem from confronting smokers to a message defending a new, uncommon and even counternormative argument. If the critical information would come from a minority, i.e from a source with low credibility, the question would then be: could we not envisage the conflict to be handled via the process of validation? Under such an appearance, cognitive activity on the persuasive information would be carried out at more indepth levels, which would lead to the elaboration of a normative dilemma bringing the smokers to adopt a new attitude and behaviour towards their smoking habits. Let us now look at some of the experimental studies that have dealt with this problem.

Some experimental evidence

Rather than putting forth a message calling for the "objective reality", arguing facts of legitimate knowledge (about health or ecology for example), in several experiments (cf. Pérez, Mugny, Roux and Butera, 1991), we confronted the smokers with a normative minority argument, expressing a "left-wing" stance not frequently heard of, and denouncing the vicious circle of production-publicity-consumption, in which the smoker is represented as a free spinning wheel in a gear, unaware but active. This way of accusing the smoker in a socio-political way is an unusual argument, and has been perceived as such at the same time as pertaining to a minority, and being rigid and conflicting. To test our hypothesis, and according to various conditions, we have attributed these arguments either to an expert ("professors in political economy") or to a minority source ("militants of a minority group"). This way, we can evaluate the impact of a highly credible source and of a source with no legitimate scientific foundation: our initial hypothesis being that the minority identity of the source should specifically focus the target's attention on the content of the normative debate. As for the results, we will limit ourselves here to changes in the intention to quit smok-

ing. That is, in the tradition of studies on influence and persuasion, the intention of stopping smoking is taken twice (on a 7-point scale); firstly before reading the message, and then a second time thereafter. Before looking at the main results, let us note that the credible source is perceived, ad hoc measures controlling them, as more expert, scientific and objective, and of course as pertaining more to a majority, than the minority source.

In a first experiment we looked at the degree of immunisation smokers have to a message that questions their smoking habits. To do this we constituted two groups of smokers: those who, resulting from a dilemma in the pretest, gave more importance to the freedom of smoking, and those who gave more importance to the respect of the non-smokers. The first group has its rights, and is thus eager to defend its position. The social influence measures do not reveal a main effect of the expert or minority identity of the source, but a first degree interaction (p<.04), their impact varying according to the type of smokers under consideration. First, the conflict induced by the minority was, as predicted, more favourable to initiate a change, but only for the smokers most anchored in their position, and the most oriented towards the defence of their own rights (m = +0.22). One can observe that it is difficult to influence them through what we have considered as an expert manner (m = –0.23). The more they feel the pressure to change, i.e. to conform to the legitimate discourse of the dominant source, the stronger they would maintain their independence and protect their identity threatened by the power struggle separating them. On the other hand, when the initial attitudes of the targets suppose some shared value with the source, i.e. when smokers give more importance to the respect of the non-smokers, the attitude becomes "polarized" through the social comparison with the expert source (m = +0.13), but does not change in front of the minority (m = –0.56). For these subjects there is no need for conflictual arguments, but rather a positive social relationship with the source, to which they can attach positively the new attitude, to consolidate the new identity that it implies. In a nut shell, a legitimate knowledge can also be convincing, but according to the route of social comparison; a source with low credibility can also be convincing, but through a validation process.

In a second study we have confirmed this interaction (p.<005) by distinguishing, on the basis of their initial intention to stop smoking expressed in the pre-test, the subjects more or less "convinced" of their tobacco consumption. The results have shown that in front of an expert source, subjects who already expressed the intention to change their behaviour, change more (m = –0.23; minority: m = –0.96), whereas in front of the minority source more convinced smokers were the most influenced (m = +1.31; experts: m = +0.58). Reasoning in terms of how people deal with the conflict, one could consider that the subjects closer to the source, from a psychological point of view, would consider more positively the argument of the source and would approach the influence situation via the social comparison route. It is the positivity of the comparison, guaranteed by the high credibility of the discourse, that would provoke the change. Here we would be in a phase where the change, having already started if one considers the initial declared intention, rests on a psychological community between targets and sources highly valued due to their expertise. For the subjects initially reluctant to stop their habit of consuming tobacco, the impossibility of a positive comparison is of no doubt, due to the high perceived descrepancy with the counter-normative discourse. Change is not to be expected via social comparison, for this one would render the opposition more saliant. These subjects only change in front of a particularly conflictual source, such as a minority, that would activate a validation process.

In a third experiment, the message against tobacco was presented as receiving social support of a large majority, or of a small minority, either of smokers, or non-smokers. As suggested by the interaction between these two variables (p<.06), two conditions were, according to our hypothesis, relatively more influential: the in-group majority of smokers (m = +0.25; majority of non smokers: m = –1.00), and the minority of non-smokers (m = –0.38; minority of smokers: m = –0.92). We find once again that once a psychological community between targets and sources exists, these then take advantage of the legitimacy of their message, founded here on consensus. Whereas,

when there is a psychological distance, in a way that it excludes any form of normative control, it is the non credible character of the source that releases the process of validation.

Let us report the main results of a fourth experiment (Pérez and Mugny, 1990). In half of the conditions the anti-tobacco texts were, as usual, attributed to militants of a minority group, and in the other half to professors in political economy. The independent variable specific to this experiment was expected to induce an interdependent or independent way of reasoning. The subjects of the *interdependent* condition were to distribute 100 points between pro- and anti-tobacco arguments. This manipulation had to make the position of the non-smokers salient and predominent, thus favouring the expert source. In the *independence* condition, subjects disposed of 100 points to judge each of the arguments separately. This manipulation had to allow the expression of diverging positions, and to favour the impact of the less credible source. The results confirm the interaction between the two independent variables (p<.02). The expert source has more influence under interdependence of the judgements (m = +0.16) than under independance (m = –0.26). Conversely, the minority source produces more influence in the context of independence of judgements (m = +0.29) than in the context of interdependence (m = –0.36).

Which resistance?

Studies on smoking cessation take place in a context of psychosocial resistance. Research on minority influence has shown the following double phenomenon: when the targets resist, focussing on the personal characteristics of minorities or their members, the minority impact is reduced (regarding effects of the psychologization, see Papastamou, 1986). However, when they resist, denying the credibility of the message content, the minority impact grows paradoxally (cf. Pérez, Mugny and Moscovici, 1986). Therefore, the content of the message would play a more important part than the characteristics of the source in front of a minority. The reverse would be true for an expert message, the characteristics of the source being more crucial than the provided information. All this contradicts the general belief (probably a dominant social representation of the influence processes) according to which experts can convince thanks to the value of their arguments.

This is illustrated by another experiment (Pérez, Moscovici and Mugny, à paraître). Subjects, all smokers, were exposed to the usual anti-tobacco arguments, attributed to an expert source or a minority. They were then asked to write down either critical arguments *against the content* of the text only, or characteristics going *against the authors* of the text only. Following instructions, they wrote in average more than four arguments or characteristics. Social approval was also measured, in asking them to express their agreement with various ideas defended in the persuasive message. Analysis reveals a main effect: subjects who have criticized the content of the message disagree more with the arguments of the message than those who have criticized the source, especially when it is a minority. This confirms that denial specifically reduces the approval of a minority source (Pérez et al, 1986).

Regarding social influence on the intention to quit smoking, we find an interaction between the anti-tobacco's message source and the target of the critical activity (p<.01). As predicted, the minority group induces more change when targets focus their critical attention on the content of the message (m = +0.79) rather than on the characteristics of its authors (m = +0.02). The reverse is true for the expert source, which induces more change when the critical activity is focussed on the caracteristics (m = +0.78) than when it is focussed on the content of the message (m = +0.24).

An a posteriori division of subjects according to whether they propose more (at least three) or less arguments or characteristics, further illustrates this double dynamic. When the critical activity concerns the attributes of the source, subjects indicating more negative characteristics change less (m = 0.00) than those who indicated less negative characteristics (m = +0.97). The less one criticizes the source, the more one changes. This effect is particularly obvious for the subjects criticizing the less the highly credible source (m = +1.60), confirming the effects of psychologization on the influence of higher status sources (Papastamou, 1986). When criticism adresses

the content of the message, subjects who write the greater number of counter-arguments change their intention to stop smoking (m = +0.90) more than those who write less (m= +0.22). This effect is stronger for the minority (m = +1.12), confirming the paradoxical effects of denial.

Conclusion

Whether as a function of the degree of immunisation in the face of non-smokers, the initial discrepancy between source and target, the possible identification with the source, the in(ter)dependence of the judgements, or the nature of counterarguing, the same pattern of influence appears. For targets psychologically closer to the source, social influence is a function of positive relationship, and depends on the legitimacy of its expert knowledge. Conversely, for more distant subjects, the impact is a function of a more intense conflict that is provided by the minority identity of the source. The former would function through a social comparison process, the latter through a validation process. The point is that in an influence relationship, either a unique point of view can prevail, or several. A source exerting legitimate informational or normative pressure would take advantage of a compelling or constraining field, that insures its superiority and its positivity. Whereas it is under the condition that the management of the normative conflict operates in an open field that a minority source (or a source of little credibility) can induce a change via a validation process.

One cannot conclude from the above that the legitimacy of expert knowledge ensures more influence than the illegitimacy of sources a priori devoid of credibility. Both of them operate according to a specific process, and it is their insertion in a particular normative context that makes more or less probable their efficiency in the control of social behaviour. If these various routes of persuasion present a theoretical and integrative interest in a field of research which is particularly dynamic, it also constitutes a potentially pragmatical contribution for professionals of mass media campaigns (especially on health), which often produce the perverse effect of reinforcing strongly anchored behaviours, rather than changing them (see Roberts and Maccoby, 1985). A first step to avoid such a perverse effect could consist in carefully questioning their social representations about the most effective tactics for persuading others.

References

Alcalay, R. (1983). The impact of mass communication campaigns in the health field. Social Science and Medecine, 1983, 17, 87–94.

Deutsch, M. & Gerard, H.B. (1955). A study of normative and informational social influence upon individual judgment. Journal of Abnormal and Social Psychology, 51, 629–636.

McGuire, W.J. (1985). Attitudes and attitude change. In G. Lindzey, E. Aronson (Eds), The handbook of social psychology (Vol. 2). New York, Random House.

Moscovici, S. (1980). Toward a theory of conversion behavior. In L. Berkowitz (Ed.), Advances in experimental social psychology (Vol. 13). New York: Academic Press.

Mugny, G., Pérez, J. A. (1991) The social psychology of minority influence. Cambridge, Cambridge University Press.

Nemeth, C. (1986). Differential contributions of majority and minority influence. Psychological Review, 93, 23–32.

Papastamou, S. (1986). Psychologization and processes of minority and majority influence. European Journal of Social Psychology, 1986, 16, 165–180.

Pérez, J. A., Moscovici, S. & Mugny, G. (à paraître). Effets de résistance à une source experte ou minoritaire, et changement d'attitude. Revue Suisse de Psychologie, à paraître.

Pérez, J. A., Mugny, G. (1990) Changement d'attitude, crédibilité et influence minoritaire: interdépendance et indépendance de la comparaison sociale. Revue Suisse de Psychologie, 1990, 43, 150–158.

Pérez, J. A., Mugny, G. & Moscovici, S. (1986). Les effets paradoxaux du déni dans l'influence sociale. Cahiers de Psychologie Sociale, 32, 1–14.

Pérez, J. A., Mugny, G., Roux, P. & Butera, F. (1991) Influences via la comparaison sociale, influences via la validation. In: J. L. Beauvois, R. V. Joule & J.M. Monteil, Perspectives cognitives et conduites sociales, vol. 3. Cousset, Delval.

Petty, R. E., Cacioppo, J. T. Communication and persuasion. New York: Springer-Verlag, 1986.

Roberts, D. F., Maccoby, N. (1985). Effects of Mass Communication. In G. Lindzey, E. Aronson (Eds), The handbook of social psychology (Vol. 2). New York, Random House.

Rule, B. G. & Bisanz, G. L. (1987). Goals and strategies of persuasion: a cognitive schema for understanding social events. In: M. P. Zanna, J. M. Olson & C. P. Herman (Eds.) Social influence: The Ontario Symposium. Vol.5. New Jersey: Erlbaum.

Zanna, M. P., Olson, J. M., & Herman, C. P. (Eds.), Social influence: The Ontario Symposium. Volume 5. New Jersey: Erlbaum, 1987.

Examining the Cultural Constitution of the Category of Person

Gün R. Semin & Monica Rubini

1. Introduction: the Cultural Relativity of the Category of Person

One of the central social and psychological categories is the "category of person" (Mauss, 1933; Sampson, 1985). The fact that there are fundamental differences in the cultural constitution of the category of the person has eluded psychological attention until recently. A closer inspection of historical, anthropological and recent cross-cultural research suggests that our notions of the person as a constitutive principle, in order to understand the individual and to predict and explain his/her behaviour, are culture specific and possibly even misleading. Our contemporary understanding of the terms "self", "identity" and "person" in the Western world is an historically and culturally "idiosyncratic" one. As Geertz (1979) pointed out:

The Western conception of the person as a bounded, unique, more or less integrated motivational and cognitive universe, a dynamic centre of awareness, emotion, judgment, and action organized into a distinctive whole and set contrastively both against other such wholes and against a social and natural background is, however incorrigible it may seem to us, a rather peculiar idea within the context of the world's cultures (p. 229).

The currently prevailing Western notion of the individual as an isolated, separated and unique entity is the product of considerable historical change. Cherry (1967, p. 463), for example, highlights this point by examining the etymology of the concept of the individual. This concept, derived form the Latin *individuum* originally appears to have had a dual meaning. Cicero, using it in Democritus' sense, referred to it as an individual "atom", very much in today's sense. Tacitus, on the other hand, in the post-Christian period used it as meaning "inseparable", which is also how it was used in mediaeval theological argument referring

"to a person as inseparably involved in some group and representing that group. "Individual" meant an "inseparable unity", as in the "Holy and individual Trinity" or (as Milton used it) "the individual (= indivisible) Catholicke Church". Even in the 17th Century, a husband and wife were "individual". It referred to a person, or thing, which had no separate existence apart from one another, or from the group." (Cherry, 1967, p. 463)

There are diverse social historical reasons which are advanced for the transformation of this understanding of the person to its current atomistic or ego-centred conception, which are beyond the scope of this contribution. These arguments, coming from literary, philosophical and social historical sources, date the origins of our present conception of the person around the 16th and 17th centuries and link it, among other things, to the emergence of social mobility, the growth of a bourgeois middle class, and the increasingly secular attitudes and questionings which arose with the becoming of "science".

Even a cursory examination of cross cultural work on conceptions of identity reveals that there are considerable divergences in the way in which identities are embedded in social relationships, along with how responsibilities for the actions of a person are attributed. Across and within societies, one finds that "person-hood" or identity can be conceptualized as relative manifestations within a social organization. For example, one finds in a variety of societies that "the individual is born with his name and his social functions ... The number of individuals, names, souls and roles is limited in the clan and the line of the clan is merely a collection (ensemble) of rebirths and deaths of individuals who are always the same" (Mauss, 1906, in Allen, 1986, p. 33). Recent cross-cultural research shows, for example, that in India, as in various other cultures, there are distinctly holistic and thus relational cultural conceptions of the person, whereby the social role is treated as the primarily normative unit rather than the "individual" (see Miller, 1984;

Shweder & Miller , 1985). Another example is to be found in traditional Japanese culture, formed under the strong influence of Confucianism, where "personhood" is not individualistic. The status of the person is a dependent one, identifying the individual in terms of his/her affiliation with a certain social group and perceiving him/her as the sum total of several autonomous "areas of duties" such as "ko" (to one's parents), "giri" (to the people to whom one is indepted socially), "jin" (humanity and loyalty), "ninjo" (duties to oneself), etc. (cf. Kon, 1984). Thus, the category of person and its assessment is related to the person's area of action. Behavior is derived from the general rule, the norm, where personality in our Western sense is not valued but "personhood" is seen as duties and responsibilities resulting from being part of the community, or family, where the self is not separable from the role (Kon, 1984). Geertz (1973) in the context of his studies in Bali notes:

"... a persistent and systematic attempt to stylize all aspects of personal expression to the point where anything idiosyncratic, anything characteristic of the individual merely because he is who he is physically, psychologically or biographically, is muted in favour of his assigned place in the continuing, and, so it is thought, never-changing pageant that is Balinese life. It is dramatic personae, not actors that in the proper sense really exist. Physically men come and go – mere incidents in a happen-stance history of no genuine importance, even to themselves. But the masks they wear, the stage they occupy, the parts they play, and most important, the spectacle they mount remain and constitute not the facade but the substance of things, not least the self." (p. 50)

Read (1955) in a discussion of the Gahuku-Gama of New Guinea argues that their conception of man does not distinguish between the "individual" and the status that the person occupies. The Gahaku-Gama fail "... to separate the individual from the social context and, ethically speaking, to grant him an intrinsic moral value apart from that which attaches to him as an occupant of a particular status" (Read, 1955, p. 257). As Shweder and Bourne (1982) point out, "exotic" conceptions of "personhood" contrast "... with a Western mode of social thought in which the "individual" is abstracted from the social role, and the moral responsibilities of this abstracted, inviolate individual are distinguished from his/her social responsibilities and duties" (p. 168).

2. The Social Psychological Implications of the Category of Person

What we have been doing so far is to identify cultural differences in the constitution of the category of the person. As Triandis, Bontempo, Villareal, Asai & Lucca (1988) point out in their recent paper, one of the possible ways of coming to social psychological terms with a fuzzy concept such as culture is by examining what they term "determining dimensions of cultural variation" (p. 323). The dimension that is pertinent to the differences in the cultural construction of the person can be termed "collectivism" versus "individualism" (Hofstede, 1980). The social psychological significance of this dimension is to be found in the differences of the person's relationship to the group or in the way identities are embedded in social relationships. Triandis (1988), in contrasting collectivism to individualism, points out that in collectivism, personal goals are subordinate to ingroup goals, greater stress is put on the social norms and duties; the types of beliefs are consensual to the ingroup; there is higher readiness towards ingroup cooperation, and emotional attachment to the ingroup is stronger, inter alia. Other comparable distinctions are made with respect to differences in the types of social activities whereby cultures that are predominantly collectivist (e. g., Chinese) display more "situation centred" rather than "individual centred" activities (Hsu, 1981); or a stronger "social orientation" than an "individual orientation" (Yang, 1981).

One psychological translation of the cultural dimension of collectivism-individualism has been to examine it as an individual difference variable, namely allocentrism – idiocentrism (e. g., Triandis, Leung, Villareal & Clack, 1985; Triandis, et al., 1988). This essentially is a translation of the cultural differences to an individual difference scale by which one can examine the degree to which individuals represent a collectivistic (allocentric) or individualistic (idiocentric) orientation. Another psychological implication is differences in everyday social interaction styles. Wheeler, Reis and

Bond (1989) demonstrate that in Hong Kong, a predominantly collectivist culture, interactions between students were longer but fewer, with a greater percentage of group and task interactions compared to students in the U.S.

It has also been shown that variations in cultural conceptions of the person are associated with differences in social-cognitive processes. Stronger situational attributions are made in societies where the social role is treated as the primary normative unit and reference in comparison with societies that have an "individual-centred" emphasis where dispositional attributions are more prominent (cf. Miller, 1984; Shweder & Miller, 1985; Shweder & Bourne, 1982). For instance, Miller (1984) reports a comparative study of the types of attributions Indian and American adults and children make for both pro-social and deviant behaviours. She demonstrates that Americans at older ages utilize more dispositional explanations and fewer contextual ones than Hindus. Her developmental study shows that whereas American subjects increasingly use dispositional explanations the reverse is the case for Hindus. These results illustrate the differential impact of cultural conceptions of the person on the attributional process.

3. Studying Insults as a Method of Uncovering the Cultural Construction of Personhood

We approached the investigation of the cultural construction of the category of the person by focussing on an everyday practice that questions or challenges what it means to be a person (Semin & Rubini, 1990). One prototypic instance of such a social practice is "... verbal abuse which involves denial of what is near and dear to a person. Thus, verbal abuse can be psychologically revealing since it enables one to examine those aspects of the person which are culturally so critical that their denial removes a central feature of the category of person prevailing in the culture" (Semin & Rubini, 1990). The types of insults we were interested in collecting were decontextualized ones, namely those that prevail in a culture generally rather than those which arise in specific contexts, between specific subgroups who share a joint biography or history, or are peculiar to

specific professional or ritualized activities, etc. The argument we advanced was the following. In the case of individualistic cultures, the person is conceptualized as an autonomous agent. Thus insults in such cultures should be directed to the person as the singular object of abuse. Conversely, for collectivist cultures, the central feature of the person is his or her relations to the "ingroup" which could involve kin, village, ethnic or regional membership, and so on. Thus, we postulated that types of verbal abuse should index cultural orientation and that we should be able to distinguish between individualistic and relational (or collectivist) verbal insults as a function of the orientation that is dominant in the culture. Our proposition was simply that the examination of the prevalence of different types of verbal abuse can provide a general methodological entry to the examination of the cultural constitution of the category of the person. The hypothesis we advanced suggested that, in collectivistic cultures, verbal abuse that is typically relational, namely involving kin or group membership, will be more pronounced in contrast to individualistic cultures where verbal abuse that is directed only to the person will be more prominent.

We examined this hypothesis by investigating insult types that can be found in three regions of Italy: Northern, Central and Southern. The idea behind this was based on the assumption that Southern Italian cultural orientations are predominantly collectivist which stems largely from a reliance upon a traditional family form (cf. Galtung, 1971; Schneider & Schneider, 1976). In Northern Italy, we expected a predominantly individualistic conception of the person largely due to the high degree of industrialization and a stronger Central European influence. In our study we operationalized this cultural variation by choosing three samples from three cities: Catania, Bologna and Trieste, and predicted that relational or collectivistic insults would be more prominent in Catania (South) than Trieste (North), with Bologna occupying an intermediary position between the two, in particular due to migration to Bologna from the South and North. What we find is in line with our expectations as can be seen from Figure 1. We find that relational insults vary as a function of town from South to North, with significantly more relational in-

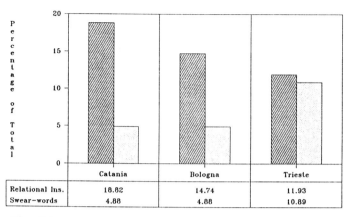

Figure 1. Types of insults/swear-words as a function of city.

▨ Relational Ins.   ☐ Swear-words

sults in the South and less in the North. The reverse is however not obtained for individualistic insults. Considering that the data for this study were obtained from three cities located in a country sharing the same language community and relatively homogeneous media (radio, TV, newspapers), the investigation of verbal abuse proves to be an important indirect method of unfolding the cultural construction of the category of the person. We would like to suggest that this tool may indeed be very powerful in the examination of how people construct identities as a function of different contexts that are experimentally controlled. For instance, if one were to provide a series of individualistic and relational insults within contexts that are experimentally manipulated, such as a group context or an individual context, then the likelihood of insult type (relational versus individual) should vary systematically. In that sense, the focus on insults provides a powerful psychological tool for the indirect examination of how identities are constructed culturally and also in different situative contexts.

4. Conclusions

More broadly, the focus on the cultural constitution of the person opens new vistas in the conceptualization of fundamental issues in psychology such as personality, focussing on personality as an independent unit of analysis with the notion of "individuality" underpining

the scientific endeavour. This individualistic reduction of personality detaches the person completely from his/her social context. The idea that we can capture the person by focussing on individual psychology and deleting the social context of the person is virtually like deleting the bases of what permits the person to be what it is in the first instance. The considerations advanced in our contribution suggest that certain central conceptions in our psychological science may very much be culturally conditioned folklore.

References

Allen, N. J. (1985). the category of person: a reading of Mauss's last essay. In M. Carrithers, S. Collins & S. Lukes (Eds). *The Category of Person.* Cambridge: CUP.

Benedict, R. (1946). *The chrysanthemum and the sword.* Boston: Houghton Mifflin.

Cherry, C. (1967). "But there is nothing I have is essential to me" (Or "The human race is not a club"). In *To honor R. Jakobson.* Vol. 1 (pp. 462–474). The Hague: Mouton.

Douglas, M. (1966). *Purity and danger.* London and Henley: Routledge & Kegan Paul.

Galtung, J. (1971). *Members of two worlds: A development study of three villages in Western Sicily.* International Peace Research Institute. Prio Monographs, 2. Oslo: Universitetsforlaget.

Geertz, C. (1973). *The Interpretation of Cultures: Selected Essays by Clifford Geertz.* N. Y.: Basic Books Inc.

Geertz, C. (1979). From the native's point of view.

On the nature of anthropological understanding. In P. Rabinow and W. M. Sullivan (eds.), *Interpretive social science*. (pp. 127–151) Berkeley: University of California Press.

Hofstede, G. (1980). *Culture's consequences*. Beverly Hills, CA: Sage.

Hsu, F. L.K. (1981). *American and Chinese: passage to differences* (3rd ed.). Honolulu: Hawai University Press.

Kon, I. S. (1984). The self as a historical-cultural and ethnopsychological phenomenon. In L. H. Strickland (Ed.), *Directions in Soviet social psychology* (pp. 29–46). N. Y.: Springer.

Mauss, (1933, transl. 1985). A category of the human mind: the notion of person; the notion of self. In Carrithers, M., Collins, S., & Lukes, S. (eds.), *The category of the person* (pp. 1–25). Cambridge: CUP.

Mead, M. (1937). Some anthropological considerations concerning guilt. In M. L. Raymert. (ed.), *Feelings and emotions*. N. Y.: Hufner.

Miller, J. (1984). Culture and the development of everyday social explanation. *Journal of Personality and Social Psychology, 46,* 961–978.

Read, K. (1955). Morality and the concept of person among the Gahuku-Rama. *Oceania, 25*(4).

Sampson, E. E. (1985). The decentralization of identity: Toward a revised concept of personal and social order. *American Psychologist, 40,* 1203–1211.

Sampson, E. E. (1989). The challenge of social change for psychology: Globalization and psychology's theory of the person. *American Psychologist, 44,* 914–921.

Schneider, J. & Schneider, P. (1976). *Culture and political economy in Western Sicily: Studies in social discontinuity*. N. Y.: Academic Press.

Semin, G. R. & Rubini, M. (1990). Unfolding the concept of person by verbal abuse. *European Journal of Social Psychology, 20,* 463–479.

Shweder, R. A. & Bourne, E. (1985). Does the concept of the person vary cross-culturally? In A. J. Marsella & G. White (Eds.), *Cultural conceptions of mental health and therapy*. Boston: Reidel.

Shweder, R. A. & Miller, J. (1985). The social construction of the person: How is it possible. In K. J. Gergen & K. E. Davies (Eds.), *The social construction of the person*. N. Y.: Springer.

Triandis, H. C. (1988). Collectivism vs. individualism: A reconceptualization of a basic concept in cross-cultural social psychology. In C. Bagley & C. K. Verma (Eds.), *Cross-cultural studies of personality, attitudes and cognition* (pp. 60–95). London: Macmillan.

Triandis, H. C., Bontempo, R., Villareal, J. M., Asai, M., & Lucca, N. (1988). Individualism and collectivism: Cross-cultural perspectives on self-ingroup relationships. *Journal of Personality and Social Psychology, 54,* 323–338.

Triandis, H. C., Leung, K., Villareal, J. M. & Clack, F. (1985). Allocentric vs. idiocentric tendencies: Convergent and discriminant validation. *Journal of Research in Personality, 19,* 395–415.

Weintraub, K. J. (1978). *The value of the individual: Self and circumstance in autobiography*. Chicago: Chicago University Press.

Wheeler, L. Reis, H. T. and Bond, M. H. (1989). Collectivism-individualism in everyday social life: the middle kingdom and the melting pot. *Journal of Personality and Social Psychology, 57,* 79–86.

Yang, K. S. (1981). Social orientation and individual modernity among Chinese students in Taiwan. *Journal of Social Psychology, 113,* 159–170.

The Organization of Individual Action Through Social Representations: A Comparative Study of Two Therapeutic Schools

Beat Thommen, Mario von Cranach & Rolf Ammann

1. Our Problem and its Theoretical Basis

Social systems can be conceived as self-active. They act as units on their environments (as can be seen for example in the politics of unions, political parties or business enterprises). They are delimited from other social systems and they are internally structured according to roles, hierarchies, power relations and personal relationships. Their acts are based on the actions of their sub-systems and individual members. Social systems develop and store knowledge about different content areas; their representations of the reality they have to cope with are very important. Thus, professional groups possess a broad and manyfold knowledge of their specific fields. Following Moscovici (1961, 1981, 1984) and many others, we refer to the knowledge of social systems as *"social representations"*. There are several reasons, which support the assumption that the study of social representations forms an essential link between the social and the psychological level:

- Social representations can be materialized and objectivated in rituals, in objects and arrangements, regulations, programs etc.
- Social systems define themselves through their social representations and thus delimit themselves from other social systems (e. g. by regulations, training programmes, ethical considerations etc.).
- By means of their social representations, social systems provide their members with patterns for the interpretation of the world and thus enable the construction of a common social reality (Schütz, 1932; Schütz & Luckmann, 1984).
- Social representations outlast individual lifes and fates. They develop in the historical processes of social change and are transferred through traditions.
- Social representations are objectivated in the individual actions of the system's members.

Social representations are neither static nor abstract. In the processes of socialization, the social system transfers its central representations to its group members (fig. 1). Thus a Rogerian psychotherapist learns and adopts in the course of his therapy-training, the central values of person-centeredness, together with the corresponding action competences. When a group member has taken over parts of a social system's social representations, we speak of *individual social representations*. These form a part of the individual knowledge structure. By the integration into the individual cognitive system the social representations are subjected to many changes (assimilation to the existing cognitive structures). According to the degree of change of the social representations in this process, we can construct a continuum between *conventionalized* and *privatized* individual social representations. Conventionalized individual social representations correspond fairly to the social representations of the social system; they are hardly modified. Privatized individual representations are changed and subjectively interpreted, so that they fit into the individual cognitive system. Besides individual social representations the individual knowledge structure comprises idiosyncratic knowledge which has not been taken from the social representations of the social system.

Social representations and individual social representations are inseparable connected. We conceive of their connection as a circular process (see fig. 1): In the course of socialization (for example professional training) the individual integrates parts of the social representations into his knowledge system. Thus, these parts are represented as individual social representations in the heads of the group mem-

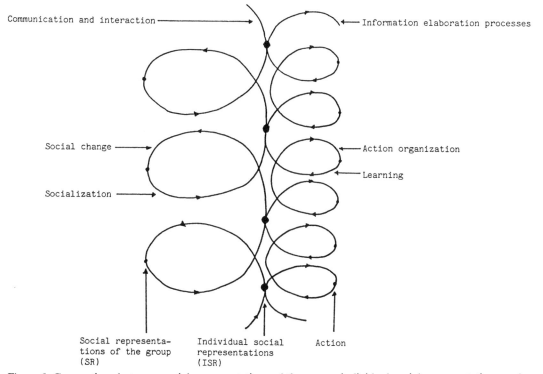

Communication and interaction

Information elaboration processes

Social change

Action organization

Learning

Socialization

Social representa-
tions of the group
(SR)

Individual social
representations
(ISR)

Action

Figure 1. Connections between social representations of the group, individual social representations and action.

bers. Among these members, there is only partial consensus concerning the social representations of the social system. Differences between members of a social system or between its sub-systems create conflicts which instigate social change and thus a change of the social representations of the larger system. The changed social representations of the system act back, through socialization processes, on the individual members, thus closing the circle of mutual influence of the individual and the social level. These assumptions about the relationship between social representations and individual social representations in consideration are based on theories of Mead (1934), Goffmann (1969), Harré & Secord (1972), Leontjev (1977), Schütz & Luckmann (1984) and Moscovici (1981, 1984).

For the individual group member, the individual social representations serve various functions:

– The identification function, which is related to the definition of group membership ("I am the member of the Swiss society of be-

haviour therapy. I support the basic attitude of behaviour therapy").
– The function of self presentation ("I am behaviour therapist" or "I am a therapist on the basis of humanistic psychology").
– The function of action organization and action justification.

By the latter function social systems control the acts of individual members. The exploration of this process in more detail is the topic of this paper. The underlying theory is also treated in the paper by von Cranach (this volume).

2. The research problem

It is a basic assumption of our theory that individual action is planned, steered and controlled by information elaboration processes which are partly consciously represented (von Cranach et al, 1980; von Cranach, Maechler & Steiner, 1985; von Cranach, 1983; von Cranach & Ochsenbein, 1985). The knowledge structure forms the basis of information elaboration which goes on during the action. By integrating parts of the social representations (in form of individual social representations) into the knowledge structure, individual action is socially steered and controlled. In exerting influence on the cognitive system, the superordinated social unit also influences the action organization – this is our central working hypothesis. In this research we investigate the question, how social groups, by imposing their social representations on their members, influence their action organization.

We consider the relationship between individual social representations and action as a mutual one. The knowledge from individual social representations influences the action organization. On the other hand, individual experiences and learning processes lead to a change of the individual social representations (fig. 1). In the present empirical investigation, we have only studied the segment of the spiral which refers to "action organization".

3. Empirical investigation

3.1 Data collection and evaluation

For our study we chose the professional group of psychotherapists. We compared the ther-

apeutic action of seven "client-centered" psychotherapists (CCT) in the sense of Rogers and seven psychotherapists working according to the method of vertical behaviour analysis (VBA), a further development of cognitive behaviour therapy (Grawe, 1980).

To analyse the connections between social representations and individual action, data from various qualitative levels had to be collected and evaluated:

1) Social representations: We reconstructed the social representations of the two psychotherapeutic schools from their basic literature and publications from the statutes, regulations and from interviews with prominent representatives of the schools. The result was a comprehensive exposé of the social representations, which was aproved by representatives of the two schools.

2) Action accompanying information processes: Immediately after the therapeutic session we confronted the therapists with videos of their own actions and asked for their remembered action accompanying cognitions, perceptions, emotions etc. (Self-confrontation method, von Cranach et. al, 1982).

3) Individual social representations: About two weeks after the therapy session, we questioned the therapists in a post-interview to give us further information in relation to

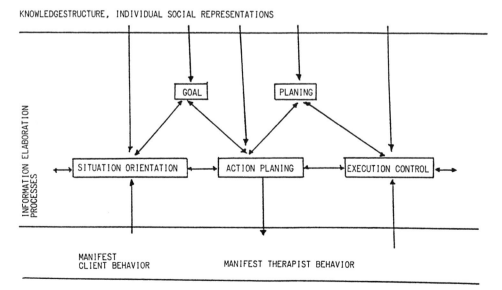

Figure 2. Model of information elaboration and action organization. Information elaboration processes within a loop.

those parts of the self-confrontation interview which seemed to relate to individual social representations. Thus we got additional information about the background of the action accompanying information processing.

The central part of the evaluation was the analysis of the self-confrontation data according to a model of cyclical information-elaboration and action organization (compare Fig. 2). The model contained constructs from three realms:

Manifest behaviour

Here we were restricted ourselves to an analysis of the verbal client-therapist interaction.

Information-elaboration processes

From many investigations of action related cognitions and in accordance with results of research in cognition, we assume that action accompanying information processes run off in a sequence of three steps: situational orientation; action planning, and execution control. We call this three-step sequence an information processing loop. The central unit of an information processing loop is the given action goal. According to the model of sequential-hierarchical action organization which has been successfully used in many empirical investigations (Hacker, 1972, 1986; Volpert, 1982), we consider the information processing loops as sequentially and hierarchically organized.

Knowledge structure

As knowledge, we consider the cognitions which are stored in the longterm memory in form of schemata (Bartlett, 1932; Aebli, 1980; Piaget, 1971 and many others). The abstracted knowledge which has been stored is recoded in the action situation and then steers situation specific information processing.

On the basis of the sketched model, we formulated differentiated assumptions about the effects of the social representations of the given therapeutic groups on the individual social representations and consequentially, on action organization.

The data were mainly qualitatively evaluated. We searched for ideal-typic patterns of action organization, which can be referred to the social representations of the given therapeutical school. Some of our questions were also quantitatively evaluated. Since our study does not correspond to the requirements of experimental design or sampling, we renounced the use of statistical inference methods.

3.2 Results

We have studied the impact of social representations on the organization of action in four problem areas. From two of these areas we shall report some examples, while we shall briefly summarize the results of the other two areas (a comprehensive report is given in Thommen, Ammann & von Cranach, 1988).

3.2.1 The client from the viewpoint of the therapist – the influence of therapeutic knowledge on attributions

The social representation of the given therapeutic school determines to a strong degree, how a therapist explains behaviour of the client and how he uses the explanation to construct knowledge about his client.

A first assumption is that VBA-therapists make more attributions than CC-therapists.

The school of VBA emphazises the functional aspects of behaviour. The theory departs from the central question: what are the plans that steer the client's behaviour? The comprehensive reconstruction of the structure of plans presupposes many attributions. Contrary to this view, the school of CCT rejects the procedure to analyse behaviour to achieve explanations. In contrast, the therapist is assumed to avoid making hypotheses about the causes of the client's problems. Therefore the social representations led us to expect that VBA-therapists should make more attributions than CC-therapists. Our results point in this direction, but the tendency is weak. 53% of all attributions in the self-confrontation which refer to the client come from VBA-therapists and 47% from CC-therapists.

A second assumption is that the attributions of CC-and VBA-therapists differ in their contents. The strong concentration of VBA on the plan concept leads to the expectation that the attributional contents are to a large degree determined through constructs like goals, plans and intentions. In addition, we expect functional explanations and processes of information elaboration. On the other hand we would expect from the CC-therapy that those attributions should play the main role which concern the actual emotional state of the client. These include statements about the depth of the clients experience of self-disclosure and his/her his self-exploration and authenticity of the client, because the central element of CC is the verbalization of the contents of emotional experience.

As shown in table 1, VBA-therapists attributed to their clients, quite in line with their social representations, more often cognitive information elaboration, goals and enduring dispositions. CC-therapists attributed to a larger degree expectations and needs. Emotions and situation-specific dispositions were attributed by both groups to a similar degree. There is a marked surplus on the VBA-Therapists' side in the interpretation of non-verbal behaviour (61% in contrast to 39% of the CC-therapists). We can explain this result post-hoc by the social representations of the VBA: the therapists are instructed to observe closely the non-verbal behaviour in order to infer the plans of the client (Grawe, 1980, pp. 127,197).

Furthermore, attributions in the organization of action, in connection with other cognitive processes, fulfill different functions for the members of the two schools. The VBA ther-

apists use the attributions to construct a comprehensive client-specific knowledge. The CC-therapists content themselves with situation-related attributions and do not use these for the further construction of client specific knowledge.

3.2.2 Vertical behaviour analysis and non-directive therapy – two different types of action?

Behaviour therapy, the basis of VBA, was considered as a technological application of behaviour theory from the beginning. The technological question was: what are the means to transfer an initial state into the desired goal state? Keupp and Bergold (1972, 123) emphasize the following characteristics as constitutive for behaviour therapy: "Behaviour modification is the explicit attempt to introduce rational and purposive action into the realm of therapy .... Behaviour modification is characterized by instrumental action." On the contrary, non-directive therapy is not based on an explicitly formulated theory. Moreover, Rogers deduced from his activity as a consultant, general attitudes of the helping person which he had experienced as therapeutically effective. The basic therapeutical attitude is imprinted by a deep respect of the dignity and autonomy of man. Rogers was convinced that the client "knows" better than the therapist which direction his development should take. In this process, the therapist has to assume the role of companion rather than that of a leading constructor of the therapy. Rogers formulated therapeutic goals only in the form of general psy-

Table 1. Percentual frequences of attribution of client-centered therapists of vertical behavior analysis.

CATEGORIY OF ATTRIBUTIONS	CLIENT-CENTERED THERAPISTS	VERTICAL BEHAVIOR THERAPISTS
Cognitive information elaboration	33%	67%
Goals	40%	60%
Enduring disposition	33%	67%
Expections/needs	64%	36%
Emotions/situation specific dispositions	48%	52%
Interpretations of verbal behavior	48%	52%
Interpretations of non-verbal behavior	39%	61%
Other categories	52%	48%

Total of coded attributions: 286

chological processes and strictly refused to the separation of diagnoses and therapy in the classic sense. A diagnosis in the service of the long-term planning of therapy would have contradicted the postulate of autonomy. The retention of the therapist to set the goals enabled him to control his action by comparison to concrete goals. Instead he was forced to measure his action directly with the criteria of ideal therapeutic behaviour. These are the famous three therapeutic attitudes of empathy, positive regard and congruency (e. g. Rogers 1942, 1951, 1961).

Habermas (1981) defined in his "theory of communicated action" the two types of action: the logical, success-oriented and the norm-(or value-)oriented. Following these suggestions, we developed the hypothesis that therapeutic action of the VBA-therapists can be described according to the model of the logical success oriented action, while the action of CC-therapists is described according to the model of norm and value oriented action.

From the content of the social representations, we derived assumptions about the effects on the therapist actions. Here we report two examples (for a comprehensive report, see Thommen et al, 1988).

Horizon of planning of the therapists. As concerns vertical behaviour analysis, the therapists can indicate the goals and the therapeutic action steps which they shall pursue in the coming therapy session. They develop long-terme strategic plans.

As concerns non-directive psychotherapy, the therapists do not know the exact goals or therapeutic action steps they are to undertake, and do not develop long-term strategic plans.

To test this assumption, we analyzed the planning interviews in respect to the goals and steps of intervention for the next therapy sessions which the therapists named. The seven VBA therapists mentioned 38 therapy goals and intervention steps which they planned to realize. (x = 5.43; SD = 1.27). The client-centered therapists only mentionned 15 goals and action steps (x = 2.14; SD = 1.27). All of these seven non-directive therapists explicitly pointed out that they wanted to leave the initiative to the client and that they did not want to structure the therapy hour according to pre-meditated guidelines.

Strategic action planning:

In vertical behaviour analysis, the therapists depart from an aspired super-goal, from which they deduce the appropriate sub-goals (e. g. the client should see his positive sides). They realized a strategy which we call "top-down-planning". The single action steps and information processing loops are sequentially ordered and hierarchically nested. Thus, their approach corresponds to the "sequential-hierarchical model". Using their self-confrontation data, we reconstructed their action organization for many information processing loops and always found the action structure which we have schematically sketched in fig. 3.

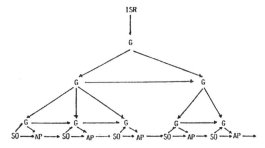

Figure 3. Strategical planning of VBA-therapists: Hierarchical sequential action organization. "Top-Down-Planning" (G = Goal, SO = Situation orientation, AP = Action planning).

From a super-goal, the therapists derive sub-goals and specific therapeutic means. The connection of the action steps is achieved through their instrumental relationship to the common super-goal of the given part of the therapy.

On the contrary, non-directive therapists did not depart from a therapy goal set for their specific clients; instead they had (consciously or subconsciously) the general goals of client-centered therapy in mind (e. g. verbalization of emotional experiences), and they tried to realize these general goals in relation to the specific situation. We characterized this strategy as inductive. The generation of goals occurs spontaneously from the given situation, as it were, from lower to higher levels or "bottom-up". Their goals are neither sequentially ordered nor hierarchically nested, which results in a "parallel" action structure. (Compare our schematic representation in fig. 4).

Figure 4. Strategic planning of client-centered-therapists: Parallel action orientation. "Bottom-Up-Planning" (G = Goal, SO = Situation orientation, AP = Action planning).

All in all, our results sustain the assumption that the action patterns of VBA- and CC-therapists represent a different type of action. VBA-therapists plan and act logically and success-oriented, while CC-therapists are norm-guided and value-oriented.

3.2.3 The formation of the relationship between client and therapist

The different roles and prescriptions concerning the therapeutic relationship have the effect that VBA-therapists set their goals more consequently, pursue them over a longer time, plan more strategically and seek and store more diagnostic informations about the patient (person-specific knowledge), than the CC-therapists.

3.2.4 Meta cognitions and emotions

How do therapists represent what they think and what they feel?

CC-therapists make their own mental system more as an object of self-reflection than do VBA-therapists. CC-therapists mentioned empathic processes considerably more often than VBA-therapists.

4. Conclusions

In four central realms of therapeutic action we found differences in the action organization of both groups of therapists, and we related these differences to the social representations of the two groups. Therefore, social representations of a group are more than just the ideological basis for the justification of individual action.

There are two extreme positions in psychology which concern the question of determination of the individual through social factors. Cognitive psychology depicts man as a solitary information processer who solves his problems alone and detached from social communication and social relations. On the other side of the continuum, there are social-psychological and sociological approaches which depart from a determination of individual action through super-ordinated social systems. We believe that the connection between action theory and the theory of social representations makes it possible to develop a more differentiated solution to this problem. We assume that the individual takes his knowledge from the social representations of his reference groups, and in doing so, he/she creates, forms and adapts knowledge in many ways. The social representations of the social system form on the one hand, the basis of individual knowledge and action, but on the other hand, they are transformed by their introduction into the individual cognitive system. A second transformation of the individual social representations lies in their application in specific situations. Through information-elaboration processes, individual social representations have to be combined and changed in a way that they correspond to the concrete requirements of the situation.

In our theory we see the individual neither as an isolated fighter nor as a marionette at the strings of the social system. Individual action is steered by social cognitions which come from the social representations of the social system, but the social representation is twice transformed before it becomes effective for action in a specific situation. This transformation and the privatization of social representations, which is connected with it, makes it possible and even necessary that social representations are subject to a constant historical change, which is achieved by the communication and interaction of the group members and of relevant sub-groups. We see development of individual social representations and action of the group members on the one hand, and of the social representations of the group on the other hand, as a co-evolution process (von Cranach, this volume).

References

Adorno, Th. et al. (1976). Der Positivismusstreit in der deutschen Soziologie. 5. Aufl. Neuwied: Sammlung Luchterhand.

Aebli, H. (1980). Denken: Das Ordnen des Tuns. Band 1: Kognitive Aspekte der Handlungstheorie. Stuttgart: Klett-Cotta.

Bartlett, F. (1932). Remembering. Cambridge: Cambridge University Press. (Reprint 1977)

Billig, M. (1976). Social Psychology and Intergroup Relations. London: Academic Press.

Cranach, M. von, Mächler, E. & Steiner, V. (1985). The Organisation of Goal-directed Action. In: G. P. Ginsburg, M. Brenner and M. von Cranach (Eds.), Discovery Strategies in the Psychology of Action. European Monographs in Social Psychology 35. London: Academic Press.

Cranach, M. von, Kalbermatten, U., Indermühle, K. & Gugler, B. (1980). Zielgerichtetes Handeln. Bern: Hans Huber. (Englisch: Goal-directed Action. London: Academic Press, 1982)

Cranach, M. von & Ochsenbein, G. (1985). "Selbstüberwachungssysteme" und ihre Funktion in der menschlichen Informationsverarbeitung. Schweiz. Zeitschrift für Psychologie, 44 (4), 221–235.

Durkheim, E. (1898). Individuelle und kollektive Vorstellungen. In: E. Durkheim (Hg.), Soziologie und Philosophie. Frankfurt: Suhrkamp. 1976, S. 45–83.

Goffmann, E. (1969). Strategic interaction. Philadelphia: University of Pensylvania Press.

Grawe, K. (1980). Die diagnostisch-therapeutische Funktion der Gruppeninteraktion in verhaltenstherapeutischen Gruppen. In: K. Grawe, (Hg.), Verhaltenstherapie in Gruppen. München: Urban & Schwarzenberg. S. 89–223.

Habermas, J. (1981). Theorie des kommunikativen Handelns. Bd. 1 & 2. Frankfurt: Suhrkamp.

Hacker, W. (1986). Allgemeine Arbeits- und Ingenieurpsychologie. Berlin. VEB, Deutscher Verlag der Wissenschaften.

Homans, G. C. (1950). The Human Group. New York: Harcourt Brace.

Harré, R. & Secord, P. F. (1972). The explanation of social behaviour. Oxford: Basil Blackwell.

Keupp, H. & Bergold, J. (1972). Probleme der Macht in der Psychotherapie unter spezieller Berücksichtigung der Verhaltenstherapie. In:

C. H. Bachmann (Hg.), Psychoanalyse und Verhaltenstherapie. Frankfurt: Fischer. 105–140.

Leontjew, A. N. (1977). Tätigkeit, Bewusstsein, Persönlichkeit. Stuttgart: Klett-Cotta.

Mead, G. H. (1934). Mind, Self and Society. Chicago: The University of Chigaco Press. (Deutsch: Geist, Identität und Gesellschaft. Frankfurt: Suhrkamp. 1968)

Moscovici, S. (1984). The phenomenon of social representation. In: R. M. Farr and S. Moscovici (Eds.), Social representations. Cambridge: Cambridge University Press.

Moscovici, S. (1981). On social representations. In: J. P. Forgas (Ed.), Social cognition: Perspectives on everyday understanding. London: Academic Press.

Moscovici, S. (1961). La psychanalyse, son image et son public. Paris: Presses Universitaires de France.

Piaget, J. (1971). Psychologie der Intelligenz. Olten: Walter-Verlag. (Orig. 1947)

Rogers, C. R. (1942). Counseling and psychotherapy. Boston: Houghton Mifflin. (Deutsch: Die nicht-direkte Beratung, 5. Aufl. München: Kindler. 1972.)

Rogers, C. R. (1951). Client-centered therapy: Its current practice, implications, and theory. Boston. Houghton Mifflin. (Deutsch: Die klientenzentrierte Gesprächspsychotherapie. München: Kindler. 1973)

Rogers, C. R. (1961). On becoming a person. Boston: Houghton Mifflin. (Deutsch: Die Entwicklung der Persönlichkeit. Stuttgart: Klett-Cotta. 1973)

Schütz, A. (1932). Der sinnhafte Aufbau der sozialen Welt. Wien.

Schütz, A. & Luckmann, Th. (1973, 1984). Strukturen der Lebenswelt. Bd. I. Neuwied: Luchterhand (1975); Bd. II. Frankfurt: Suhrkamp (1984).

Thommen, B. Ammann, R. & Cranach, M. von (1988). Handlungsorganisation durch soziale Repräsentationen. Bern: Hans Huber.

Volpert, W. (1982). The model of hierarchical-sequential organization of action. Paper to the XXII International Psychological Congress, Leipzig. In: W. Hacker, W. Volpert & M. von Cranach (Eds.) (1982), Cognitive and motivational aspects of action. Amsterdam: North Holland Publishers.

Subject Index

Name Index